Poor Places, Thriving People

Poor Places, Thriving People

How the Middle East and North Africa Can Rise Above Spatial Disparities

THE WORLD BANK
Washington, D.C.

ISBN: 978-0-8213-8321-6
eISBN: 978-0-8213-8423-7
DOI: 10.1596/978-0-8213-8321-6

Library of Congress Cataloging-in-Publication Data
Poor places, thriving people : how the Middle East and North Africa can rise above spatial disparities.
  p. cm.
  Includes bibliographical references and index.
  ISBN 978-0-8213-8321-6 — ISBN 978-0-8213-8423-7 (electronic)
1. Industrial location—Middle East. 2. Industrial location—Africa, North. 3. Middle East—Economic conditions—Regional disparities. 4. Africa, North—Economic conditions—Regional disparities. 5. Space in economics. I. World Bank.
  HC415.15.Z9D576 2011
  339.4'60956—dc22   2010038030

Cover photo: Loïc Whitmore/World Bank

Contents

List of Figures

List of Maps

List of Tables

Preface

It is now well known that the clustering of production in major cities is a driving force of economic growth. However, the governments of the Middle East and North Africa (MENA) are determined to make sure that their citizens benefit from their national development no matter where they live. The principle of economic justice makes wide gaps in living standards between leading and lagging areas politically intolerable.

So the key question is this: how can MENA reap the benefits of economic agglomeration while mitigating geographic disparities in well-being?

It is hard for policy makers to find straightforward advice on lagging area development. This is not surprising, given the controversy that exists among the experts and the diversity of locations. Following the 2009 World Development Report titled *Reshaping Economic Geography*, the moment was right to draw together the World Bank's thinking on lagging areas in MENA.

The main messages of *Poor Places, Thriving People: How the Middle East and North Africa Can Rise Above Spatial Disparities* can be summarized in four words: people, connections, clusters, and institutions.

- The surest way to help a lagging area to catch up is to invest in its *people*. A lack of education (especially for girls) and high dependency ratios are the essence of the lagging region phenomenon.

- MENA has a proximity premium: its lagging areas' populations are rarely far from its growth hubs. This report shows how smart investments and policies in transport can *connect* poor places to the dynamic economies of their rich neighbors. There is also a wide-open field of opportunity for telecommunications to bring electronic proximity to lagging areas.

- Many countries have spent huge sums on subsidies to entice investors to lagging areas—usually without any sustainable impact. This report recommends that governments turn their efforts toward the new approach to local economic development, which is gaining ground around the world, and is based on economic *clusters*, local competitive advantage, private initiative, and public-private dialogue.

- MENA's historical legacy is one of centralized and sectorally-compartmentalized *institutions*. However, as the region's governments increase their focus on integrated local development, they are exploring new institutional models that are more suited to their needs. The report describes the state-of-play in territorial planning, public financial management, targeted programs, deconcentration, and decentralization, and it sketches some emerging lessons.

The World Bank is committed to the development of MENA's lagging areas. In Sohag, one of the Arab Republic of Egypt's poorest governorates, for example, the Bank financed community-identified local infrastructure such as schools and sanitation systems. The Republic of Yemen's rainfed agriculture project is raising farmers' yields and incomes in the highlands and in the *wadis* of Tihama and the Eastern Plateau. In Tunisia, the Bank has partnered with the Agency for Rural Development in the northwest since 1982. Our analytical and advisory services to MENA governments have included reports on the international experience of technology poles, briefings on the latest trends in local economic development policy, an options paper on the allocation of investment funds for public infrastructure in Saudi Arabia, and econometric analyses of the causes of spatial disparities in welfare.

This report combines the insights of specialists in the majority of the World Bank's key sectors: agriculture, development economics, education, health, poverty analysis, social protection, and transport. It is the report's modest aim, if not to offer a single formula for reducing spatial disparities, at least to propose a range of policy options that the region's leaders can reflect on in the light of their national objectives.

Shamshad Akhtar
Vice President, Middle East and North Africa
The World Bank

Acknowledgments

This report was prepared by a team led by Alex Kremer and including Loïc Whitmore, Ted Alcorn, Hayat Al-Harazi, Omar Aloui, Brian Blankespoor, Heba Elgazzar, Rose-Marie Esber, Luca Etter, Fatou Fall, Hassene Kassar, Hiromichi Katayama, Stephen Kennedy, Mourad Khaladi, Stephen King, Anat Lewin, Andrea Liverani, Abdoul Mijiyawa, Claudio Montenegro, Siddig Muneer, Charbel Nahas, Ziad Nakat, Magalie Pradel, Rachidi Radji, Gudivada Rao, Joana Silva, Estelle Sommeiller, Mehmet Tohsun, Michael Wilson, Serdar Yilmaz, and Ayman Zohry.

The peer reviewers were Chorching Goh, Daniel Lederman, and Marisela Montoliu Muñoz.

Many people provided advice, but the team gives special thanks to the representatives of Middle East and North African (MENA) countries at the consultations in 2008 and 2009 in Marseille, as well as Indermit Gill, Marisela Montoliu Muñoz, Nada Eissa, and the OECD Public Governance and Territorial Development Group. Andrew Stone, Ruslan Yemtsov, and Vivian Hon provided valuable technical advice. Jeff Lecksell of the World Bank's Printing, Graphics, and Map Design Unit assisted in the formulation and finalization of the maps.

The team acknowledges the support of the multi-donor Gender Action Plan.

Abbreviations

ABB	Activity-Based Budgeting
AERI	Agricultural Exports and Rural Income
ARC	Appalachian Regional Commission
ASEAN	Association of Southeast Asian Nations
BRT	bus rapid transport
CCT	conditional cash transfer
CGDR	*Commissariat Général de Développement Régional* (General Commissariat for Regional Planning)
CIAT	Interministerial Committee for Territorial Planning
DALYs	disability-adjusted life years
DECRG	Development Economics Research Group (of the World Bank)
DHS	Demographic and Health Survey
DT	Tunisian dinar
EEI	Egyptian Education Initiative
ELMO index	a measure of economic justice; acronym formed from the surnames of its inventors: Elbers, Lanjouw, Mistiaen, and Özler
ERVET	*Ente Regionale per la Valorizzazione Economica del Territorio* (Regional Institution for Territorial Economic Development)
ESFD	Economic and Social Fund for Development
ESSBs	*Établissements de soins de santé de base* (primary health care facilities)
EU	European Union
EUN	Egyptian Universities Network
FAO	Food and Agriculture Organization
FAOSTAT	FAO statistical database
FNS	Fund of National Solidarity
GAEB	General Authority for Education Buildings

GCC	Gulf Cooperation Council
GDP	gross domestic product
GIS	geographical information system
GNI	gross national income
GRDP	gross regional domestic product
HIECS	Household income, expenditure, and consumption survey
HRM	Human resource management
ICT	information and communications technology
IFPRI	International Food Policy Research Institute
IHSES	Iraq Household Socio-Economic Survey
IMCI	Integrated Management of Childhood Illnesses
IMR	infant mortality rate
INDH	National Human Development Initiative
INS	*Institut National de la Statistique* (National Statistics Institute) (Tunisia)
ISSIP	Integrated Sanitation and Sewerage and Infrastructure Project
ITU	International Telecommunications Union
JEI	Jordan Education Initiative
LPI	Logistics Performance Index
MAUP	Modifiable Areal Unit Problem
MCIT	Ministry of Communications and Information Technology
MDCI	Ministry of Development and International Cooperation
MEHAT	Ministry of Environment, Habitat, and Territorial Planning
MENA	Middle East and North Africa
MENA13	Specifically Algeria, Djibouti, the Arab Republic of Egypt, the Islamic Republic of Iran, Iraq, Jordan, Lebanon, Libya, Morocco, the Syrian Arab Republic, Tunisia, the Republic of Yemen, and the West Bank and Gaza
MERCOSUR	Southern Cone Common Market (*Mercado Común del Sur*)
MoE	Ministry of Education
MPO	Management and Planning Organisation
NAF	National Aid Fund
NAFTA	North American Free Trade Agreement
NHHS	National Household Survey
NRENs	National Research and Education Networks
NRRP	National Rural Roads Program

NSDP	National School Development Plan
ODESYPANO	Office for Forestry and Livestock Development in the northwest
OECD	Organisation for Economic Co-operation and Development
ORMVAs	*Offices Régionales des Mise en Valeur Agricole*
PCBS	Palestinian Central Bureau of Statistics
PEM	public expenditure management
PHC	primary health center
PISA	Program for International Student Assessment
PMT	proxy means testing
POS	point-of-sale
PPP	purchasing power parity
SDIs	School Development Initiatives
SEZs	special economic zones
SMEs	small and medium enterprises
SNAT	Territorial Master Plan (*Schéma National d'Aménagement du Territoire*)
SSN	Social Safety Net
TFR	total fertility rate
TIMSS	Trends in International Mathematics and Science Study
TME	total managed expenditure
UK	United Kingdom
ULO	Urban Land Organization
UN	United Nations
UNDP	United Nations Development Programme
UN-WIDER	United Nations World Institute for Development Economics Research
USO	universal service obligation
WDI	World Development Indicators
WDR	World Development Report
WFP	World Food Programme (of the UN)
WUAs	Water Users' Associations
WVS	World Values Survey
ZDR	*Zones de Développement Régional*

All dollars are in US$ unless otherwise noted.

CHAPTER 1

Overview

This is a summary of the World Bank's 2010 *Middle East and North Africa Development Report* on spatial disparities. The full report has more in-depth analysis and examples from the region and beyond. It will be available online and from booksellers in August 2010.

For the international experience of spatial development and regional policy, readers may be interested in the World Bank's 2009 World Development Report, *Reshaping Economic Geography*.

The Political Demand: Spatial Equity with Productivity

Leaders in the Middle East and North Africa (MENA)[1] are concerned about the development gap between leading and lagging areas. Spatially uneven development may be seen as a failure of economic justice, or as a betrayal of the social contract between the government and the governed, and that migration may translate into urban discontent or changes in political and social relations.

But MENA governments have another concern that is no less pressing. Unemployment rates are on average more than twice as high as those in middle-income countries worldwide. Creating jobs requires competitiveness and growth.

Can MENA raise living standards in lagging areas without compromising economic productivity? This report answers yes and proposes a policy framework for doing so.

Spatial Concentration with Spatial Equity

Everywhere in the world, economic activity is spatially concentrated for the simple reason that production is more efficient when it is agglomerated.

As a result, 54 percent of the world's economic activity is concentrated in countries that make up 10 percent of its area; within countries, economic activity is squeezed into the major cities. In MENA, the same pattern exists: the productivity of capital and labor is measurably higher in the Arab Republic of Egypt, Morocco, and Tunisia's leading areas.

But we have to distinguish two spatial patterns:

- *Agglomeration*—the tight concentration of businesses in certain *places*

- *Spatial disparities*—the gaps in living standards between *people* in different places

The broad pattern of spatial disparities in the Middle East and North Africa is typical of low- and middle-income countries: living standards are highest where economic activity is densest and where connections to economic density are closest.

- Urban areas are better off than rural areas.

- Areas close to urban centers are better off than isolated areas.

- The same pattern of spatial disparities applies to indicators of both economic and human development.

- The same pattern of disparities is found within subnational divisions.

- Women and men experience spatial inequalities differently.

However, living standards between rich and poor places can converge even as economic agglomeration grows. With effective policies in place, disparities in social indicators—such as poverty, health, and education—can and do shrink.

Spatial Disparities Are a Political Issue

If spatial disparities are a by-product of economic growth, why are they of such concern to policy makers?

From a sociopolitical perspective, spatial disparities can have worrisome effects. They can become a source of political grievance for residents of low-income areas. In addition, by fueling migration, spatial inequalities bring political risks to the better-off areas where the migrants settle.

The policy maker's challenge is, therefore, to sustain spatial and political balance without sacrificing the efficiencies gained from agglomeration. The aim of this report is to offer MENA's policy makers a framework for doing so.

A Policy Framework for Spatial Equity with Economic Efficiency

The solution to the spatial disparity problem lies in careful local analysis and an appropriate mix of policies tailored to the characteristics of each lagging area.

Adapting the 2009 World Development Report, this study examines three policy packages (summarized in table 1.1):

Package 1 levels the playing field and the opportunity for human development in lagging areas by allowing better access to social services and an improved environment for business. Policy Package 1 applies to all lagging areas because it reduces spatial disparities without compromising the efficiencies of spatial agglomeration.

Package 2 connects poor places to the poles of development. Policy Package 2 applies to lagging areas that are close to leading areas, where spillover effects can reduce spatial disparities.

Package 3 underpins private sector interest in nonleading areas and does so without relying on subsidies. Policy Package 3 applies to lagging areas where competitive potential is manifested by private investor interest. The aim is encouraging local economic growth to reduce spatial disparities.

Spatial Disparities in Living Standards: Uncovering the Truth

The spatial concentration of MENA economies is apparent to all. But the reality of spatial disparities—differences in living standards—requires careful examination. To match the policy package to the place,

TABLE 1.1

Matching Policy Packages to Lagging Areas

Policy package	Area of applicability
Package 1. Level the playing field and the opportunity for human development in lagging areas	All lagging areas
Package 2. Connect poor places to the poles of development	Lagging areas close enough to leading areas to benefit
Package 3. Underpin private sector interest in nonleading areas	Areas where the private sector might see unrealized growth potential

Sources: Study Team and World Bank 2009.

policy makers must understand the unique characteristics of each lagging area.

Some pointed questions can help indicate the way forward. First, is geography really a major contributor to socioeconomic inequality? Second, is an area lagging because of low economic opportunity or because of poor human development? Third, assuming a genuine spatial inequality problem does exist, how has it evolved over time? Are lagging areas converging with leading areas, or are disparities becoming wider? Is redistribution of population from lagging to leading areas helping to solve the problem?

This analysis will grapple with the problem of diagnosing spatial inequality, showing first how to identify degrees of spatial inequality and then how to separate lagging areas into distinctive types.

Fast Urbanization but a Delayed Transition out of Agriculture

MENA differs from other developing regions in at least one key respect. The region's populations are more agglomerated (urbanized) than one would expect for their level of economic development. Why is that? For one thing, most of the land in the MENA region is too arid or mountainous to support settlement and farming. Consequently, rural populations here have historically been concentrated in coastal strips, in mountain valleys, and along the rivers. By necessity, therefore, MENA's settled areas have had high population densities from an early date. One implication of this fact is that the region needs less additional population agglomeration to obtain the economies of agglomeration found in developed countries.

MENA is urbanizing fast: on average, countries were 65 percent rural in 1960 but 65 percent urban in 2007. Normally, urbanization is accompanied by a shift of labor from agriculture to services and manufacturing. In MENA, that labor transition has been delayed. Agriculture has lost its share of value added, but rural areas remain centers of low-productivity employment and poverty. Moreover, MENA has an unusually high rate of agricultural employment growth (figure 1.1), and too many people on too little land has become a common feature of MENA's lagging rural areas. One reason is that the region has an unusually high rate of growth in the working-age population (figure 1.2). Given the land and water constraints, the region's agricultural sector cannot continue to absorb surplus labor. A shift of labor out of agriculture is overdue; when it comes, it will shift population into the cities. Climate change is likely to accelerate this process.

FIGURE 1.1

MENA's Agricultural Labor Force Is Growing Fast Relative to Its Level of Development

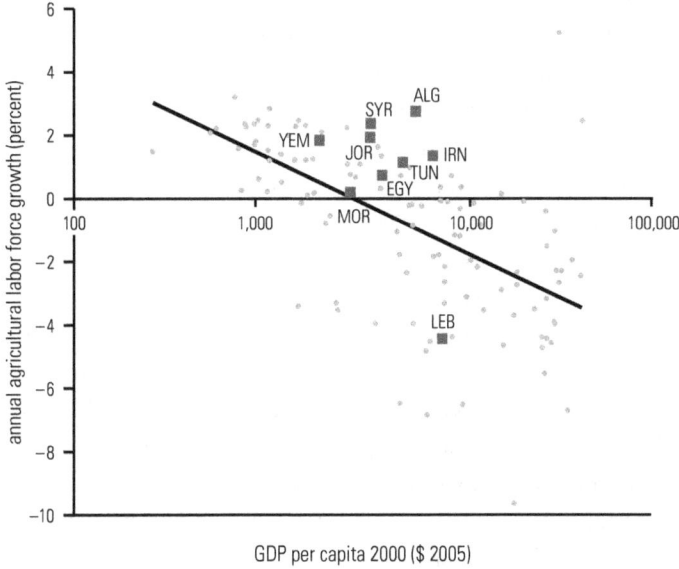

GDP per capita 2000 ($ 2005)

Source: World Development Indicators Database, accessed May 17, 2009.

Note: ALG = Algeria; EGY = Egypt, Arab Rep.; IRN = Iran, Islamic Rep.; JOR = Jordan; LEB = Lebanon; SYR = Syrian Arab Republic; TUN = Tunisia; YEM = Yemen, Rep.

FIGURE 1.2

MENA's Working-Age Population Has Been Booming Compared with Other Countries and Economies at the Same Level of Development

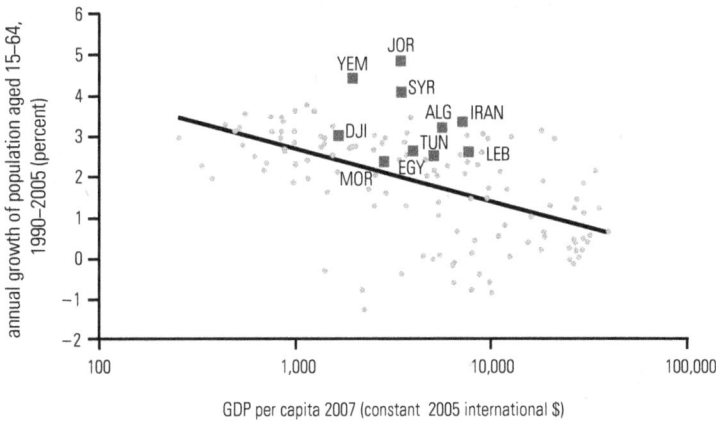

GDP per capita 2007 (constant 2005 international $)

Source: World Development Indicators Database, accessed May 29, 2009.

Note: DJI = Djibouti; MOR = Morocco.

Spatial Disparities Are Smaller Than They Seem

Geography is highly political, so it is essential for policy makers to have an objective understanding of how location affects household welfare.

Things are not always as they seem at first glance. For example, economic elites bump up the average consumption levels in leading areas, but the living conditions of the vast majority of people in those areas may actually be similar to those in lagging areas. Urban slums may have levels of poverty and human development similar to or even worse than rural areas. Simply by using median instead of average values of household welfare can alter the appearance of spatial disparities.

It is also important to focus on absolute poverty numbers as opposed to poverty rates. Focusing on poverty rates can overlook the large absolute numbers of poor people living in high-density urban areas.

Location matters more with respect to living standards in some countries than others. The spatial component of inequality is biggest in Morocco, followed by Egypt and the Republic of Yemen. Nevertheless, in no MENA country or economy for which data were available does rural-urban inequality account for more than 20 percent of total inequality of household expenditure. Overall, MENA's urban-rural and interprovincial divides are no greater than those in other developing regions of the world.

Spatial Disparities Are Often Social Disparities

Household characteristics explain a large share of spatial disparities. The following example will help to clarify the concepts at work. Although Upper Egypt has only 40 percent of the population of Egypt, it accounts for 60 percent of its poverty and 80 percent of its severe poverty. Economic geography, however, is not the main factor holding Upper Egypt back. In fact, demography explains 62 percent of the consumption gap between Upper Egypt and Lower Egypt. The problem is that Upper Egyptian workers have to share their earnings with more family members who are too young or too old to work. In other words, Upper Egypt has a high "demographic dependency"—the ratio of dependents to people of working age. Households with unfavorable demographic characteristics would be at a disadvantage wherever they lived.

Likewise, a household's education level can influence its success. While leading areas may have better-educated people and lagging areas may provide inadequate educational opportunity, households with low educational achievement will do worse than better-educated households, regardless of location.

Three factors explain why household characteristics in MENA's lagging areas differ so greatly from those in leading areas: fertility, sorting, and education.

MENA's demographic transition has been and remains spatially uneven. Although fertility rates are falling across the region, they began falling in leading and urban areas first and in lagging and rural areas later. In the short run, therefore, MENA's demographic transition has caused spatial disparities in dependency ratios, and this disparity is a major cause of the region's rural-urban and interprovincial disparities in well-being. As the demographic transition reaches MENA's lagging areas, however, it will become a major contributor to spatial *convergence* in living standards.

Many factors influence fertility rates, including female education, gender empowerment, female labor participation and income growth, and access to quality reproductive health services. Spatial considerations influence all of these determinants, which explain why MENA's demographic transition has been geographically uneven.

The available data on internal migration in MENA confirm the sorting effect: the people with the highest earning potential leave lagging areas. This is due partly to the tendency of people with greater education to place greater value on city amenities, and partly to the fact that the jobs that make education productive tend to be concentrated in cities.

Finally, people in lagging areas are less able to acquire human capital, whether from the educational system or from family members and social networks. This is the education effect.

These three effects—fertility, sorting, and education—are related and mutually reinforcing, and they account for much of what makes a household rich or poor. Improving living standards in lagging regions is, therefore, as much a question of developing people as it is of developing the place itself.

The demographic and educational components of spatial disparities differ significantly from country to country, as shown in the following examples.

- *Egypt*. Demography is a major contributor to Egypt's disparities. If all of Egypt's governorates had the same demographic profile, the rural-urban gap would be a full 17 percentage points lower than it is. Educational disparities are also significant, albeit less so than demography.

- *Djibouti*. Unusually, the demography of rural Djibouti mitigates the rural-urban gap. If rural and urban areas had the same demographic characteristics, the gap would be 4 percent *higher* than it is. Conversely, educational disparities add 11 percentage points to the rural-urban gap.

- *Jordan*. Average rural per capita consumption is 24 percent behind urban levels in Jordan. If demographic disparities are removed, this difference dwindles to an insignificant 12 percent. Controlling for educational disparities, the gap becomes just 3 percent.

- *Lebanon.* In looking at what separates Mount Lebanon, the North, and Bekaa from Beirut, the differences in household characteristics and earnings per worker are not significant. Labor force participation and mobility are the key factors.

- *Morocco.* Morocco features only modest interprovincial disparities but a significant urban-rural gap: per capita household consumption in rural areas is only 54 percent of that in Morocco's urban areas. Even if rural and urban areas had the same demographic characteristics, the rural-urban gap would still be 41 percent. And controlling for education, rural Morocco's per capita household consumption would still be 32 percent lower than urban Morocco's.

- *The Syrian Arab Republic.* Syria's northeast regions lag far behind Damascus City in terms of average per capita household expenditure. Without demographic disparities, however, the northeast would not be a lagging area at all. Spatial disparities in education seem to play no role.

- *The Republic of Yemen.* Without the demographic and educational components of intergovernorate disparities, the Republic of Yemen's poorest governorate would trail only 40 percent (instead of 65 percent) behind the city of Sana'a in terms of per capita consumption. The rural-urban gap would be 25 percent instead of 40 percent.

The implication for policy makers is clear: one cannot assume that observed spatial disparities in economic welfare are due to spatial disparities in economic opportunity. For many lagging areas, the population would be disadvantaged wherever they lived, so human development is likely to be a key component of effective spatial development almost everywhere in MENA.

Convergence and Migration: Sometimes Spatial Disparities Resolve Themselves

Once policy makers have a clear profile of spatial disparities, it can be useful to know whether those disparities are narrowing or widening over time (box 1.1).

In some countries, the redistribution of population from lagging to leading areas can take place quickly enough to solve the lagging-area problem. If this is the case, then it makes sense to focus economic investment wherever the return is highest, which is usually in agglomerations. In other countries, the population will not shift from lagging areas to leading areas, perhaps because lagging areas have higher fertility rates or because inflexible social structures limit migration. In this situation, the lagging areas may require spatially targeted economic development policies to bring about an increase in earnings.

BOX 1.1

Convergence Trends for the Islamic Republic of Iran, Tunisia, and the Arab Republic of Egypt

The Islamic Republic of Iran. In the Islamic Republic of Iran, the convergence in living standards between leading and lagging areas was more a result of leading areas losing ground owing to economic decline than of lagging areas gaining from growth. The urban-rural convergence occurred during 1976–85, when per capita household expenditure fell much more in urban areas than in rural areas. Once the economy resumed steady growth in the early 1990s, however, the urban-rural gap widened once again.

Tunisia. Between 1980 and 2000, Tunisia experienced significant interregional convergence. The rural-urban gap also narrowed, although it fluctuated from year to year, probably according to rainfall. Tunisia's convergence was uneven, however, as regions split into rich and poor clubs. The case of Tunisia shows that spatial convergence at the national level may take the form of a "breakout" by middle-ranking regions. For that reason, policy makers should resist the temptation to focus their convergence concerns solely on the most lagging regions.

Egypt. The country appears to be facing widening spatial disparities within lagging Upper Egypt, even though divergence is not taking place between Upper and Lower Egypt. Some villages in rural Upper Egypt are being left behind as others "break out" and reduce their poverty rates. Therefore, Egypt's current strategy of targeting social investments toward low-income villages in low-income governorates may indeed be appropriate.

Source: Authors.

Throughout the MENA region, people are moving from the countryside to the cities. The redistribution of MENA's population, however, tends to take the form of a gradual shift from rural to urban areas *within* provinces instead of a lateral migration from lagging provinces to leading provinces.

Why is the redistribution of population from lagging to leading provinces slow in MENA? One reason is that fertility rates are higher in lagging provinces. The role of social networks may also be critical. In the absence of transparent job and housing markets, the opportunity to migrate may depend on the presence of friends and family in the destination. So while the poorest may have the greatest desire to migrate, the best connected have the greatest *opportunity* to do so. Studies of Egypt confirm the importance of social networks in determining internal migration flows. Gender relations in MENA may also slow interprovincial migration. Social conventions constrain female mobility and labor market participation.

From the preceding considerations, we can see that the population in MENA is urbanizing but not "metropolitanizing." Even though political concerns may focus on the specter of an uncontrolled human tide flooding the primary cities, this picture is not the reality of internal migration in MENA. The implication is that lagging provinces' development will depend on local growth poles for some time to come.

Three Ways to Lag, with Three Policies to Match

Lagging areas' diverse geographical characteristics call for different policy responses.

For the purposes of spatial analysis, MENA's area can be classified along three dimensions.

- *Lagging versus nonlagging.* The question of living standards

- *Dense versus sparse.* The question of population density

- *Near versus distant.* The question of travel time to a major city

A map of the region that uses these classifications emphasizes MENA's varied geography (map 1.1). Much of MENA's population is clustered in islands of density. The 3 percent of MENA's surface area that is densely populated is home to 92 percent of the population. Thus, most lagging areas' populations are reasonably agglomerated. The proximity of populations to economic density is another distinctive characteristic of MENA.

Once we know a lagging area's character, we can match it to the appropriate policy package.

For example, in the lagging area of Djelfa in Algeria on the Trans-Saharan Highway, Djelfa looks like a *fringe* area: sparsely populated, distant from economic density, and with economic potential constrained by a lack of agglomeration and resources. Djelfa may, therefore, be suited only for Policy Package 1 (level the playing field and the opportunity for human development in poor places).

The Jordanian governorate of Al-Mafraq is another lagging area. Like Djelfa, it is sparsely populated and arid. Yet its provincial capital is only 50 kilometers from Jordan's capital. Al-Mafraq is, therefore, a *belt* area. It could benefit from Policy Package 1's level playing field for development, but it is also close enough to the capital to benefit from spillover connectivity. Therefore, Policy Package 2 might be appropriate.

The urban governorate of Aleppo in Syria is a lagging area although it has a large population of educated people, several major employers, and an environment of fertile farmland. It would seem to be a *pocket* of unrealized economic potential. As well as being a candidate for Policy Package 1, therefore, it could be a candidate for Policy Package 3, a package that is aimed at facilitating private investment in lagging areas.

Analyzing a given lagging area at different levels of spatial disaggregation also reveals new policy-relevant information. Upper Egypt is a case in point.

As a region within a country, rural Upper Egypt appears as a lagging area. Yet 80 percent of the difference in per capita consumption between Upper Egypt and Lower Egypt is due to demography. At the regional level, therefore, the policy emphasis should be on overcoming Upper Egypt's demographic handicap.

As a governorate, Upper Egypt shows wide disparities from district to district in access to public services and health care, so it is crucial for authorities to allocate public social investment projects to priority areas. The government's logical policy response has, therefore, been to emphasize bottom-up, participatory planning of social infrastructure, with financial allocations targeting the poorest districts.

As a collection of communities, Upper Egypt can benefit from the new technique of poverty mapping, which allows policy makers to analyze spatial disparities below the province level. In MENA, this technique reveals the disparities in welfare between neighboring villages, as well as geographically small pockets of dense poverty in large cities. At this level, policy responses should include village-level targeting of public social investment projects and targeting of dense poverty pockets in richer urban areas.

With the importance of diagnosis for matching policies to places made clear, we are now ready to present the three policy packages described at the outset.

Policy Package 1. Level the Playing Field and the Opportunity for Human Development in Poor Places

All lagging areas have one thing in common: they deserve equal policy treatment—a level playing field for development, one that will reduce spatial disparities in living standards while letting the market determine the spatial distribution of economic activity, thus securing both the economic benefits of agglomeration and the political benefits of spatial

MAP 1.1

A Policy-Oriented Spatial Typology of the Middle East and North Africa

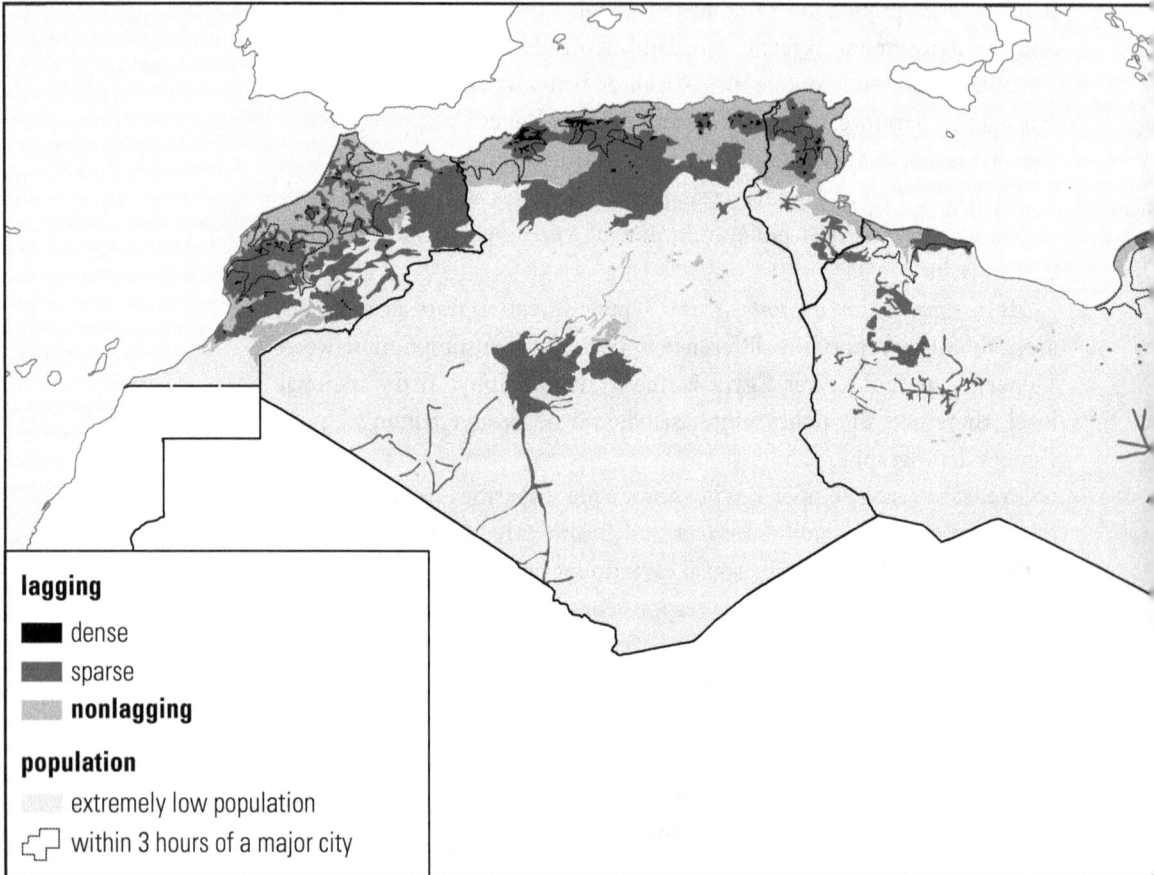

lagging
- ■ dense
- ▨ sparse
- ▨ **nonlagging**

population
- ▨ extremely low population
- ⬡ within 3 hours of a major city

Sources: Elevation, SRTM30 (2000); land cover, GLC2000 (2000); population, Landscan (2005); rail, VMAP0 (1997); rivers, CIA World Data Bank II (1980s); roads, Euro-med (2000) and VMAP0 (1997); slope, in degrees, SRTM30 (2000); urban areas, GPW3-GRUMP (2000); water bodies, Global Lakes and Wetlands Database layer 1 (2004).

Note: Lagging areas represent 40 percent of the administrative units by country that have the highest rates of poverty, and nonlagging areas represent the remaining administrative units. Using Nelson's (2008) methodology to calculate a travel time model, "near" is defined as a travel time less than or equal to 3 hours from a city of 500,000, and "distant" refers to any travel time greater than 3 hours. According to population density data from Landscan (ORNL 2005), "dense" is defined as more than 50 people per square kilometer, and "sparse" covers the remainder. Areas with population density less than 1 are displayed in white.

equity. This is the goal of our first policy package, which is applicable in all circumstances and the only package suitable for fringe areas.

History Has Left an Uneven Playing Field for Development

There is a strong statistical relationship between political institutions and spatial development: the less accountable a state, the more agglomerated its population. This finding might be because undemocratic states tend to neglect people in outlying areas.

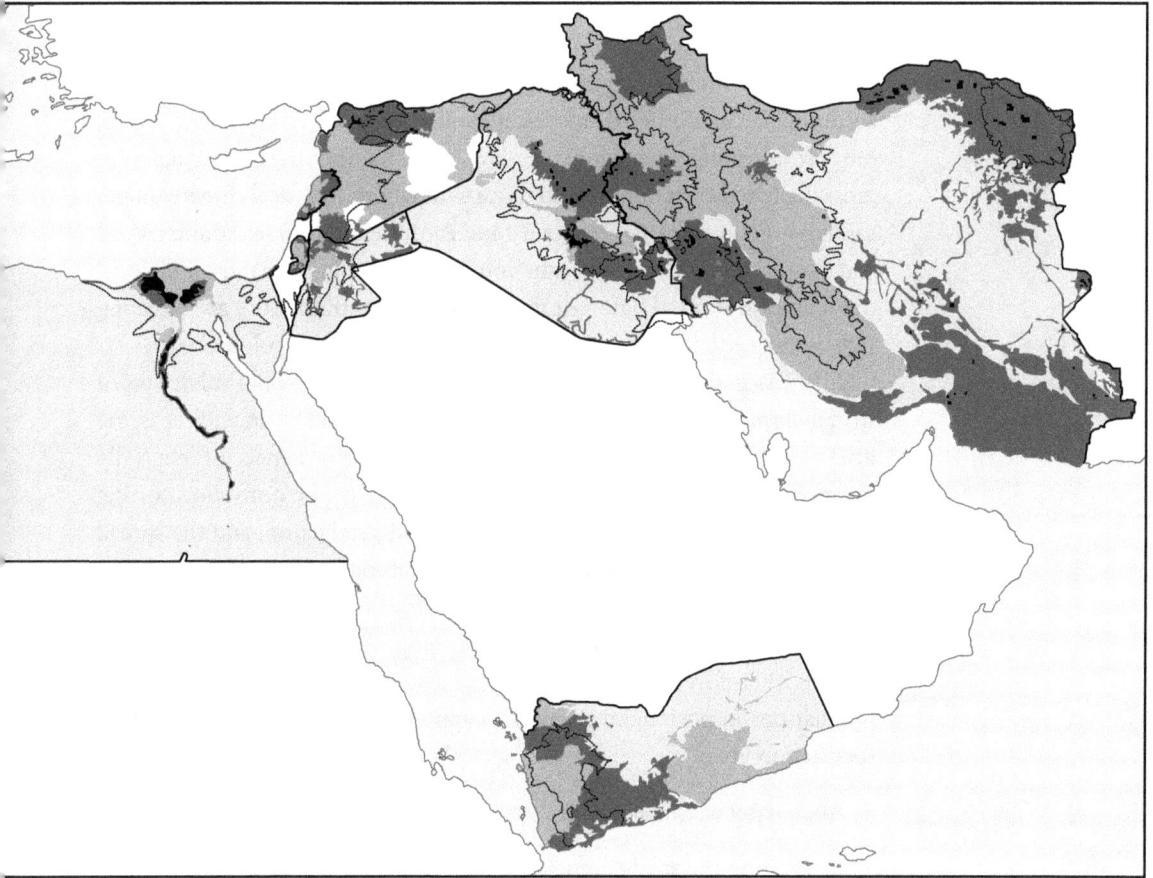

MENA's political history has left behind a spatial bias in favor of metropolitan areas. Many of the contemporary drivers of spatial bias go back to the colonial era.

At independence, most of today's MENA states were founded on belief in the state's capacity to regulate social and economic relations. Governance under Ottoman and European rule was based on the development of strong central bureaucracies. Colonial tax systems encouraged a neglect of lagging regions and shifted a large share of tax revenues away from the provinces to the capital region. In the years immediately following independence, central administrations expanded, and power remained concentrated at the capital.

In catering essentially to the metropolis, colonial management avoided redressing regional inequalities. Under both Ottoman rule and European colonization, states served as providers to the metropolis. In favoring resource extraction over economic development, the colonial powers created an economic geography of "useful versus useless" regions. Disadvantaged people were divided along ethnic and religious lines to prevent their alliance against the government. The development of metropolis- and export-oriented economies subsequently encouraged coastal agglomeration.

Empirical metrics suggest that the MENA states are less externally accountable than other countries at similar levels of development. Without formal arrangements for spreading accountability, decision makers are most likely to be accountable to those with whom they deal directly in the capitals—giving rise to an urban bias. And recently, some countries' oil and gas revenues placed huge amounts of resources in the hands of the central administration. These factors encouraged centralization, accentuating features that modern MENA states inherited from their colonial past.

MENA's governments are now seeking to reverse the political drivers of spatial disparities in response to several developments, including rising urban unemployment; the relatively poor performance of centrally planned economies worldwide; the limited ability of non-oil-exporting countries to subsidize public employment and production; and the spread of telecommunications, migration, and the broadcast media, which has made the populations of lagging areas more aware of spatial inequalities.

To create a level playing field for development, MENA's policy makers will, therefore, need to remove the historical disadvantages faced by populations in peripheral areas. The approach can be broken down into four action areas:

- Improving the investment climate in lagging areas

- Integrating the spatial dimension into public expenditure management

- Making education, health, and safety nets serve lagging-area populations

- Facilitating urban growth

How to Level Subnational Disparities in the Investment Climate

Data for the MENA Region suggest that disparities in the investment climate (consisting of the institutional context and infrastructural base) are affecting the spatial distribution of economic activity. Studies in Morocco and Egypt found an empirical link between spatial disparities in the investment climate and spatial disparities in firm productivity. We cannot be sure from the data that there is a systematic investment climate bias against lagging regions. It is clear, however, that MENA has significant spatial disparities in the investment climate, which have the potential to influence the location of economic activity (figure 1.3).

FIGURE 1.3

A Composite Index of Objective Measures of the Subnational Investment Climate in Algeria, the Arab Republic of Egypt, Jordan, Morocco, and the West Bank and Gaza

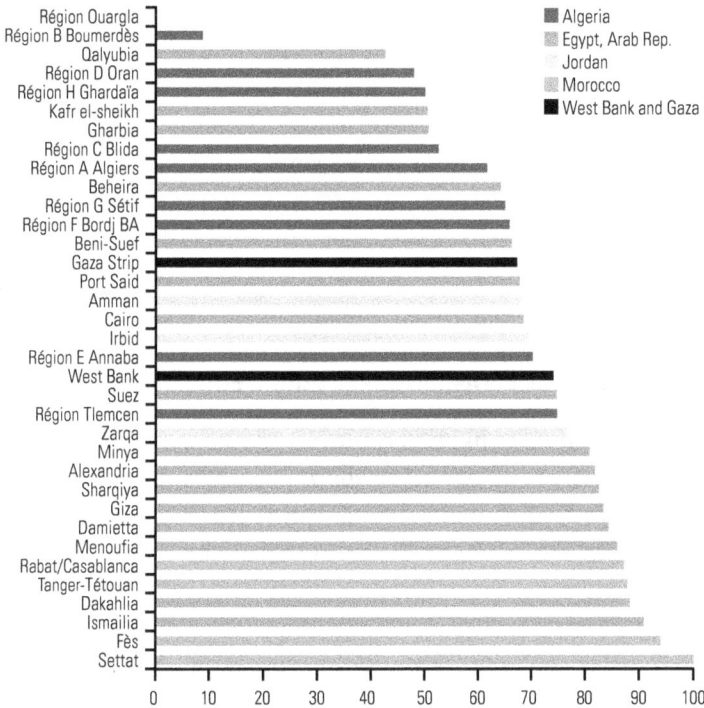

Source: Staff calculations from World Bank investment climate surveys.

How can policy makers begin to level the playing field for private investment across MENA? Possibilities include more transparency in the application of business regulations in lagging areas and the provision of critical infrastructure services in their cities. Not all lagging areas have the economic potential to benefit from improvements in the investment climate. Evidence from Egypt and Morocco, however, suggests that improvements in the institutional environment could be achieved at a relatively low cost and would strongly benefit enterprise productivity.

Public Expenditure Management Has a Spatial Dimension

Several countries outside MENA have systems and rules for tracking the spatial incidence of expenditure and for ensuring that intragovernmental transfers reflect different areas' needs. But MENA's spatial public expenditure management systems are a clear priority for action.

Most MENA countries or economies cannot monitor where central government spending takes place, which is in itself a problem for spatial policy. Moreover, the systems for allocating fiscal transfers to local governments are usually ad hoc, with the result being that poorer areas are often not compensated for their high level of needs or low resource base.

For Egypt and Jordan, the data suggest that resource transfers and governorate GDP per capita were not correlated: the highest transfers were not given to governorates with the weakest economic base. Conversely, the data from the Islamic Republic of Iran suggest that the apportionment of transfers from the central government to ostans (provinces) does give priority to lagging areas.

Correction of Spatial Disparities in Public Education Systems

Rural-urban disparities in primary and secondary enrollment rates (and other indicators of educational attainment, such as school completion and math achievement) are an obvious feature of MENA's education profile (table 1.2). But spatial analysis of the determinants of educational performance is critical; it is not just a question of building more schools in lagging areas.

What causes the spatial disparities in education? To what extent are they due to spatial disparities in children's socioeconomic status (demand-side factors) and to what extent to spatial disparities in education services (supply-side factors)? We examined the determinants of educational attainment (staying in school) in one country with high spatial disparities in attainment (Morocco) and in another with low disparities

TABLE 1.2

Lower Enrollment Rates for Rural Children, Especially the Poor
(Percent)

			Urban		Rural	
			Poor	Nonpoor	Poor	Nonpoor
Algeria	1995	Primary	96.0	95.0	89.0	89.0
		Secondary	77.0	82.0	59.0	66.0
Egypt, Arab Rep.	1999	6–15	95.8	98.5	93.5	96.7
		15–19	72.4	84.9	64.7	72.9
Iran, Islamic Rep.	2001	6–10	99.0	100.0	98.0	98.0
		11–13	92.0	97.0	76.0	84.0
Morocco	1998	7–15	69.4	87.2	36.4	49.8
Tunisia	2000	6–18	79.4	82.2	67.0	70.7
Yemen, Rep.	1998	10–14	83.0	92.1	59.6	62.0

Source: World Bank 2008.

(Jordan). The results for Morocco suggest that after the respondent's age and the household head's level of education were taken into account, the rural-urban factor explained only a very small percentage of attainment gaps. Instead, most of the disparities were explained by household characteristics. Similarly in Jordan, household economic status was the main determinant of attainment. Put simply, this finding means that the priority is to make it easier for poor households to keep their children in school, not to build more facilities in poor places.

While spatial disparities in educational attainment are mostly due to household characteristics, spatial disparities in educational achievement (learning) are largely due to geographic differences in the quality of schooling. It seems that students in rural schools receive education of lower quality than do those in urban schools. Although there have been spectacular increases in enrollment in the MENA Region, the economies have been less effective than comparator economies in converting those investments and enrollments into retention and learning. The idea that spatial disparities in learning achievement might be largely due to geographical differences in educational quality reflects the same diagnosis, but this is at the subnational rather than the international level of analysis.

Gender disparities in education are also wider in rural areas in several MENA economies. Reducing these disparities will help reduce spatial disparities in development overall.

These analyses have important implications for policy makers seeking to reduce spatial disparities in education. They lead to four priority axes to combat spatial disparities in education.

- Reducing spatial disparities on the demand side

- Reducing spatial disparities in quality

- Reducing gender disparities in lagging areas

- Using spatial planning techniques to deploy appropriate infrastructure

Each theme is illustrated with examples from our case studies on Egypt, Jordan, Morocco, and the Republic of Yemen.

Reducing Spatial Disparities through Demand-Side Interventions

We have already seen that the low economic status of children in lagging areas may be more of an obstacle to educational attainment than are disparities in educational supply. Therefore, one strategy for reducing spatial disparities is to make it more economically attractive for families to keep their children in school. For example, in conditional cash transfer programs, the transfer of a welfare benefit depends on the receiver's actions.

The education components of such programs address demand-side obstacles to education by contributing toward the costs of sending a child to school. Data from Mexico, Colombia, and Nicaragua clearly show the potential of conditional cash transfer programs to improve enrollment.

Reducing Spatial Disparities in Quality

The spatial deployment of teachers and administrators creates inequities in the quality of education. In Morocco, difficult living conditions in rural areas lead young teachers to move to urban areas as soon as they can. In addition, levels of absenteeism are high, and teachers are underused, working less than the legal minimum of 24 hours per week. In Jordan, teaching posts are awarded to those who have waited the longest to get the next job in line. In Egypt, as in Morocco, teachers migrate from rural to urban areas as they gain experience. Finally, in the Republic of Yemen, teachers are haphazardly placed on the basis of local influence, so schools in lagging areas are unlikely to obtain experienced teachers.

It is clear that improving human resource management in public education services is critical for reducing spatial disparities in education quality. Local recruitment of teachers and incentives such as improved living conditions and housing are necessary to draw experienced teachers and principals to lagging areas. And more formal, systematic, and needs-based posting procedures are needed to better match teachers to vacancies.

"School development initiatives" have demonstrated great potential for improving education quality in targeted geographic areas. These initiatives are development plans managed at the school level by school boards, teachers, and parents. This approach relies on the capacity and motivation of the local school governance committee. It also presupposes that school principals have the skills and motivation to act as community leaders.

Reducing Gender Disparities in Education in Lagging Areas

The interaction of gender disparities and spatial disparities creates wide gender gaps in lagging areas. In Morocco, for example, the gender gap for literacy is 5 percentage points in urban areas, compared to 35 percentage points in rural areas. Reducing spatial disparities in girls' education would also remove one of the causes of spatial disparities in fertility rates, which would, in turn, reduce spatial disparities in dependency ratios and living standards.

Any intervention aimed at reducing spatial-gender disparities in education should be made with girls' unique needs in mind. For example, programs in the Republic of Yemen are improving living conditions for female teachers in lagging areas and recruiting women teachers locally. Conditional cash transfer programs can be designed to provide families with special incentives to keep girls in school. Spatial planning of public investment in educationsuch as shorter distances between schools and residences, and adequate water and sanitation can reflect girls' educational needs.

Using Spatial Planning Techniques to Improve the Spatial Efficiency of Infrastructure

The race to achieve the Millennium Development Goal of full primary level completion has given strong emphasis to school construction across the MENA region, but the need for robust spatial planning of investments is becoming urgent. As the goal of universal primary enrollment and completion comes close to achievement, policy makers are shifting their focus to secondary schools, which are more expensive and farther from home. In addition, population distributions are changing rapidly with urbanization and the spread of the demographic transition from leading to lagging areas.

The situation in several MENA economies bears out the assertion that robust spatial planning is necessary. The Republic of Yemen faces a number of spatial imbalances in education. Despite Egypt's high population densities, there are significant spatial inequalities in access to educational infrastructure. Jordan suffers from a serious spatial disequilibrium in the distribution of basic and secondary schools, leading to high maintenance costs and low utilization rates.

Health: Correcting Spatial Disparities in Outcomes

Geographical differences in health status are a major concern for policy makers. MENA governments spend an average of 3.3 percent of GDP on health services, and, as a matter of equity, the impact of that spending should not depend on a person's location. Moreover, the performance of health systems in the MENA region will increasingly be measured in terms of each system's ability to reach marginalized people.

Changing Health Services and Health Outcomes in Poor Places

Large spatial disparities exist within the MENA economies in health outcomes and access to services. There are localized pockets of bad health indicators in countries such as Lebanon, Egypt, Tunisia, Jordan, and Morocco. Health care personnel are concentrated in urban areas, which are likely to offer higher wages, better living conditions, and greater opportunities for professional development; however, low-density areas have more facilities per capita. This situation may be due to the desire of policy makers to make facilities geographically accessible to all citizens, which inflates the proportion of facilities in areas of low density. If we put these two trends together, rural facilities are understaffed and underused compared with those in cities. Thus, building facilities in lagging areas is not the answer.

Bringing Better Health to Lagging Areas in Different Ways

How, then, can MENA governments reduce the health status divide between leading and lagging regions? The key is improving the quality of health service delivery, rather than its scale.

When it comes to strengthening public health delivery facilities in lagging areas, successful interventions have focused on staff incentives and nonstaff recurrent funding. Morocco's Integrated Management of Childhood Illnesses program, for example, focused explicitly on staff motivation, with training and free housing for personnel in lagging areas. Spatially adapted delivery systems have also proved cost-effective for low-density areas. For example, the Islamic Republic of Iran has strengthened communities through training of local health workers to provide family planning and reproductive health care. As a result, service coverage in rural areas has increased from nearly 40 percent to 90 percent in 15 years.

Empirical evidence from countries as disparate as Costa Rica, the Islamic Republic of Iran, Singapore, Sri Lanka, and the United Kingdom reveals the efficacy of demand-side interventions in improving health status in lagging areas. A multitude of demand-side factors may be limiting the expansion of health services in lagging areas, notably limited insurance coverage. MENA's health insurance systems tend to be limited to wealthier urban residents. Strategies that aim to expand education, transportation, nutrition, water, sanitation, and incomes in lagging areas may have a stronger effect on spatial disparities in health outcomes than a simple emphasis on the stock of health facilities. In Egypt, programs have focused on increasing women's awareness of health issues and empowering women to take advantage of family planning services. Expanding insurance plans into poor areas, as the Islamic Republic of Iran has done, can also encourage public and private providers to deliver appropriate care by stimulating demand.

Improved management information systems can help health departments ensure efficient targeting of resources. Implementation of better monitoring and IT systems in the Islamic Republic of Iran and the West Bank and Gaza resulted in strong improvements in resource distribution and usage rates of health facilities.

How to Target Social Safety Nets to Mitigate Spatial Disparities

Although many MENA economies have some kind of social safety net program, they are rarely considered a component of spatial policy. When well targeted, these programs can reduce spatial disparities, but poorly targeted programs actually increase the gap between rich and poor places.

In terms of spending, energy (and food) subsidies are by far the major social transfers in the region; however, for policy makers concerned with spatial equity, a major drawback of commodity subsidies—and energy subsidies in particular—is that they are regressive. The people who consume the most, the nonpoor in leading areas, receive the lion's share of the subsidy.

Conversely, social funds and conditional cash transfers have been shown to effectively target lagging areas. Geographical targeting distributes benefits to people who are likely to be poor or vulnerable, depending on where they live. Proxy means testing uses easily observed household indicators to predict household income and to determine who is eligible for benefits. But these positive examples of transfer schemes are not prevalent in MENA, and many existing programs could contribute more to reducing spatial disparities if better targeted.

How to Smooth the Path for City Growth

The development of MENA's lagging rural areas depends on labor shifting out of farming into the cities. As MENA's farm workforce continues to grow, it becomes harder and harder for limited land and water resources to sustain its productivity. Two-thirds of the farm labor productivity difference between MENA and Spain is explained by MENA's higher ratio of labor to land. The data also show that agricultural productivity growth in MENA is driving farmgate prices down rather than farmer incomes up because supply is outstripping urban demand. *In short, long-term rural development in MENA depends on urbanization.*

Urbanization helps to reduce spatial disparities by shifting labor from lagging to leading areas. Therefore, smoothing the path for urbanization is a recipe for spatial convergence in living standards. Urbanization is proceeding apace in MENA13, where the average rate of growth of the urban population is 3.3 percent per year, compared with 2.6 percent for national populations. The question, therefore, is not how to slow down the growth of cities, but rather how policy makers can ensure that urbanization occurs as smoothly as possible. This approach involves three topics: land markets, urban public services, and institutional frameworks.

Having Land Markets that Support Smooth Urban Growth

Well-functioning land markets are critical for smooth urban development. In MENA, however, there are signs that land markets could be performing better.

Land for housing. While the supply of housing in MENA compares favorably with other countries at a similar level of development, MENA's housing is expensive, and the affordability problem is most acute for low-income households. Although housing subsidies in countries such as Algeria, Egypt, the Islamic Republic of Iran, Jordan, Morocco, Tunisia, and the Republic of Yemen are sometimes massive, low-income households may have difficulty making the investments that give them access to these subsidies. MENA's housing stock is also underused, with high vacancy rates. These factors act as a brake on rural-urban migration, thereby denying people in lagging areas a key pathway out of poverty.

Land for business. Surveys of MENA entrepreneurs indicate that difficulties in accessing land are one of their main obstacles to competitiveness. While MENA13 economies perform well with respect to the time required to purchase property, they are worse than any region of the world except Sub-Saharan Africa in terms of transaction costs.

Land for the rural transition. Efficient agricultural land markets will be important to facilitate the shift of labor out of agriculture in the future and to increase the earnings of those who remain in farming. In MENA's agricultural land markets, however, it is often difficult for landowners to obtain and maintain registration. Therefore, the actual pattern of recognized ownership is not reflected in the official record. This lack can create problems in accessing credit or consolidating fragmented land holdings.

Planning Urban Services

The integration of new arrivals into the city depends upon their ability to access public and private services. Here we illustrate a few key principles for an agenda for MENA urban service development.

Planning ahead, rather than reacting to in-migration. Public authorities have a tendency to delay the provision of services to new informal settlements because of perceptions that they are temporary or unwelcome. But these settlements instead should be seen as part of the housing solution rather than a problem. The earlier that services for emerging settlements are planned, the greater the efficiency of road, power, water, and sanitation networks. Urban planning can also limit MENA's vulnerability to climate change by minimizing construction in vulnerable areas and by ensuring investment in protective infrastructure.

Responding to the "spatial flow" of market-led city growth. Service provision and new developments should follow people's settlement preferences rather than attempt to lead them. For example, the Islamic Republic of Iran created 18 new towns since the Revolution at a considerable distance from their parent cities with the aim of protecting farmland and preventing informal settlements around major cities. These towns, however, became dormitory communities for salaried employees of the mother city and had no economic base of their own. Therefore, the authorities have refocused their attention on increasing the supply of housing within the metropolis itself.

Similarly, in 1969, Egypt created distant satellite cities in the desert around Cairo intended to limit the city's growth. These cities suffered from the opposite problem as the Iranian new towns; they had significant business but few residents, and this created a pattern of reverse commuting. Meanwhile, the forces of agglomeration were accelerating the growth of Cairo's metropolis. By the early 1990s, therefore, the government had refocused its efforts on slum upgrading, using services to improve the quality of growth in the metropolis.

In both the Iranian and the Egyptian cases, the authorities shifted their approach, using service provision to improve the quality of metropolitan agglomeration rather than trying to discourage it.

Having Institutional Arrangements for Smooth Urban Growth

The institutional capacity of municipalities to respond to urban growth through planning, regulation, and service provision differs greatly throughout the region. Various initiatives to strengthen those capacities are ongoing.

Policy Package 2. Connect Poor Places to the Poles of Development

Spillovers from agglomerations into their peripheries are one of the most powerful forces in spatial development, thereby offering the potential to reduce spatial disparities by yoking lagging regions to the growth of leading regions.

MENA's lagging areas have a proximity advantage: 61 percent of their population lives within three hours of a major city. How, then, can MENA connect its lagging areas to agglomeration hubs so that they maximize the benefit from spillover effects? The answer has three components:

- Transport

- Trade facilitation

- Information and communication technologies

Improvement of Spillover Transport Connections

MENA's transport infrastructure is basically road-based. The extensive primary road network generally provides adequate intercity (that is, long-distance) connectivity. In measures for road network coverage, MENA performs well in comparison to other developing regions.

Given that 61 percent of MENA's lagging-area populations already live within three hours of a city, MENA governments should not assume that long-distance connectivity is a major component of the lagging-areas problem. The positive outlook on long-distance connectivity in MENA, however, masks a problem: the predisposition toward expanding higher-class roads in MENA at the expense of other key transportation investments.

MENA's broad pattern of public expenditure in transport could benefit from a reallocation of resources away from expansion of the domestic trunk road network toward maintaining the existing network, improving rural access, creating transborder networks, and improving traffic management to reduce congestion and improve safety. Urban and peri-urban mass transit systems are critical if people from lagging areas are to benefit from demand for labor from nearby agglomerations.

Degradation of road surfaces. The expansion of the trunk road network is taking place at the expense of regular maintenance. World Bank studies identify road deterioration as a major problem in Algeria, Egypt, the Islamic Republic of Iran, Iraq, Libya, and the West Bank and Gaza.

Rural connectivity deficits. MENA also suffers from a comparative neglect of rural accessibility. The rural index indicator for MENA, defined as the percentage of rural population with access to an all-season road, was an estimated at 60 percent in 2004 (figure 1.4), outperforming only Sub-Saharan Africa and South Asia. Recent rural road investments in Morocco and the Republic of Yemen, however, have delivered measurable and cost-effective impacts in lagging areas.

Urban congestion. Too many private cars and poor public transportation lead to congestion in MENA's cities. Motorization rates are set to

FIGURE 1.4

Rural Access Index: MENA versus Comparator Regions, 2004

(percentage of rural population with access to all-season road)

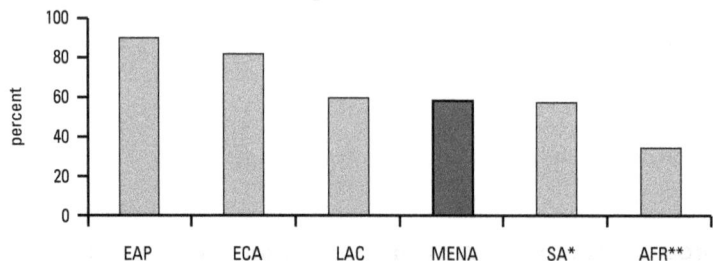

Source: Roberts, Shyam, and Ragstogi 2006.

Note: * Year 2003/04 **Year 1999–2004. AFR = Africa, EAP = East Asia and Pacific, ECA = Europe and Central Asia, LAC = Latin America and the Caribbean, MENA = Middle East and North Africa, SA = South Asia.

increase with economic growth, but these rates lean toward private cars instead of public transportation. Mass transit in MENA consists largely of low-quality, publicly owned bus services. Unaffordable public investment in light rail is often seen as the main alternative; however, other potential strategies include lifting barriers to private investment in urban buses and the development of bus rapid transport (BRT).

Road safety. MENA has, by far, the developing world's most dangerous roads. The situation is particular worrisome in Morocco, Jordan, and the Islamic Republic of Iran.

Low efficiency of road use. In some MENA economies, the return on road investment is being undermined by inappropriate regulation of commercial operators.

Smoother Border Crossings

Land borders create artificial lagging areas by restricting the movement of people and freight. Constructing transborder connections, improving logistics infrastructure, and easing border formalities, therefore, function not only as trade-promotion policies, but also as a part of national strategies to reduce spatial disparities.

Electronic Proximity: A New Tool for the Integration of Lagging Areas

Isolation from information is part of the lagging-area problem. As mobile phones and the Internet become the default communication media, those without access to them will become marginalized. Information and communication technologies (ICTs), therefore, give policy makers a new set of options for attacking spatial disparities.

MENA's rural areas generally have poor access to mobile telephone and Internet services. In 2007, cellular connections in Egypt, the Islamic Republic of Iran, Lebanon, Libya, and Syria were lower than in other countries at similar levels of development (figure 1.5). MENA is the only world region in which the rate of rural mobile phone usage has not overtaken that of fixed lines.

The challenge of ICT access in MENA's lagging areas has two components: the market efficiency gap and the access gap.

- *Closing the market efficiency gap.* The market efficiency gap is the difference between the current level of service penetration and what is achievable in a liberalized and stable regulatory environment. However, although telecommunications liberalization in MENA is a work in progress, tariffs are generally not high (except in Lebanon and Morocco). So MENA's problem is possibly more one of . . .

• *Closing the access gap.* The access gap is the difference between leading and lagging areas remaining under efficient market conditions.
Competitively awarded public-private partnerships are an efficient
instrument for bringing ICT infrastructure and services into less
profitable, low-density areas.

Policy Package 3. Underpin Private Sector Interest in Nonleading Areas

Although economically marginal areas usually miss out on private investment because of the forces of agglomeration, there are exceptions to the
rule. Tunisia's center-east region, the Tanger-TÈtouan region in Morocco,
and some governorates in the Islamic Republic of Iran are examples of lagging areas that converged with leading areas. What can governments do to
facilitate this desirable process?

In this section, we will begin by examining failed regional economic
development policies in lagging areas around the world. We cast a similarly critical eye on regional economic development policies targeting
lagging areas in MENA13, and we describe an alternative approach to
regional economic development.

Global experience has little positive to teach about the potential of big
spending programs to encourage economic growth in lagging areas.

FIGURE 1.5

Some MENA Economies Are Well Below the Trend in Terms of Cellular Connections

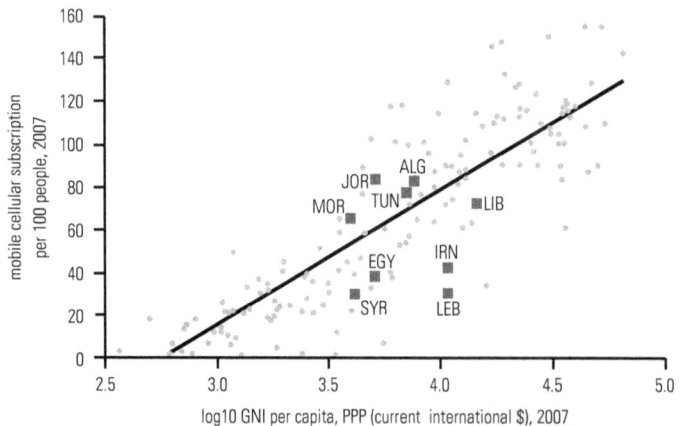

Source: ITU International Telecommunications Union Database.
Note: ALG = Algeria; EGY = Egypt, Arab Rep.; GNI = gross national income; IRN = Iran, Islamic Rep.; JOR =
Jordan; LED = Lebanon; LIB = Libya; MOR = Morocco; PPP = purchasing power parity; SYR = Syrian Arab
Republic; TUN = Tunisia.

While the traditional approach has been to focus public infrastructural investment on lagging areas, a number of studies indicate that returns to public investment are highest in leading areas, which offer the benefit of economies of agglomeration. Governments have also attempted to steer private investments toward lagging areas through financial incentives—with typically poor results. Even where spatially targeted incentives have induced firms to invest in lagging areas, the gains are often short-lived.

In MENA, the focus has been on using financial incentives to *override* economies of agglomeration, despite the global evidence that this approach is ineffective. In Algeria, regional economic development programs, which included investment in state-owned industries, attempted to spread economic activity beyond Algiers' sphere of influence. Yet both public and private investments remained centered on Algiers. Syria experienced similar difficulties during the 1990s in using industrial zones as incentives to encourage economic activity in lagging rural areas. Despite these efforts, economies of agglomeration prevailed, and the private sector continued to locate in major cities.

Coordination Instead of Financial Incentives

Some governments are now adopting a new approach to regional economic development policy. This approach accepts that the forces of agglomeration are too strong to be overridden by public money. The role of the government becomes that of facilitator rather than steerer. Table 1.3 compares the old and new paradigms of regional economic development policy.

TABLE 1.3

Old and New Paradigms of Regional Economic Development Policy

	Old paradigm	New paradigm
Objectives	Trying to compensate for locational disadvantages of lagging regions	Tapping underused potential to enhance regional competitiveness
Unit of intervention	Administrative units	Functional economic areas
Strategies	Sectoral approach	Integrated approach
Tools	Subsidies and state aids	Mix of soft and hard capital (capital stock, labor market, business environment, social capital, and networks)
Actors	Central government	Different levels of government (with private sector)

Source: OECD 2009.

Infrastructure and education are effective only in combination. A recent analysis of the determinants of regional growth found that the infrastructural investment influences growth only when combined with human capital and innovation; infrastructure alone has little impact.

If regional development is to be based on local potential, regions need a decentralized, bottom-up approach to policy design and implementation. Regional actors are better able to use information about local capacities and needs than are central authorities, and local actors are more likely to support projects they have helped design. Mobilizing local stakeholders may require decentralization and a structured dialogue between the different levels of government. A successful example is the EU's LEADER Community Initiative, which aims to promote endogenous growth through decentralized local action groups.

The public-private interface is a key source of regional productivity, growth, and innovation. Although governments cannot force agglomeration, they can play an important role in encouraging interchanges between regional actors and assembling the links on which agglomerations are built. For example, a Moroccan initiative identified four sectors as candidates for cluster development and fostered a continuous dialogue between public and private institutions aimed at identifying and coordinating investments and regulatory reform.

Because cluster-driven growth is multisectoral, policy makers need to shift increasingly to a territorial perspective rather than a sectoral one. The "green clusters" approach for rural areas provides a good example.

Realization of Agricultural Potential: Green Clusters

Agriculture is still central to MENA's lagging area economies. So what kind of agricultural growth can lead development there?

MENA's agricultural policy has long involved *public spending on water diversion and price subsidies.* Water diversion is reaching its ecological limit, however, and production subsidies can exacerbate inequality because the better-off residents of better-off rural areas receive a disproportionate share of the subsidy. Sector analysis suggests that the main potential engine of agricultural growth in MENA's lagging areas needs to be cluster development around high-value product supply chains. Therefore, we can apply the general principles of the new paradigm of regional economic development to agriculture: first, begin with a cross-sectoral territorial diagnosis that identifies latent potential; second, ensure that the full range of private stakeholders will have a leadership role, beginning in the diagnostic stage.

Proximity for All: Public Institutions for Spatial Policies

MENA governments can, therefore, beat the trade-off between agglomeration economies and spatial inequality—if they tailor their policies to the specific characteristics of their lagging areas. The three policy packages just described are designed to capitalize on those opportunities, as shown in figure 1.6.

So how can the state best organize and mobilize itself to resolve spatial disparities?

Many MENA governments have similar structures. Sector ministries are centralized, which makes local coordination difficult, and subnational administrations have very limited resources and capacity.

Global experience suggests that states can use five basic approaches to integrate the management of the various sectoral strands of spatial policy: territorial development planning, needs-based spatial allocation of fiscal resources, area-based programs, deconcentration, and decentralization.

Territorial development planning involves a central institution responsible for monitoring and analyzing spatial development trends and feeding

FIGURE 1.6

A Framework for Addressing Spatial Disparities

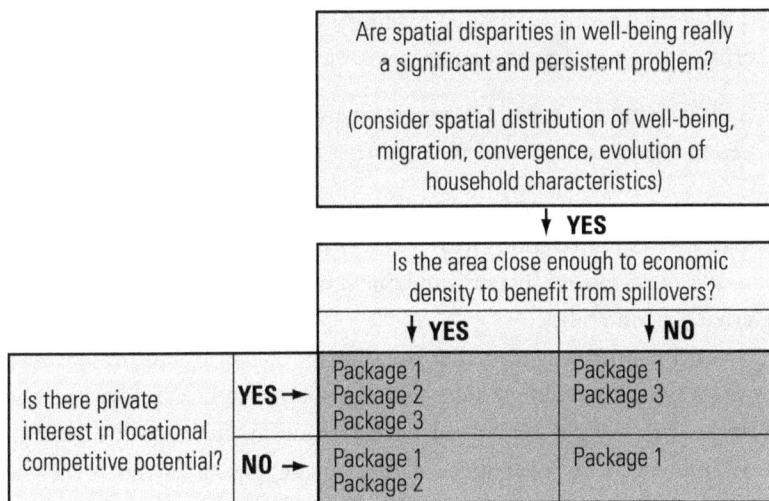

		Are spatial disparities in well-being really a significant and persistent problem? (consider spatial distribution of well-being, migration, convergence, evolution of household characteristics)	
		↓ **YES**	
		Is the area close enough to economic density to benefit from spillovers?	
		↓ **YES**	↓ **NO**
Is there private interest in locational competitive potential?	**YES →**	Package 1 Package 2 Package 3	Package 1 Package 3
	NO →	Package 1 Package 2	Package 1

Sources: Study Team and World Bank 2009.

spatial orientations into the national public investment planning process. Algeria, Morocco, and Tunisia are currently implementing this approach.

Needs-based spatial allocation of fiscal resources can take the form of untied grants or program funding. A formula-based approach to the spatial allocation of fiscal grants is common in federal states, where the government's political credibility depends on transparent and equalizing resource transfers. In the absence of simple and transparent allocation rules, however, political bargaining is likely to prevail. As we have seen, there is much room for improvement when it comes to using needs- or formula-based fiscal allocation rules to support the development of lagging regions.

Central governments can also steer fiscal resources toward poor areas by financing nationwide programs in which the level of activity is based on a location's need. Several MENA economies, including Morocco and Egypt, have programs of this type.

Area-based programs bring the spatial dimension to policy by dedicating funds and creating institutions for specific areas. The challenge lies in integrating the program with the activities of local governments without undermining them.

Deconcentration is on the agenda in all the MENA13 economies. Key lessons for MENA's policy makers include the following:

- Deconcentration requires a strong institutional champion and coordinator.

- Deconcentration involves the delegation of decision making on activities, finance, and human resource management; it works best when all three are deconcentrated in parallel.

- The central ministry's policy-making and oversight functions remain critical when policy execution is deconcentrated.

- A clear definition for the respective mandates of elected local authorities and deconcentrated sector ministries becomes extremely important.

Decentralization involves the transfer of resources and decision making to subnational administrations with political accountability to local citizens. It makes for a more efficient implementation of policies and enhances external accountability.

A vast literature suggests that the transfer of power and resources to lower levels of government helps match resources to local priorities. The problem, however, is that fiscal decentralization increases the lagging area's influence only over its own (inadequate) resources, not over the national allocation of resources. Therefore, decentralization can widen spatial disparities because there is a risk (a) of a mismatch between fiscal responsibilities and spending mandates and (b) of the overloading of subnational governments' limited managerial capacity. Fiscal decentralization is usually a political response to spatial disparities or ethnic division, and so it is often implemented without sufficient attention to the potential negative economic consequences. Cross-country analysis reveals that decentralization in low- and middle-income countries is linked to, if anything, a faster increase in spatial disparities over time.

So what is the verdict on decentralization and spatial disparities in MENA? We can sum up the evidence with three propositions:

- There are good reasons to continue decentralization in MENA: to improve accountability, responsiveness, and service quality.

- Decentralization will not necessarily reduce spatial disparities, and decentralizing mandates without resources and capacity will increase the disparities.

- What is most important is creating transparent and predictable arrangements for equalizing intragovernmental fiscal transfers and building local governments' capacity in lagging areas.

In conclusion, although most MENA governments are strongly committed to the development of lagging regions, few have asked what type of institutional platform is needed for a spatial approach to development policy.

In Short ... Seven Policy Axioms

If we draw the previous arguments together, seven brief messages can sum up the report's policy implications for MENA.

1. *Spatial development begins with clear institutional roles and processes.* Spatial policy making is multisectoral and multi-institutional. The "process platform" for spatial development includes arrangements for monitoring and coordination, resource allocation, planning, and role definition.

2. *Analysis is vital.* MENA needs better spatially disaggregated statistics, especially broken down by gender. It is critical to check that spatial disparities really are a major development issue; very often they are not as important as politics portrays them. Diagnosing the lagging area will identify the right policy package(s).

3. *Good development is good spatial development.* First and foremost, lagging areas need a level playing field for development. Simply by fulfilling their existing mandates to provide a positive business environment and services to the poor, sector ministries will be making a full contribution to national spatial development objectives. Girls' education in lagging areas is the win-win-win-win priority for

spatial development. And erasing spatial disparities in the business environment should offer a high benefit at a particularly low cost.

4. *Bringing social services to lagging areas* usually means (a) finding the incentives for high-quality personnel to work in underprivileged areas and for poor people to use public services and (b) tailoring delivery mechanisms to lower-density areas. Simply building more facilities will not solve the problem.

5. *Commodity subsidies channel a lot of public money to leading areas.* Targeted social protection schemes are more spatially equitable.

6. *Short-distance spillover connectivity* between leading and lagging areas is the transportation priority for MENA's lagging areas. Depending on a lagging area's specific geography, this priority could mean investment in rural feeder roads, road maintenance, intraurban public transportation, border logistics or peri-urban radial connections, and better regulation of transport operators. It is up to MENA governments to encourage private investment and innovation in electronic connectivity, which offers new potential for lagging areas to obtain the benefits of proximity.

7. *The best practice approach to local economic development* emphasizes the coordination of multiple actors to facilitate private sector interest in an area's latent potential. Attempts to use financial incentives to shunt private investment toward lagging areas have a very bad track record.

In short, agglomeration may be an inevitable part of growth, but governments can mitigate spatial disparities. It is a matter of policy choice.

Endnote

1. This study covers the MENA Region, as follows: Algeria, Djibouti, the Arab Republic of Egypt, the Islamic Republic of Iran, Iraq, Jordan, Lebanon, Libya, Morocco, the Syrian Arab Republic, Tunisia, the West Bank and Gaza, and the Republic of Yemen. We use the acronym MENA (or MENA13 when necessary) to signify these 13 economies. The members of the Gulf Cooperation Council (GCC) are not covered in this report because their geographic and economic characteristics are so different from those of the rest of the region.

References

ITU (International Telecommunications Union) database. ITU, Geneva.

Nelson, A. 2008. *Travel Time to Major Cities: A Global Map of Accessibility*. Ispara, Italy: Global Environment Monitoring Unit, Joint Research Centre of the European Commission. http://gem.jrc.ec.europa.eu/.

OECD (Organisation for Economic Co-operation and Development). 2009. "Investing for Growth. Building Innovative Regions." Policy Report, Meeting of the Territorial Development Policy Committee at the Ministerial Level, OECD, Paris.

ORNL (Oak Ridge National Laboratory). 2005. *Landscan Global Population Database*. http://www.ornl.gov/landscan.

Roberts P., K. C. Shyam, and C. Ragstogi. 2006. "Rural Access Index: A Key Development Indicator." Transport Papers 10, World Bank, Washington, DC.

World Bank. 2008. *Islamic Republic of Iran: Spatial Patterns of Poverty and Economic Activity*. Washington, DC: World Bank.

———. 2009. *World Development Report 2009. Reshaping Economic Geography*. Washington, DC: World Bank.

World Bank Investment Climate Surveys. World Bank, Washington, DC.

World Development Indicators Database. World Bank, Washington, DC.

CHAPTER 2

The Political Demand: Spatial Equity without Compromising Productivity

In Morocco in 1999, His Majesty King Mohammed VI begins his first Revolution Day speech by asking how rural development can stem rural-urban migration.[1] In 2006, the Arab Republic of Egypt's prime minister, Ahmed Nazif, promises members of Parliament from the south that "The aim is to direct close to 40 per cent of the budget to Upper Egypt. . . . We will do this despite the fact that Upper Egypt is not where 40 percent of Egyptians live. The president is seeking to make up for the decades-long bias against the south." (Al-Ahram 2006) In the Islamic Republic of Iran, President Mahmoud Ahmadinejad states that 40 percent of the 2008 fiscal year budget will be spent in rural areas (Christian Science Monitor 2007). All Middle East and North Africa (MENA) governments state that the spatial distribution of population requires change. Nearly all have policies that explicitly aim to reduce rural-urban migration. Twelve out of 13 also have policies that specifically aim to reduce migration into urban agglomerations (United Nations 2006).

This is where our report begins: with the concerns of national leaders and politicians. Leaders are concerned about high poverty rates in outlying areas, concerned that uneven development may translate into a flood of migrants into the cities, concerned that migration may translate into urban discontent, and uneasy that spatially uneven development may be seen as a failure of economic justice or a betrayal of the social contract between the government and the governed.

But MENA governments have another concern no less pressing. Average unemployment rates in MENA are more than twice those of middle-income countries worldwide. Creating jobs requires competitiveness and growth.

So can MENA raise living standards in lagging areas without compromising economic productivity? This report answers, "Yes."

MENA's Spatial Disparities in Living Standards: Six Facts

From the start we have to distinguish between two different spatial patterns:

- *Agglomeration*, the tight concentration of businesses in certain *places*, and

- *Spatial disparities*, the gaps in living standards between *people* in different places.

These may coincide. In fact, they often do. But they are not the same thing.

The pattern of MENA's *spatial disparities* (table 2.1) is typical of low- and middle-income countries: living standards are highest where economic activity is densest and where connections to economic density are closest. The next chapter will offer a richer exploration of the geography of inequality. For the moment, therefore, five simple facts can usefully summarize the geography of MENA's spatial disparities:

- Urban areas are, on average, better off than rural areas.

- Areas close to urban centers are better off on average than isolated areas.

- The same broad spatial pattern of disparities usually applies both for indicators of economic welfare, such as mean per capita consumption or the poverty rate, and for human development indicators, such as educational attainment and child mortality.

- The same pattern of disparities exists within subnational divisions: provinces, cities, and even rural districts have economic hubs that are better off and peripheral areas that are worse off.

- Women and men experience spatial disparities differently.

One more simple fact is required to set the scene: the entire MENA region is undergoing urbanization. The average MENA country or economy[2] was 65 percent rural in 1960 but 65 percent urban by 2007.

But so what? All countries are full of inequalities: between the educated and the uneducated, the healthy and the sick, the lucky and the unlucky, the inheritors and those whose parents had nothing, the powerful and the powerless. Economic injustice is everywhere. What is so special about spatial disparities that policy makers care so much?

Spatial Disparities in Economic and Human Development in MENA

	Mean per capita consumption (capital region/national)	Year	Poverty rate (% urban)[a]	Poverty rate (% rural)[a]	Year	Mean per capita consumption (urban/rural)	Year	Access to improved sanitation (% urban)	Access to improved sanitation (% rural)	Stunting (% urban)	Stunting (% rural)	Under-5 mortality rate (urban)	Under-5 mortality rate (rural)
Algeria	—	—	8.9	19.3	1995	—	—	98	87	10	12	40	56
Djibouti	1.24	2002	—	—	—	1.69	2002	70	19	32	44	95	73
Egypt, Arab Rep.	1.75	2005	10.1	26.8	2004/05	1.92	2005	85	52	16	18	39.1	56.1
Iran, Islamic Rep.	1.54	2005	0.8	7.2	2005	1.87	2005	86	78	11	22	36.8	34.6
Iraq	1.02	2007	16.1	39.3	2007	1.58	2007	98	82	19	24	41	41
Jordan	1.54	2002	12.9	18.7	2002	1.32	2002	92	76	12	13	22	27
Lebanon	1.34	2004	8	>25	1995	—	—	100	87	—	—	—	—
Libya	—	—	—	—	—	—	—	99	98	4	6	27.5	36.3
Morocco	1.16	1998	4.8	14.5	2007	2.17	1998	98	58	13	24	38	69
Syrian Arab Republic	1.55	2004	7.9	14.5	2004	1.52	2004	100	94	22	23	19	23
Tunisia	1.33	2000	1.6	8.3	2000	1.86	2000	96	64	4	10	—	—
West Bank and Gaza	—	—	16	15	2003	1.18	2005	100	93	11	9	29.7	29.9
Yemen, Rep.	1.70	2005	30.8	45	1998	1.67	2005	92	34	44	56	56.7	86.1

Sources: Poverty: Algeria, World Bank 1999; Egypt, World Bank 2007; the Islamic Republic of Iran, World Bank 2008a; Iraq, Shlash 2009; Jordan, World Bank 2008a; Lebanon, Haddad 1996; Morocco, Haut Commissariat au Plan, 2007; Syria, El Laithy and Abu-Ismail 2005; the West Bank and Gaza, World Bank 2003; Republic of Yemen, World Bank 2002. Consumption: Djibouti, Egypt, the Islamic Republic of Iran, Iraq, Lebanon, Jordan, Morocco, Syria, the Republic of Yemen: national household surveys, years as specified (Egypt July–September only); Tunisia, INS 2000; West Bank and Gaza, PCBS 2006. Sanitation, stunting, and under-five mortality: Alcorn 2009.

Note: — = not available.

a. Poverty lines vary between countries, so poverty rates in different countries cannot be compared from this table.

Politics Makes Geography Important

Spatial disparities begin to matter when politics enters the equation. Consider two countries: Country A and Country B. Both countries have the same poverty rate, 20 percent (figure 2.1). Poor people have annual per capita income of $600. Nonpoor people have twice as much. Both countries, therefore, have a GDP per capita of $1,080 per year. Both countries have the same income distribution and a Gini coefficient of 0.44. Both have the same poverty gap.

Each country could design the same social program to target the poor and probably achieve approximately the same results at approximately the same cost. From the point of view of individuals' economic welfare, Country A and Country B are identical. Seen from this strictly individualistic viewpoint, therefore, the question of place is of zero relevance: it is literally a nonissue.

From a broader sociopolitical viewpoint, however, the two countries are materially different. Whereas the poverty rate in Country A is the same in all regions, Country B has a poverty rate of 50 percent in the southeast, but only 10 percent in the other provinces. This spatial

FIGURE 2.1

Spatial Distribution of Disparities

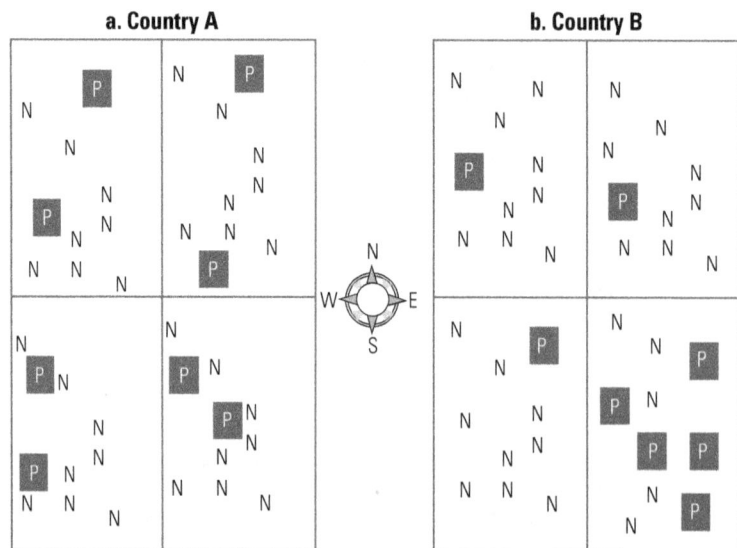

Source: Study Team.

Note: P = poor, N = nonpoor.

clustering of low-welfare people could lead to a number of sociopolitical phenomena:

- *Perceived spatial injustice*. The residents of Country B's southeastern province may conclude that their birth location has deprived them of opportunity, through no fault of their own effort or ability.

- *Perceived spatial agency of the state*. It may be inferred that Country B's government and those who hold political power are in some way responsible for the lagging area status of the southeastern province.

- *Spatial political association*. Residents of Country B's southeastern province may form geographically based political ties in order to further their perceived common grievances. Ethnic and religious divisions may provide a framework for political association, in which case the spatial disparities become particularly worrisome (Kanbur and Venables 2005).

- *Spatial social and political reorganization*. Natives of Country B's southeast province may migrate north and west in order to share in the higher incomes of other regions. Internal migration might involve the reconfiguration of family and social networks; informal social protection systems; patronage systems and political allegiances; a shift in power; and the spatial redistribution of ethnic, religious, and age groupings. Any of these rearrangements of the existing order could be perceived as a source of sociopolitical stress in Country B's four provinces.

As the UN-WIDER study on spatial inequality (Kanbur and Venables 2005) concluded, "Even when spatial units do not represent ethnic or other cleavages, but command the allegiance of the population as political entities, increasing disparities in group averages may lead to tensions and conflict." These sociopolitical phenomena are real. MENA politicians' concern about them is genuine.[3] Tackling them is a political imperative, as we shall see. But tackling them *in the wrong way* can impose an unacceptable cost upon national development.

MENA Needs Economic Agglomeration

MENA needs the spatial concentration of productive activity. No country has ever achieved developed-country status without urbanizing. Even the populations of great agricultural exporters such as Australia, Argentina, Chile, New Zealand, and Uruguay are more than 85 percent urbanized.

Among the earliest thinkers to identify the relationship between agglomeration and productivity was the North African father of economics, Ibn Khaldun (1332–1406). Ibn Khaldun observed that people concentrate in high-density areas in order to achieve economic specialization and a division of labor. The larger and denser the agglomeration, he wrote, the greater its level of prosperity (Al-Alwani 1982).

Economic activity is spatially concentrated for a good reason: production is more efficient when it is agglomerated (Henderson, Shalizi, and Venables 2001; World Bank 2009a, 128–29).

1. There is a "*home market effect*"; firms keep transport costs low by locating close to their customers. These firms' employees then become customers themselves, attracting more businesses into the area (Krugman 1991). A firm can keep its transportation costs down by locating near other firms if it is a producer of intermediate goods. So consumers in agglomerations attract firms that employ workers who become more consumers.

2. "*Localization economies*" arise from having many companies in the same sector in the same place. They can learn from each other, keep in touch with the market, and share the same pool of suppliers and skills.

3. "*Urbanization economies*" appear when different industries gather together. They exchange technologies, information, and skills. Places grow economically by producing and diffusing knowledge (Romer 1994).

These "economies of agglomeration" are the founding principles of the new economic geography, a subdiscipline of economics that explains where growth takes place. Economies of agglomeration attract investment to places where economic activity is already densest. So 54 percent of the world's economic activity is concentrated in countries with 10 percent of its area (Henderson, Shalizi, and Venables 2001). Within countries, economic activity is squeezed into the major cities. Ten metropolitan areas in Mexico account for a third of the country's population and 62 percent of its output. Vietnam's cities have 30 percent of the nation's population but produce 70 percent of its output (World Bank 2009a). Shanghai has only 1.2 percent of China's population but produces 12.5 percent of its economic value (UN Habitat 2004).

Seven centuries later, the current spatial distribution of economic activity in MENA confirms Ibn Khaldun's predictions. Map 2.1 shows the agglomeration of economic activity in Libya and Iraq, estimated by gridding the distribution of employment by sector. Tripoli and Baghdad are the prime foci of production. They dwarf the secondary poles of

MAP 2.1

Spatially Concentrated Economic Activity in Libya (left) and Iraq (right)

Spatially concentrated economic activity

Libya   Iraq

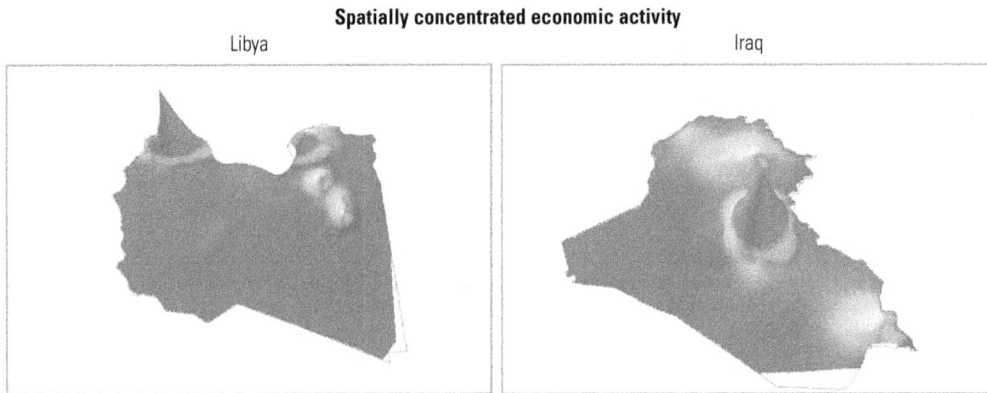

Source: http://gecon.yale.edu/data.php. Accessed August 18, 2009. Methodology described in Nordhaus 2006.

Benghazi, Basra, and Kirkuk, as investment and labor are drawn into the metropolis by the economies of agglomeration.

The evidence from MENA confirms that investment and production are indeed more efficient in areas of dense economic activity.

In Egypt (World Bank 2009c) researchers broke down the determinants of labor productivity in industrial firms. They looked at the companies' sector, years of operation, size, and so on. Controlling for all these variables, they found that a firm in Upper Egypt, Egypt's lagging area far from Cairo, had labor productivity 44 percent lower than elsewhere.

The Tunisian government collects investment data and household consumption data by governorate. It is, therefore, possible to see how much investment it took in each governorate to generate the same increase in household consumption. The calculations confirm the power of agglomeration economies. It takes much more investment to support a given value of consumption growth in the lagging areas of the south and the northwest than it does in the leading areas of Tunis, the northeast and the center-east (table 2.2).

The Tunisian figures may understate the spatial disparities between the rates of return on investment in different regions. First, firms sometimes register their investment at the location of their head office, even if the actual physical investment takes place elsewhere. Investment in the Tunis area may, therefore, be overstated. Second, remittances usually flow from rich areas to poor areas, so spatial disparities in income are bigger than disparities in consumption. But conversely, the ratios do not capture the nonconsumption benefits of investment in social services.

TABLE 2.2

Investment in the Poorest Areas of Tunisia Gives the Poorest Returns

(in millions TD, 2000 prices)

	Increase in annual consumption, 1985–2000	Public and private investment, 1986–2000	Investment needed to raise consumption by 1 m TD/year
Tunis and Northeast	2,018	23,594	11.6
Northwest	409	6,455	15.8
Center-west	395	5,316	13.5
Center-east	1,843	15,591	8.4
South	483	9,225	19.2

Sources: INS 2000;. Enquête nationale sur le budget, la consommation et le niveau de vie des ménages [National survey of household budgets, consumption, and living standards], Commissariat Général de Développement Régional (CGDR).

Therefore, the location of investment in Tunisia can contribute to the sociopolitical objective of raising living standards in the south, northwest, and center-west lagging areas on the one hand, or the economic objective of maximizing growth nationwide on the other. Figure 2.2 shows the hypothetical range of outcomes if investment were to be redistributed between leading and lagging areas while earning the same average return by region in terms of household consumption increases that it did in 1985–2000. The cost of increasing consumption in the lagging regions by 1 million Tunisian dinars (TD) per year is a reduction in *nationwide* consumption of TD 610,000 per year.

Morocco publishes industrial production and investment figures by province and prefecture, which allows one to calculate the how much investment it takes to produce a dirham of additional production in each region. Figure 2.3 illustrates the agglomeration economies: regions with more industry have tended to achieve greater increases in production relative to the cost of investment. This finding seems to confirm that there is a trade-off between investing to achieve the political goal of shifting production to lagging areas and investing for national growth. Figure 2.4 illustrates the hypothetical trade-off between the objective of increasing the geographical spread of industrial activity in Morocco and promoting national growth. It takes less investment to generate Moroccan dirham (MD) 1 million of industrial growth in Morocco's three most industrialized provinces—Grand Casablanca, Doukala-Abda, and Tanger-Tétouan—than it does in the other eleven. Applying the average provincial returns on investment for 1996–2005, it seems that the same investment could either generate a MD 1 million increase in industrial production in the 11 nonleading provinces or a MD 1.2 million increase in *national* industrial production, depending on where it takes place.

A measure of the power of economies of agglomeration is that they are the main factor determining where firms locate across the developing

FIGURE 2.2

Hypothetical Range of Outcomes between National Consumption Growth and Consumption Growth in Tunisia's Poorer Areas, 1985–2000

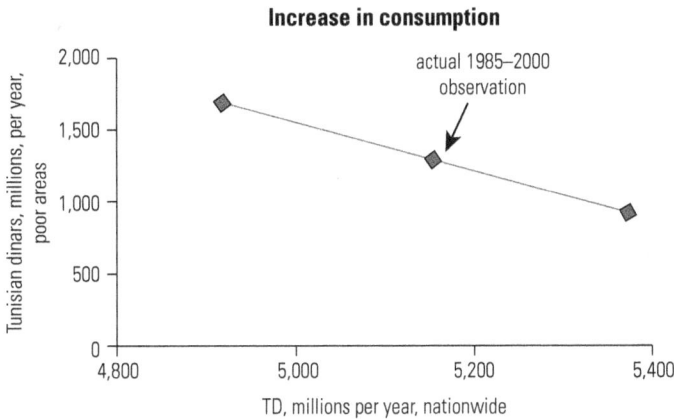

Source: Table 2.2.

Note: The poor areas are the northwest, center-west, and south.

FIGURE 2.3

In Morocco, Provinces with Large Industrial Sectors Provide the Highest Returns to Industrial Investment

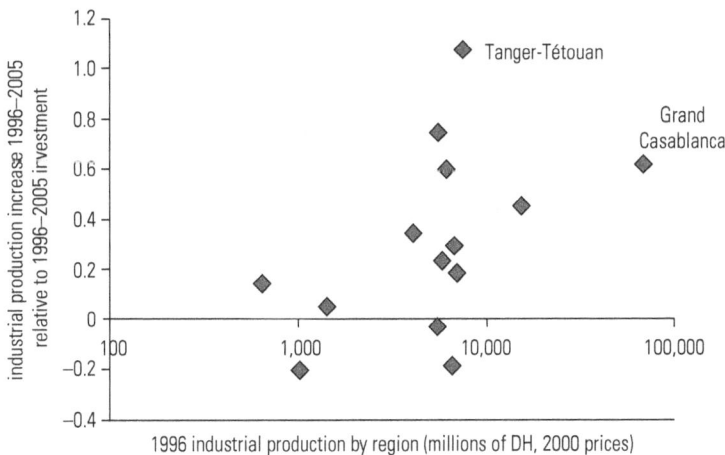

Source: Annuaires Statistiques du Maroc (Statistical Directory of Morocco), 1998–2007.

Note: All figures converted to 2000 prices.

world (Deichmann, Lall, Redding, and Venables 2008). Tehran province's density of economic activity (value added per square kilometer) is six times higher than that of the next-densest province (World Bank 2008a). In Morocco, industrial employment growth is focused on Casablanca and then on spillovers from that metropolis into adjoining areas (Catin,

FIGURE 2.4

Consequences of Splitting MD 1 Billion Industrial Investments between Leading Three and Lagging Eleven Provinces in Morocco, 1996–2005

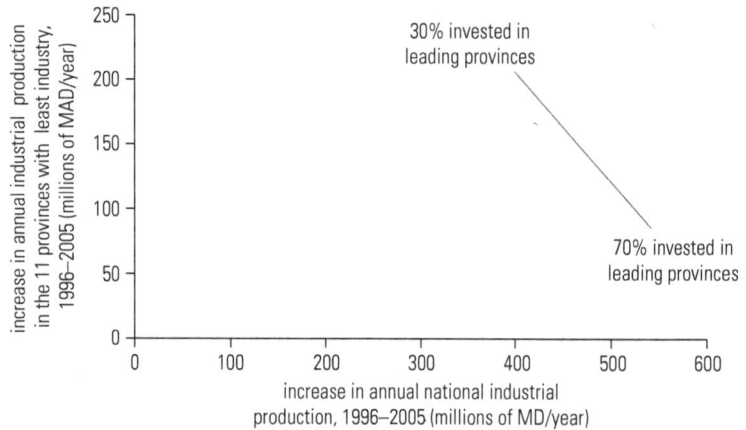

Source: Annuaires Statistiques du Maroc [Statistical Directory of Morocco], 1998–2007.

Note: All figures converted to 2000 prices.

Hanchane, and Kamal 2007). In Tunisia, agglomeration is one of the most easily identifiable determinants of a region's growth (Karray and Driss 2008).

However, there are exceptions to the general rule that economic activity becomes increasingly concentrated. Some countries have "breakaway" regions that pulled away from the peloton of middle-ranking regions to achieve accelerated growth. In the Islamic Republic of Iran, it was the southwestern ostans of Bushehr and Ilam that broke out. In Tunisia, it was the center-east, and in Morocco it was Tanger-Tétouan. So, while economies of agglomeration may be primordial in determining spatial competitiveness, we must also ask what conditions make for a "breakaway region" and what role governments can play in facilitating breakaways. We will explore this question in later sections.

Nonetheless, breakaway areas are the exception, not the general rule. It is a statement of fact that agglomeration is a major source of productivity and economic growth in MENA and elsewhere.

Spatial Disparities Create Political Stresses

In MENA as elsewhere, spatial disparities are a hot issue because they put pressure on governments.

The regional disparities that developing countries inherited at independence were a challenge to postindependence nation building. Tackling inherited spatial inequalities was a crucial objective for the state-building agenda. By highlighting the developmental divides within national boundaries, lagging areas encouraged the preservation of a traditional *asabiyyah*—a form of group identity and solidarity promoting regionally based agendas and hampering the development of fully integrated national communities (Hudson 1997; Owen 1992, 67–68; Esman and Rabinovitch 1988). (See box 2.1.)

Moreover, by fueling migration, spatial inequalities bring political risks to the better-off areas. MENA has experienced rural-urban migration,

---

BOX 2.1

Ibn Khaldun and the Political Economy of Spatial Disparities

Ibn Khaldun (1332–1406), the North African polymath, is considered one of the fathers of modern social science and economics. His career took him to many of the great cities of the Arab world: Granada, Fès, Tunis, Cairo, Alexandria, and Damascus. His masterpiece, *The Muqaddimah*, elaborates a theory of the political economy of the urban-rural divide (Omran 1980).

Ibn Khaldun observed that the stability and prosperity of society depended on the existence of *asabiyyah*, which has been translated as "social cohesion," "social capital," or "group solidarity." *Asabiyyah* is strong among rural populations and provides the foundation for a stable society within which urbanization, economic specialization, and economies of agglomeration can be constructed.

Ibn Khaldun argues, however, that the economic growth resulting from agglomeration carries the seeds of political tension. Increasing disparities between cities and rural areas lead to corruption, conspicuous consumption, and a breakdown of *asabiyyah* and of the legitimacy of the state in the eyes of the governed. These in turn lead to political instability and maybe a change of government.

Although Ibn Khaldun speaks to us from six centuries ago, his observations about how political stability depends upon the perceived fairness of the relationship between rich places and poor places are echoed in the concerns of MENA's politicians today.

However, MENA's twenty-first-century politicians have policy instruments that fourteenth-century rulers would not have dreamed of: public schools and health centers, targeted social protection schemes, planning capacity, and infrastructure budgets. Modern governments can deploy these services to reinforce *asabiyyah*—social cohesion—at the same time that market forces are building agglomeration.

So perhaps if Ibn Khaldun were alive today, he might be more optimistic.

urban unemployment, and degrading living conditions in slums and shantytowns, and finally political radicalization in urban areas.

Spatial disparities are, therefore, more than economics; seen through the lens of MENA's recent history, they are also a challenge to the equilibrium of the state. Therefore, the question is how to sustain this spatial-social equilibrium without sacrificing the economic efficiency of agglomeration.

Women and Men Experience Spatial Inequalities Differently

In MENA, as in other parts of the world, women's lives are conditioned by society's expectations and norms. The traditional gender paradigm in MENA, combined with gender-specific legal provisions, determines to a great extent women's access to and interaction with the state and the public sphere. Key elements of the traditional gender paradigm in MENA include centrality of the family, establishment of the man as the principal breadwinner and as head of household, the "code of modesty," and unequal decision making and economic power in the private sphere (World Bank 2008b, 94, 132).

Thus, living in a lagging area affects women differently from men. Their experience of distance differs according to their mobility. Their experience of disparities in services differs according to their ability to interact with officialdom. Their experience of migration differs according to their access to the job market and social networks.

This study, therefore, commissioned field surveys in Egypt, Saudi Arabia, and Tunisia to investigate how spatial inequality and gender roles interact (Esber 2008). They confirmed that spatial inequality sometimes can combine with gender inequality to create a double perception of marginalization. The main findings from the surveys are summarized below.

Women are particularly affected by spatial disparities in access to services. Gender disparities in access to public, social, and administrative services tend to be higher in lagging areas. This finding is borne out by MENA's data on education access and outcomes; in Morocco, the literacy gap between men and women is 5 percentage points in urban areas and 35 percent in rural areas. In Tunisia, the gender literacy gap in 2004 was 5 percentage points in Ettadhamoun, a low-income suburb of Tunis, and was 12 percentage points in Kasserine, a provincial town in a lagging governorate. Two-thirds of women in the lagging area town of Kasserine cited improvement in relations with public administrations and government authorities as a priority for improvement in their living conditions, a higher score than any other issue such as education or access to credit.

When men from lagging areas migrate in search of work, the female members of the family who remain sometimes have difficulties dealing with male officials (see box 2.2 for an example). This issue is particularly important for the design of MENA's agricultural extension services. Many rural women assume day-to-day responsibility for the household's farming activities when men of working age migrate in search of employment, but these women are socially and physically constrained from obtaining advice and services from male extension agents.

Women are especially affected by the lack of appropriate transport options in peripheral areas. Social and physical constraints on women's use of transportation are, of course, particularly important in low-density areas. Women in lagging areas of Saudi Arabia have particular difficulty in accessing all levels of education and services, in addition to limited social interactions, because of their partial mobility. The transportation disparity exists but is less pronounced in Egypt and Tunisia. In the Republic of Yemen, 56 percent of rural women, but only 25 percent of men, reported that transportation options were unresponsive to their needs (World Bank forthcoming). Rural girls have to pay 50 percent more than boys for transportation to school; boys can hitch a lift, but girls have to pay for a private car for themselves and their *muhrams* (male companions).

The costs and benefits of migration are different for women. Displacement from home results in physiological, psychological, and social stress (Shami 1993), but men and women may have very different experiences of the pros and cons of moving to the big city. This finding was clear from our survey of residents of Manshiyet Nasser, a low-income area of Cairo, who were asked to compare life in the capital with Qena, a lagging

---

BOX 2.2

A Migrant's Wife Has Difficulties with the Local Authorities

"My husband worked in the Sahel for a few years. At the time, I was entitled to receive social security from the authorities but often didn't receive it. The *shaykh* [local authority] did not want to give it to us, because I sent him away from my home. I was a woman alone with my children, and if the neighbors saw that I received him at home, they would say bad things about my conduct, and I would have problems when my husband returned. Unfortunately, the shaykh considered it his right to go to people's homes; it is not the case for me [to permit it in order] to have social security. I should have made a complaint against him to his superiors, and I would have won my case."

Source: Khadija, a 40-year-old woman from Kasserine, a lagging area of Tunisia.

area town in Upper Egypt. The economic motive for migrating to Cairo appeared more positive to men than to women: 82 percent of men but only 36 percent of women saw job opportunities as an advantage of living in Cairo compared with Qena. For women, the main advantage of living in Cairo was the ability to build strong social networks and was cited as an advantage of Cairo by 55 percent of women but only 36 percent of men. When asked about the advantages of Qena compared with Cairo, men and women again had very different viewpoints. For men, Qena's primary positive points were transportation and the ease of obtaining official papers. For women, Qena's main attractions were the low crime rate and the healthier environment.

In Tunisia, however, men and women both saw the advantage of the capital city over a lagging area town (Kasserine) in the same light: income and employment. And both men and women saw the lagging area town having the same advantage over Tunis: greater family solidarity, respect for tradition, and freedom from crime. More than 80 percent of women said that they would support their son's or daughter's migration. Women were particularly pragmatic in their attitude that economic factors justified migration. A majority of female respondents quoted the saying, "Your country is where you earn your bread."

One cannot be certain why the Tunisian women surveyed seemed much less worried by the negative social effects of migration than their counterparts in Egypt; however, it may be that the comparative weakness of Tunisia's social restrictions on women makes migration less of a challenge when it comes to mobility, to the labor market, and to establishing social networks.

Therefore, the social roles apportioned to women in MENA mean that they experience the lagging region syndrome of distance and isolation even more acutely than men. The gender dimension of spatial disparities may not be as visible as the political dimension, but it is, nonetheless, an element to be taken into account when policy makers attempt to balance the sociopolitical with the economic.

Spatial Equity with Spatial Efficiency

So we begin with two firm facts. First, investment and employment are more productive when they take place in areas of economic agglomeration in leading areas. Second, the strongest political demand from governments and the governed is for improvements in living standards in lagging areas.

The purpose of this report is to suggest how MENA policy makers can turn the tension between spatial politics and spatial economics into a win-win: a policy package that satisfies both the political argument for equity and the economic argument for efficiency.

- First, by analyzing MENA's lagging areas, we will see that MENA economies can get greater improvements in living standards in lagging areas than they think for any given economic cost. The reason, as our detailed diagnosis of MENA's lagging areas will show, is that many of the factors holding lagging areas back are social and institutional rather than economic. This means that MENA governments can address the root causes of spatial disparities through administrative reforms and human development interventions, such as education, and health and social protection programs, rather than relying on the doubtful and costly strategy of luring economic activity to lagging areas.

- Second, we will show how governments can maximize the benefit-cost ratio of policies to reduce spatial disparities by tailoring them to different lagging areas. Later sections of this report will explore, in turn, the potential of human development, connectivity, and targeted regional economic development to narrow MENA's spatial disparities.

- Finally, the report will examine how some MENA economies are attempting to reverse the historical legacy of centralization and build a new institutional framework for managing territoriality. We will then discuss whether such reforms will give MENA politicians more room to maneuver in the future, setting up a new and more propitious trade-off between spatial economics and spatial politics.

Matching Policy Packages to Lagging Areas: A Three-Way Framework

It is a cliché that development policies must fit the local context, and this is especially true for spatial development. Lagging areas (see box 2.3) come in many different varieties; an arid rangeland is not a peri-urban slum.

Which policies, then, are appropriate in which places? With some adjustment, the framework of the 2009 World Development Report, *Reshaping Economic Geography* (World Bank 2009a), provides a starting point for matching policy packages to places.

Drawing on the World Development Report, we propose three policy packages for MENA:

- Policy Package 1. Level the playing field and the opportunity for human development in lagging areas.

- Policy Package 2. Connect lagging areas to the poles of development.

BOX 2.3

Mind Your Language!

This report will use the word "lagging" nearly 500 times, so we need to agree what it means.

Our definition of a "lagging area" combines the spatial distribution of economic activity and living standards. It uses the phrase "lagging area" to denote a place with low production per capita and low living standards compared with other places in the same country. If a subnational measure of GDP were available for a lagging area, it would be significantly lower than the national average. Welfare measures such as per capita consumption and human development indicators will also be low.

A lagging area can be big or small. In the context of a country, it might be a region. In the context of a region, it might be a district or an agro-ecological zone. In the context of a district, it might be a village.

The phrase "spatial disparities," however, refers solely to the gaps in *living standards* between lagging areas and the rest of the country. It says nothing about the distribution of *economic activity*.

This terminology underlies the critical distinction illustrated in figure 2.5. Overcoming spatial disparities is about raising people's living standards in lagging areas, but it does not necessarily involve a change in the spatial distribution of economic activity.

- Policy Package 3. Underpin private sector interest in nonleading areas.

The three packages are not mutually exclusive; they can overlay each other. Policy Package 1 applies everywhere. Governments can choose to add packages 2 or 3 or both if the lagging area meets specific criteria.

Policy Package 1. Provide a Level Playing Field and the Opportunity for Human Development in Lagging Areas

Breaking the link between the spatial concentration of production and spatial disparities. Just because economic activity is attracted to agglomerations (density) does not mean that people living in peripheral areas must suffer from growing spatial disparities in well-being. Unfortunately, it is very difficult to analyze the spatial distribution of economic activity in MENA, as authentic subnational GDP estimates are scarce.[4] However, the experience of developed countries shows that economic agglomeration does not necessarily mean greater spatial disparities in living standards (World Bank 2009a).

In France, for example, the concentration of economic activity around the Paris metropolitan area grew more and more pronounced between 1982 and 2002. At the same time, however, the distribution of per capita income became more and more equal (Martin 2005), as the taxation and benefits systems transferred the value of metropolitan areas' production to poorer people in the provinces. In the United Kingdom (UK), conversely, both economic activity *and* people's incomes became more concentrated during the 1990s (Duranton and Monastiriotis 2002). The reason was a growing gap in education levels between the leading southeast and the poorer parts of the UK. In the United States during the twentieth century, the gap in posttax incomes between the poorer and the richer states narrowed whenever the tax rate increased (World Bank 2009a) and widened when it fell again. Long-term convergence between richer and poorer states in the United States was achieved by investments in education (Lall and Yilmaz 2000). A study of Eastern Europe and Central Asia found that the correlation between a region's GDP and its level of poverty was very strong in some countries and weak in others (Dillinger 2007).

In short, the spatial distribution of production and spatial disparities in welfare are different outcomes. The decisions of governments determine how far agglomeration translates into spatial disparities in living standards (figure 2.5).

The implication is that policy makers who are concerned about spatial disparities in people's well-being should focus first and foremost on

FIGURE 2.5

**Agglomeration and Spatial Disparities in Well-Being:
Two Separate Outcomes**

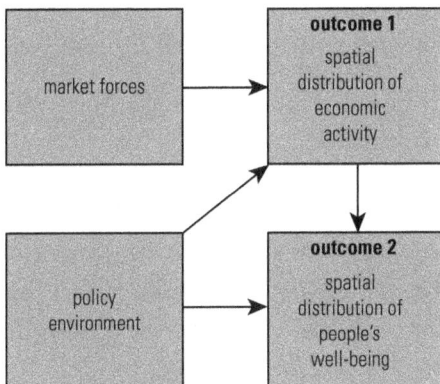

Source: Authors.

developing the people who live in poor places. Such policies could include improving educational services, arranging health services and social protection, and making it easier to take advantage of migration opportunities.

The core principle of Policy Package 1 is that governments should try to give poor places the same institutional environment and opportunities for human development as those in rich places—in other words, a "level playing field for development."

Leveling the playing field involves understanding how the historical accretion of centralizing policies has created implicit spatial biases in policy, and then setting out to correct them. As we shall see in later sections, a legacy of MENA's colonial and postcolonial history was often an implicit prometropolitan bias in the application of policies. The institutional environment; patterns of government expenditure; pricing policies; and education, health, and social protection systems were most favorable to metropolitan, urban, or leading areas. For example, energy subsidies, which obviously favor urban and metropolitan areas the most, averaged 7.1 percent of GDP for all MENA countries, even before the fuel price increases of 2008.

The policy package of investing in people and leveling the playing field for development can be applied to any area with lagging development indicators. Clearly, it does not depend upon the lagging area having specific geographic characteristics, such as proximity to agglomeration, or on a specific source of economic potential, such as natural resources or access to markets. It is based upon the universally applicable principles that institutions and human development are critical to spatial development and that nondiscriminatory treatment of different target groups is nondistorting.

The two policy packages that follow, however, are applicable only to areas that meet defined criteria.

Policy Package 2. Connect Lagging Areas to the Poles of Development

Economic growth spreads out and spills over from cities to hinterlands. And if a lagging area is close enough to a leading area, linking the two can help prosperity to spill over from the latter to the former. Being connected to markets will increase consumer welfare in the lagging area, as residents face lower prices because of market integration. Workers and producers will also realize higher value added as they benefit from better access to jobs and markets. Therefore, connectivity infrastructure is always a backbone of spatial development.

In Vietnam, for example, a highway from Hanoi to Hai Phong created a corridor of growth and poverty-reduction penetrating deep into a lagging area (ADB, JBIC, and World Bank 2005). Rural road investments raised GDP by 30 percent between 1993 and 1998, as well as expanding school enrollment and improving health service utilization. In India, investment in rural roads was one of the most effective forms of public expenditure in terms of promoting growth and poverty reduction at the subnational level (Fan, Hazell, and Thorat 1999).

MENA has a special advantage over other world regions when it comes to using connective infrastructure to develop lagging areas. MENA's settlement patterns are compact. Lagging areas are often close to leading areas; only 39 percent of its lagging areas' populations live more than three hours from a major city.

The benefits of linking lagging areas to nearby hubs are proven. A study by the World Bank found that improved rural feeder roads in Morocco generated substantial positive effects compared with areas without new roads for transport, agriculture, health, education, and gender. Farmers' production, productivity, and output values increased, and they shifted toward higher-value crops. And enrollment in primary education increased much faster, particularly for girls (Levy 2004).

However, connectivity investments do have a side effect: cheaper transport often means more economic agglomeration. As transportation costs between the leading and the lagging area fall, producers in the lagging area can be undercut by competition from the leading area, which has lower costs because of its economies of agglomeration (Venables 2005). Looking at the arrival of new interstate highways in rural America, Chandra (2000) found that rural-based companies that had been trading nationally expanded after the arrival of the roads, presumably because they could now access their distant markets more cheaply. Companies that had been trading within the local region, conversely, tended to shrink as their home market was left more exposed to competition from other areas. Italy's *intervento straordinario*, which mobilized billions of dollars per year to build roads and railways for Italy's lagging southern region, is now credited with having led to the *out*-migration of two million workers from the target area in the 1950s (World Bank 2009a).

The literature cited earlier suggests that effects of short-distance connections (such as rural feeder roads) are more likely to be unambiguously positive for the lagging area than the effects of trunk roads. This finding may be because the artisans and farmers in the small villages that benefit from feeder roads are usually not in competition with larger towns. The village benefits from cheaper consumer goods and farm inputs, as well as better access to agricultural markets and services and the possibility of commuting to larger settlements. The availability of feeder roads can be a major influence on farmers' costs to market and decision to invest in cash crops (Lall, Wang, and Munthali 2009); however, it should be noted that it is difficult to measure the impact of rural roads programs ex-post, because it is hard to know whether a new road in a place led to its development or whether a place's high level of development made the government decide that it needed a new road (Van de Walle 2009).

Transportation is no longer the only critical mode of connectivity. Improving information and communication technology (ICT) connectivity is now of growing importance in linking lagging areas to national economic growth. Not only can cheap and efficient communications improve access to market information, but also they can support the delivery of education. They help people from poorer areas to migrate and integrate into leading areas by acquiring contacts and "cultural markers" from more advanced parts of the country.

This report will, therefore, assess the state of connectivity in MENA and will identify thematic priorities for lagging areas in the transport and ICT sectors.

Policy Package 3. Underpin Private Sector Interest in Nonleading Areas

We suggested earlier that the people-based approach is the most applicable solution for all lagging areas.

Sometimes, however, the people-based approach *alone* is not enough. Sometimes there are places whose populations need new economic opportunities nearby to sustain their livelihoods. Governments will look to place-based economic development interventions under the following three circumstances:

- There is no prospect of growth spilling over from leading areas fast enough.

- There is no prospect of migration solving the lagging area problem fast enough.

- There is genuine private investor interest in the lagging area, requiring only that government puts the necessary facilitating institutions and infrastructure in place.

The critical point is that governments should underpin private sector interest, not seek to steer it toward lagging areas.

The ability of the population to redistribute itself from lagging to leading areas is a key criterion for deciding whether place-based approaches are appropriate (World Bank 2009a). Clearly, the easier it is for people to move to leading areas with high economic potential, the less sense it makes to allocate productive investment to lagging areas with low economic potential. In this report we will see that most of MENA's populations are urbanizing but not redistributing from lagging to leading provinces. MENA's policy makers, therefore, cannot always rely upon metropolitan growth and migration toward leading provinces to take care of underemployment in lagging provinces. This finding gives some weight to the case for place-based economic development policies, perhaps targeting lagging areas' secondary agglomerations.

However, place-based regional economic development policies that aim to secure spatially balanced growth have earned a bad reputation, and rightly so. The problem is that governments have usually tried to use financial incentives to create investor interest where it did not really exist. In fact, the forces of economic agglomeration are so strong and so persistent that governments' attempts to combat them with incentives to invest in lagging areas have usually been overwhelmed. Even the greatest catastrophes, such as the near-destruction of German and Japanese cities by Allied bombs at the end of World War II, seem unable to redirect the spatial distribution of economic activity in the long term (Davis and Weinstein 2002; Brakman, Garretsen, and Schramm 2004).

The history of policies aimed to stimulate investment in lagging areas is, therefore, littered with costly failures, as this report will describe in detail.

When nonleading areas move to the front, it is not because government has deployed subsidies and incentives to influence firms' location. It is because the market has responded to potential locational competitiveness, whether it be human resources (Ireland, southern United States), natural resources, or market access (Tanger-Tétouan and center-east Tunisia).

This finding, therefore, means a new paradigm for the state's role in promoting regional development. The government's role is no longer to use incentives to steer investment toward lagging areas by distorting market forces; it is to help ensure that the *private sector's market-led decisions are underpinned* by the necessary infrastructure, information, networks, and regulations. The key is not incentivization but coordination.

However, the corollary of the new paradigm of regional economic development is that it just cannot apply to all lagging areas. It needs private investor interest in a lagging area's unrealized commercial potential. So it is likeliest to succeed in middle-ranking regions or in areas with a strong skills or natural resource base. Conversely, it is least likely to work in very poor regions without such assets.

This report will examine in more detail the lessons learned from global practice on this "new paradigm" for regional economic development. It will examine MENA experience and derive principles for MENA policy makers.

How to Put It All Together: Three Policy Approaches

So we have three policy packages, each applicable to a different set of lagging areas (table 2.3 and figure 2.6). First, all lagging areas need fair access to decent institutions and human development. Second, lagging areas near to economic poles can gain from improved spillover connectivity. Third, places with private sector interest in unrealized economic potential could benefit from the government's coordinating the underpinning of private investment with the necessary infrastructure, information, networks, and regulations.

Figure 2.6 restates this framework and also serves as a map for the rest of this report. The process begins by checking the real size and trajectory of spatial disparities, because the spatial dimension of inequality is sometimes not as important at it appears. But if policy makers deem that the spatial disparities problem is serious enough to warrant intervention, the next stage is to identify the characteristics of the lagging areas in question. We will discuss these diagnostic stages in detail. The following three sections explore the three policy packages themselves: level the playing field and the opportunity for human development in lagging areas, connect lagging areas to the poles of development, and underpin private sector interest in nonleading areas' economic potential. The last section concludes by exploring how MENA's institutional structures can become more supportive of such territorial approaches.

TABLE 2.3

Matching Policy Packages to Lagging Areas

Policy packages	World Development Report 2009 terminology	Why?	Where?
Package 1. Level the playing field and the opportunity for human development in lagging areas	"Institutions" ("spatially blind policies")	Spatial disparities in well-being can narrow even while production is agglomerating, so long as policies are appropriate. MENA has a historical legacy of policies' widening disparities.	Applicable to all lagging areas
Package 2. Connect lagging areas to the poles of development	"Infrastructure" ("spatially connective policies")	For growth to spill over from economic poles into lagging areas, they have to be connected.	Lagging areas close enough to density to benefit
Package 3. Underpin private sector interest in nonleading areas	"Incentives" ("spatially focused policies")	Sometimes nonleading areas do move ahead to leading-area status (e.g., Tunisia's center-east, Morocco's Tanger-Tétouan)	Areas where the private sector sees unrealized growth potential

Sources: Study Team and World Bank 2009a.

FIGURE 2.6

Matching Policy Packages to Lagging Areas

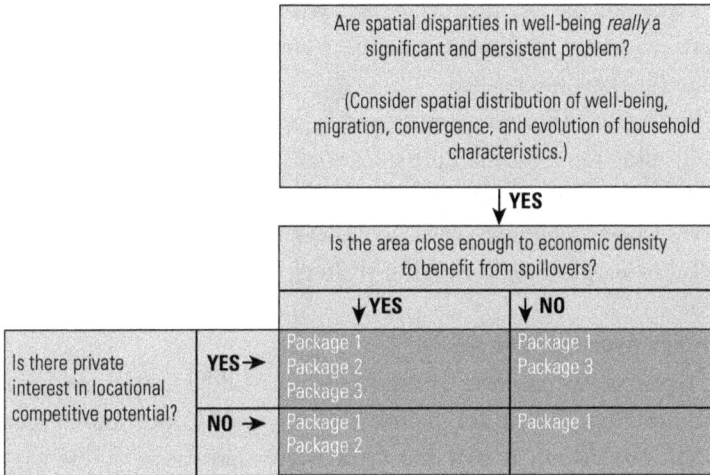

Sources: Study Team and World Bank 2009a.

What This Report Covers and What It Doesn't

From Examples to Recommendations

Spatial analysis needs spatially disaggregated data, but spatially disaggregated data in MENA are scarce. Household consumption surveys are generally representative at the province-governorate level, but poverty maps are usually required to access finer levels of disaggregation. Other subnational data in MENA are generally a by-product of sectoral analyses. Rural-urban breakdowns are sometimes available and provincial breakdowns are rarer. Where subnational data do exist, the use of administrative boundaries for demarcation makes cross-country comparison a hazardous exercise.

The approach of this report has, therefore, been to illustrate general principles from specific examples. In the chapters that follow, key spatial development issues are exemplified by the available data. The message to the policy maker is always the concept and the analytical method rather than a locality-specific conclusion.

In addition, this report contains little spatial econometrics. We could have spent a lot of time, money, and effort analyzing the forces of spatial agglomeration in MENA, but we would have concluded only what MENA's policy makers know well already: that economic activity is drawn inexorably toward existing agglomerations. We could have attempted to quantify the returns to public spending on spatial development, but with such analyses showing inconclusive results even in countries with abundant data (Glaeser and Gottlieb 2009), there was little hope that they would have been more productive in MENA. Indeed, even if we had had more data, there was the risk that deeper analysis would merely have led to the truisms that every locality's experience is unique and that yet more disaggregated analysis was needed.

This report, therefore, emphasizes operational implications. We hope to illustrate some simple questions that policy makers can pose in order to anatomize the spatial disparities situation in their country. Every section concludes with an "Ideas for Policy Makers" box—a handful of suggestions for taking strategy toward implementation.

Country Coverage: The MENA13

This report does not cover Israel, Malta, or Middle Eastern and North African economies that are members of the Gulf Cooperation Council (GCC). The reason is that the GCC states have very different geographical and economic characteristics from the rest of the region: their economic geography results from the absence of widespread sedentary agriculture because of their aridity and their abundance of mineral resources. So, while the GCC states do indeed face a number of critical spatial development issues, they would require a separate and distinctive analysis. The study, therefore, covers the following Middle Eastern and North African economies: Algeria, Djibouti, Egypt, the Islamic Republic of Iran, Iraq, Jordan, Lebanon, Libya, Morocco, the Syrian Arab Republic, Tunisia, the West Bank and Gaza, and the Republic of Yemen.

The report uses the abbreviation "MENA" to signify these 13 economies. Sometimes, for example, to distinguish them from the broader set of MENA economies, it will refer to them as the "MENA13." When a secondary source refers to "MENA" as the whole region, including the GCC, we will say so.

The report uses national definitions of "rural" and "urban" areas. Unless otherwise stated, when the report states an indicator for "lagging areas," this refers to the worst-off 40 percent of governorates or provinces.

Endnotes

1. Speech of H. M. King Mohammed VI of Morocco on the occasion of the forty-sixth anniversary of the revolution.
2. Algeria, Djibouti, Egypt, the Islamic Republic of Iran, Jordan, Lebanon, Libya, Morocco, the Syrian Arab Republic, Tunisia, the West Bank and Gaza, and the Republic of Yemen.
3. In an unscientific poll, the report team surveyed 27 MENA policy makers in April 2009 concerning spatial development policies in their countries.

Seventy-eight percent said that government had favored the metropolis at the expense of peripheral areas in the past, though half of them thought that this bias had been corrected. Two-thirds said that spatial policy was primarily based on political or social considerations; one-third said it was based on efficiency considerations.

4. Egypt's National Human Development Reports (HDR) publish estimates of GDP per capita by governorate. These figures are obtained by applying a constant multiplier to consumption data. GECON's publicly available datasets assume that a given sector's labor productivity is equal in all locations within the same country. Morocco issued its first provincial GDP estimates after this report went to press.

References

ADB (Asian Development Bank), JBIC (Japanese Bureau for International Cooperation), and World Bank. 2005. *Connecting East Asia: A New Framework for Infrastructure.* Washington, DC: World Bank.

Al-Ahram. 2006. "Focus on Upper Egypt." *Al-Ahram Weekly Online.* March 23–29.

Al-Alwani, M. 1982. "The Arabs and the Science of Population Distribution." *Population Bulletin of ECWA* 22: 159–77.

Alcorn, E. 2009. "Regional Overview of Spatial Disparities in Health Care Access and Health Outcomes." Unpublished.

Brakman, S., H. Garretsen, and M. Schramm. 2004. "The Strategic Bombing of German Cities during World War II and Its Impact on City Growth." *Journal of Economic Geography* 4 (2): 201–18.

Catin, M., S. Hanchane, and A. Kamal. 2007. "Structure Industrielle, Externalités, Dynamique et Croissance Locale au Maroc." *Région et Développement* 25: 1–18.

Chandra, A. 2000. "Does Public Highway Infrastructure Affect Economic Activity? Evidence from the Rural Interstate Highway System." *Regional Science and Urban Economics* 30: 457–90.

Christian Science Monitor. 2007. "Ahmadinejad: Rock Star in Rural Iran." December 7.

Davis, D., and D. Weinstein. 2002. "Bones, Bombs, and Break Points: The Geography of Economic Activity." *American Economic Review* 92 (5): 1269–89.

Deichmann, U., S. Lall, S. Redding, and A. Venables. 2008. "Industrial Location in Developing Countries." *World Bank Research Observer* 23 (2): 219–46.

Dillinger, W. 2007. *Poverty and Regional Development in Eastern Europe and Central Asia*. Europe and Central Asia Chief Economist's Regional Working Paper Series. Washington, DC: World Bank.

Duranton, G., and V. Monastiriotis. 2002. "Mind the Gaps: The Evolution of Regional Earnings Inequalities in the U.K., 1982–1997." *Journal of Regional Science* 42: 219–56.

El Laithy, H., and K. Abu-Ismail. 2005. "Poverty in Syria: 1996–2004." Unpublished.

Esber, R. 2008. "Gender and Spatial Disparities in the Middle East and North Africa: A Study of Saudi Arabia, Egypt and Tunisia." Unpublished.

Esman, M. J., and I. Rabinovitch. 1988. *Ethnicity, Pluralism and the State in the Middle East*. Ithaca, NY: Cornell University Press.

Fan, S., P. Hazell, and S. Thorat. 1999. *Linkages between Government Spending, Growth and Poverty in Rural India*. Washington, DC: IFPRI (International Food Policy Research Institute).

Glaeser, E. L., and J. D. Gottlieb. 2009. *The Economics of Place-making Policies*. Washington, DC: National Bureau of Economic Research.

Haddad, A. 1996. *Poverty in Lebanon*. Beirut: UN Economic and Social Council for Western Asia (ESCWA).

Haut Commissariat au Plan. 1998, 1999, 2000, 2007. "Annuaires Statistiques du Maroc" (Statistical Directory of Morocco). Rabat, Morocco.

———. 2007. *Activité, Emploi, et Chômage*. Rabat: Direction de la Statistique.

Henderson, J. V., Z. Shalizi, and A. Venables. 2001. "Geography and Development." *Journal of Economic Geography* 1 (1): 81–105.

Hudson, M. 1997. *Arab Politics: The Search for Legitimacy*. New Haven, CT: Yale University Press.

INS (Institut National de la Statistique). 2000. *Enquête Nationale sur le Budget. La Consommation et le Niveau de Vie des Ménages*. Tunis: INS.

Kanbur, R., and A. Venables. 2005. *Rising Spatial Disparities and Development*. Helsinki: World Institute for Development Economic Research (UNU-WIDER).

Karray, Z., and S. Driss. 2008. *Regional Growth in Tunisia: Economic Geography Forces and Industrial Structure*. Cairo: Economic Research Forum.

Krugman, P. 1991. "Increasing Returns and Economic Geography." *Journal of Political Economy* 99 (3): 483–99.

Lall, S., H. Wang, and T. Munthali. 2009. "The Where of Infrastructure Investments in Malawi: Insights from a Spatial Analysis." Unpublished background paper for World Bank.

Lall, S., and S. Yilmaz. 2000. "Regional Economic Convergence: Do Policy Instruments Make a Difference?" *Annals of Regional Science* 35 (1): 153–66.

Levy, H. 2004. "Rural Roads and Poverty Alleviation in Morocco." Paper presented at Scaling Up Poverty Reduction: A Global Learning Process and Conference, Shanghai, May 25–27, World Bank.

Martin, P. 2005. "The Geography of Economic Inequalities in Europe." *Swedish Economic Policy Review* 12: 83–108.

Nordhaus, W. D. 2006. "Geography and Macroeconomics: New Data and New Findings." *PNAS* 103 (10): 3510–17.

Omran, A. R. 1980. *Population in the Arab World: Problems and Prospects.* New York: United Nations Fund for Population Activities.

Owen, R. 1992. *State, Power, and Politics in the Making of the Modern Middle East.* London: Routledge.

PCBS (Palestinian Central Bureau of Statistics). 2006. *The Palestinian Expenditure and Consumption Survey 2005.* Ramallah: PCBS.

Romer, P. 1994. "The Origins of Endogenous Growth." *Journal of Economic Perspectives* 8 (1): 3–22.

Shami, S. 1993. "The Social Implications of Population Displacement and Resettlement: An Overview with a Focus on the Arab Middle East." *International Migration Review* 27 (1): 4–33.

Shlash, A. 2009. Iraq High Committee for Strategy Reduction. Draft Strategy Review presentation. June. Amman.

UN Habitat. 2004. *The State of the World's Cities 2004/5: Globalization and Urban Culture.* New York: United Nations.

United Nations. 2006. *World Population Policies 2005.* New York: United Nations, Department of Economic and Social Affairs, Population Division.

Van de Walle, D. 2009. "Impact Evaluation of Rural Roads Projects." *Journal of Development Effectiveness* 1 (1): 15–36.

Venables, A. 2005. "Spatial Disparities in Developing Countries: Cities, Regions, and International Trends." *Journal of Economic Geography* 5: 3–21.

World Bank. 1999. *Democratic and Popular Republic of Algeria. Growth Employment and Poverty Reduction.* Washington, DC: World Bank.

———. 2002. *Yemen: Poverty Update.* Washington, DC: World Bank.

———. 2003. *Deep Palestinian Poverty in the Midst of Crisis.* Washington, DC: World Bank.

———. 2004. *Jordan: Poverty Assessment.* Washington, DC: World Bank.

———. 2007. *Arab Republic of Egypt: Enhancing the Performance of the Road Sector.* Washington, DC: World Bank.

———. 2008a. *Islamic Republic of Iran: Spatial Patterns of Poverty and Economic Activity.* Washington, DC: World Bank.

———. 2008b. *Gender and Development in the Middle East and North Africa.* Washington, DC: World Bank.

———. 2009a. *World Development Report 2009: Reshaping Economic Geography.* Washington DC: World Bank.

———. 2009b. *Arab Republic of Egypt. Upper Egypt: Pathways to Shared Growth.* Washington DC: World Bank.

———. 2009c. "Egypt Investment Climate 2009: Accelerating Private Enterprise-led Growth." World Bank, Washington, DC.

———. Forthcoming. *Gender and Transport in the Middle East and North Africa Region: Case Studies from West Bank and Yemen.* Washington, DC: World Bank.

CHAPTER 3

Diagnose to Prescribe: Uncovering the Truth about Spatial Disparities

Lagging areas are different from each other. Upper Egypt is not the Moroccan Rif, and the Moroccan Rif is not Baluchistan. The moment one starts to dig into the data, one discovers that every backward area has its own individual character. To misquote Tolstoy, all lagging areas are lagging in their own way.

Recognizing the different species of lagging area is, therefore, the key to adopting the right package of policies. The symptoms might be the same, but the causes—and the required interventions—are very different.

So, what questions must we ask when we diagnose a lagging area?

First of all, does the country in question really have a spatial disparities problem in the first place? The immediate answer may be, "Obviously, yes." As the analysis below will show, however, spatial disparities are not always a significant part of overall socioeconomic inequality. If location is not a major determinant of household welfare, then it makes more sense for government to focus on general poverty reduction than on the development of specific places.

The next question to ask is whether a location has a low level of welfare because of its lack of economic opportunity or because of the population's characteristics. Even if household welfare *is* linked to location, this link might be because certain areas contain people with low earning potential. If household characteristics are the main factor behind spatial inequality, then it makes more sense to focus on improving the potential of targeted groups of people—"investing in people"—than on developing the economy in targeted places.

Supposing that we have proved that we have a genuine spatial inequality problem, it is then necessary to characterize the lagging area in question. How is its level of development changing over time? Is it converging with leading areas? Is its population dwindling as people migrate in search of better opportunities? These trends will tell policy makers whether the lagging area problem is resolving itself over time without government intervention. Is it a high-density or a low-density area? Is it well connected to poles of economic activity, or is it isolated from them? As we shall see, the answers to these geographic questions will indicate to policy makers how the different options for action might work.

What Kind of Spatial Inequality Does the Country Have?

This section will take the reader through the process of spatial inequality diagnosis. A problem thus defined clearly is the first step to selecting an appropriate policy response.

Where Is the Country, on the Path to Agglomeration?

The measurement of agglomeration has traditionally depended on indicators of urbanization. Measuring urbanization, however, is not straightforward. The first problem is that there is no standard definition of "urban" and "rural," which obstructs cross-country comparisons. The second problem is that areas change from rural to urban, which obstructs comparisons over time. Egypt is a case in point. Its census distinguishes urban and rural population according to an *administrative* definition that labels most peri-urban settlements as rural, even if their appearance, habitat, and lifestyle are clearly urban (box 3.1). According to national and United Nations (UN) statistics, Egypt's population was 42.5 percent urban in 2000. If Egypt adopted the definition used by India, however, which defines urban areas as communities with 5,000 or

---

BOX 3.1

The Nile Delta: Urban, Rural ... or Rurban?

"Follow the Nile north out of Cairo on the old agricultural road, and you find it hard to pinpoint where the city ends and the lotus-shaped Delta begins. Carpeted with redbrick apartment blocks and spliced with streets in every direction, the lush greenery of the Nile's splintered arteries is almost impossible to appreciate in isolation. This is where the urban and the rural get lost in each other, with livestock living in doorways and workers camping out in fields. In the past, literary giants venerated the Delta's wild marshlands; today, any clear-cut divisions between the metropolis and the countryside have long faded away."

Source: Shenker 2009.

more inhabitants, then 86 percent of Egypt's total population would be classified as urban (World Bank 2009b). Then, as cities grow and overflow into rural areas, population spreads from the city centers into new urban settlements, which might explain the curious statistic (Wahba 2007) that urban-rural migrants outnumber rural-urban migrants by a ratio of three to one.

Researchers have recently surmounted this problem of definitions by creating an index of agglomeration that depends only on the distribution of population across space (Uchida and Nelson 2008; World Bank 2009a), so it is not affected by different countries' administrative definitions of urban and rural areas. This "agglomeration index" measures the proportion of the population living in an area with a population density of 150 people per square kilometer, which is also no more than an hour's travel time from a city (table 3.1). The index, therefore, provides an objective measure of agglomeration (although it seems to underestimate urbanization in desert city-states such as Djibouti or the United Arab Emirates).

Using the agglomeration index, we can see that MENA's populations are more agglomerated than one might expect for their level of economic development; most of them are well above the trend line (figure 3.1). Egypt, Jordan, Lebanon, and Libya have levels of agglomeration that would normally be found in the most agglomerated of the richest developed countries. The populations of the Syrian Arab Republic, Morocco, and

TABLE 3.1

How Agglomerated Are the Economies of the Middle East and North Africa?

Economy	Share of urban population (UN database)	Rank	Agglomeration index	Rank
Algeria	59.8	9	56.9	9
Djibouti	83.4	2	50.4	12
Egypt, Arab Rep.	42.5	12	92.6	1
Iran, Islamic Rep.	64.2	7	62.8	7
Iraq	67.8	6	72.2	6
Jordan	80.4	4	79.4	5
Lebanon	86	1	86.8	3
Libya	83.1	3	83.4	4
Morocco	55.1	10	53.6	10
Syrian Arab Republic	50.1	11	59.1	8
Tunisia	63.4	8	51.9	11
West Bank and Gaza	71.5	5	90	2
Yemen, Rep.	25.4	13	25.5	13

Source: Uchida and Nelson 2008.

Note: The index is the percentage of population living in areas with a population density of at least 150 people/km² who are no more than an hour's travel time from a city of 50,000 people.

FIGURE 3.1

MENA Is Agglomerated for Its Level of Development

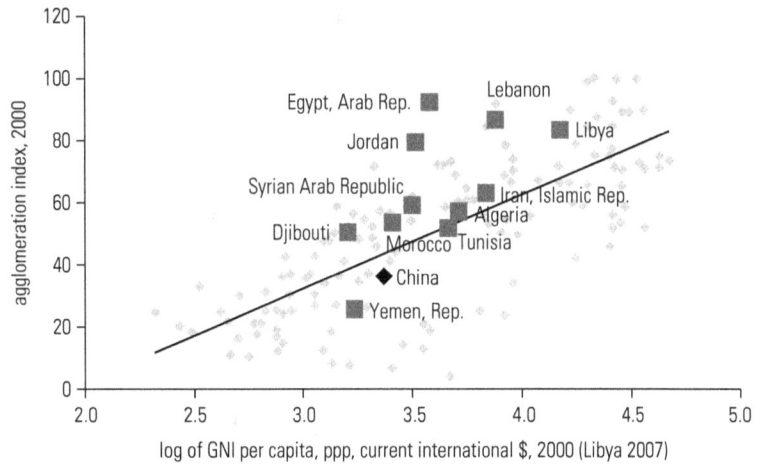

Sources: World Bank, World Development Indicators database, Uchida and Nelson 2008.

Note: GNI = gross national income; PPP = purchasing power parity.

Djibouti are agglomerated to the extent found in countries 50 percent richer. Only the Republic of Yemen is below the trend line, while Algeria and Tunisia are on it.

Why is MENA a region with such high agglomeration of its populations? One possible reason is water. Before humans learned to build long water conveyance systems or to drill deep tubewells, the only places fit for settlement and farming were areas with good soils plus plentiful rainfall, surface water, or shallow aquifers. Most land in the MENA region does not meet these conditions; it is either too arid or too mountainous to support settlement and farming.

One can take the percentage of a country's land that is either arable or forested as an indicator of the area with adequate water for agrarian settlement. In the European Union (EU), this ratio is usually above 50 percent and is never lower than 30 percent (Cyprus). In MENA, this ratio never rises above 28–30 percent (Lebanon, Morocco, and the Syrian Arab Republic) and is lower than 5 percent in Algeria, Djibouti, Jordan, Libya, and the Republic of Yemen (World Bank 2009a).

So historically, MENA's rural populations were concentrated in coastal strips, in mountain valleys, and along rivers such as the Nile, Tigris, and Euphrates. As populations grew, there was little new fertile rainfed land to bring under cultivation. By necessity, therefore, MENA agriculture was from an early date characterized by high labor-land ratios, and settled areas had high population densities. The famous Middle Eastern cities of antiquity were often either riverine commercial hubs for irrigated farming areas, such as Jericho and Babylon, or coastal hubs for maritime trade, such as Alexandria and Tyre.

Map 3.2 illustrates how water availability has shaped settlement patterns in Iraq. In the mountainous areas of northern Iraq, where rainfed agriculture has been practiced for centuries, settlements are evenly spread, interrupted only by high mountain ranges, the arched bands visible to the north of the map. Average population per settlement is relatively low in these scattered villages (Ameen 2008). In the rest of Iraq, however, agriculture has historically been based on irrigation from surface water. Its population is, therefore, concentrated in riverine bands, with a higher level of population per settlement.

But high-density agriculture is not the whole story of MENA's high level of agglomeration. (See map 3.1.) MENA's political and governance history has also played a role in driving population concentrations. The politics of agglomeration is a question that we will examine in chapter 4.

Whatever the cause, why does it matter to policy makers to know that their country is more agglomerated than other countries at the same level of development? Put simply, it may be an indication that a country does not need significant additional population agglomeration to obtain developed-country economies of agglomeration. Rather, the policy

MAP 3.1

MENA's Pockets of Nonaridity

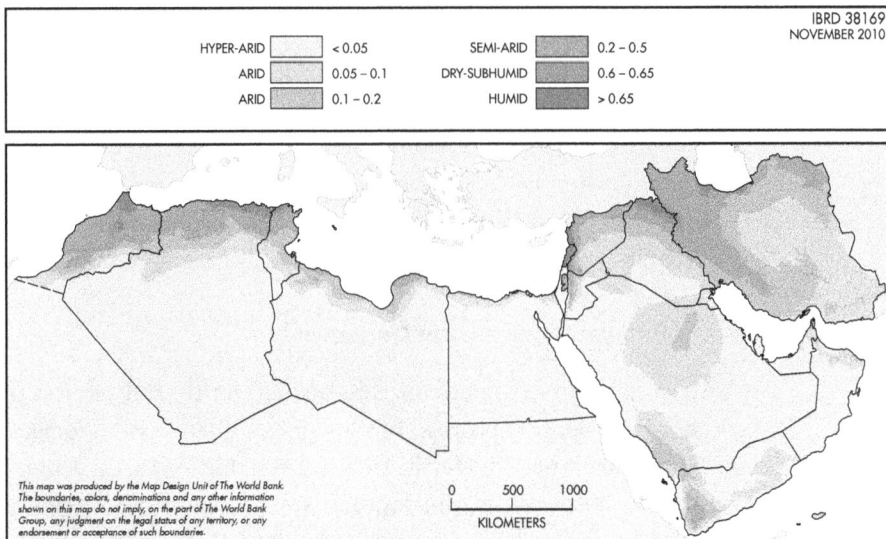

IBRD 38169		
NOVEMBER 2010		
HYPER-ARID < 0.05	SEMI-ARID 0.2 – 0.5	
ARID 0.05 – 0.1	DRY-SUBHUMID 0.6 – 0.65	
ARID 0.1 – 0.2	HUMID > 0.65	

This map was produced by the Map Design Unit of The World Bank. The boundaries, colors, denominations and any other information shown on this map do not imply, on the part of The World Bank Group, any judgment on the legal status of any territory, or any endorsement or acceptance of such boundaries.

0   500   1000

KILOMETERS

Sources: World Bank Spatial Analysis Team and DECRG.

MAP 3.2

Water-Based Settlement Patterns in Iraq: Rainfed and Riverine

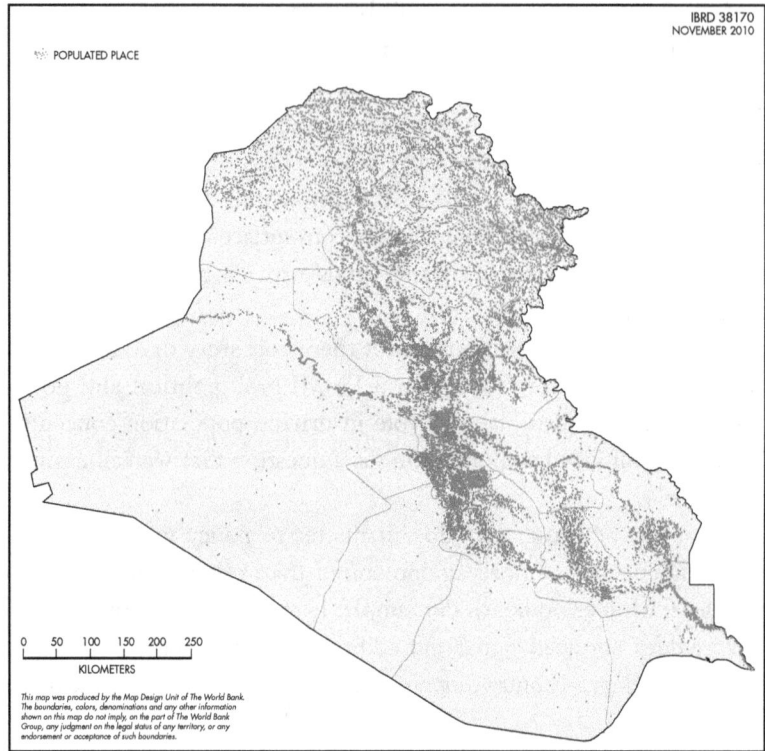

Source: National Geospatial Intelligence Agency, http://earth-info.nga.mil/gns/html/cntyfile/iz.zip, accessed July 2009, reproduced in Ameen 2008.

Note: A dot = a settlement.

emphasis should be on managing urban density to avoid excessive congestion costs and overloading of infrastructure and services.

The Republic of Yemen's level of population agglomeration, however, is the exception. It is far below what one would expect for its level of GDP per capita. This finding suggests that Yemeni policy makers should expect, plan for, and certainly not attempt to discourage, urbanization.

A Case of Delayed Agricultural Transition?

The shift of labor from agriculture into manufacturing and services is part of the agglomeration process. In a low-income, farm-based society, people have to live where the fertile land is. Even the first urban centers grow as "market towns" within farming areas. But as the economy grows and households become richer, agricultural output becomes a smaller share of total consumption. Manufacturing and services begin to dominate the economy, and most enterprises are no longer tied to the location of a natural resource. Therefore, they cluster into urban centers to take advantage of economies of agglomeration. So economic growth, the shift out of farming, and agglomeration are all interconnected strands of spatial development.

The transition out of agriculture is a two-stage process (World Bank 2008a). First comes the change in the economy's sectoral composition, with manufacturing and services overtaking farming as the main source of value added. Then comes the shift in employment, with labor moving away from the land into workshops and offices. In between, there is an interim period, when agriculture has lost its share of value added, but rural areas are still a reservoir of low-productivity employment and poverty. If agriculture has lost its share of value added but has not yet lost its share of employment, this inevitably means that the labor productivity gap between the farm and nonfarm sectors is temporarily even bigger than normal. Then eventually the higher labor productivity in manufacturing and services will draw labor out of agriculture and rural areas into the urban agglomerations to work in manufacturing and services.

As figure 3.2 shows, most MENA13 countries are in that interim period—the bottom right-hand quadrant—when agriculture has ceded its share of value added, but rural areas have retained their share of poverty. This is the time of transition when rural-urban disparities are most acute, because the gap in labor productivity between rural and urban areas is at its highest. If MENA economies are to follow the normal path, the way forward is for labor to shift out of farming, raising land-labor ratios, labor productivity in agriculture, and rural incomes.

If MENA is to raise agricultural incomes, much of the gains will probably have to come from a shift of labor out of farming, so that the area of fertile land per worker can increase. Table 3.2 breaks down the difference between labor productivity in MENA agriculture and labor productivity in a developed country with similar agro-climatic conditions (Spain). It shows that most of the difference in labor productivity is due to Spanish farmers having more land to work with, rather than Spanish land being economically more productive than MENA land. The exception is Iraq, which has comparatively high land-labor ratios but low land productivity. Improving land productivity through improved irrigation efficiency, higher-value cropping, slicker marketing chains, and agronomic improvement, will of course always be important for MENA; nevertheless, rare are the countries that have reduced the productivity gap between farm and nonfarm labor without workers leaving agriculture.

But something very special seems to be happening to MENA's agricultural labor force. At middle-income levels of GDP per employed

FIGURE 3.2

Poverty Is Rural and Growth Is Nonagricultural, in MENA Economies

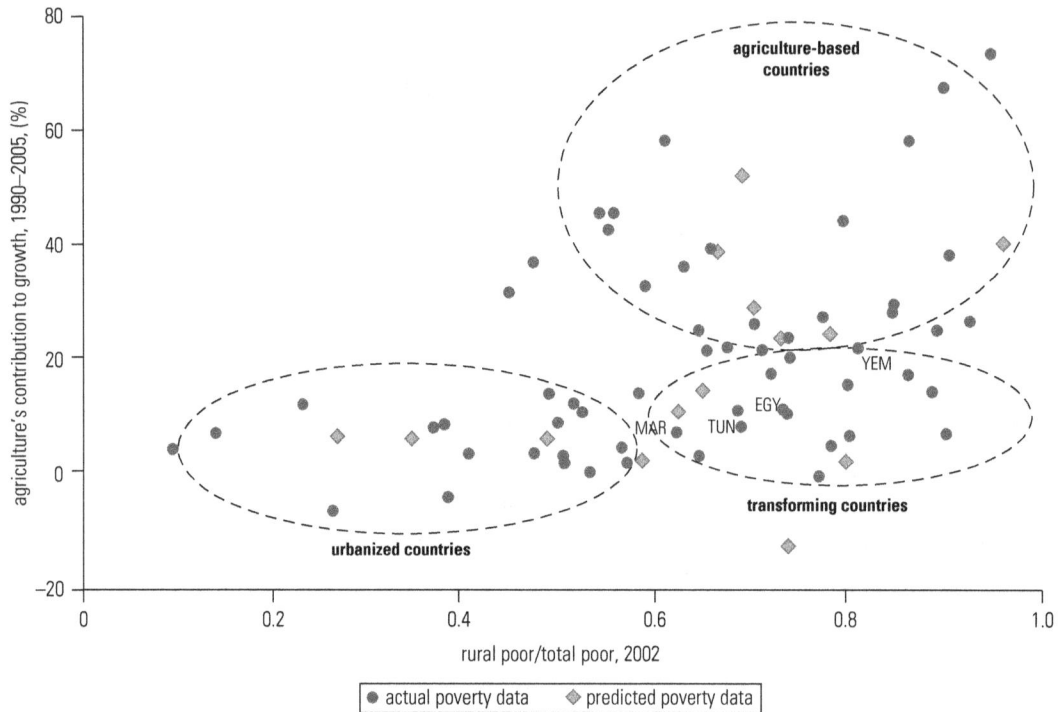

Source: World Bank 2008a.

Note: The contribution of agriculture to growth is defined as the agricultural growth rate times the sector average share over the period divided by the GDP growth rate. Rural shares in poverty marked with a circle are from Ravallion, Chen, and Sangraula (2007), using the $2.15-per-day poverty line. Rural shares of poverty marked with a diamond are predicted with an estimated regression of the rural share of poverty on rural share of population, agricultural share in GDP, log of GDP per capita in 2000 US$, and regional dummies. EGY = Egypt, Arab Rep., MAR = Morocco, TUN = Tunisia, YEM = Yemen, Rep.

person, it is usual for employment in agriculture to stabilize or shrink as workers move out of farming into manufacturing and service jobs. Figure 3.3 presents data for 162 countries on the relationship between a country's overall labor productivity and the growth rate of employment in agriculture: the richer the country and the higher labor productivity, the lower the rate of growth of agricultural employment. Countries usually have a declining farm labor force when they reach the level of development of the Syrian Arab Republic, Egypt, Jordan, Algeria, Tunisia, or the Islamic Republic of Iran.

However, in MENA there is growing agricultural employment—and quite rapid growth too: more and more people are trying to make a living out of MENA's limited land and water resources. Between 1990 and 2005, the number of people working in farming grew by 32 percent in

TABLE 3.2

Difference between Agricultural Labor Productivity in MENA and Spain: How Much Is Due to the Land-Labor Ratio?
percent

	Share due to difference in land productivity (%)	Share due to difference in land per worker (%)
Egypt, Arab Rep.	–64	164
Djibouti	–47	147
Jordan	2	98
Syrian Arab Republic	15	85
Iran, Islamic Rep.	17	83
Yemen, Rep.	19	81
Tunisia	24	76
Algeria	26	74
Morocco	27	73
Iraq	90	10

Source: Log-divisia decomposition, using WDI data accessed May 17, 2009.

FIGURE 3.3

MENA's Agricultural Labor Force Is Growing Fast for MENA's Level of Development

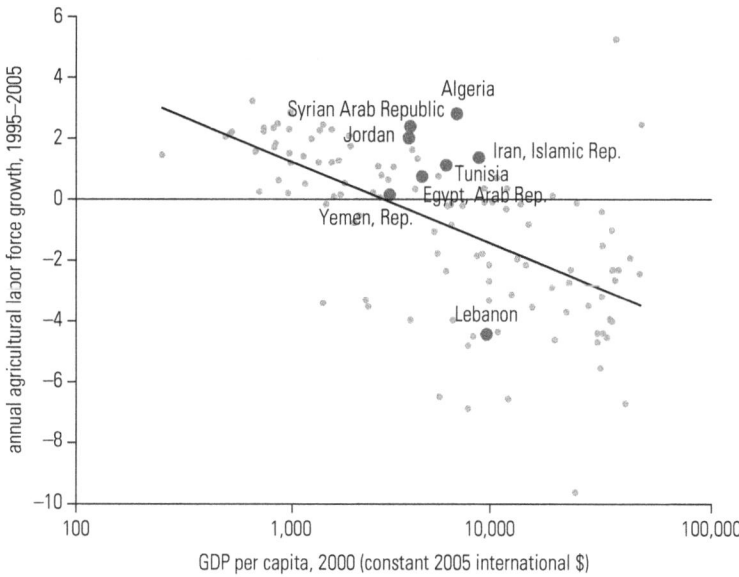

Source: WDI.

the West Bank and Gaza, 58 percent in Jordan, 24 percent in Tunisia, 44 percent in the Republic of Yemen, 43 percent in the Syrian Arab Republic, 60 percent in Algeria, 13 percent in Egypt, and 24 percent in the Islamic Republic of Iran.

Morocco, Lebanon, and Libya are the only countries whose agricultural workforce is following the usual (stabilizing or downward) trend. Farm employment in Lebanon and Libya, however, is dominated by foreigners, which may affect the statistical reporting. Lebanese nationals are thought to provide only about a fifth of the country's agricultural workforce (World Bank 2007a), the remainder being Syrians and Palestinians.

The retention of labor in agriculture is reducing land-labor ratios and farm sizes, which, in turn, depresses the productivity of agricultural labor. Between 1990 and 2005, the land-labor ratio fell by at least 15 percent in Algeria, Djibouti, Jordan, the Syrian Arab Republic, Tunisia, the West Bank and Gaza, and the Republic of Yemen, with smaller decreases in the Islamic Republic of Iran and Morocco.[1] It is predicted that climate change will aggravate the decline in land-labor ratios in agriculture, as marginal land becomes unsuitable for cultivation. One estimate (FAO 2009, 15) predicts that MENA (including the Gulf Cooperation Council [GCC]) will lose 7 percent of its arable land by 2050, compared with a 9 percent *increase* worldwide.

Tunisia is a case in point of the delayed transition of labor out of agriculture (World Bank 2006a). Agricultural employment grew by 20 percent between 1993 and 2002, but there was no trend increase in labor productivity in agriculture. During the same period, productivity in manufacturing and services rose by 4.4 percent and 4.7 percent per year, respectively. As Tunisia's agricultural labor force grows, therefore, farm sizes shrink. The share by number of landholdings less than 5 hectares rose from 41 percent in 1976 to 53 percent in 2005.

Many people trying to live off little land is a recipe for a lagging rural area in MENA. If one divides the Republic of Yemen's rural districts into three groups according to their poverty rates, the high-poverty districts have 24 people per hectare of arable land—three times as many as the low-poverty districts (World Bank 2009c). If one compares (richer) rural Lower Egypt with (poorer) Upper Egypt, the difference in agricultural incomes cannot be blamed on inefficient farming in Upper Egypt. In fact, Upper Egypt makes 36 percent *more* net income from a feddan (approximately 0.42 hectares) of land than Lower Egypt (World Bank 2009b). Upper Egypt's problem is that it has 0.17 feddan per capita in an average village instead of Lower Egypt's 0.32 feddan (World Bank 2009b). So the retention of labor in farming is a major correlate of lagging area status in MENA's rural areas.

One reason why MENA has an unusually high rate of agricultural employment growth is that MENA has an unusually high rate of growth in its working-age population (figure 3.4). There is a trend relationship between population growth and development: richer countries have lower population growth. But MENA economies tend to have had higher-than-expected rates of growth of the population ages 15–64 for

FIGURE 3.4

MENA's Working-Age Population Has Been Booming, Compared with Other Countries at the Same Level of Development

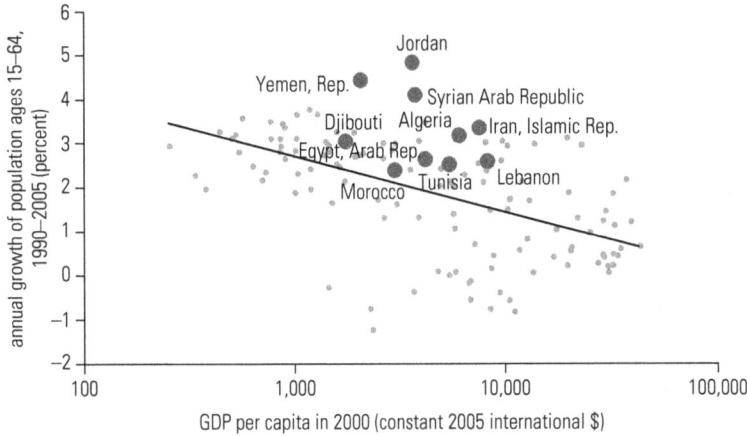

Source: WDI.

their levels of GDP. Other reasons for MENA's high rate of agricultural employment growth may include the following:

- Disappointing employment growth in manufacturing

- Limited alternative opportunities for women in rural MENA societies

- Increasing recognition, by statistical offices, of women's participation in the labor force as unpaid labor on the family farm

Moreover, environmental degradation and climate change might increase urbanization pressures. Climate models predict that the MENA region will be particularly hard hit by climate change, with more frequent droughts, heat waves, and heavy storms. Between 1990 and 2002, all economies of MENA for which data were available experienced increased drought frequency.[2] A continued deterioration of weather patterns would reduce the productivity of agriculture relative to other activities, and thus—other things being equal—further encourage rural-urban migration. Cline (2007) forecasts that agricultural production in Algeria, the Islamic Republic of Iran, Iraq, and Morocco will fall by about 30 percent between now and 2080. The International Food Policy Research Institute (IFPRI) (Nelson and others 2009) predicts drops in production of 25–35 percent and 11–24 percent, respectively, for MENA's irrigated and rainfed wheat between 2000 and 2050. It has also been estimated that a one-meter rise in sea level, which may be brought about by the melting of polar ice, would compromise 13 percent of Egypt's agricultural land.

Syria's drought of 2007–09 provided a stark illustration of a link between weather and movement to the cities, and the potential for climate change to accelerate future urbanization. According to a UN study, an estimated 200,000–250,000 farmers and their families were forced to abandon their land due to this drought. Peri-urban areas close to the cities of Damascus, Aleppo, and Hama received the majority of the displaced (Oweis 2009; IRIN News 2009).

MENA's burgeoning farm workforce and stressed natural resource base matter for spatial policy. The region's agricultural sector has already done an exceptional job in absorbing surplus labor. Given the region's land and water constraints, a shift of labor out of agriculture is, in a sense, overdue. With a shift of labor out of agriculture will come a shift of population into urban settlements.

Are Poverty and Inequality Really a Lagging Areas Question?

Without exception, all MENA governments see lagging area development as important for inclusive development. But how much attention should actually be given to the spatial dimension in the design of policies for socioeconomic inclusion?

At one extreme, poverty could be completely nonspatial, with the mix of people of different standards of living being the same at all locations across the territory. Obviously in this case, it would make little sense for national or sectoral development policies to focus on specific locations. At the other extreme, however, poverty could be a highly spatial phenomenon, with all the worse-off people living in certain locations and all the better-off in others. In this case, location-based development policies would be more justified. In reality, of course, every country will be somewhere in between these two impossible extremes.

In the words of Sherlock Holmes, "There is nothing more misleading than an obvious fact." As we have seen earlier, strong political forces are pushing decision makers to focus their attention and resources on some places more than others. It is therefore essential for policy makers to have an empirical, evidence-based understanding of the degree to which location really does affect household welfare.

Or, to put it in other words, what if spatial disparities are actually less important than they seem?

If we put the spatial dimension of household welfare into its proper perspective, three principles are worth bearing in mind:

- Mistrust averages

- Focus on the *absolute* numbers in poverty

- Break down household welfare into its spatial and nonspatial components

Mistrust Averages: Don't Let a Few Very Rich People Distort the Picture of Spatial Inequality

Welfare inequalities are usually greater in leading areas than in lagging areas. This inequality is what one would expect: the country's economic elite usually lives in the richest places. This means that a few very well-off households can bump up the mean development indicators of leading areas, even though the living standards of many people in the leading area might be low.

Using median instead of average values of household welfare therefore stops spatial disparities from looking bigger than they really are. In Syria in 2004, for example, the *average* per capita household consumption in the richest province, Damascus, was 90 percent higher than in the poorest province, El Quneitra. But the difference between consumption per capita in the *median* households in the two provinces was significantly narrower: 64 percent (WDR 2009). Table 3.3 shows how average per capita household consumption typically gives a stronger impression of spatial disparities than the median.

This is not merely a statistical curiosity; it indicates the very real tension between first impressions and underlying reality in spatial diagnostics.

Focus on the Absolute Numbers in Poverty

It is important to focus on the absolute number of poor people living in different areas. MENA's poverty rates tend to be highest in the semi-arid, desert, and mountainous areas, where population density is lowest. The risk of focusing on poverty rates, therefore, is that one might overlook the large absolute numbers of poor living in high-density urban areas.

Libya provides a good example of the poverty mass being located where poverty rates are low. According to the 2003 household survey,

TABLE 3.3

Mean versus Median per Capita Consumption

Country	Coefficient of variation of area per capita household consumption		Number of areas
	Average	Median	
Djibouti (2002)	0.33	0.29	5
Egypt, Arab Rep. (2005)	0.35	0.30	24
Jordan (2002)	0.19	0.14	12
Morocco (1998)[a]	0.20	0.19	13
Syrian Arab Republic (2004)	0.20	0.18	14
Yemen, Rep. (2005)	0.34	0.26	21

Source: National household surveys, years as specified, Egypt July–September.

Note: a. Excluding data from Guelmine Es-Semara.

the three *Shabiyat* (administrative subdivisions) with the highest poverty rates are Al Kufrah, Ghat, and Mizdah.[3] Al Kufrah is a massive desert area in the southeast of the country, bordering Egypt and Sudan on the east and Chad on the south. Its capital, Al Jawf, receives less than 3 mm of rain per year. Ghat is another desert province, in the far southwest, bordering Algeria. Mizdah is in a hilly area further north. Between them, these three inhospitable Shabiyat had a combined population of 81,000 in the 1995 census, of which around 25,000 were living below the poverty line. The coastal capital province, Benghazi, on the other hand, has an estimated 50,000 people living in poverty, despite having a much lower poverty rate. This is not to claim that Benghazi is a lagging area. The point is that a focus on lagging areas should not mean that one overlooks the larger absolute numbers of poor people in leading areas.

The Iraqi experience shows how poverty rates and absolute numbers both enter into policy making. In 2009, the High Committee for Iraq's Poverty Reduction Strategy Paper was pondering the implications of the Iraq Household Socioeconomic Survey (IHSES), Iraq's first postwar nationwide household income and consumption survey. The survey had revealed huge disparities in poverty rates between governorates, from 10 percent in Kirkuk and 13 percent in Baghdad right up to Sala'alddin, Babel, and Muthanna governorates, all with poverty rates above 40 percent. The High Committee's analysis of the poverty data rightly focused on the high poverty *rates* in the lagging rural governorates, and the first pillar of its Poverty Reduction Strategy placed emphasis on raising poor people's earnings from agriculture. But the High Committee also noted that the *numbers* of poor people were concentrated in the big cities: 13 percent of the poor lived in the capital and another 11 percent in the port city of Basra (figure 3.5). In fact there were a third *more* poor people in Iraq's four richest governorates than in the four poorest governorates because of the higher populations of the rich governorates. Therefore, another pillar of the High Committee's poverty strategy focused on housing, a critical issue for the poor in Iraq's major cities.

Similarly, although the urban-rural divide may show urban areas to be better off, this should not obscure the existence of poor places within cities. Urban slums, for example, may have levels of poverty and human development similar to or even worse than rural areas. Table 3.4 shows a selection of human development indicators for slums in Egypt, Morocco, and the Republic of Yemen. Child health seems to be as poor in slums as in rural areas. Literacy rates are higher, which may be to due to the tendency of educated people to migrate toward the cities. In Egypt, however, the net primary education enrollment rate for boys and girls combined is about 7 percentage points higher in rural areas than in slums (UN Habitat 2006, 122).

FIGURE 3.5

High Poverty Rates Did Not Mean High Poverty Numbers in Iraq, 2007

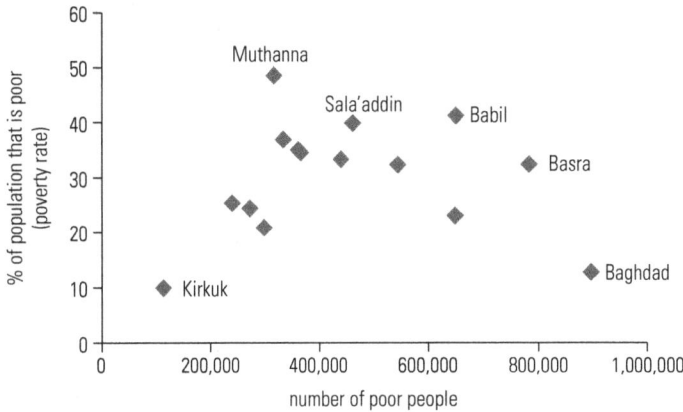

Source: Shlash 2009.

TABLE 3.4

Human Development Indicators in Slums

Country	% of malnourished children under five years (children underweight)			% of births attended by skilled health personnel			% of children under five years with diarrhea			Female literacy rate (%)		
	Urban	Rural	Slum	Urban	Rural	Slum	Urban	Rural	Slum	Urban	Rural	Slum
Egypt, Arab Rep.	6.8	9.6	10.7	86.7	59.0	76.6	16.8	20.2	23.7	73.7	42.9	60.2
Morocco	6.5	13.9	13.9	85.3	39.5	39.1	11.5	12.4	13.4	67.5	24.6	53.4
Yemen, Rep.	24.5	30.7	29.5	45.8	10.0	35.1	25.7	35.8	32.6	37.4	6.2	24.0

Source: UN Habitat 2006.

In 8 of 10 MENA13 countries, the data show that the ratio of the slum population to the rural population is on the increase (table 3.5). The exceptions are Tunisia, which has implemented a successful program of slum improvement, and Egypt, where the slum population data need some other explanation. In the Islamic Republic of Iran, Iraq, Lebanon, and Libya, the slum population already matches or exceeds the rural population. In short, the problem of poor people in rich areas is catching up with the problem of poor people in poor areas.

Break Down Household Welfare into Its Spatial and Nonspatial Components: Check That Spatial Disparities Are Really a Big Part of the Inequality Story

If we are to know for certain how important spatial disparities are as a part of overall inequality, it is necessary to have some objective, statistical

TABLE 3.5

Rural and Slum Populations in MENA
(thousands)

Country	Slum population 1990	Slum population 2005	Rural population 1990	Rural population 2005	Ratio rural to slum 1990 (%)	Ratio rural to slum 2005 (%)
Algeria	1,508	2,370	12,110	12,057	803	509
Egypt, Arab Rep.	14,087	11,015	31,152	41,816	221	380
Libya	1,242	1,867	1,060	1,361	85	73
Morocco	4,457	6,054	12,470	3,564	280	224
Tunisia	425	188	3,433	3,480	808	1851
Iran, Islamic Rep.	17,094	21,763	23,773	22,868	139	105
Iraq	6,825	9,992	n.a.	5,610	n.a.	56
Jordan	388	741	881	1,174	227	158
Lebanon	1,142	1,811	503	537	44	30
Syrian Arab Republic	629	1,012	6,500	8,842	1033	874
Yemen, Rep.	1,787	3,803	9,740	14,999	545	394

Sources: UN Habitat 2006; World Bank World Development Indicators.

Note: n.a. = not available.

measure of how inequality breaks down into its spatial and nonspatial components. One well-tested technique for doing so takes a measure of overall inequality, the Theil index, and divides it into two parts: that which is attributable to inequality within locations and that which is attributable to inequality between locations (Bourguignon 1979; Shorrocks 2005).

Comparing different countries' spatial components of inequality raises methodological complications (box 3.2); nonetheless, there are good reasons to trust the main messages from the exercise.

Applying the decomposition to data on per capita household consumption in MENA shows some striking differences between economies. In some, spatial inequalities are a big part of the inequality story, but in others they are not.

Table 3.6 gives the picture for disparities between urban areas and rural areas. It looks at two different measures of inequality in households' economic welfare. The National Household Survey (NHHS) data measures per capita household expenditure. The Demographic and Health Survey (DHS) data measure a wealth index based on the household's ownership of physical assets (Rutstein and Johnston 2004).

The second column of table 3.6 gives the overall Theil index for households' economic welfare from each survey. The third column gives the component of the overall Theil index explained by urban-rural disparities. The fourth column is the one to focus on: it shows the share of total inequality that takes the form of urban-rural disparities (the third column divided by the second column).

The results show dramatic differences between MENA countries. In Jordan and Djibouti the rural-urban issue is not at all an important

BOX 3.2

Decomposing MENA's Inequality into Its Spatial and Nonspatial Components: A Worthwhile Exercise, Despite the MAUP

The problem with comparing different countries' inequality decompositions is that comparisons depend on the geographical unit of analysis. This "Modifiable Areal Unit Problem" (MAUP) consists of a "Scale Problem" (the size of the unit of analysis) and an "Aggregation Problem" (where the boundaries are drawn). The effect of the Scale Problem is that the smaller the geographical unit, the more important spatial inequality appears to be. Imagine an analysis, for example, in which the units were so small that each contained only one household. In this case, inequalities would appear to be 100 percent spatial. At the other extreme, if all the households in the study were listed in the same location, the spatial component of inequalities would appear to be zero.

However, despite this flaw, the decomposition analysis for MENA may still be worth presenting. First, the two-way rural-versus-urban analysis standardizes the breakdown at two very large populations, reducing intercountry scale effect differences. Second, the interprovincial analysis produces nearly the same ordering of countries as the rural-versus-urban analysis, suggesting that there is more to the ranking than scale effects. Third, despite Morocco's high number of provinces and a large rural-urban divide, the decomposition portrays Morocco's interprovincial inequality as a very low share of total inequality. This is the opposite of what one would expect if the Scale Effect were the main determinant of the decomposition results.

Source: Openshaw 1984.

component of overall inequality, which is what one might expect for small, urbanized countries. In Egypt and Morocco, on the other hand, the rural-urban divide explains 16–29 percent of total inequality, depending on which survey one considers.

There is a straightforward policy implication here. Policies that target the development of lagging (rural) areas are not likely to make a sizeable impact on socioeconomic disparities in countries toward the top end of table 3.6, such as Jordan, Djibouti, the Republic of Yemen, and Syria. Policies that target poor *households*, whether in urban or rural areas, would stand a better chance. Spatially targeted development initiatives for rural areas might make more sense for countries toward the bottom of table 3.6, such as Egypt and Morocco.

Even so, in no country in the table does rural-urban inequality account for more than a fifth of total inequality of household expenditure. Does this mean that spatial inequality is relatively unimportant? Some authors (Elbers 2007) argue that this Theil decomposition calculation understates the problem. The main reason is that society's aim is usually not to abolish

TABLE 3.6

Where Does the Urban-Rural Divide Count?

Households' economic welfare, by urban and rural	Overall Theil index	Urban-rural component of Theil index	Share of Theil index explained by urban-rural disparities (%)	Maximum possible urban-rural component of Theil index	ELMO index = actual urban-rural disparity versus maximum possible urban-rural disparity (%)
Jordan DHS 2002	0.20	0.00	2	0.12	3
Jordan NHHS 2002	0.29	0.01	2	0.18	4
Djibouti NHHS 2002	0.32	0.01	3	0.16	7
Yemen, Rep. NHHS 1999	0.24	0.01	5	0.15	8
Syrian Arab Republic NHHS, 2004	0.30	0.02	7	0.15	14
Yemen, Rep. NHHS 2005	0.38	0.03	9	0.17	20
Egypt, Arab Rep. DHS 2005	0.24	0.04	16	0.14	28
Egypt, Arab Rep. NHHS	0.29	0.05	17	0.13	39
Morocco NHHS 2001	0.31	0.05	17	0.16	34
Morocco NHHS 1999	0.28	0.05	19	0.15	37
Morocco DHS 2004	0.33	0.10	29	0.19	51
Lebanon NHHS[a]	—	—	—	—	—

Source: Sommeiller 2008, using household data from the sources listed in the first column, years as specified, Arab Republic of Egypt July–September only.

Note: — = not available. DHS = Demographic and Health Survey, NHHS = National Household Survey.
a. No urban-rural variable in the Lebanon dataset.

inequality altogether but to give different social groups the same opportunities. In other words, the goal is economic justice, not economic equality. So what matters is not whether rural-urban disparities account for a high proportion of total inequality, but whether rural people and urban people have the same chance of being at the same position in the socioeconomic hierarchy.[4]

The "ELMO index,"[5] therefore, serves as a measure of economic justice. It takes the existing income distribution, imagines that all the richest people lived in urban areas and all the poorest people lived in rural areas, and calculates the Theil measure of rural-urban disparities on this basis. This is the "maximum possible urban-rural component of Theil index," in the fifth column of table 3.6, and represents a situation of "maximum economic injustice" between urban and rural areas. It represents the situation in which the rural population gets all the worst places on the socioeconomic ladder. Then the ELMO index in the last column compares the actual urban-rural disparity with the maximum urban-rural disparity.

Using the ELMO index, we can see that the ranking of countries is more or less the same. Jordan, Djibouti, the Republic of Yemen, and Syria have ELMO scores of 20 percent or less, meaning that their rural-urban divide could be five times bigger given the current level of overall economic inequality. Egypt and Morocco again stand out as the countries in which rural-urban disparities are a significant part of the inequality picture.

MENA is not particularly badly off, compared with the rest of the world, when it comes to the urban-rural divide. To put MENA's rural-urban disparities into perspective, one can compare them with other developing country regions. Rural-urban disparities in Sub-Saharan Africa, East Asia and the Pacific, and Latin America and the Caribbean average 14–18 percent of overall disparities (world region averages). Their ELMO indexes average 25–28 percent. By this measure, Morocco is at or just above the global norm, while several other MENA economies are well below it.

The differences among MENA economies in the importance of spatial disparities are again quite dramatic when one considers interprovincial disparities rather than urban-rural disparities. Table 3.7 repeats the exercise for administrative subdivisions, such as provinces, governorates, and *mohafazat*. Interprovincial inequality is a very small component of overall inequality for Syria, Jordan, and the Republic of Yemen. This inequality means that "lagging area" policies targeting specific provinces might be less effective at attacking inequality than policies that target disadvantaged sections of society nationwide. In Lebanon and

TABLE 3.7

Where Does the Interprovincial Divide Count?

Households' economic welfare by province[a]	Overall Theil index	Interprovincial component of Theil index	Share of Theil index explained by interprovincial disparities (%)	Maximum possible interprovincial component of Theil index	ELMO index = actual interprovincial disparity versus maximum possible interprovincial disparity (%)
Syrian Arab Republic NHHS, 2004	0.31	0.01	3	0.21	5
Jordan DHS 2002	0.20	0.01	4	0.17	4
Yemen, Rep. NHHS 1999	0.24	0.01	5	0.21	6
Morocco NHHS 1999	0.28	0.02	8	0.22	10
Jordan NHHS 2002	0.29	0.03	9	0.21	12
Yemen, Rep. NHHS 2005	0.38	0.03	9	0.24	14
Morocco NHHS 2001	0.32	0.03	10	0.23	14
Egypt, Arab Rep. DHS 2005	0.24	0.04	17	0.22	19
Djibouti NHHS 2002	0.32	0.06	17	0.26	21
Egypt, Arab Rep. NHHS	0.29	0.06	21	0.19	31
Lebanon NHHS	0.28	0.06	21	0.22	27
Morocco DHS 2004	0.33	0.10	29	0.29	33

Source: Sommeiller 2008, using household data from the sources listed in the first column, years as specified, Arab Republic of Egypt July–September only.

Note: a. To calculate the interprovincial component of inequality, provinces are divided into four sets, from richest to poorest.

Egypt, however, interprovincial inequality accounts for more than a fifth of total inequality. In Djibouti, where the rural-urban divide was insignificant, interdistrict inequality is about a sixth of overall inequality. In Morocco, the situation is very interesting. Although rural-urban disparities were quite important in Morocco, the household expenditure survey data from 1999 and 2001 revealed that interprovincial inequality was a very small part of overall inequality. And yet the wealth index of the Demographic and Health Survey makes out that a full 29 percent of overall economic inequality is accounted for by interprovincial disparities. This finding means that interprovincial disparities in ownership of assets such as housing, livestock, land, and consumer durables are important, but interprovincial disparities in household expenditure are not.

Disparities that May Not Be as Spatial as They May Seem

The bottom line is that socioeconomic disparities might not be as important in measured living standards as they are in politics. We have seen earlier that politics tends to "spatialize" issues. Therefore, it is all the more important for policy makers to perform some cold, objective analysis of the real role of location in determining people's life-chances.

Low Economic Opportunity . . . Or Low Human Development?

As we saw in table 3.7, Egypt's interprovincial disparities account for around a fifth of total inequality. The lagging area is the Nile Valley south of Cairo, also known as Upper Egypt. Although Upper Egypt has only 40 percent of the country's population, it has 60 percent of its poverty and 80 percent of its severe poverty.

Here is a striking fact: demography explains 62 percent of the consumption gap between Upper and Lower Egypt (World Bank 2009b) (table 3.8).

Much thought has gone into identifying which geographical handicaps have blocked Upper Egypt's development: its distance from Cairo and major ports, a lack of transportation infrastructure, or a shortage of land and other productive natural resources. The fact is, however, that Upper Egyptian workers earn only 8 percent less on average than their Lower Egyptian counterparts and have only a slightly higher employment rate, so economic opportunity might not be the main factor holding them back. The problem is that when Upper Egyptian workers return home, they have to share their earnings with more nonworking family members who might be too young or too old, or excluded from the labor market by social constraints on women. In other words "demographic dependency," the ratio of dependents to people of working age, is higher in Upper Egypt than in Lower Egypt. Unfavorable household

TABLE 3.8

Explaining the Difference between per Capita Consumption in Upper and Lower Egypt

	All households	Farming is main income source	Farming is a subsidiary income source	No farming, but agricultural wages	Nonfarm activities only
Total gap	−18%	−13%	−19%	−23%	−21%
	of which:	of which:	of which:	of which:	of which:
Demographic dependency	−11%	−12%	−13%	−11%	−9%
Earnings per worker	−8%	−2%	−8%	−13%	−12%
Employment rate	+1%	+1%	+2%	+1%	+1%
Percentage of total gap	100	100	100	100	100
Demographic dependency	62	95	67	46	46
Earnings per worker	45	13	41	57	57
Employment rate	−6	−8	−9	−4	−3

Source: World Bank 2009b.

characteristics are therefore causing Upper Egypt's purchasing power to lag. Such households would be worse off wherever they lived.

Various measures of a household's composition need to be considered as part of the demography question:

- The size of the household: the more household members there are, the lower consumption per capita will be for any given amount of earnings

- The number of people of working age in the household

- The number of females in the household, because there are cultural limitations on women's earning opportunities

- The gender of the head of the household, because female and male households heads have different opportunities to access markets and services on behalf of their household members

- The age of the head of the household, because a person's earning power typically peaks in midlife before falling again as old age approaches[6]

Education is another—nondemographic—household characteristic that affects a household's chances of succeeding. A household with more education will tend to fare better than a household with less education, wherever it lives. Leading areas usually have more than their share of well-educated people, so part of the difference between the well-being of leading and lagging areas might be because of the differing education levels of their populations. Spatial disparities in education levels might be because educational services are better in leading areas, because parents in leading areas are rich enough to afford better education, or because educated people in lagging areas migrate to leading areas.

One can, therefore, break down spatial disparities in households' consumption levels into three components:

- Spatial disparities caused by spatial differences in economic opportunity

- Spatial disparities caused by differences in household demography

- Spatial disparities caused by differences in education

The relative importance of these three components should determine the policy response. If demography and education are important causes of spatial inequality, then it makes sense to focus on human development. Investments in education, opportunities for women, and reproductive health are then a win-win policy; they reduce spatial disparities without the economic inefficiency of pushing production into lagging areas.

One way of distinguishing between the influences of human development and economic opportunity is to work out what the economic welfare of households with the *same* characteristics would be in different geographical locations. The separation of spatial disparities into their demographic and educational components is presented next for 8 of the 13 MENA economies: Djibouti, Egypt, Iraq, Jordan, Lebanon, Morocco, Syria, and the Republic of Yemen. The findings are powerful, inasmuch as they show important differences in the form of spatial disparities among different countries of the MENA region. Each set of data tells a unique story and points each economy toward its own specific policy direction.

Before looking at each economy, it is important to mention a key point. The analysis only uses the limited range of household characteristics mentioned earlier, and for education, it measures only the household head's level of schooling. If more household characteristics had been included, these characteristics would have appeared even more important compared with spatial differences in economic opportunity.

The statistical technique described next works only with average consumption values and not with medians. Otherwise, medians would have been used to give a more representative picture of spatial inequalities.

Figures 3.6 and 3.7 confirm that demography is a critical cause of Egypt's spatial disparities. If all of Egypt's governorates had the same demographic profile, the coefficient of variation of mean governorate per capita household consumption would be 0.27 instead of 0.35. The rural-urban gap would be two-thirds of what it actually is, a full 17 percentage points lower. A lagging governorate in Upper Egypt, like Fayoum, would be 36 percent behind Cairo instead of 55 percent. Assiut, deeper into Upper Egypt, would be 59 percent behind Cairo instead of 71 percent

FIGURE 3.6

Demography Matters for Intergovernorate Disparities in the Arab Republic of Egypt

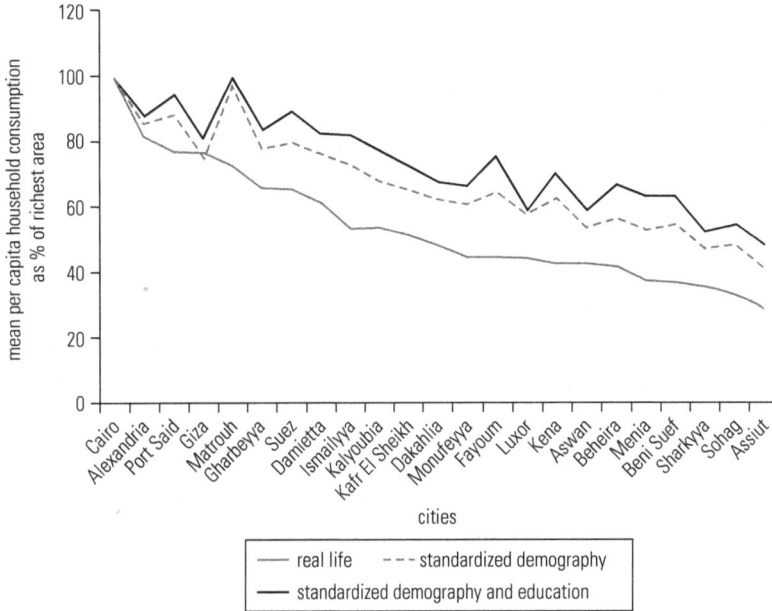

Source: World Bank staff calculations, from 2004–05 HIECS, July–September.

FIGURE 3.7

Remove Demographic and Educational Differences, and the Arab Republic of Egypt's Urban-Rural Divide Shrinks Away, 2005

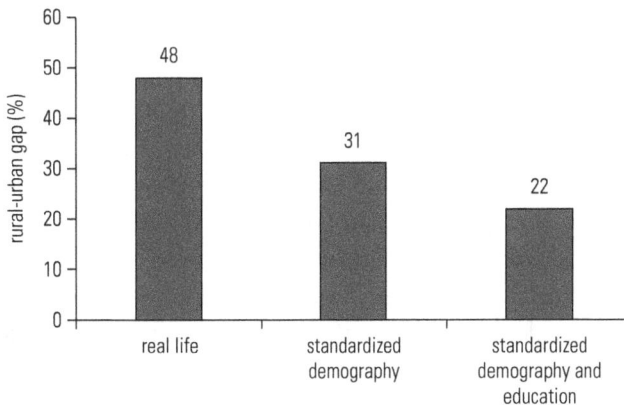

Source: World Bank staff calculations from 2004–05 HIECS, July–September only.

behind. The governorates that share Cairo's favorable demography are either urban (Alexandria, Port Said, and Giza) or new developments (S. Sinai).

Overall, education is important too, albeit less so than demography, as illustrated by the gap between the top line and the middle line in figure 3.6 and between the middle and right-hand columns in figure 3.7. The metropolitan governorates of Cairo, Alexandria, and Giza share the same educational advantages. If there were no spatial disparities in demography and education, the rural-urban gap might be less than half of what it is (figure 3.7).

In Djibouti, different lagging districts have different types of spatial disparity (figure 3.8). The districts of Tadjoura, Obock, Ali-Sabieh, and Dikhil all appear at first sight to be in the same situation, with per capita household consumption well below Djibouti City's, but the breakdown of causes is different. In fact, disparities between Tadjoura and Obock on the one hand, and Djibouti City on the other, *increase* when one takes away their demographic differences, meaning that these two outlying districts have more favorable demographic characteristics than the capital. For Ali-Sabieh and Dikhil, demographic differences do play a role in creating spatial disparities, as witnessed by the upward curling tail in the demography-adjusted curve. For Dikhil, demography is particularly crucial. If all of Djibouti's districts had the same demography, mean per capita consumption in Dikhil would be 65 percent of that in Djibouti City as opposed to the observed 46 percent, and Dikhil would be the richest district outside Djibouti City instead of the poorest.

For education it is the other way around; there are significant educational differences between Djibouti City on the one hand and Tadjoura and Obock on the other. For Ali-Sabieh and Dikhil, however, educational disadvantage is not a major factor after demography has been taken into account.

If one compares urban (mostly Djibouti City) with rural Djibouti (figure 3.9), the demography of rural Djibouti helps to mitigate the rural-urban gap. If rural and urban areas had the same demographic characteristics, the gap would be 4 percentage points higher. This is a very unusual finding, as we shall see when we look at the other countries. Education, however, has the usual prodisparity effect. With demographic characteristics accounted for, education disparities add 11 percentage points to the rural-urban gap.

Jordan is an interesting case, because at the time of this writing, the country is considering a strategy of regionalization and regional development to combat spatial inequality. In fact, Jordan has low intergovernorate disparities (figure 3.10). The coefficient of variation of governorate means per capita household consumption is only 0.19, compared with

FIGURE 3.8

Djibouti's Interdistrict Disparities: Tadjourah and Obock Lag in a Different Way from Ali-Sabieh and Dikhil

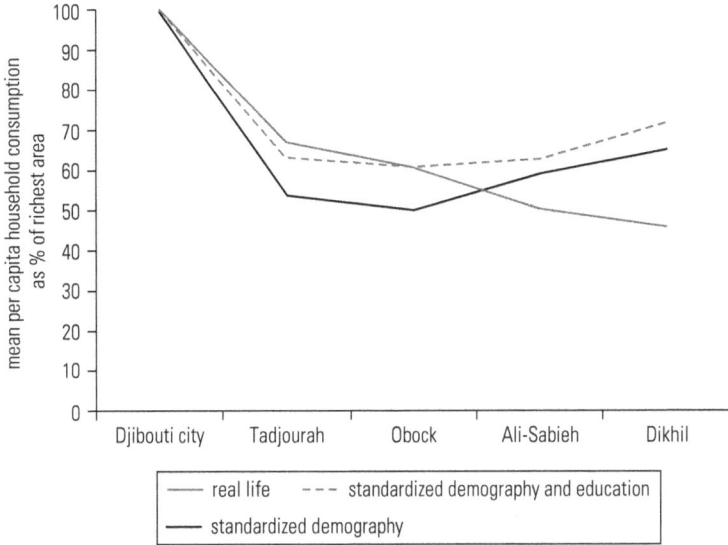

Source: 2002 National Household Survey.

FIGURE 3.9

Djibouti's Rural-Urban Gap, 2002

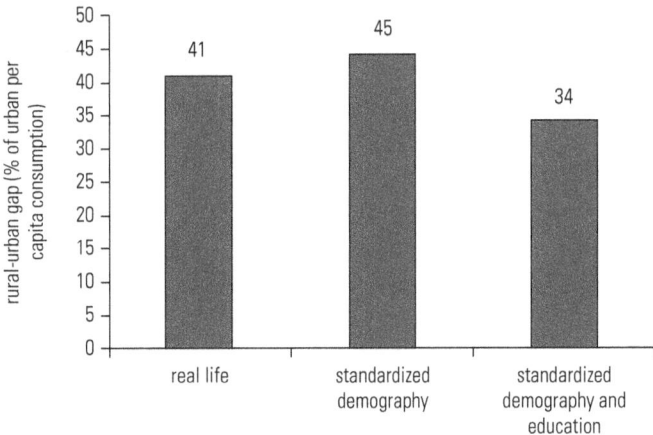

Source: 2002 National Household Survey.

FIGURE 3.10

Intergovernorate Disparities Are Small and Largely Demographic in Jordan

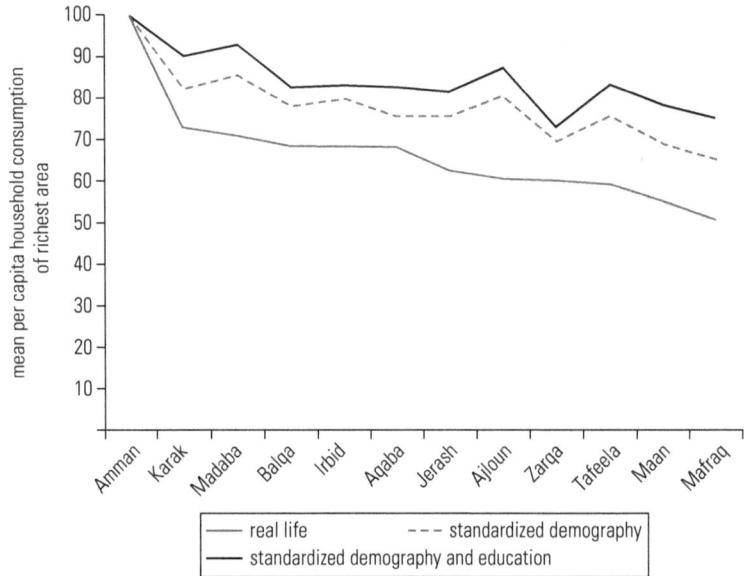

Source: World Bank staff calculations from 2002 National Household Survey.

0.35 in Egypt and a full 0.46 in Morocco. And if there were no demographic disparities in Jordan, the coefficient of variation would be only 0.12. The poorest governorate, Al-Mafraq, would be only 35 percent behind Amman instead of 49 percent behind. Apart from Maan and Zarqa, every other governorate would be within 25 percentage points of Amman. Moreover, this result is before the dispersing effect of educational disparities is taken into account. The importance of demography for the rural-urban comparison is even more dramatic. Average rural per capita consumption is 24 percent behind urban levels. Take away demographic disparities, and this difference dwindles to an insignificant 12 percent. Allow for education, and it becomes a mere 3 percent.

In short, urban-rural disparities in economic opportunity should not be considered a priority policy challenge for Jordan.

Lebanon, another small country, is a total contrast from Jordan.[7] At 0.29, the intermohafaza (province) coefficient of variation of mean mohafaza per capita household consumption is moderate. Lebanon, however, is the only country in the sample for which there is no spatial disparity in demography or education to account for the gap between Beirut and the rest of the country (figure 3.11). (Data are not available for Nabatieh or S. Lebanon.) One possibility is that opportunities to

FIGURE 3.11

Demography and Education Do Not Cause Interregional Disparities in Lebanon

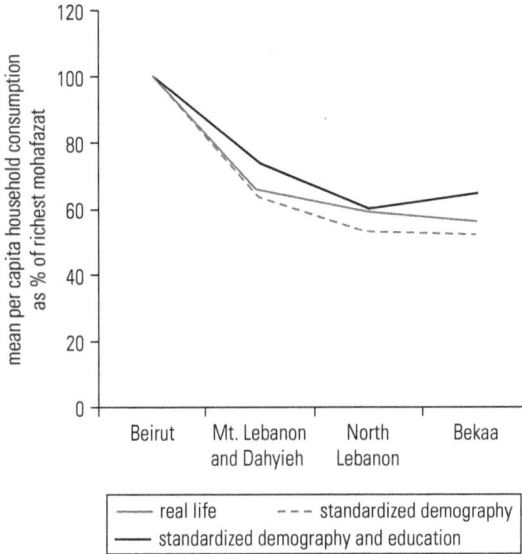

Source: World Bank staff calculations, from 2002 National Household Survey.

relocate in Lebanon are more limited than in other countries for socio-cultural reasons, even though the distances involved are quite small. Another possibility is that congestion and the high cost of living and housing in Beirut is encouraging high-potential households to stay in the provinces.

One can divide Lebanon into a center (Beirut and Mount Lebanon) and a periphery (the north, south, Bekaa, and Nabatieh). The apparent gap between the center and the periphery is big enough—a 63 percent difference in per capita household consumption (UNDP 2008)—but the cost of living in the center is 20 percent higher than in the periphery. Adjust for that, and the gap falls to 36 percent. And the periphery has a lower percentage of its population economically active. Beirut, for example, has a 48 percent higher labor force participation rate than Nabatieh. Adjust for that, and per capita consumption per economically active person is a trivial 3 percent.

The implication is that a spatial development strategy for Lebanon's periphery should lean toward improving labor mobility and increasing lagging areas' labor force participation rate. Disparities in earnings per worker, education, and family size, however, are not the major issues.

Morocco's interprovincial spatial disparities are modest (figure 3.12): the coefficient of variation of provincial mean per capita household

FIGURE 3.12

Interprovincial Disparities Are Quite Modest and Not the Fault of Demography in Morocco

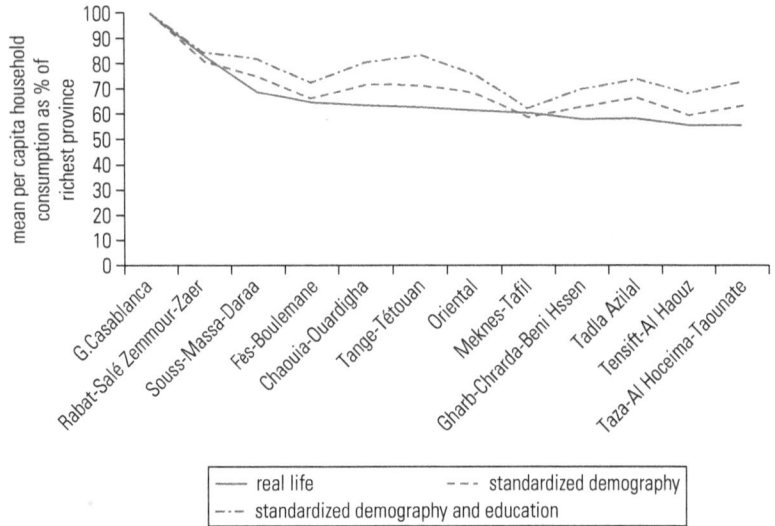

Source: World Bank staff calculations, from 1998 household survey.

Note: Guelmime Es-Semara is not inculded.

consumption is only 0.20.[8] However, Morocco's urban-rural gap[9] is quite large: 54 percent of mean urban per capita household consumption compared with 48 percent in Egypt and 40 percent in the Republic of Yemen. The education of the household head and demography are factors to be considered but of less importance than in some of the other countries under consideration. Rabat-Salé Zemmour-Zaer, Fès-Boulemane, Meknes-Tafil, and Tensift-Al Haouz have practically the same demographic composition as the leading area of Grand Casablanca, and elimination of the demographic disparities would not bring any province more than 9 percentage points closer to Casablanca's per capita consumption. Even if rural and urban areas had the same demographic characteristics, the rural-urban gap would still be 41 percent. Controlling for the level of education of the household head, rural Morocco's per capita household consumption would still be 32 percent lower than urban Morocco's. So Morocco is a case of significant rural-urban differences in economic opportunity, which household characteristics cannot explain away (see figure 3.13).

In Syria, the issue of the north and northeast regions weighs heavily upon policy makers. Average per capita household expenditure in the northeast governorates of El Hassakeh, El Quneitra, and Al Raqqa

FIGURE 3.13

The Rural-Urban Gap Is Large and Cannot Be Explained Away by Demography or Education in Morocco, 1998

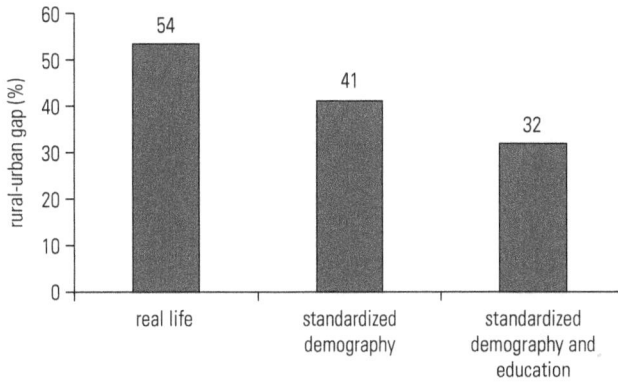

Source: World Bank staff calculations, from 1998 household survey.

is 45–53 percent lower than in Damascus City. Poverty is particularly high among the Kurdish population, which is concentrated in the north and northeast (UNHCR 2009) and includes some 300,000 stateless or unregistered persons (Lowe 2006). The northeast is also home to some of the poorest Iraqis to settle in Syria. Partly in order to support living standards and employment in the northeast, the government has maintained subsidies for cotton prices worth 0.9 percent of GDP (World Bank 2008b). Three years of drought, starting in 2006–07, have spurred migration out of the northeast toward Damascus. So what can the analysis tell us about the plight of Syria's lagging areas?

It is striking that Syria's intergovernorate disparities can in no way be linked to spatial disparities in the level of education of the household head (figure 3.14); when one simulates the equalization of education levels across governorates, it makes no difference to per capita household consumption. Even when one compares the urban population with the rural population, disparities in the level of education of the household head do not count for much. Controlling for the education variable reduces the urban-rural gap only by 4 percentage points, which compares with a reduction of 7 to 11 percentage points in the other countries in the sample. This difference could be because educational attainment is evenly spread across the territory or because the returns to educational attainment are low due to low wage differentials.

However, demographic disparities do matter. Outside Damascus, Syria's governorates can be divided into two groups. There are the

FIGURE 3.14

**Lagging Governorates Are a Demographic Phenomenon;
Education Is Not the Issue in the Syrian Arab Republic**

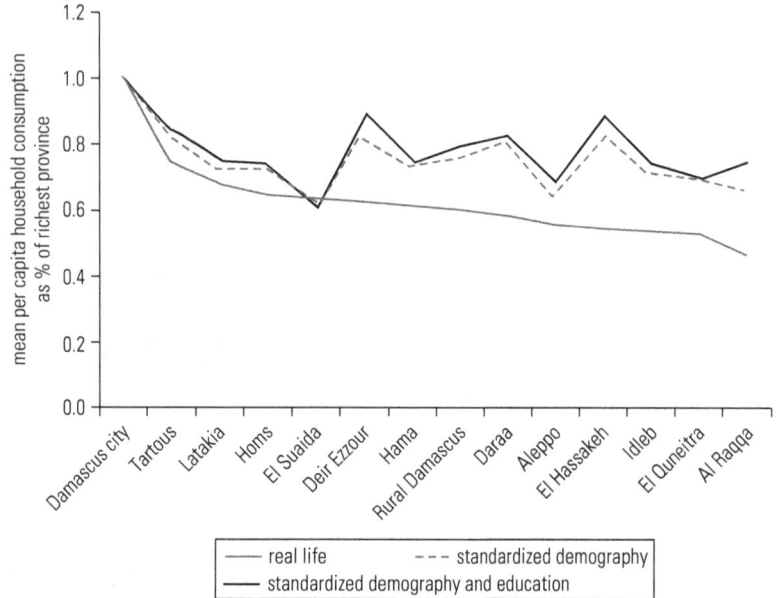

Source: World Bank staff calculations from household survey, 2004.

governorates of the central band (Tartous, Latakia, Homs, El Suaida, and Aleppo), which have a nearly identical demographic makeup to Damascus City, even though they lag 20 to 40 percent behind Damascus City in terms of per capita consumption. But then there is a second set of governorates to the north and south of this central belt (Deir Ezzour, Hama, Rural Damascus, Daraa, El Hassakeh, El Quneitra, and Al Raqqa) where demography is a major source of lagging area status. This group of governorates includes the northeast region.

In fact, the demography factor is so strong that without it the northeast would not be a lagging area at all. If all of Syria's governorates had the same demographic profile (figure 3.14), El Hassakeh would be no worse off than Tartous, the leading governorate outside Damascus City—and significantly better off than the port city of Latakia and the urban provinces of Homs, Hama, Aleppo, and El Suaida. The northeastern lagging governorates of El Quneitra and Al Raqqa would be on a par with the leading governorates of Latakia and Homs.

The northeast, therefore, may be a lagging region, but it is not necessarily a region lacking in economic opportunity. Its households have a demographic composition that would fare badly wherever it was located (and household heads have a level of education similar to that in other areas).

In the Republic of Yemen (figure 3.15), demography is worth a 15 percentage-point handicap, on average, for governorates outside Sana'a City. The demographic disadvantage is particularly strong (20 percentage points) for the Sana'a Region governorate (Sana'a City's peri-urban and rural fringe), for Al-Maharh, and for Sa'adah (the location of a religious insurgency and approximately 80,000 internally displaced people). Without the demographic and educational components of inter-governorate disparities, the poorest governorate, Amran, would only be 40 percent behind Sana'a City in terms of per capita consumption, instead of 65 percent. The vast, arid, and sparsely populated gover-norate of Al-Maharh would be 17 percent richer than Sana'a City instead of 20 percent poorer; thanks to its position on the Oman bor-der, it offers its inhabitants more economic opportunity than any other governorate. Without differences in education and demography, the rural-urban gap would be 25 percent instead of 40 percent.

FIGURE 3.15

Demography and Education Explain about a Third of Intergover-norate and Rural-Urban Inequality in Republic of Yemen

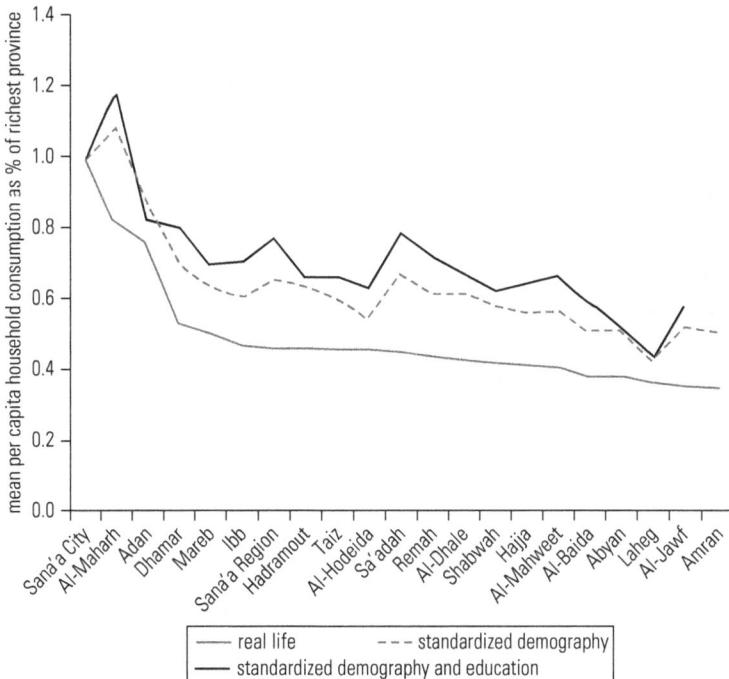

Source: World Bank staff calculations from 2005 household survey.

The implication for MENA's policy makers is clear: before assuming that observed spatial disparities in welfare are the fault of spatial disparities in economic opportunity, one should check whether the households in the lagging areas are actually able to take advantage of economic opportunities. As the data previously have shown, the situation varies from country to country. For many lagging areas, however, the population of lagging areas consists of households who would have low per capita consumption *wherever they lived*—because of their household composition or their educational level. This observation means that human development is a key component of effective spatial development in MENA.

Where Does Lagging Areas' Demographic Disadvantage Come From?

Why do MENA's lagging areas have household characteristics that are so different from those of leading areas? The differences can be broken down into three effects:

• The *fertility effect*—Women in lagging areas have more children.

• The *sorting effect*—People with high potential are the most likely to move out of low-potential areas.

• The *education effect*—Children in lagging areas have less opportunity to acquire human capital.

The *fertility effect* comes from MENA's demographic transition being spatially uneven. Fertility rates are falling across MENA, but they fell in leading and urban areas first and in lagging and rural areas last. Lagging areas with a history of higher fertility have higher dependency ratios now.

Figure 3.16 tells the story of the Islamic Republic of Iran's demographic transition. In 1986, the rural total fertility rate[10] was 1.1 points higher than the urban rate. (In other words, a typical rural woman was having 1.1 more children over her lifetime than a typical urban woman.) By 1990, the gap had widened to 1.7 points, as the urban rate fell faster than the rural rate. By 2000, however, the rural rate had caught up, and the gap had closed to 0.4 points.

The spatially uneven demographic transition has been similar in other MENA economies. The rural-urban fertility rate gap in Tunisia closed from 2.3 in 1988 to 0.8 in 2006. In Jordan, the gap was 1.7 in 1990 but had practically vanished at 0.1 by 2007. In Egypt, the rural-urban fertility gap suddenly began to shrink around 1992; since then, it has fallen from 2.0 to 0.7. Egypt had massive spatial disparities in contraceptive use in the mid-1990s. The highest rate of use was in urban Lower Egypt, while the rate in rural Lower Egypt (53 percent) was more than twice as high as in rural Upper Egypt (24 percent) (Chelala 1996). In Morocco

FIGURE 3.16

The Islamic Republic of Iran's Demographic Transition
Began in Urban Areas

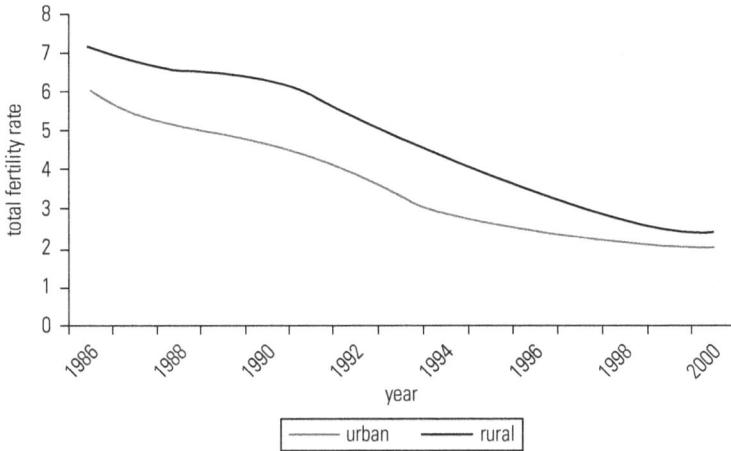

Source: Sutton 2001.

the fertility rate gap was widening until 1992, when it hit a massive 3.0, but it was as low as 0.9 in 2003. In Algeria, the fall in fertility spread spatially like a wave, starting in coastal and urban wilayate (governorates) and only coming later to the high plateaus and then to the Saharan and Saharan Atlas *wilaya* (Sutton 2001). The result was that "interior and Saharan Algeria contain regional pools of demographic vitality and potential population growth" (map 3.3); according to the 1995 house-hold survey, the ratio of people of nonworking age to people of working age was 25 percent higher in rural areas than in urban areas (World Bank 1999). In the Republic of Yemen, however, the trend is not yet clear. The gap narrowed from 2.6 to 2.0 between 1991 and 1997, but then widened again to 2.2 by 2006.

This "radiating demographic transition" conveys both bad and good news. In the short run, it is the cause of spatial disparities in dependency ratios that, as we have seen, are a major cause of MENA's rural-urban and interprovincial disparities in well-being. As the demographic transition reaches MENA's lagging areas, however, it will become a major long-term force for spatial convergence in living standards. Therefore, it is possible that a significant fraction of the spatial disparities "problem" may be already in the process of mitigating itself.

Fertility rates are known to be influenced by many factors: female education, gender empowerment, female labor participation, and income growth, as well as access to quality reproductive health services (World Bank 2007b). All of these determinants of fertility vary from place to place, which is precisely why the demographic transition has been

MAP 3.3

Interior and Saharan Algeria Contain Regional Pools of Demographic Vitality and Potential Population Growth

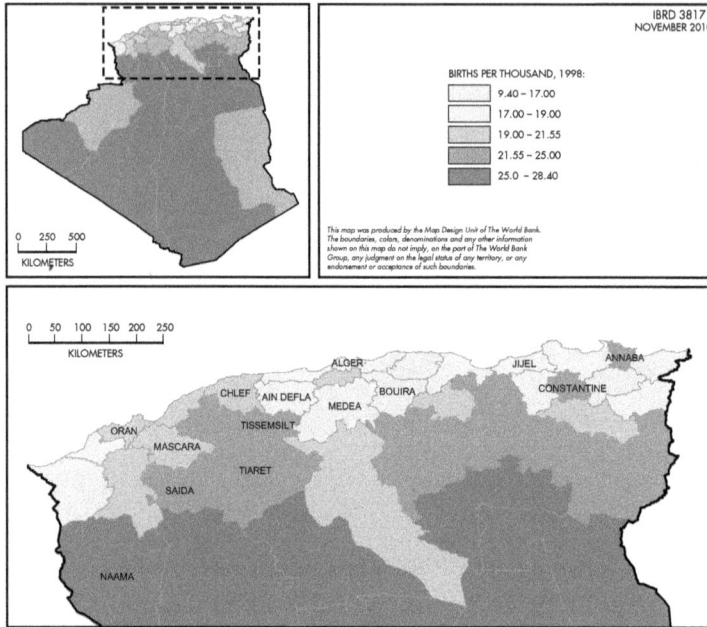

Source: Sutton 2001.

geographically uneven. For example, in Tunisia (Ayadi and Amara 2009) the relationship between household size and poverty is strongest in coastal (leading) areas, suggesting that the motivation to limit one's number of children might be highest there. As MENA governments develop population policies, they could, therefore, focus on the spatial dimension of fertility (see map 3.3).

The *sorting effect* means that people with the highest earning opportunities leave lagging areas. This is because people with more education set greater store by city amenities, and because the jobs that make education productive tend to be concentrated in cities (Henderson 1986). In Morocco in the 1980s, people with secondary or higher education were 120 percent more common among rural-urban migrants than among the rural population overall (Centre d'Études et de Recherches Démographiques 1989). Lifetime rural-urban migration rates in Egypt are twice as high for university graduates as for people without intermediate-level education (Wahba 2007). People with more education, moreover, tend not to migrate out of large cities (McCormick and Wahba 2005). In Syria, a male with secondary education is twice as likely to migrate as one with less than primary education (Khawaja 2002).

The *education effect* is about people in lagging areas being less able to acquire human capital, whether from the educational system or from family members and social networks. Given the centrality of education for spatial development, therefore, later sections will discuss the spatial dimension of education and how MENA governments can use education as an instrument for achieving their spatial development objectives.

The three household characteristic effects—fertility, sorting, and education—are interrelated, inseparable, and mutually reinforcing. Women who have received less primary and secondary education tend to have more children at any given level of household income (Akin 2005). Educated people who leave the lagging area take their education with them, rather than transmitting their human capital to the lagging area's next generation. Those who remain behind are more likely to be female and less educated—that is, the section of the population most associated with child-rearing.

Developing People to Take Opportunities

The conclusion, then, is that lagging areas' poor economic situation is linked to household characteristics. This point is of critical importance for policy makers. It means that stimulating economic development in MENA's lagging areas is *as much a question of developing people to take opportunities as of developing places to make opportunities.* Delivering quality education in lagging areas is critical, not just because educated people can take more opportunities, but also because education is a key factor in the demographic transition toward lower fertility rates and lower dependency ratios in lagging areas.

What Are the Differences in the Cost of Living?

It costs less to live in lagging areas than in leading areas. Housing is less expensive, and food can sometimes be cheaper too. When measuring spatial disparities in living standards, therefore, it is important to allow for differences in the cost of living.

One way of gauging spatial disparities in the cost of living is to look at the difference between urban and rural poverty lines, which is the cost of maintaining a minimum standard of living for one person. However, one cannot assume that the rural-urban gap in the average cost of living will be exactly the same as the rural-urban gap in the poverty line, because poor people's spending has a distinct composition.

In MENA, the urban poverty line averages 10 percent higher than the rural poverty line (table 3.9). This is a smaller gap than for most other

TABLE 3.9

Urban-Rural Differences in the Cost of Living Partially Cancel Out Spatial Disparities in Spending Power

Country or region	Year of survey(s)	Ratio of urban to rural poverty lines
Middle East and North Africa		1.10
Egypt, Arab Rep.	1995, 1999/00	1.09
Iran, Islamic Rep.	1994, 1999	1.13
Jordan	2002–03	1.13
Morocco	1990–91, 1998–99	1.29
Tunisia	1995, 2000	1.18
East Asia and the Pacific		1.30
Europe and Central Asia		1.05
Latin America and the Caribbean		1.44
South Asia		1.30
Sub-Saharan Africa		1.29

Source: Ravallion, Chen, and Sangraula 2007.

regions; however, it still cancels out a large part of the apparent urban-rural disparity in living standards. For example, per capita expenditure in urban Morocco in 1998–99 was 54 percent higher than per capita expenditure in rural Morocco, but the poverty line in urban Morocco was 29 percent higher than in rural Morocco. In Jordan, the urban poverty line in 2002 was 13 percent higher than the rural poverty line. This gap is actually higher than what the urban-rural gap in per capita per consumption would be if rural and urban Jordan shared the same demographic characteristics. Moreover, spatial disparities in demography could reinforce spatial disparities in prices, if the cost of living for a dependent is lower than for a worker—for example, in terms of food, travel, and clothing expenses.

Spatial Disparities Are Not as Wide as They Seem

The implication of all the earlier discussion is that the political economy of space, sorting effects, fertility effects, education effects, and price differences all combine to magnify the appearance of spatial inequalities in economic opportunity. A key recommendation of this report is, therefore, to check that inequalities in economic opportunity are really as big as one imagines.

Does Spatial Convergence Come in Many Qualities?

Once policy makers have a clear profile of spatial disparities at a moment in time, it would be useful to know how they are changing across time. The crucial question is, are living standards converging spatially? If they are, governments may decide that it is not necessary to focus resources on resolving an issue that is on its way to a solution.

The 2009 World Development Report (World Bank 2009a) shows how spatial disparities follow a general pattern as countries experience economic growth:

- The living standards gap between leading and lagging areas first grows, as industrialization gathers pace, and then shrinks. The initial divergence happens as economies of agglomeration concentrate economic activity in leading areas and cities. The subsequent convergence results from migration out of lagging areas, making labor scarcer and pushing up wages, from investments spilling out of congested cities into peri-urban areas and from greater spending on public social services in lagging areas (2009a, 62). The same goes for disparities between subnational regions and rural-urban disparities (2009a, 65). The divergence-convergence cycle can be a long-term process; countries such as Sweden, Spain, the United Kingdom, the United States, and Japan took 40 to 100 years for the income gap to rise and fall back to preindustrialization levels (2009a, 86). But the trends are not always smooth or simple. Massive divergence can happen very quickly, as it did in India, the Russian Federation, and Vietnam in the 1990s (Shankar and Shah 2003). Countries can converge and then diverge, as China did, or can diverge and then converge, like Brazil.

- It is possible for disparities in social indicators, such as poverty, health, and education, to shrink at the same time that economic agglomeration is growing. Reducing social spatial disparities depends on the state; it requires a progressive taxation system and for lagging areas to receive quality social services (2009a, 238).

The MENA examples below are specimens of the kind of convergence narrative that could inform policy decisions. They examine the Islamic Republic of Iran, Tunisia, and Egypt.

The lesson that our analysis of these countries teaches is that, while the divergence-convergence cycle might be a useful generalization, every country's convergence experience has its own quality. A simple statement that development is converging or diverging across space does not capture the potential variety of trends required to inform policy makers' decisions.

The Islamic Republic of Iran: Spatial Convergence in Living Standards, but for the Wrong Reason. The Islamic Republic of Iran has enjoyed inter-ostan (province) spatial convergence in spending power since the Revolution. The population-weighted[11] coefficient of variation of mean per capita household expenditure was 0.40 in 1976, about the same as in India. By 2005, it was 0.28. Underlying the inter-ostan convergence was an urban-rural convergence. In 1976, the urban-rural gap in per capita household expenditure was 53 percent. By 2005, the gap was down to 37 percent.

However, the story of living standards convergence is not as happy as it seems. The leap forward in convergence, both inter-ostan and rural-urban, occurred from 1976 to 1996 (figure 3.17), when the economy was affected by conflict, urban private assets were expropriated (Behdad 1989), and GDP per capita averaged 34 percent lower than its 1976 peak. The urban-rural convergence came from urban per capita household expenditure falling by 21 percent from 1976 to 1985, while rural per capita household expenditure "only" fell by 7 percent. In fact, the reduction in inequality came with an increase in overall poverty (Assadzadeh and Paul 2004). The rural sector also benefited from the revolutionary government's decision to adjust the terms of trade in favor of rural areas. Between 1976 and 1984, agricultural value added grew by 31 percent, twice the rate of the non-oil economy (Behdad 1989). One sure reason was that farmgate prices rose 55 percent in real terms from 1977 to 1985 (Mojtahed and Esfahani 1989).

But once the overall economy began to resume steady growth, from the early 1990s onward, the spatial convergence trend changed.

FIGURE 3.17

Inter-Ostan Disparities Shrink over Time in the Islamic Republic of Iran

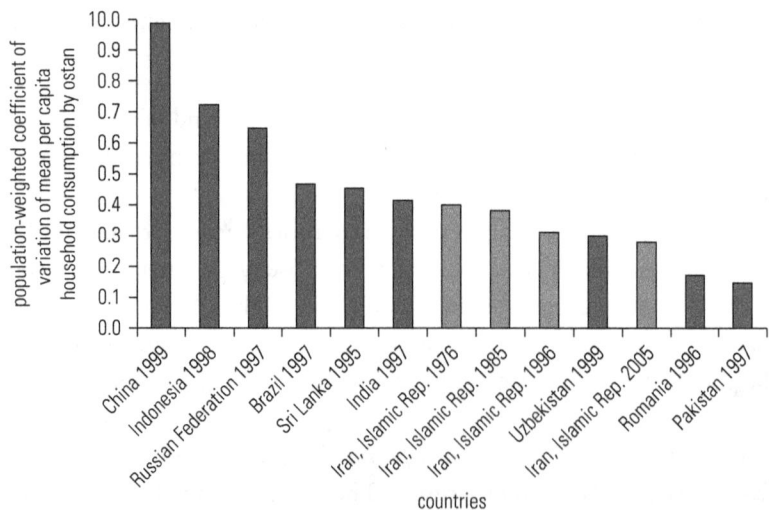

Sources: World Bank staff calculations using government of the Islamic Republic of Iran unpublished data, http://www.unescap.org/esid/psis/population/popin/profiles/iran/popin15.htm; Shankar and Shah (2003).

Inter-ostan convergence stagnated, and the urban-rural gap began to widen once again, from 29 percent in 1996 to 37 percent in 2005—when the rural-divide was a major theme of political campaigning in the run-up to the presidential election. In the Islamic Republic of Iran, therefore, the story is that spatial divergence can be part of a positive growth process.

Tunisia: A Case of Bipolar Convergence. Tunisia has seen significant interregional convergence. The population-weighted coefficient of variance of median household consumption by region fell from 0.32 in 1980 to 0.24 in 2000. This fall brought Tunisia's interregional disparities down into the Western European range. There has been an identifiable trend for governorates with higher poverty rates to enjoy higher growth rates (Boulila, Gabsi, and Trabelsi 2009).

Although the rural-urban gap also narrowed over the same period, the convergence trend is not clear. The ratio of "communal" to rural mean per capita household expenditures was 2.11 to 1.00 in 1980 and 1.85 to 1.00 in 2000. The rural-urban gap, however, fluctuates from year to year, probably according to rainfall; in 1975, it was as low as 1.81, even slightly lower than in 2000, so one cannot be totally certain of a converging trend.

A critical feature of Tunisia's spatial convergence is the trajectory of the middle-ranking regions, namely the center-east, the northeast, and the south. In 1980, these three regions had more or less the same standard of living as each other, sandwiched between the prosperous Greater Tunis region and the lagging center-west and northwest regions. Since 1980, however, each of the middle-ranking regions has taken its own course. On the one hand, living standards in the center-east have shot up to converge with Greater Tunis. On the other, the south and the northeast have stagnated, in relative terms, to converge with the center-west and the northwest (figure 3.18). Zooming in, we see that the center-east's success was focused on a breakout by Mahdia and Monastir governorates (figure 3.19). Monastir's mean per capita household consumption in 1980 was 31 percent lower than Tunis's and around the same as that of its neighbors. By 2000, however, it had split away from its neighbors, even those closer to the metropolis, and joined Tunis.

There are important policy lessons in Tunisia's regional convergence experience. First, economic agglomeration is a more selective process than simple agglomeration theory suggests (that is, economic density leading to more economic density). Clearly, Tunisia's center-east region built on some kind of potential competitive advantage, despite being further from the Tunis metropolis than the equally rich northeast area. The implication is that distance from economic density is not the whole story

FIGURE 3.18

Regions Split into Rich and Poor Clubs, While Converging Overall in Tunisia

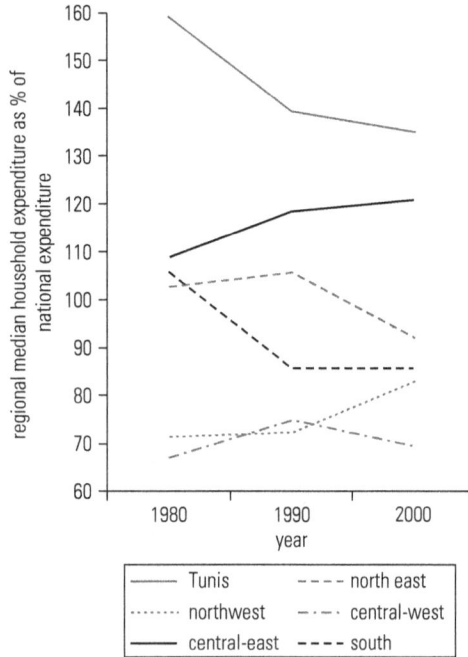

Sources: INS 2000, 1990, 1980: Enquête nationale sur le budget, la consommation, et le niveau de vie des ménages [National survey of household budgets, consumption, and living standards].

FIGURE 3.19

Proximity of Eastern Governorates to the Metropolis Does Not Explain Performance in Tunisia, 1980–2000

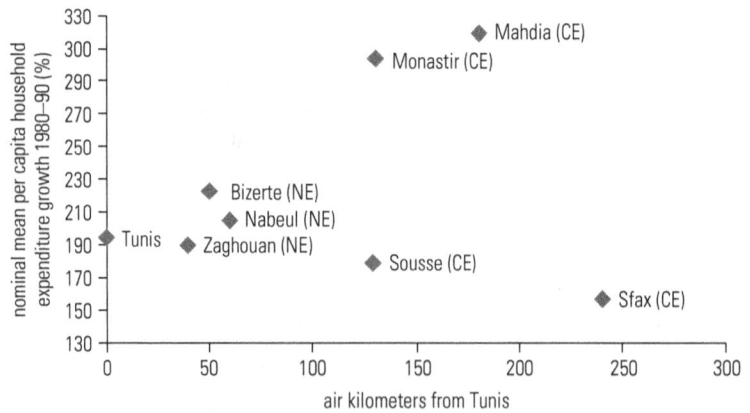

Source: INS 2000, 1980, Enquête nationale sur le budget, la consommation et le niveau de vie des ménages [National survey of household budgets, consumption, and living standards].

Note: CE = center-east, NE = northeast.

when it comes to predicting an area's success; effective spatial development strategies can tap other sources of development potential. This is a theme that we will discuss further in later sections. Second, spatial convergence at the national level may take the form of a "breakout" by middle-ranking areas. Therefore, policy makers should not focus their convergence concerns solely upon the most lagging areas.

The Arab Republic of Egypt: Agglomeration of Poverty within the South. The rural-urban gap has been widening in Egypt (table 3.10). Between 2005 and 2008, the fastest per capita household consumption growth was in metropolitan, Upper Egypt urban, and Lower Egypt urban areas. The fastest growth, however, at 5.6 percent per annum, was in the urban areas of the poorer Upper Egypt governorates. Overall, it is not possible to identify clear convergence or divergence across governorates. The population-weighted coefficient of variation of the gross regional domestic product (GRDP) estimates published by the United Nations Development Programme's (UNDP's) national Human Development Reports was unchanged at 0.39 between 1998–2009 and 2003–04.[12]

However, there is a growing spatial concentration of poverty over time. Between 1995 and 2008, the number of Egyptians living below the poverty line rose by 3,070,000, with an increase of 3,796,000 in the governorates of Upper Egypt.

What seems to be happening is that Egypt is facing a situation of widening spatial disparities at the micro level within Upper Egypt, even if there is no overall divergence at the national level. Not only is the gap between urban and rural Upper Egypt widening, but also some villages in rural Upper Egypt are being left behind while others "break out." As figure 3.20 shows, poverty reduction in Upper Egypt's villages was a two-speed affair. In 1996, most villages had poverty rates in the 50 to 75 percent band. Some villages broke away, reducing their poverty rates to 10 to 20 percent. But an equal number of villages remained stuck with

TABLE 3.10

The Arab Republic of Egypt, 2005–08: Urban Convergence with Rural Divergence

Annual growth in mean real household consumption, 2005–08	Urban (%)	Rural (%)
Metropolitan	3.3	n.a.
Lower Egypt	4.2	3.1
Upper Egypt	5.6	1.6

Source: World Bank 2009b.

Note: n.a. = not applicable.

FIGURE 3.20

Two-Speed Development in Rural Upper Egypt, 1996–2006

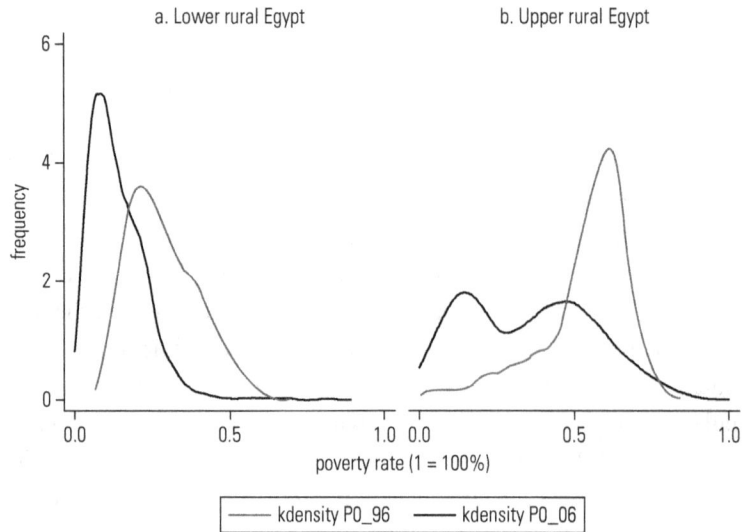

Source: World Bank 2009b.

their poverty rates in the 40 to 60 percent range. The Egyptian government's strategy of targeting assistance toward low-income villages in low-income governorates does indeed fit the evidence on the spatial distribution of poverty.

Convergence in Human Development Indicators: A Mirage?

When it comes to social indicators such as health, education, and poverty outcomes, appearances of spatial convergence can be deceptive. As long as the national picture is improving, spatial convergence in basic social indicators will usually be observed. When the national picture is deteriorating (as in the poverty case for Egypt 1995–2008 mentioned earlier) divergence may be noted; however, this change might be more to do with the choice of indicator than with spatial patterns in human development.

For example, the Islamic Republic of Iran's human development indicators have improved and converged spatially during recent decades. Between 1976 and 1996, the female literacy rate rose 45 percentage points from 17 percent to 62 percent, while for urban women it rose by only 26 percentage points from 56 percent to 82 percent (UNDP 1999). During 1994–2000, infant and under-five mortality rates fell fastest in the poorest provinces (Mehryar 2004). Rates of stunting, wasting, and underweight fell in all provinces, with some of the biggest gains in lagging ostans. Inter-ostan inequalities in basic education have decreased over time; in the 10 years to 2006, the gap between the highest and the lowest literacy rates narrowed by 10 percentage points (World Bank 2008c).

However, such indicators of basic social welfare do not tell the full story. Poverty rates, malnutrition rates, illiteracy rates, and so on *can hardly fail to converge if the overall human development situation is improving*, because it is impossible for the rates in leading areas to fall below zero. In the United Kingdom, for example, spatial disparities in maternal mortality are minuscule because they are close to zero percent everywhere. The United Kingdom still has significant spatial disparities in health, however. For example, a child from Wales is 77 percent more likely to be overweight than a child from the East of England (Hawkins and others 2007). The United Kingdom still has spatial disparities in health, but indicators of basic social welfare achievement no longer pick them up. So it may be with the Islamic Republic of Iran and other MENA economies. Convergence of basic social welfare indicators may be taking place, but this does not mean that other social indicators are not showing wide—and may be increasing—disparities.

Understanding the potentially misleading convergence conclusions to be drawn from the standard basic social indicators is particularly important in MENA economies where the social service agenda is a rapidly advancing frontier: from primary school enrollment toward postprimary access and quality in education (World Bank 2008c, 83–114);[13] from the communicable toward noncommunicable disease; from water connections toward water and sanitation service quality; and from extreme poverty toward borderline poverty and vulnerability (Iqbal 2006).

Is Internal Migration Resolving MENA's Lagging Area Problem?

Internal migration should reduce spatial disparities, as several processes come into play:

- When people move from lagging areas to leading areas, they reduce the supply of labor in their place of origin, causing earnings per head to rise in lagging areas.

- Migrants send remittances back home. For example, in Sub-Saharan Africa remittances account for 15 percent of rural income, and in China, migrant-sending households become richer in terms of consumption, production, and ownership of consumer durables (De Brauw and Giles 2006).

- Prolonged migration leads to a reduction in the importance of the lagging area's development needs, for the simple reason that fewer people live in the lagging area.

The 2009 World Development Report (World Bank 2009a, 146–69) classifies countries into two groups. On one side, there are countries in which the movement of labor from lagging to leading areas can bring about spatial convergence in living standards. The United States, with its northward wave of African American migration after the Civil War and its continuing tradition of long-distance relocation is one example. China, where migrants account for a third of urban employment, is another. On the other side are countries where the populations of lagging areas cannot or will not migrate to leading areas, perhaps because of social, ethnic, religious, or linguistic divisions. Although 40 percent of India's urban population are migrants, for example, only 4 percent of migrants cross state lines. This finding means that the migration solution is not going to resolve the lagging area problem for lagging states such as Bihar, Orissa, or Madhya Pradesh.

The appropriate policy response to the lagging areas problem depends on which category a lagging area falls into. The more the population is locked into its current spatial distribution, the more spatially targeted economic development is required to improve economic opportunities in lagging areas.

Note the difference between changes in the spatial distribution of population and the propensity to migrate. A high propensity to migrate is a necessary but insufficient condition for a redistribution of the population from lagging to leading areas. Many migrants, both men and women, practice seasonal or temporary "circular" migration; they migrate, but their long-term domicile does not change. Spatial disparities in the fertility rate can also cancel out migration. And migration into and out of a lagging area can cancel itself out. In the Islamic Republic of Iran, for example, gross provincial outmigration numbers 1986–96 were seven times larger than net interprovincial migration figures.

Where, then, does MENA lie? Is its spatial distribution of population fluid or fixed?

Urbanization, but Not Metropolitanization

All over MENA, the center of demographic gravity is moving from the countryside to the cities, with rapid increases in the urban sector's share of population.

Overall population growth, however, is still fast enough to keep MENA's rural populations growing. Here the exception is Lebanon, whose rural population peaked pre-1960, reached a nadir around 1990, and has been creeping back up ever since.

Despite the popular view that there is a headlong rush of migrants to the capital cities and main metropolitan areas, official data show that in Algeria, Egypt, the Islamic Republic of Iran, Morocco, and Syria the main city's share of total population has stayed more or less constant. Only Tripoli in Libya and Sana'a in the Republic of Yemen have significantly increased their shares of the national population, while Amman and Beirut have lost population share. Most main cities have also seen their share of the urban population fall.

Therefore, urbanization is spread across entire territories, and is not, as is popularly believed, taking the form of a unipolar concentration of population in each country's biggest city or cities. MENA's observation is consistent with the worldwide observation (Henderson, Shalizi, and Venables 2001) that the relative size of cities changes little as economic growth occurs. In North Africa in 1960, 25 percent of the urban population was living in cities of more than 1 million inhabitants, a figure that had risen to only 33 percent by 2005. In the Islamic Republic of Iran, the share rose from 26 percent to 33 percent over the same period; and in Iraq, from 32 percent to 35 percent. Meanwhile, Amman's share of the urban population fell from 48 percent to 24 percent, Beirut's from 70 percent to 51 percent, and Damascus's from 34 percent to 23 percent. Sana'a was the exception, with its share of the urban population doubling to 30 percent (United Nations Department of Economic and Social Affairs 2007).

MENA's urbanization is on a par with that of other developing country economies and not, as is sometimes feared, a phenomenon of uniquely overgrown megacities. Henderson (2000) estimated the relationship between growth and the size of the "prime" (main) city for a sample of countries using 1965–95 panel data. Of the 70 prime cities for which results were available, 24 appeared so large as to be restricting economic growth. Only one of these was from the MENA region: Cairo. The other MENA cities in the study, Algiers, Tehran, Amman, Damascus, and Tunis, were among the 30 prime cities that came out as being appropriately sized.

Table 3.11, therefore, summarizes the trend of the past three decades with respect to the urban-rural continuum: urbanization, but without an emptying of rural areas and without a concentration of the urban population within prime cities.

Very Little Lateral Redistribution toward Leading Provinces

The redistribution of MENA's population tends to be a gradual shift from rural to urban areas within provinces rather than a lateral agglomeration from lagging provinces to leading provinces. This shift is very different from what happened in the United States in the late nineteenth century or in China since the 1990s, where there were massive lateral redistributions of the population across long distances. To visualize MENA's case,

TABLE 3.11

Urbanization without Deruralization or Metropolitanization

1980–2007	Increase in urban % of population	% Decrease in rural population	Increase in biggest city's % of total population	Increase in biggest city's % of urban population
Algeria	22	–13	1	–5
Djibouti	15	–15	—	—
Egypt, Arab Rep.	–1	–77	–1	–2
Iraq	—	—	—	—
Iran, Islamic Rep.	18	–16	–2	–10
Jordan	18	–41	–5	–18
Lebanon	13	26	–13	–27
Libya	7	–52	10	9
Morocco	15	–20	–1	–8
Syrian Arab Republic	7	–92	2	0
Tunisia	15	–10	—	—
West Bank and Gaza	10	—	—	—
Yemen, Rep.	14	–124	6	12

Sources: Staff calculations; World Bank GDI database.
Note: Gray = An indicator of agglomerating population redistribution. Brown = An indicator of nonagglomerating population redistribution. — = data not available.

one can extrapolate from the different observed population growth rates of a country's provinces across consecutive censuses to project how its population might be allocated across the territory in future (table 3.12). The resulting scenarios are not a forecast in the strict sense because they do not reflect future changes in migration numbers or the fertility rate; however, they do give a clear sense of the current stasis in the interprovincial distribution of MENA's population.

Although many studies of international migration from MENA exist, analysis of internal migration flows is scarce and mostly focused on Wahba and Assaad's work in Egypt. What research is available tends to confirm its noncentripetal character. Data from the Egypt Labor Market Panel Survey (Wahba 2007) show that the overall propensity to migrate is low; only 1.6 percent of the population changed its governorate of residence during the eight years between the 1998 and 2006 surveys. The lifetime intergovernorate migration rate is significantly lower for men than for women—7 percent compared with 11 percent—suggesting that much intergovernorate migration is determined by marriage patterns rather than by opportunities of higher-paying employment. Moreover, migration flows between better- and worse-off areas can cancel each other out; during 1990–98, 0.2 percent of the population moved from rural to urban areas, while 1.1 percent of the population relocated in the opposite direction (Wahba 2007). Syria's Internal Migration Survey Project (Khawaja 2002)

TABLE 3.12

Little Lateral Redistribution of Population toward Leading Provinces, Save in Tunisia

In …		the poorest …		provinces' share of		to …	
	Egypt, Arab Rep.	the poorest …	13	provinces' share of	58.0 in 1996	to …	54.7 in 2036
	Iraq		7	the population	37.7 in 1997	(%)	39.6 in 2037
	Iran, Islamic Rep.		15	is heading from	36.0 in 1996		33.4 in 2036
	Jordan		6	… (%)	32.2 in 1994		32.6 in 2036
	Morocco		27		48.4 in 1994		43.6 in 2034
	Syrian Arab Republic		7		45.4 in 1981		44.9 in 2021
	Tunisia		12		39.0 in 1986		15.0 in 2026

Sources: Arab Republic of Egypt, National Human Development Report and censuses; Iraq, http://cosit.gov.iq/english/2007/15-13.htm and http://cosit.gov.iq/english/2007/2-3.htm (accessed July 7, 2010); Islamic Republic of Iran, National Household Survey, http://www.unescap .org/esid/psis/population/popin/profiles/iran/popin15.htm and http://www.statoids.com/uir.html (accessed January 23, 2008); Jordan, http://www.statoids.com/ujo.html (accessed April 24, 2009) and National Household Survey; Morocco, http://www.statoids.com/yma.html (accessed April 23, 2009) and World Bank 2004a; Syrian Arab Republic, http://www.undp.org.sy/publications/national/Poverty/ Poverty_In_Syria_en.pdf, http://www.statoids.com/usy.html (accessed April 24, 2009) and http://www.populstat.info/Asia/syriap.htm; Tunisia, INS 2000: Enquête nationale sur le budget, la consommation et le niveau de vie des ménages [National survey of household budgets, consumption, and living standards].

found a lifetime migration rate of 14 percent, which is low by middle-income country standards. Again, there was no sense of migrants being particularly drawn toward the larger cities; Damascus, Idlib, and Hama all had a negative lifetime net migration rates (2002, 26), and provincial capitals had a lower share of lifetime migrants in them than smaller urban centers (2002, 17). In the Islamic Republic of Iran during 1996–2006, 36 percent of migratory moves between 1996 and 2006 were within the same district (*shahrestan*), and another 26 percent between different districts of the same province (ostan).[14]

MENA's internal migration patterns deserve more research. At this stage, one can only hypothesize as to why the redistribution of population from lagging to leading provinces is slow.

The role of social networks may be critical. In the absence of transparent market information for jobs and housing, the opportunity to migrate toward economic opportunity may depend upon having friends and family at one's destination. From the employer's point of view, it is important to hire workers one can trust, especially if labor laws and slow legal procedures make it difficult to fire staff. (In India, World Bank enterprise surveys reveal that employers believe it harder to find an employee they can trust than an employee with the right skills [Amin 2009].) This finding would mean that patterns of internal migration are dictated by social connections across space; the poorest may have the greatest desire to migrate, but the best connected have the greatest opportunity.

The primacy of social networks in determining internal migration flows is illustrated by studies of Egypt (box 3.3). Setting aside the employees who found work through public channels (that is, essentially public sector jobs), 55 percent of employed workers said they found their jobs through friends

Caffeine-Based Networking among Cairo Construction Craftsmen

"A craftsman has to be recognized by his peers as an insider to be able to get work. This is typi-cally done through socializing at the coffeehouse. After long discussions with craftsmen and sub-contractors, I discovered that besides having their own jargon, craftsmen also had secret signs that they would not reveal to me as an outsider. There were clear indicators that there was an insid-ers' culture [into] which one had to be initiated in order to belong.

"A coffeehouse is frequented by a stable group of craftsmen who usually live nearby and who rely largely on relationships they forge in the coffeehouse to get work. Most craftsmen agree that there is no point extending their job search beyond the local coffeehouse."

Source: Assaad 1993, 935.

and relatives (Wahba and Zenou 2005). Moreover, *where* one lives is critical in determining one's chances of using a network. People already residing in cities, where social networks are densest, are on the inside track; 60 percent of Cairenes used friends and relatives to find a job, compared with 40 percent of residents of rural Upper Egypt, and increasing popula-tion density by 10 percent increases the probability of using social networks by 2.2 percent. Some regions of origin are more propitious for job seekers than others. For construction labor, employers rely on ties of kinship and place of origin to determine who gets hired and who remains unemployed (Assaad 1993). In fact, one of the reasons that it is difficult to use national household survey data to analyze migration patterns is that a small propor-tion of villages provides a high proportion of migrants, so cluster samples estimate migration rates with huge margins of error.

Map 3.4 shows how the networking effect plays out in the Republic of Yemen. Areas sending migrants can be identified from receipts of remit-tance income, which are clustered around three poles, one in the arid center of the country and two in the southwest. None of these three areas is exceptional in terms of household incomes or poverty. What appears to be happening is that migrant networks are centered on certain send-ing localities, irrespective of their levels of income.

Are gender relations in MENA a brake on interprovincial migration? It is known that there are social constraints upon female mobility (Assaad 2005) and labor market participation (Khawaja and others 2009). Gender inequality plays a major role in shaping the consequences of migration and spatial disparities (Chant 1992).

However, a study of gender and spatial disparities in MENA commis-sioned for this report (Esber 2008) did not find clear evidence that

MAP 3.4

Remittance Income Clusters in the Republic of Yemen

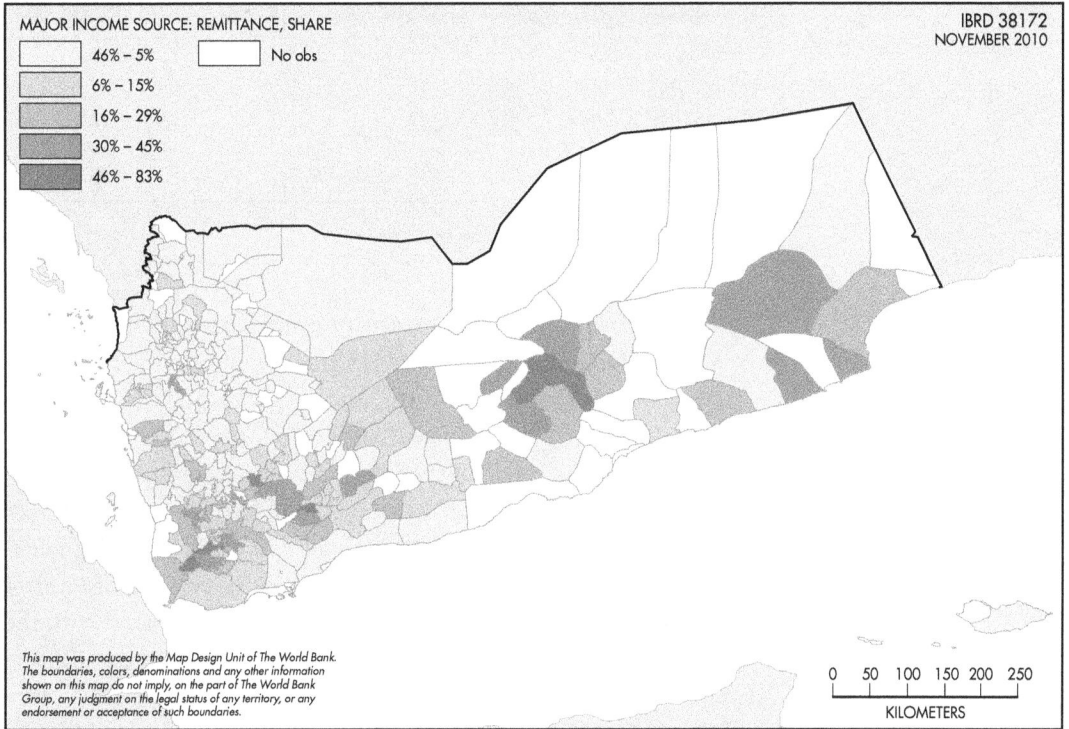

MAJOR INCOME SOURCE: REMITTANCE, SHARE

- 46% – 5%
- 6% – 15%
- 16% – 29%
- 30% – 45%
- 46% – 83%
- No obs

IBRD 38172
NOVEMBER 2010

This map was produced by the Map Design Unit of The World Bank.
The boundaries, colors, denominations and any other information
shown on this map do not imply, on the part of The World Bank
Group, any judgment on the legal status of any territory, or any
endorsement or acceptance of such boundaries.

0   50   100   150   200   250

KILOMETERS

Source: World Bank 2009c.

women's social status was limiting migration. The women interviewed
tended to view internal migration as an attractive strategy to improve
their livelihoods. An Egyptian woman spoke for many when she said, *"It
makes no difference to me whether we stay here or anywhere; the most important
thing to me is to find a job with a good income for my husband so that we, as a
family, live a decent life."* In Qena, Egypt, there was no significant difference between men and women in their average estimate of the minimum
required increase in household income to justify the decision to migrate
to Cairo: LE 1,155 versus LE 1,167 per month. In Tunisia, women interviewed were nearly as supportive as men of their sons migrating in search
of a better life: 81 percent of women and 91 percent of men surveyed said
that migration was beneficial for the young. An oft-repeated phrase was
"Your country is where you earn your bread." Women even looked more
favorably than men, by a rate of 100 percent to 39 percent, upon their
daughters' migrating: 81 percent of women said that they would actively
encourage their daughters to migrate.

TABLE 3.13

Lebanon's Population Distribution Becomes Less Agglomerated

Share of national population	1970 (%)	1996 (%)	2004 (%)
Central Beirut	22	10	10
Greater Beirut	44	32	35
Central Lebanon (Greater Beirut plus Mount Lebanon)	62	48	50
All Lebanon	100	100	100

Source: Nahas 2009.

In Lebanon, a disproportionate rate of external emigration may have been a factor in limiting the redistribution of population toward leading provinces. The interprovincial distribution of the population deagglomerated during the civil war (Nahas 2009), with Greater Beirut's share of the country's population falling and then stabilizing during the postwar period (table 3.13). This change was despite the fact that migration from the periphery to Beirut and its environs had boosted the center's populations. In 2004, only 61 percent of the Lebanese population of Greater Beirut and Mount Lebanon had been born there, compared with the 93 percent of the peripheral areas' population (the north, the south, and Bekaa) that was native to those regions.

The overall conclusion, therefore, is that the redistribution of population in MENA economies is urbanizing but not metropolitanizing. The process of agglomeration is taking place more within subnational regions than among them. There are important implications for MENA's spatial development strategies. First, one cannot overemphasize the importance of confronting preconceptions with robust subnational data. Even though political concerns may focus on the specter of an uncontrolled human tide flooding the prime cities, this is not the reality of internal migration in MENA, or at least not the whole reality. Second, provincial cities are critical poles for lagging areas' demographic transformation, and should, therefore, be central to spatial development strategies.

Is the Lagging Area a Fringe, Belt, or Pocket?

Lagging areas come in many varieties. The governorate of Aleppo in Syria is a second lagging area. Its mean per capita household expenditure is 56 percent of that of the capital. It is home to a great conurbation of 4.4 million people—possibly the oldest continuously inhabited city in the world—and a number of major employers, including the headquarters of the national railways. It is surrounded by fertile farmland.

The northeastern governorate of Al-Mafraq in Jordan is a a second lagging area. Its mean per capita household expenditure is 51 percent of that of the capital, but it could hardly be more different from Aleppo. With a population density of only nine people per km^2 and a yearly average of 150 millimeters of rainfall, it represents MENA's vast swathes of sparsely populated dryland. Yet its provincial capital is only 50 kilometers from the national capital—a 45-minute drive—and sits on the intersection of two four-lane highways, a crossroads between three capital cities: Amman, Baghdad, and Damascus.

A third lagging area is the wilaya of Djelfa in Algeria, where the high plateau meets the Sahara. More than half of Djelfa's population older than six years of age is reported as being without education. The private car ownership rate is only a tenth of that in Algiers. It lies on the Trans-Saharan Highway. Unlike Mafraq, though, it is far from the nearest big city; Algiers is 300 kilometers across the mountains.

Aleppo, Al-Mafraq, and Djelfa all have lagging development indicators in common, but their geographical characteristics set them apart from each other. Aleppo has economic and demographic density and diverse resources; Al-Mafraq and Djelfa do not. Al-Mafraq is close enough to a major agglomeration to benefit from spatial spillovers. Aleppo and Djelfa are not.

If one is apply the correct mix of policies as suggested in figure 2.6 and table 2.3, it is, therefore, necessary to diagnose which kind of lagging area we are dealing with. Aleppo, Al-Mafraq, and Djelfa provide good specimens of three types: the fringe, the belt, and the pocket.

- Djelfa looks like a "fringe" area. It is sparsely populated, it is distant from economic density, and its economic potential is constrained by the lack of agglomeration or a resource base for growth. If this diagnosis is correct, then Djelfa is a prime candidate for Policy Package 1 as outlined in table 2.3: a level playing field for development in terms of access to health, education, social protection, and the business environment, so that its citizens can make the most of a very difficult geographic context.

- Al-Mafraq appears as a "belt" area. It could benefit from the level playing field for development, but it is also close enough to benefit from good connectivity with the capital nearby, Policy Package 2 in table 2.3.

- Aleppo seems to be a "pocket" of unrealized economic potential. It already has population density and economic agglomeration, and just the brief description above should indicate its potential as a location for tourism and agriculture-related growth. Aleppo may, therefore, be a candidate for Policy Package 3 in table 2.3, facilitating private sector interest in investment in lagging areas.

MAP 3.5

A Policy-Oriented Spatial Typology of the Middle East and North Africa Region

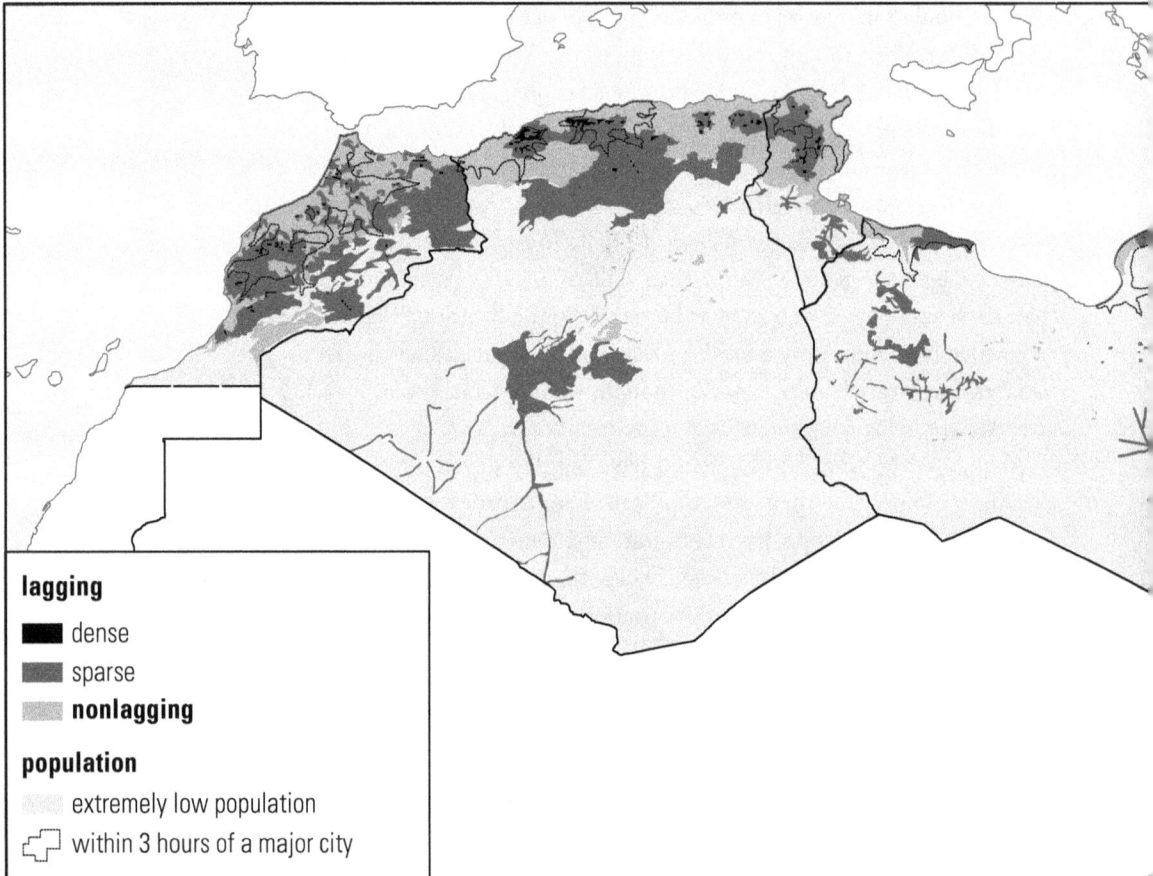

lagging

■ dense

■ sparse

▨ **nonlagging**

population

▨ extremely low population

⊏⊐ within 3 hours of a major city

Sources: Elevation, SRTM30 (2000); land cover, GLC2000 (2000); population, Landscan (2005); rail, VMAP0 (1997); rivers, CIA World Data Bank II (1980s); roads, Euro-med (2000) and VMAP0 (1997); slope, in degrees, SRTM30 (2000); urban areas, GPW3-GRUMP (2000); water bodies, Global Lakes and Wetlands Database layer 1 (2004).

Note: Lagging areas represent 40 percent of the administrative units by country with the lowest consumption, or 40 percent of the administrative units by country that have the highest rates of poverty, and the nonlagging designation comprises the remaining of administrative units. Using Nelson methodology (2008) to calculate a travel-time model, "near" is defined as a travel time of less than or equal to four hours from a city of 500,000; likewise, distant is any travel time greater than four hours. Based on population density data from Landscan (ORNL 2005), "dense" is defined as greater than 50 people per square kilometer, and "sparse" is the remainder. Areas of population density less than 1 are displayed in grey.

It is, of course, beyond the scope of this report to recommend a development strategy for any given lagging area. That would require location-specific studies; however, it has been possible, by means of Geographic Information System (GIS) technology, to summarize the characteristics of MENA's leading and lagging areas.

Map 3.5 shows our policy-oriented typology of the MENA region. Locations are classified according to three dimensions:

- *Dense versus sparse population.* The criterion for a dense area in map 3.5 is that it should have at least 50 inhabitants per km². To put this in

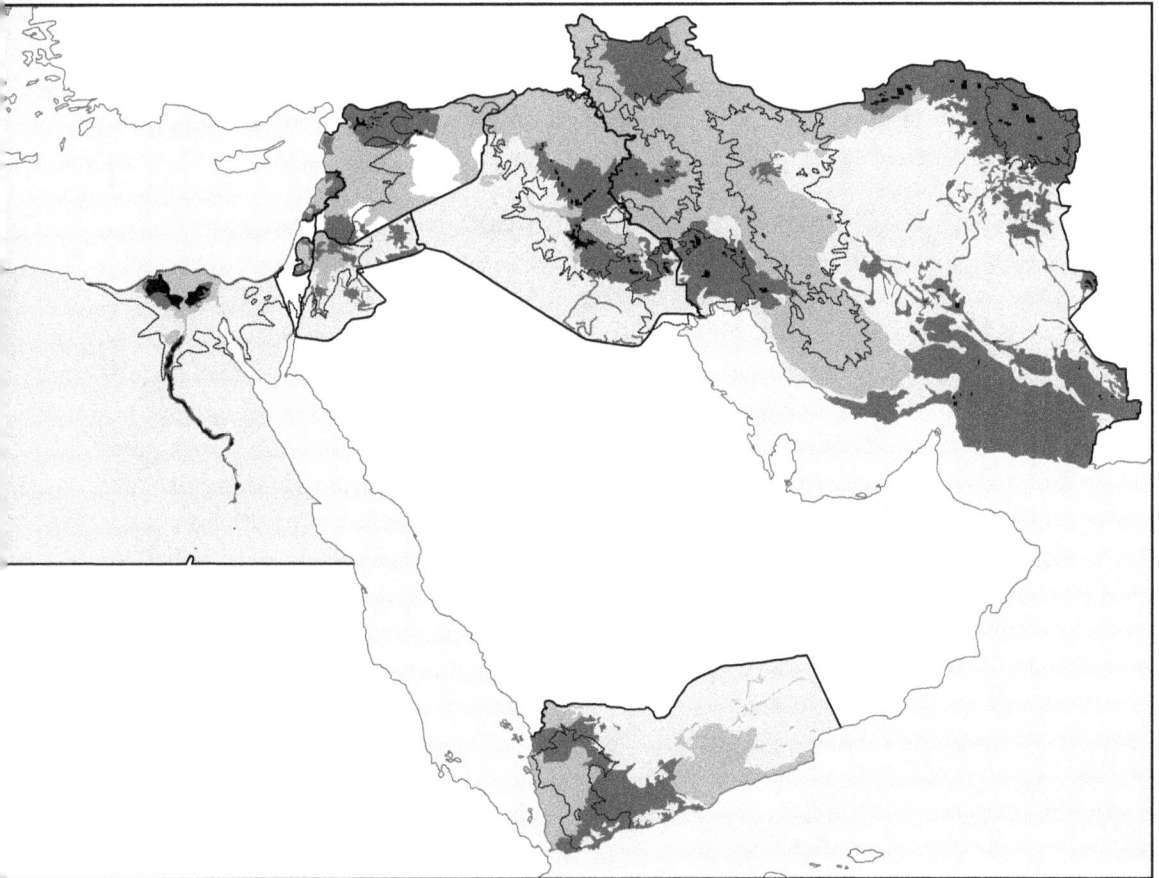

perspective, this is approximately the average population density of
Ireland, Mexico, and Lithuania, or one person for every two hectares
of land. It is notable that the areas of high population density in
MENA appear as small islands in a wide sea of sparsely inhabited
areas. These high-density areas cluster in six strings: along the
Maghreb coastline, in the Levantine hinterland, in the valleys of the
Nile and Euphrates, among the western highlands of the Republic of
Yemen, and along the central north-south axis of the Islamic Republic
of Iran. Each of these strings is cut off from the others by arid desert
or semi-desert areas.

- *Near versus distant.* The criterion for a "near" area is that it should be
  no more than three hours' travel by road from a city of at least half a
  million people. These areas benefiting from proximity to agglomeration of course extend radially from areas of high density.

- *Lagging versus nonlagging.* For the purposes of map 3.5, lagging areas were defined as the least developed 40 percent of administrative divisions. Mean per capita household consumption was used as a default indicator of development. If consumption data were not available, poverty data were used. Neither consumption nor poverty data were available for Algeria, so a composite index of development, which was based on the ratios of people without education, business registration, and car ownership, to wilaya population, was applied.

The mapping emphasizes MENA's fragmented geography. As much as 86 percent of the region's territory is more than three hours' travel from a city of half a million people. As little as 3 percent of MENA's surface area has a population density greater than 50 persons per km^2.

But the mapping exercise also reveals how MENA's human population is clustered into islands of density (table 3.14). Ninety-two percent of the population is squeezed into that 3 percent of the surface area with population density greater than 50 persons per km^2. Eighty-four percent of the population lives in areas with population density greater than 200 persons per km^2 (the average population density of Italy or Luxembourg), and 81 percent lives in areas with a density greater than 400 persons per km^2 (the average population density of the Netherlands). And 72 percent of MENA's population lives in the 14 percent of MENA's land area that is within three hours of a city of at least half a million people.

TABLE 3.14

Indicators of Population Concentration

Country	Percentage of population living in areas of		
	<50 persons per km^2 (%)	<100 persons per km^2 (%)	<200 persons per km^2 (%)
Algeria	12	17	22
Egypt, Arab Rep.	1	2	3
Iran, Islamic Rep.	11	14	18
Iraq	9	13	15
Jordan	5	8	11
Lebanon	4	6	10
Libya	8	10	11
Morocco	13	19	25
Syrian Arab Republic	11	15	20
Tunisia	15	22	28
West Bank and Gaza	2	5	9
Yemen, Rep.	12	19	28
Total	**8**	**12**	**16**

Source: See Appendix.

Lagging areas are, of course, more likely to have low population densities and to be far from cities. A resident of a lagging area in MENA is 79 percent more likely to live more than three hours from a major city than a resident of a nonlagging area. And a resident of a lagging area is 56 percent more likely to reside in an area of population density of less than 50 persons per km^2 than someone from a nonlagging area. In fact, the average population density of a lagging administrative division in MENA is less than half that of a nonlagging administrative region, 22 persons per km^2 compared with 55.

However—and this is the single most critical message from the mapping exercise—a significant proportion of the lagging area population lives in the small fraction of the total land area that is densely inhabited and close to agglomeration. Sixty-one percent of the lagging area population lives within three hours of a city with half a million people or more, and 89 percent of the lagging area population lives in places where the population density is 50 persons per km^2 or more, 85 percent in areas of 100 persons per km^2 or more, 81 percent in areas of 200 persons per km^2 or more, and 77 percent in areas of 400 persons per km^2 or more, which is the average population density of the Netherlands. *In other words, most lagging areas may be sparsely inhabited, but most lagging area populations are reasonably dense.*

The proximity of populations to economic density seems to be a distinctive characteristic of MENA when compared with other parts of the world. GIS analysis (Hon, Rojchaichanintorn, and Schmidt 2009) has estimated the average travel time for various countries from home to a city of *100,000* or more, which is obviously a less demanding criterion than the half-million used for MENA earlier. The results in table 3.15 suggest that MENA, with 72 percent of its population less than 3 hours from a city of half a million, enjoys a proximity-to-density advantage over major developing countries such as Brazil, Chile, Pakistan, and

TABLE 3.15

Proximity Comparators

Country	Average travel time to a city of 0.1 million or more (hours)
Brazil	3.0
Chile	2.9
China	2.1
India	2.2
Mexico	1.8
Pakistan	2.9
Thailand	3.4

Source: Hon, Rojchaichanintorn, and Schmidt 2009.

Thailand. It is not surprising that this finding should be so, given MENA's relatively high agglomeration indexes.

The character of MENA's lagging areas varies from country to country (table 3.16 and figure 3.21). Basically, one can split MENA's economies into three groups according to the human geography of their lagging areas:

- *The Maghreb+ group* (Tunisia, Morocco, Algeria, and Libya, plus the Republic of Yemen and the Islamic Republic of Iran). These countries' lagging areas have a relatively high share of their lagging area populations in low-density areas and areas that are distant from major cities. Note, however, the use of the word "relatively"; as noted earlier MENA's lagging area populations tend to be denser and closer to agglomeration than those of other parts of the world.

- *The Mashreq group* (Syria, Iraq, Jordan, Lebanon, and the West Bank and Gaza). Their lagging area populations are even more likely to live in densely populated areas or near to major cities.

- *Egypt.* Egypt's lagging area populations are not in sparsely populated areas, but a high proportion of them (basically Upper Egyptians) live far from major cities.

TABLE 3.16

Geographic Character of Lagging-Area Populations in MENA

% of total population	% of country's lagging area population			
	>3 hrs from city of >0.5 million		<3 hrs from city of >0.5 million	
	<50 people per km^2 (%)	>50 people per km^2 (%)	<50 people per km^2 (%)	>50 people per km^2 (%)
Algeria	15	48	4	33
Egypt, Arab Rep.[a]	0	43	0	56
Iraq	2	9	9	80
Iran, Islamic Rep.	8	36	6	50
Jordan	4	1	4	91
Lebanon	1	3	5	91
Libya	4	37	5	54
Morocco	19	34	11	36
Syrian Arab Republic	4	8	8	80
Tunisia	16	37	13	34
West Bank and Gaza	0	5	2	93
Yemen, Rep.	11	24	7	57
MENA12[b]	**6**	**33**	**5**	**56**

Source: See Appendix.

Note: a. Leading and lagging categorization data unavailable for 1 percent of the Arab Republic of Egypt's population. b. Djibouti is not included in MENA12.

FIGURE 3.21

The Mashreq's Lagging Area Populations Are Denser and Closer to Density than the Maghreb's

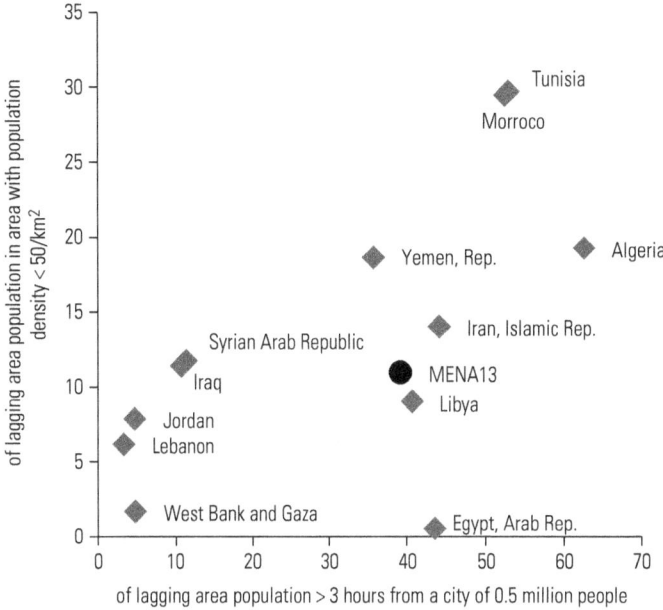

Source: Study Team.

What does this mean for lagging area policies? Again, it must be emphasized that any lagging area deserves its own made-to-measure diagnosis. But the general implication is that the Mashreq's lagging area populations are more likely to have the necessary proximity to agglomeration to benefit from spillover connectivity (Policy Package 2). These are the "belt" areas, of which Al-Mafraq was an example. They and Egypt's lagging areas are also more likely—other things being equal—to get an economic competitiveness boost from their agglomeration of population, giving regional economic development approaches (Policy Package 3) a better chance of success. These are the "pockets" of density, of which Aleppo was a specimen. In the Maghreb, however, a lagging area's population is relatively more likely to be living in a "fringe" area of low density and high distance from agglomeration, like the good citizens of Djelfa. In such areas, as in all lagging areas, it is critical to remove any spatial biases in access to services or the business environment (Policy Package 1).

The purpose of the discussion earlier was to develop a general framework for analysis. Geographic generalizations, however, are hazardous when applied to specific places. The only way to identify the appropriate policy approach for a given lagging area is to recognize its specificities, by zooming in to the appropriate level of detail, which is the subject of the following section.

To Understand a Lagging Area, Zoom In and Zoom Out

Analyzing a lagging area at different levels of spatial disaggregation makes for better policies. Each time the analysis zooms in by one level, new policy-relevant information appears.

Take the lagging area of Upper Egypt, for example. The analytical focus shifts depending on whether one is looking at Upper Egypt at a regional, governorate, district, or village level. The richest insights and policy options come from thinking at different spatial scales (box 3.4).

As a region within a country. A standard breakdown of spatial disparities in Egypt is between broad regions: metropolitan Egypt, Lower Egypt, Upper Egypt, and frontier governorates. At this level of aggregation, Upper Egypt as a whole appears as the lagging area (table 3.17). The analysis, therefore, focuses on the broad differences between Upper Egypt and Lower Egypt: their distances from the Cairo metropolis, household composition, and land availability. When the World Bank analyzed Upper Egypt at the regional level (2006b), the policy conclusions therefore focused on trunk connectivity and agricultural productivity and marketing. But the regional-level analysis is overshadowed by the observation that 80 percent of the differences in per capita consumption between Upper Egypt and Lower Egypt is due to demography: the higher ratio of children and old people to people of working age in

---

BOX 3.4

The Arab Republic of Egypt's Human Development Reports: A Model for MENA?

The Arab Republic of Egypt's annual Human Development Reports, a joint product of the Egyptian government and the United Nations Development Programme (UNDP), have helped the country to focus on governorate- and district-level approaches. Every year, this publication puts subnational indicators of economic, human, and social development into the public domain. At the same time, they have documented the continuing challenge of mobilizing governorate- and district-level administrations to deliver more responsive public services (see, for example, UNDP 2004). The reports have been posted online for every year since 1997, giving an overview of spatial development that is unmatched in MENA. As a public data resource on subnational development trends, Egypt's National Human Development Reports could serve as a model.

TABLE 3.17

Contrasting Broad Regions in the Arab Republic of Egypt

Indicator	Lower Egypt	Upper Egypt
UN Human Development Index (2008)	0.719	0.693
GRDP per capita (2005–06; LE)	6,911	5,867
Life expectancy at birth (2006)	71.1	69.8
Women as % of labor force (2005)	27	20
Maternal mortality per 100,000 live births (2005)	47	55
Percentage of unfit school buildings (2003–04)	20	26

Source: UNDP Egypt National Human Development Report 2008.

Note: GRDP = gross regional domestic product; LE = Egyptian pounds.

Upper Egypt (World Bank 2009b). At the regional level, therefore, the emphasis was on realizing Upper Egypt's agricultural potential in the face of an intractable demographic handicap.

As a governorate of Upper Egypt. But when one zooms in to the governorate (province) level, new issues come into sharper focus. In 1998, the Egyptian government launched the Sohag Rural Development Project. Governorate-level analysis had shown that Sohag was the poorest governorate in Upper Egypt. In fact, Sohag was the core of a "Middle Upper Egypt" lagging subregion of the lagging region of Upper Egypt. And when the analysis concentrated on Sohag's development challenges, a new set of issues came to the forefront: the wide disparities among different districts' access to public services such as sanitation and health care; and the difficulties experienced by the governorate and district authorities in allocating public investment budgets to priority projects in the priority district, with all investment decisions being taken in Cairo by sectoral ministries and the Ministry of Economic Development. Based on the governorate-level perspective, therefore, the government's policy response was a program that emphasized the bottom-up, participatory planning of social infrastructure investments, with financial allocations going to the poorest districts.

As communities of Upper Egypt. Measuring spatial disparities at subprovincial level used to be problematic. The options available were to use national household survey data, which are usually unreliable at subprovincial level because of the cluster sampling approach, or made-to-measure village surveys, which are either very localized or very expensive.

The new technique of poverty mapping (Demombynes and others 2002), however, has given policy makers this option. Poverty mapping uses the household survey to identify poor households. It then looks up the census responses for these same households and thus finds out which census responses are associated with poverty. Finally, it looks in the census for other households that gave similar census responses. In this way, it can plot a map of where the poor people are, right down to village level. In MENA, Egypt and Morocco have completed poverty-mapping exercises.[15]

A poverty map instantly deepens one's understanding of spatial disparities. It brings into sharp focus the wide gap in development between communities separated by only a few kilometers. It helps identify the factors that determine whether a village develops. Figure 3.20, above, illustrates the importance of village- or community-level information. It shows how poverty reduction over time was a village-level process in Egypt, with the residents of entire villages breaking out as a group to join the "club" of more advanced villages, while the residents of other villages got left behind as a group. The conclusion is clear: if households in a village succeed together or fail together, it is critical for policy makers to know the correlates of village-level success.

As the Morocco poverty-mapping exercise illustrated, the closer one zooms, the larger the proportion of differences in welfare that can be linked to location. Location represented only 18 percent of inequality when the breakdown was at the regional level, but it accounted for 40 percent of inequality at the commune level (Lanjouw 2004). The finer the disaggregation, therefore, the easier it is to target the poor geographically, with public investments or social protection spending. Morocco's poverty-mapping exercise was, therefore, critical to the design of the National Human Development Initiative (INDH), which is budgeting US$0.26 billion per annum on spatially targeted public social and economic infrastructure investments.

Lebanon's Economic and Social Fund for Development (ESFD) managed to improvise a useful fine-resolution poverty map in 2004 to underpin its social strategy, despite the lack of census data or household consumption data (Nahas 2009). The spatial divisions used were the cadastral limits, the smallest division available to estimate population on the basis of the buildings census. To estimate living standards, the map used the distribution of retail stores, restaurants and hotels, services, construction activity, electricity consumption, and the number of "minutes talked" per head on each telephone exchange. The resulting map was detailed enough to reflect poverty pockets within suburbs (Hay Al Sillum, Biddawi, and Palestinian camps) and the persistent influence of the wartime frontlines in seven distinct areas.

A key conclusion of the ESFD analysis was that the geographically small pockets of dense poverty in the suburbs of the large towns, which would have been overlooked by a less detailed map, contained more poor

TABLE 3.18

Policy Implications of Multi-Level Spatial Analysis in Rural Upper Egypt

Level of analysis	Focus of analysis	Focus of findings	Emphasis of policy implications
Leading versus Lagging region	Decomposing the interregion gap in per capita productivity and consumption	Upper Egypt's high dependency ratio, dependence on low-value agriculture, and remoteness from Cairo's demand for farm products	Linking rural Upper Egypt farmers to urban markets through supply chain development, trunk road improvements, and high-value cropping
Province and district	Improving service delivery by governorate and district administrations	Responsiveness of investment decisions at governorate and district level	Deconcentration and decentralization of public investment planning
Village and community	Poverty mapping and small-scale surveys	Disparities in the welfare of neighboring locations Residing in a successful village, which is an important part of escaping from poverty	Village-level targeting of public investment projects Targeting dense poverty pockets in richer urban areas

Source: Study Team.

households than the extensive areas of rural deprivation. In other words, high-resolution analysis helps to remind policy makers that rich areas can contain many poor people.

Table 3.18 summarizes the case for a multilevel analysis, taking the example of Egypt and zooming through the national, provincial and sub-provincial, scales. Although all MENA economies have major budgetary commitments to lagging areas, much analysis is required at every level to optimize their strategies.

We can close this exploration of lagging area diagnostics in MENA with the conclusion that better information would make for better policies. We have seen that every lagging area is different and that spatial variation is just as evident at the micro level as at the macro level. Indeed, the study of spatial disparities is reminiscent of fractal geometry, where each pattern contains an infinite series of smaller patterns nested within it. And yet the foundation of subnational data and analysis in MENA is currently simply too weak to support policy makers' demands for an effective and evidence-based response.

This chapter has attempted to show what kinds of analysis can inform spatial development policy. It has shown how subnational data can give critical insights to policy makers, such as the importance of demography, education, dense populations, suspended rural transition, and within-province migration. The question is, therefore, whether MENA can afford to continue spending billions of dollars on spatial development programs without adequate subnational data.

Endnotes

1. FAOSTAT, http://faostat.fao.org, accessed August 14, 2009. The data show increases in the arable land-labor ratio for Egypt, Iraq, Lebanon, and Libya. The figures showing a dramatic increase in arable land for Egypt from 1990 to 1995 are surprising.

2. *Source:* Palmer Drought Severity Index map from (IPCC 2007).

3. Personal communication: Director of national statistical service.

4. Another reason is that comparing rural-urban disparities with overall inequality downplays the well-being of minorities: if rural people are a small share of the overall population, they will never account for a large share of over-all inequality, no matter how poor they are.

5. Named after the surnames of its inventors: Elbers, Lanjouw, Mistiaen, and Özler.

6. The rise and fall of the household head's earning capacity with increasing age is captured by the coefficient on the square of the household head's age.

7. The household survey data did not include a rural-urban field, or data for two southern mohafazat (Nabatieh and S. Lebanon).

8. Excluding data from Guelmime-Es Semara.

9. Also with data from Guelmime-Es Semara and the areas of Oued Ed-Dahab Lagouira and Laayoun-Boujdour-Sakia El-Hamra.

10. The total fertility rate (TFR) is a synthetic indicator denoting births per woman per lifetime, and is based on the age profile of women in a given year and the number of births per woman in each age group in that year.

11. Weighting the coefficient of variation by population stops provinces with small populations from having a disproportionate impact on the statistic.

12. The UNDP GRDP estimates published in the national Human Development Reports are based upon incomes reported in the national household income and expenditure surveys (HIECS). The reliability of income survey responses is usually low.

13. "As more children were enrolled in school, the quality and efficiency of education came to the forefront. In response, MENA economies experimented with a variety of mechanisms, including decentralization, engaging the private sector in the provision of education, and the adoption of quality assurance programs (World Bank 2008d, 4)."

14. Statistical Bureau of the Islamic Republic of Iran, census 1375.

15. Algeria's *Carte de la Pauvreté* (UNDP 2006) follows a different approach, using local government revenues as an indicator of the level of development of different administrative divisions.

References

Abbasi-Shavazi, M. J., and P. McDonald. 2005. "National and Provincial-Level Fertility Trends in Iran, 1972–2000." Working Paper in Demography No. 94. Australian National University, 10.

Akin, M. S. 2005. "Education and Fertility: A Panel Data Analysis for Middle Eastern Countries." *Journal of Developing Areas* 39 (1): 55–69.

Ameen, J. 2008. "Kurdistan's Genocide: A New Insight." *Xebat*, April 16.

Amin, M. 2009. *How Tough Is It to Find an Employee You Can Trust?* October 2, http://psdblog.worldbank.org/psdblog/2009/10/labor -issues-in-india-beyond-labor-laws.html#more (private sector development blog, accessed October 5, 2009).

Assaad, R. 1993. "Formal and Informal Institutions in the Labor Market, with Applications to the Construction Sector in Egypt." *World Development* 21 (6): 925–39.

Assadzadeh, A., and S. Paul. 2004. "Poverty, Growth, and Redistribution: A Study of Iran." *Review of Development Economics* 8 (4): 640–53.

Ayadi, M., and M. Amara. 2009. *Spatial Patterns and Geographic Determinants of Poverty in Tunisia.* Cairo: Economic Research Forum.

Behdad, S. 1989. "Winners and Losers of the Iranian Revolution: A Study in Income Distribution." *International Journal of Middle East Studies*, 327–58.

Boulila, G., C. Gabsi, and M. Trabelsi. 2009. *Regional Pro-Poor Growth and Convergence in Tunisia.* Cairo: Economic Research Forum.

Bourguignon, F. 1979. "Decomposable Income Inequality Measures." *Econometrica* 47 (4): 901–20.

Centre d'Études et de Recherches Démographiques. 1989. *Education et Changements Démographiques au Maroc.* Rabat: Royaume du Maroc, Ministère du Plan, Direction de la Statistique.

Chant, S. 1992. *Gender and Migration in Developing Countries.* London: Belhaven.

Chelala, C. 1996. "Egypt Faces High Population Growth." *The Lancet* (December 14): 1651.

Cline, W. 2007. *Global Warming and Agriculture: Impact Estimates by Country.* Washington, DC: Center for Global Development; Peterson Institute for International Economics.

De Brauw, A., and J. Giles. 2006. *Migrant Opportunity and the Educational Opportunity of Youth in Rural China.* IZA Discussion Paper 2326. Bonn: Institute for the Study of Labor.

Demombynes, G., C. Elbers, J. Lanjouw, P. Lanjouw, J. Mistaien, and B. Ozler. 2002. *Producing an Improved Geographic Profile of Poverty.* United Nations University, WIDER.

Elbers, C. L. 2007. "Re-interpreting Sub-Group Inequality Decompositions." Policy Research Working Paper WPS 3687. World Bank, Washington, DC.

Esber, R. 2008. "Gender and Spatial Disparities in the Middle East and North Africa. A Study of Saudi Arabia, Egypt, and Tunisia." Unpublished.

FAO (Food and Agriculture Organization). 2009. *Food Security and Agricultural Mitigation in Developing Countries: Options for capturing synergies.* Rome: FAO.

Hawkins, S., L. Griffiths, T. Cole, C. Dezateux, and C. Law. 2007. "Regional Differences in Overweight: An Effect of People or Place?" *Archives of Disease in Childhood* 93 (i): 407–13.

Henderson, J. V. 1986. "Urbanization in a Developing Country: City Size and Population Composition." *Journal of Development Economics* 22 (2): 269–93.

Henderson, V. 2000. "The Effect of Urban Concentration on Economic Growth." Working Paper 7503. National Bureau of Economic Research, Cambridge, MA.

Henderson, J. V., Z. Shalizi, and A. Venables. 2001. "Geography and Development." *Journal of Economic Geography* 1 (1): 81–105.

Hon, V., J. Rojchaichanintorn, and E. Schmidt. 2009. "A Framework for Bank Engagement in Lagging Areas." Unpublished. World Bank, Washington, DC.

INS (Institut National de la Statistique). 1980, 1990, 2000. *Enquête Nationale sur le Budget. La Consommation et le Niveau de Vie des Ménages.* Tunis: INS.

IPCC (International Panel on Climate Change). 2007. *Fourth Assessment Report.* Geneva: IPCC.

Iqbal, F. 2006. *Sustaining Gains in Poverty Reduction and Human Development in the Middle East and North Africa.* Washington, DC: World Bank.

IRIN News. 2009. "Syria: Drought Driving Farmers to the Cities." September 2. http://www.irinnews.org/report.aspx?ReportID=85963.

Khawaja, M. 2002. *Internal Migration in Syria: Findings from a National Survey.* Oslo: Fafo.

Khawaja, M., R. Jurdi, S. Assaf, and J. Yeretzian. 2009. *Unmet Need for the Utilization of Women's Labor: Findings from Three Impoverished*

Communities in Outer Beirut, Lebanon. Cairo: Economic Research Forum.

Lanjouw, P. 2004. "The Geography of Poverty in Morocco: Micro-Level Estimates of Poverty and Inequality from Combined Census and Household Survey Data." World Bank. http://siteresources.worldbank .org/INTMOROCCOINFRENCH/Resources/Lanjouw.Geography PovertyMorocco.pdf.

Lowe, R. 2006. *The Syrian Kurds: A People Discovered.* London: Chatham House.

McCormick, B., and J. Wahba. 2005. "Why Do the Young and Educated in LDCs Concentrate in Large Cities? Evidence from Migration Data." *Economica* 72 (285): 39–67.

Mehryar, A. 2004. "Primary Health Care and the Rural Poor in the Islamic Republic of Iran." Paper presented at Scaling Up Poverty Reduction: A Global Learning Process and Conference, Shanghai, May 25–27.

Mojtahed, A., and H. S. Esfahani. 1989. "Agricultural Policy and Performance in Iran: The Post-Revolutionary Experience." *World Development* 17 (6): 839–60.

Nahas, C. 2009. "Spatial Inequalities in Lebanon: Development Trends and Public Policy." Unpublished background paper for this report.

Nelson, A. 2008. *Travel Time to Major Cities: A Global Map of Accessibility.* Ispra, Italy: Global Environment Monitoring Unit, Joint Research Centre of the European Commission. http://gem.jrc.ec.europa.eu/.

Nelson, G. C., M. W. Rosegrant, J. Koo, R. Robertson, T. Sulser, T. Zhu, et al. 2009. *Climate Change: Impact on Agriculture and Costs of Adaptation.* Washington, DC: International Food Policy Research Institute.

Openshaw, S. 1984. *The Modifiable Areal Unit Problem.* Norwich: Geo Books.

ORNL (Oak Ridge National Laboratory). 2005. *Landscan Global Population Database.* http://www.ornl.gov/landscan.

Oweis, K. Y. 2009. "Water Crisis Uproots Syrian Farmers." *Jordan Times,* July 31.

Ravallion, M., S. Chen, and P. Sangraula. 2007. "New Evidence on the Urbanization of Global Poverty." Policy Research Working Paper 4199. April. World Bank, Washington, DC.

Rutstein, S. O., and K. Johnston. 2004. *The DHS Wealth Index.* DHS Comparative Report No. 6. Calverton, MD: ORC Macro.

Shankar, R., and A. Shah. (2003). "Bridging the Economic Divide within Nations: A Scorecard on the Performance of Regional Development Policies in Reducing Regional Income Disparities." *World Development* 31 (8): 1421–41.

Shenker, J. 2009. "We Are Going Underwater. The Sea Will Conquer Our Lands." *The Guardian* (Manchester), August 21.

Shlash, A. 2009. "Iraq High Committee for Strategy Reduction. Draft Strategy Review Presentation." June. Amman.

Shorrocks, A. 2005. "Spatial Decomposition of Inequality." *Journal of Economic Geography* 5 (1): 59–81.

Sommeiller, E. 2008. "Spatial Analysis of Social Welfare in MENA Countries." Unpublished background paper for this report.

Sutton, K. 2001. "Demographic Transition and Regional Population Change in Algeria, 1987–1998." *Arab World Demography* 4 (3): 206–16.

Uchida, H., and A. Nelson. 2008. "Agglomeration Index: Towards a New Measure of Urban Concentration." Background paper. http://siteresources.worldbank.org/INTWDR2009/Resources/4231006-1204741572978/Hiro1.pdf.

UN Habitat. 2006. *State of the World's Cities 2006/7: The Millennium Development Goals and Urban Sustainability.* Nairobi: United Nations Human Settlements Program.

UNDP (United Nations Development Programme). 1999. *Human Development Report of the Islamic Republic of Iran.* Tehran: UNDP.

———. 2004. *Egypt Human Development Report 2004—Choosing Decentralization for Good Governance.* Washington, DC: UNDP.

———. 2006. *Affinement de la Carte de la Pauvreté.* Algiers: UNDP.

———. 2008. *Poverty, Growth and Income Distribution in Lebanon.* Beirut: UNDP.

UNHCR (United Nations High Commissioner for Refugees). 2009. "Refworld: The Leader in Refugee Decision Support." Accessed June 16, 2009, from http://www.unhcr.org/refworld/topic,463af2212,464dbe362,49ce361e28,0.html.

United Nations Department of Economic and Social Affairs. 2007. *World Urbanization Prospects: The 2007 Revision Population Database.* New York: United Nations.

Wahba, J. 2007. "An Overview of Internal and International Migration in Egypt." Working Paper 0703. Cairo: Economic Research Forum.

Wahba, J., and Y. Zenou. 2005. "Density, Social Networks, and Job Search Methods: Theory and Application to Egypt. *Journal of Development Economics* 78: 443–73.

World Bank. 1999. *Democratic and Popular Republic of Algeria: Growth Employment and Poverty Reduction.* Washington, DC: World Bank.

———. 2006a. *Tunisia: Agricultural Policy Review.* Washington, DC: World Bank.

———. 2006b. *Upper Egypt: Challenges and Priorities for Rural Development.* Washington, DC: World Bank.

———. 2007a. *Lebanon: Economic and Social Impact Assessment: From Recovery to Sustainable Growth.* Washington DC: World Bank.

———. 2007b. *Population Issues in the 21st Century. The Role of the World Bank.* Washington, DC: World Bank.

———. 2008a. *World Development Report 2008: Agriculture for Development.* Washington, DC: World Bank.

———. 2008b. *Syrian Agriculture: Towards the Social Market.* Washington, DC: World Bank.

———. 2008c. *The Road not Traveled. Education Reform in the Middle East and North Africa.* Washington, DC: World Bank.

———. 2009a. *World Development Report 2009: Reshaping Economic Geography.* Washington, DC: World Bank.

———. 2009b. *Arab Republic of Egypt. Upper Egypt: Pathways to Shared Growth.* Washington, DC: World Bank.

———. 2009c. *Yemen: Pathways Out of Rural Poverty.* Washington, DC: World Bank.

World Development Indicators Database. http://data.worldbank.org/data-catalog. World Bank, Washington, DC.

CHAPTER 4

Policy Package 1. Level the Playing Field and the Opportunity for Human Development in Lagging Areas

Apply in All Circumstances: The Only Package for "Fringe" Areas

Matching Policy Packages to Lagging Areas (from table 2.3)

Policy packages	World Development Report 2009 terminology	Why?	Where?	Downside risk
Package 1. Level the playing field and the opportunity for human development in lagging areas	"Institutions" ("spatially blind policies")	Spatial disparities in well-being can narrow even while production is agglomerating, so long as policies are appropriate. MENA has a historical legacy of policies' widening disparities.	Applicable to all lagging areas (whether or not Package 2 or 3 applies)	High cost of replicating metropolitan services inappropriately in lagging areas

Source: World Bank 2009a.

As we have seen in the previous chapter, lagging areas have many different qualities. Some lagging areas are close enough to agglomerations to benefit from growth spillovers, but some are not. Some lagging areas are sparsely populated, but many have high population densities. Some even believe in "lagging cultures" (box 4.1).

But all lagging areas have one thing in common: they deserve fair policy treatment—a level playing field for development. As we saw in chapter 2, countries can reduce spatial disparities in living standards without having to spread economic growth across the territory. In fact, reducing spatial disparities in living standards, while letting the market determine the spatial

---

BOX 4.1

Lagging Areas: Is Culture to Blame?

Many people believe that poor places remain poor because of the culture of their inhabitants. Every country has a deep stock of jokes and insults about the backwardness of the citizens of their lagging regions.

We, therefore, wanted to see if we could find any evidence for a correlation between cultural values and geography in MENA. Data from the World Values Survey (WVS) were analyzed to assess whether people's views were correlated with the size of the settlement where they lived. The questions analyzed were those that tested social beliefs that might constrain economic development:

- If jobs are scarce, should men have more of a right to a job than women?

- Is an opportunity to use initiative important in a job?

- Are thrift and saving money important qualities in a child?

- Is education an important trait in a woman?

- Should a person follow his individual beliefs or secular and religious authorities?

The analyses did not reveal any trends. If cultural beliefs are a cause or an effect of spatial backwardness, we could not find any evidence.

---

distribution of economic activity, is a win-win strategy; it brings both the economic benefits of agglomeration and the political benefits of spatial equity.

So what is this "level playing field for development"?

To answer this question, we need to delve into MENA's past. This chapter will show that the centralized state is the legacy of MENA's colonial and postindependence history. We will show how MENA's governance characteristics have been inherited. We will then provide statistical evidence that those with such governance characteristics tend to follow a more spatially concentrated development path.

MENA's policy makers therefore face a dilemma. They have the task of promoting development in peripheral areas. But they are obliged to do so within the framework of administrative and political structures that are intrinsically centralizing. In short, the explicit policies are pushing in one direction, while the implicit structures and systems are pulling back in the opposite direction.

Building a "level playing field for development" therefore means adjusting sector policies so that they are no longer biased in favor of metropolitan or central areas. The latter part of this chapter will thus move away from political theory to the nitty-gritty of a range of government functions: public expenditure management, business environment regulation, education, health, the management of urbanization, and social protection.

How Governance Affects Urbanization—Some Numbers and an Explanation

Political organization has a spatial impact. The lower a country's level of political accountability, the more urbanized and agglomerated it is.

Following the example of Ades and Glaeser (1995), but using a fixed effects panel data model with observations from 1975 to 2004 (tables 4.1, 4.2), we estimated the relationship between governance

TABLE 4.1

Politics Affects the Size of a Country's Largest City

Explaining (log) population of largest city				
logNonUrbanPop	0.41	0.42	0.4	0.41
	(7.81)**	(8.10)**	(7.97)**	(7.97)**
logOtherUrbanPop	0.72	0.74	0.71	0.71
	(25.85)**	(26.13)**	(26.55)**	(26.51)**
logPerCapGDP	−0.2	−0.23	−0.21	
	(8.73)**	(9.97)**	(8.60)**	
Poor: logPerCapGDP				−0.21
				(8.09)**
Rich: logPerCapGDP				−0.21
				(8.48)**
Trade (logOpenc)	−0.01			
	(0.24)			
Trade (logOpenk)		0.06		
		(2.81)**		
Trade (logTradeShare)			−0.01	−0.01
			(0.29)	(0.29)
DictatorDummy	0.06	0.06	0.06	0.06
	(2.95)**	(3.22)**	(2.78)**	(2.78)**
FreeDummy	−0.04	−0.04	−0.04	−0.04
	(1.90)	(1.99)*	(2.02)*	(2.03)*
Ethnic conflict	0.03	0.03	0.04	0.04
	(3.25)**	(3.32)**	(3.60)**	(3.59)**
Constant	3.15	2.79	3.27	3.26
	(5.80)**	(5.03)**	(6.11)**	(6.03)**
Observations	563	563	588	588
Number of countryid	77	77	77	77
R-squared	0.91	0.91	0.92	0.92

Source: Study Team.

Note: Fixed effects for countries and years included, but not reported. Absolute value of t statistics in parentheses. * significant at 5%; ** significant at 1%.

TABLE 4.2

Political Rights Reduce Agglomeration

Ordinary least squares	Agglomeration index
Political right	−16.657
	(2.80)***
Political stability	2.367
	(1.60)
Log (GDP per capita)	32.255
	(4.95)***
[Log (GDP per capita)]	−1.730
	(3.69)***
Log (population size)	16.702
	(7.02)***
Trade openness	−0.061
	(2.64)***
Log (land area)	−4.038
	(5.17)***
Share of paved roads	2.537
	(0.82)
Log (population in agricultural sector)	−10.358
	(4.36)***
MENA	5.561
	(1.22)
Constant	−152.426
	(6.74)***
Observations.	157
R-squared (adjusted)	0.75

Source: GDP per capita, trade openness, land area, population in agricultural sector: World Development Indicators. Political rights: http://www.freedomhouse.org/template. Political stability: Kaufman, Kraay, and Mastruzzi 2009.

Note: ***, ** respectively denote significant coefficients at 1% and 5% level. Figures in parentheses are robust *t*-student.

indicators and the size of a country's main city. The governance indicators were measures of political rights and freedom (Freedom House) and measures of political and social instability (Political Instability Task Force). We see that politics matter. All else being equal, population in the largest city rose when countries became dictatorships and fell when countries become "free" (as defined by Freedom House). There was also a tendency for ethnic conflict to cause rises in the population in the largest city.[1]

Looking beyond the growth of the largest city to urbanization more generally, we conducted a similar analysis using the urban population in a country as the dependent variable. The patterns were similar. Being a "free" country (as defined by Freedom House) is associated with slower urbanization. Ethnic conflict increases urbanization. Interestingly, a dictatorship does not increase urban population—which makes sense if an effect of dictatorship is to attract people from secondary cities to the center of power in the main city.

Finally, the relationship between governance indicators and the World Bank's (2009a) agglomeration index was estimated for a worldwide sample of 182 countries. The governance indicators in question were the index of political rights from Freedom House (2009) and the index of political stability of Kaufman, Kraay, and Mastruzzi (2009). The exercise also took account of a number of other factors known or thought to be related to agglomeration: GDP per capita, population size, land area, trade openness, road quality, and the share of the population employed in agriculture. A dummy variable for MENA economies was also added.

The variables explained 75 percent of the variation in the agglomeration index. The coefficients on GDP represent the strong link between agglomeration and growth. The MENA dummy variable was not statistically significant, suggesting that the other variables in the equation captured all of MENA's special characteristics.

The key finding was the extremely strong negative correlation between political rights and the agglomeration index, significant at the 1 percent level. In other words, more political rights meant less agglomeration. This correlation was significant for all the specifications tested.

This matters for the MENA13, which has a lower average political rights score (0.18) than non-MENA lower-middle-income economies (0.26), other developing countries (0.31), and the rest of the world (0.40). The impact of MENA's low political rights on agglomeration, though not massive, is very clear. If MENA13 economies' political rights indicator increased to that of the average country in the world, this would be accompanied by a 4–percentage point reduction in the agglomeration index.

What is happening here? One can think of political rights as spreading political accountability not only across the population but also across places. Democratic processes and public service accountability give citizens across the territory a voice in policy making. But in the absence of formal mechanisms for sharing political accountability across the territory politicians and bureaucrats are disproportionately influenced by the people who are physically closest to them: their face-to-face contacts and the metropolitan population more generally.

Contemporary drivers of spatial bias go back to MENA's colonial history. The institutions responsible for spatial policies are themselves the product of earlier spatial policies (North 1990; Kuran 2004). Yesterday's historical anti–poor area biases thus constrain the performance of today's explicit pro–poor place policies. In the MENA region, these patterns have their roots in colonial times, as far back as Ottoman rule.[2] Four features of MENA's colonial legacy are important in this context:

- A belief in the state's mission to regulate society centrally, supported by a highly centralized administrative machinery and fiscal system

- A condition of "state autonomy," which manifested itself in a lack of representative institutions articulating local demands

- An outward orientation of economic, trade, and fiscal policies that catered to the metropolis to the detriment of lagging areas

- A concentration of the colonial elite in urban and coastal areas

MENA's colonial legacy is interventionist government. At independence, most modern MENA economies were characterized by ideologies based on a belief in the state's capacity to regulate social and economic relations (Richards and Waterbury 1990; Owen 1992; Luciani 1989; Ayubi 2008; Ozbudun 1997). The statist tradition derived partly from the Ottoman rule. In addition to collecting taxes and waging wars, the Ottoman administration provided welfare services, fixed prices for basic staples, administered public procurement schemes to keep certain prices low, and set up public enterprises to produce strategic commodities such as food staples and gunpowder. These features of Ottoman rule persisted—and in some cases were reinforced—during European colonization. They influenced MENA's state-driven development approaches and were further accentuated by Kemalist ideologies throughout MENA (Brown 1997).

Colonial statehood was based on the development of strong central bureaucracies. During the 1950s and 1960s, MENA experienced a regionwide process of bureaucratization: administrations grew, increased prestige attached to public office, and a strong belief in the developmental role of the bureaucracy prevailed (Ayubi 1988, 13). This feature was not born at independence either; MENA economies inherited key features of their government organization and administration structure from the Ottoman Empire and European powers. The Ottoman administration was a strong bureaucratic machine (Findlay 1980, Findlay 1997). Rather than deriving their status and power from the ownership of economic assets such as land, the local elites in the Ottoman provinces sought direct political power though positions in the state bureaucracy (Ozbudun 1997). Statism and bureaucratic rule in the provinces were based on the Ottoman fiscal system, which is widely considered to have shaped governance structures (Tosun and Yilmaz 2008).

Colonial rule stifled the representation of local interests. Under the Ottoman rule, the governing apparatus was insulated from social pressures. The bureaucracy was rendered "autonomous," through a deliberate policy of recruitment and compensation aimed at cutting identity and economic links with the dominant landed, commercial, and industrial classes, but also from regional entities (Ozbudun 1997). The separation between rulers and ruled was reinforced by the absence of representative systems. The Ottoman Empire did not evolve from feudal pluralism to constitutionalism and representation (via the estates and the corporate autonomy of bodies such as the church, cities, and the guilds) that characterized the rise of European states. Neither centrally nor in the provinces did Istanbul develop representative mechanisms until the last quarter of the nineteenth century (Ozbudun 1997). No substantial progress was achieved during European colonization either. So the economic grievances of marginal areas were neither articulated nor addressed.

Colonial tax systems encouraged a neglect of lagging areas. First, they discouraged economic development in marginal areas. Particularly during the classical period (1453 to the 1600s), the Ottoman Empire had very low provincial tax rates compared with Europe and other empires (Karaman 2009). Both taxation and internal security in the Ottoman provinces were delegated to local elites. This presented the central administration with a trade-off in setting tax rates. On the one hand, the center and their delegated authorities shared an interest in maximizing gross tax revenue. On the other, the center was concerned about the power balance between itself and its tax-collecting delegates. So the central administration sometimes capped tax rates in the provinces to limit the power of local elites. This cap also discouraged the development of the tax base because neither the central administration nor the local elites stood to gain from economic growth. The tax ceilings induced, at best, economic neglect of lagging areas and, at worst, inefficient or outright detrimental economic policies.

Second, colonial tax systems diverted fiscal resources away from local investments. The Ottoman fiscal system shifted a large share of tax revenues away from the provinces and toward the capital region. The tax receipts that remained with provincial governors were only for security and administration expenses, not local investments. The bias toward police and security spending continued and was reinforced during French and British rule, during which some two-thirds of total expenditure was typically security related (Owen 1992).

In catering essentially to the metropolis, colonial management avoided redressing regional inequalities. In addition to diverting taxes, colonial rule diverted actual output. Ottoman governors owed their ultimate allegiance to Istanbul. Their performance was assessed on the basis of whether they catered to the security and consumption needs of the Porte, rather than on their development of the provinces. During European colonization, the colonial states continued to serve as providers of goods to the metropolis. Agriculture focused on export crops, such as wine, cereals, and tobacco. In the initial stage, industry was developed only for the processing in situ of certain goods. In favoring resource extraction over economic development, the colonial powers instated an economic geography of "useful versus useless" regions. The agriculturally rich areas of Morocco—the coastal plains and plateaus as well as the north and west of the Atlas ranges—were known to the French and Spanish colonial powers as "*Le Maroc Utile*" (Pennell 2001, 169; Thomas 2005, 212; Eickleman 1976). Similarly, "*l'Algérie utile*" was where mineral, agricultural, and demographic resources could allow quick economic extraction. This spatial breakdown of colonies was reflected in "divide and rule" politics. Rather than seeking the consent of disadvantaged groups (and regions) through investments and economic benefits, European powers kept these groups divided along ethnic and religious lines, to prevent their alliance against the government. Particularly in the colonial territories, which are today the Syrian Arab Republic, Lebanon, Iraq, Morocco, and Algeria, this maintained spatial disparities (Cleveland 1999; Owen 1992; Bengio and Ben-Dor 1999).

The development of metropolis-oriented economies encouraged coastal agglomeration. Export orientation resulted in an increase in the importance and size of coastal cities. New business opportunities and improving living conditions attracted populations from inland rural areas, as well as Europe. Between the early nineteenth century and the early twentieth century, the population in Tunis more than doubled. With the French colonial period after 1881, the influx of Europeans grew substantially, reaching close to 100,000 in 1936—that is, 45 percent of total city residents.

Resources were directed toward urban settler communities. Investments were primarily oriented to the infrastructure necessary to support colonial economic activity and trade in coastal cities and allowing adequate transportation and connection links, but they also aimed to improve the living conditions in settler areas. A classic example is the Constantine Plan of 1955–63—one of the last development plans to be attempted under colonial administration. Conveniently located between Algiers and Annaba (called Bône at the time, and the second-largest city in Algeria), Constantine was a crossroads for the transport of agricultural products and primary resources coming from the inland, as well as an important internal market. The plan provided for the increase of European settlements in the main coastal cities and their ancillary towns, the building of railway links between main port cities and internal hubs, the expansion of irrigation within settlement estates, and the expansion of settler agricultural development. Policies were explicitly aimed at favoring new settlers, such as the establishment of a housing authority in Tunis to facilitate the construction of inexpensive housing for French immigrants. Such policies left nonsettler regions behind and often occurred at the expense of the local national community. For example, in 1932 an infrastructure development project in education and health, financed with Moroccan taxpayer money and profits from the local phosphate industry, benefited nearly exclusively the settler community that was just 4 percent of the total population. European hospitals in the predominantly Muslim cities of Marrakech, Fès, and Meknès received up to 10 times more funding than hospitals of the majority population. The local population, representing more than 90 percent of total inhabitants of the three cities, received just over 10 percent of hospital funding (Thomas 2005). Sometimes, regional disparities were also a result of being subject to different colonial administrations. Morocco is a good example. Although facing the Mediterranean and strategically controlling the Gibraltar Strait, northern areas under Spanish rule were much neglected compared to areas under the French protectorate because of the lack of resources of the Spanish government. At independence, economic activity was limited and infrastructure scarce, with path dependency encouraging backwardness and an economic lag behind other areas.

Strong spatial disparities therefore existed at the moment of independence. The pro-settler and coastal bias of colonial development processes— already distinct under the Ottomans—resulted in a deepening of the spatial divide. At independence, many areas faced dire poverty. The predominantly urban politics characterizing the colonial period, with the capital city as the center of a political arena dominated by a small elite, continued through independence. Administrative expansion proceeded in parallel with a centrally planned approach to economic management. The central government extended its interventions into rural areas, as large land estates were expropriated.

As the central administrations expanded, power remained concentrated at the core. Whether the path to independence had been smooth or characterized by struggles, power remained centralized in the years following independence. As mentioned earlier, postindependence governments confronted a series of challenges, both internal and external (Korany 1987). Internally, weak bureaucratic capacity constrained the development of influence over the entire territory. Empirical metrics suggest that MENA economies remain less externally accountable than others at a similar level of development.

Oil and gas revenues placed huge amounts of resources in the hands of some central administrations, permitting large bureaucracies, a centrally driven development policy, and state autonomy, as the state does not need to penetrate society and develop the economy to raise revenues (Luciani 1989; Beblawi and Luciani 1987; Henry 2004).

Discontent with government policies is sometimes deeper in cities. (See table 4.3 and figure 4.1.) This is despite the fact that cities often fare better in terms of a variety of indicators. (The exception, shown in table 4.3, is the Islamic Republic of Iran, where inhabitants of Tehran expressed more confidence in the Khatami administration than did the rest of the country.) Given the increased opportunities for association

TABLE 4.3

Nonmetropolitan People State More Confidence in Their Governments

	Percentage of interviewees who said they have "a great deal of confidence" in the government	
	Outside the capital area	Capital area
Egypt, Arab Rep. (2000)	**19.8**	10.9
Iran, Islamic Rep. (2000)	24.5	**33.4**
Iraq (2004)	**13.1**	6.8
Jordan (2001)	**54.8**	48.0
Morocco (2001)	**33.1**	26.5

Source: World Values Survey Association, European and World Values Surveys Four-Wave Integrated Data File, 1981–2004.

Note: Boldface identifies the larger number in the row.

FIGURE 4.1

People in Smaller Settlements State More Confidence in their Government in the Arab Republic of Egypt

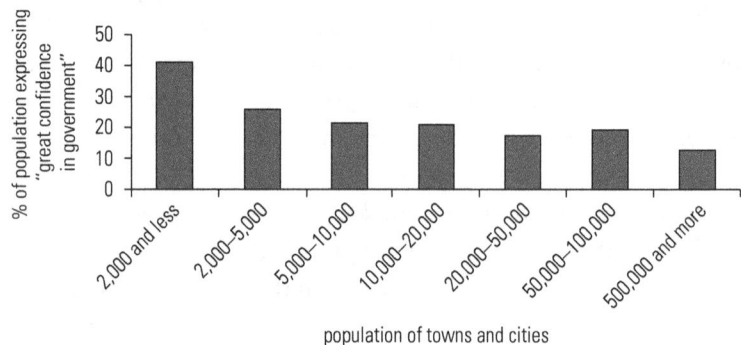

Source: World Values Survey Association, European and World Values Surveys Four-Wave Integrated Data File, 1981–2004.

and protest in urban areas, it is understandable that governments might be more responsive to urban demands.

But MENA's governments are now seeking to reverse the historical drivers of spatial disparities. The state-led model of economic development and its centralizing policies have been losing steam since the 1990s, for a number of reasons:

• The rapid growth of urban population has increased the cost of subsidizing metropolitan areas. Urban growth and unemployment have driven policy makers to reduce the incentives for rural-urban migration.

• The performance of centrally planned economies worldwide has been disappointing, compared with that of market economies.

- In non–oil exporting countries, fiscal constraints have limited the state's ability to continue the subsidization of public employment and production.

- Frustration with the poor performance of centralized bureaucracies has led policy makers to seek out alternative models of delivery—for example, quasi-autonomous agencies, public-private partnerships, and of course deconcentration and decentralization.

MENA governments are, therefore, now seeking to reverse the historical legacy of disadvantage that peripheral areas' populations have experienced in their relationship with the state. The rest of this section will, therefore, examine what MENA policy makers can do and are already doing to create "a level playing field for development."

How Differences in the Subnational Investment Climate Can Handicap Lagging Areas

The literature on economic geography emphasizes agglomeration economies as an influence over where economic activities take place; entrepreneurs invest where their customers, suppliers, and potential labor force are already clustered. The implication is that low investment in lagging areas is an efficient market response to economies of agglomeration.

This implication is true—but it is not the whole story. The investment climate is also an important determinant of the geographical spread of economic activity.

The phrase "investment climate" can be defined as the "policy, institutional, and behavioral environment, both present and expected, that influences the returns, and risks, associated with investment" (Stern 2002). It consists of the macroeconomic environment, the institutional context, and the infrastructural base. There is abundant evidence on the relationship between the investment climate and the level of economic activity at the country level. By logical extension, therefore, one would expect subnational disparities in the investment climate to affect the spatial distribution of investment and economic activity. Although all locations within a country share the same macroeconomic environment, spatial differences in the institutional and infrastructural situation are perfectly possible. Box 4.2 recounts a microscale anecdote of a business location decision based on spatial disparities in the investment climate.

Within-country differences in the local institutional environment in Bangladesh, China, India, and Pakistan have a clear impact on firm productivity (Dollar, Hallward-Driemeier, and Mengistae 2005). The authors

BOX 4.2

An Entrepreneur's Experience of Spatial Disparities in the Business Environment

"I wanted to create a small center of Internet and video games. I could provide a little money as personal financing. So I presented an application for credit to banks of the town of Kasserine to finance my project so that I could settle in Thala or Kasserine. Unfortunately, all my requests were refused. I came to Tunis, and I settled in with cousins in Ettadhamoun [a low-income area in Tunis]. I presented the same request, and it was accepted."

Source: A 35-year-old unemployed graduate from the lagging area of Kasserine, Tunisia.

conclude, "Most of the existing work on the relationship between institutions and growth assumes that the important institutions are constant within a country. The empirical link that we establish between investment climate indicators and firm performance . . . reveals that there is significant variation in the investment climate across locations within countries. So, local governance is important." A study of India (Lall and Mengistae 2005) again finds that within-country differences in the institutional environment (represented by labor regulations and access to reliable electric power) explain a greater share of the variation in firm productivity than economic geography (agglomeration effects plus market access). Indeed, cities in locations with poor market access seem to receive the biggest productivity boost from a good institutional environment.

Figure 4.2 presents a composite index of the subnational investment climate for Algeria, the Arab Republic of Egypt, Jordan, Morocco, and the West Bank and Gaza. The index uses Investment Climate Survey (ICS) indicators that are common to all economies and are objectively quantifiable. National-level conditions remain important; the Algerian subnational indicators cluster toward the bottom end of the range, the Jordanian and Palestinian indicators are grouped in midrange, and the Moroccan indicators are toward the top. However, the range of within-country investment climate variation is quite large in Algeria. And it is particularly striking for Egypt, where it stretches almost from the bottom to the top of the measured range. It is possible that the range of within-country variation would also have been significantly larger for Morocco had a greater number of locations been surveyed.

The data for MENA economies are often insufficient to measure the impact of subnational investment climate disparities on enterprise performance. One of the reasons is that enterprise survey responses usually represent a narrow range of locations. Another is that multiple independent datasets are needed to separate different kinds of location-specific

FIGURE 4.2

A Composite Index of Objective Measures of the Subnational Investment Climate in Algeria, the Arab Republic of Egypt, Jordan, Morocco, and the West Bank and Gaza

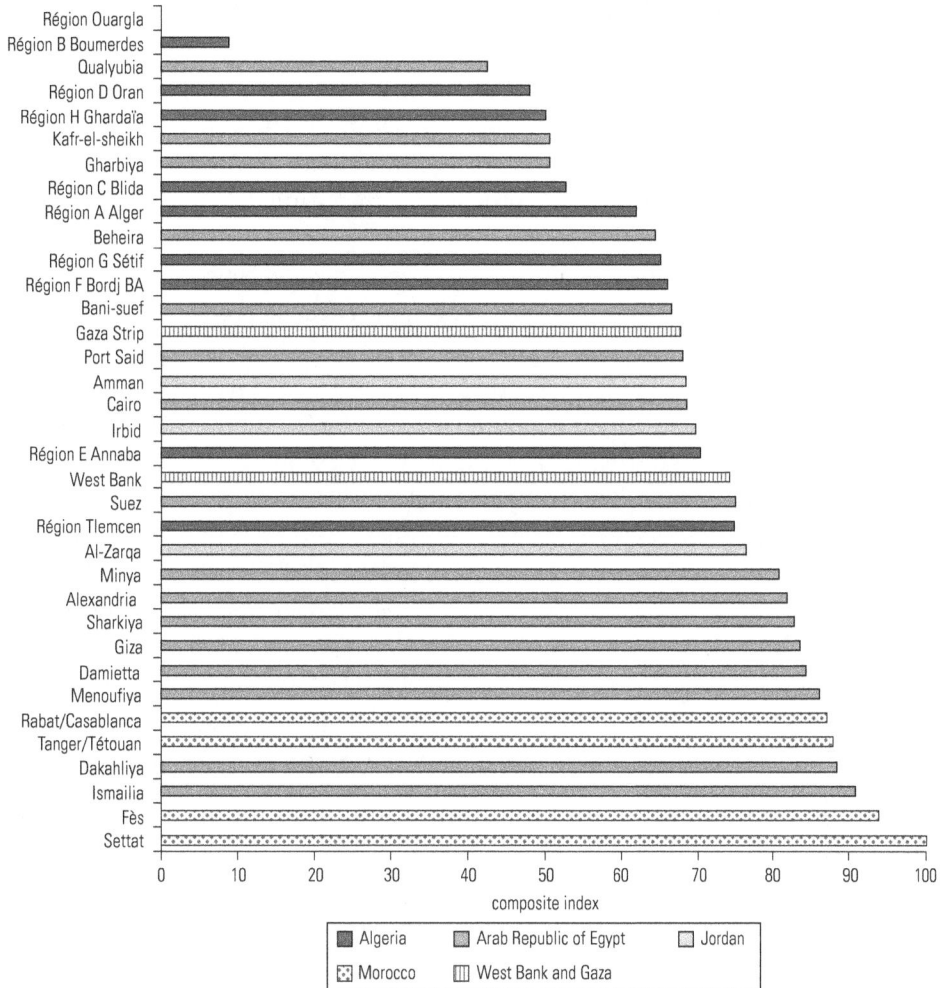

composite index

Legend: Algeria | Arab Republic of Egypt | Jordan | Morocco | West Bank and Gaza

Source: World Bank staff calculations from World Bank Investment Climate Surveys.

Note: The indicators used are the cost of corruption as a percentage of total annual sales, weeks of delay in filling a technical vacancy, percentage of workforce with less than primary education, percentage of firms making informal payments to government officials, percentage of input value available on credit, weeks of waiting period for a construction permit, weeks of delay in obtaining a water connection, and percentage of firms using own generators. Each indicator is normalized from best (100) to worst (0), and a simple average of the normalized values is taken for each administrative division. Région Ouargla's score is zero.

effects. Therefore, this is a potential area for further data collection and research; however, there is suggestive evidence that investment climate disparities are affecting the spatial distribution of economic activity.

It is possible to link spatial disparities in the investment climate and spatial disparities in firm productivity. Mengistae and Thompson (2006) used enterprise survey and industrial census data from Morocco to analyze the spatial dispersion of productivity among manufacturing plants.

Their aim was to separate out three causes of disparities in productivity: natural geography, economies of agglomeration, and the institutional environment. The investment climate variables in the analysis were infrastructural (entrepreneurs' perceptions of electricity, telecommunications, and transport), institutional (corruption, tax administration, the legal system, and access to credit), and educational (availability of skilled labor). Natural geography, agglomeration economies, and the investment climate were all significant, but their relative importance was striking: disparities in the institutional environment explained more variation in firms' productivity than natural geography and agglomeration externalities combined.

Although there was no clear correlation between leading-lagging and the investment climate effect, the effect on productivity appeared to put nonmetropolitan provinces at a disadvantage for the two sectors analyzed. For food, tobacco, and beverages, the investment climate's effect on productivity was most unfavorable for Taourirt, Fès, and Tanger-Assilah. For apparel, leather, and footwear the most unfavorable effect was for Berkane, Tanger-Assilah, and Fès.

MENA governments have been concerned to bring financial services into lagging areas. Although commercial banks in MENA13 economies have branch networks that match those in other middle-income regions, such as Latin America and East Asia, MENA has fewer accounts per branch than any other region (table 4.4), even Sub-Saharan Africa and South Asia. This may be because MENA economies have encouraged state-owned banks to open branches as a social mandate.

TABLE 4.4

MENA's Commercial Banks Have Extensive Networks with Few Accounts

Country group	Accounts per 1,000 adults, commercial banks (unweighted average)	Number of branches per 100,000 adults, commercial banks (unweighted average)	Accounts per branch, commercial banks (unweighted average)
Middle East and North Africa	**574**	**14**	**4,200**
Europe and Central Asia	1,282	23	5,600
High income: OECD	1,964	30	6,500
Sub-Saharan Africa	366	5	7,100
Latin America and the Caribbean	1,099	15	7,500
East Asia and the Pacific	1,123	12	9,400
South Asia	608	7	8,900
High income: non-OECD	2,842	21	13,700

Source: World Bank FinStats database.

Note: MENA data are from Algeria, Jordan, Lebanon, Morocco, the Syrian Arab Republic, Tunisia, and the Republic of Yemen.

How to bring financial services to lagging areas is an important topic that cannot be covered in adequate detail in this report; however, the data presented in table 4.4 suggest that branch density is not the constraint on the geographical reach of the financial sector in MENA. Answers should be sought rather in the development of financial products and transactions technologies that meet the needs of people in poorer and more remote areas.

What does the spatial dimension of the investment climate mean for lagging areas? One can break the investment climate–spatial development linkage into two components:

- First, an overall improvement in a country's investment climate at the national level might reduce the spatial concentration of business activity. Although the degree of liberalization of MENA's economies is average for middle-income countries, regulations are applied unequally; MENA economies suffer from abnormally high levels of corruption for their level of national income, and the private sector is dominated by long-standing ties between business and government elites (World Bank 2009d). This situation is likely to make it critical for business owners and senior management to be located close to the capital, where they can maintain face-to-face contacts with senior government figures. Conversely, greater transparency in the application of business legislation would make it safer for businesses to locate far from the seat of power.

- Second, within-country disparities in the application of business regulation might penalize lagging areas.

Policy makers should, therefore, take heart that the evolution of their country's economic geography is not entirely predetermined by the forces of agglomeration. The spatial distribution of economic activity is at least partially amenable to policy intervention via the investment climate (see box 4.3).

BOX 4.3

Making the Subnational Investment Climate Work for Lagging Areas: An Idea for Policy Makers

Survey enterprises in leading and lagging areas to identify

- The key factors determining choice of location

- The key investment climate handicaps faced by lagging areas

Source: Study Team.

How to Manage the Spatial Dimension of Public Expenditure

Public expenditure management (PEM) systems are the transmission mechanisms between the political will to reduce spatial disparities on the one hand and the allocation of resources to disadvantaged territories on the other. Historically, MENA's public expenditure management systems were often set up to centralize and sectoralize the public budget, so they do not automatically lend themselves to managing and monitoring expenditure by location. Now that MENA governments have an increasing interest in the spatial dimension of public policy, their spatial political objectives must be underpinned by accounting and budgeting systems that allow one to manage the spatial incidence of public expenditure.

This is not to say that it is efficient to redirect all forms of public expenditure toward lagging areas. On the contrary, investment in economic infrastructure and productive activities is likely to offer a higher rate of return in leading areas benefiting from economies of agglomeration; however, robust spatial data on public funding for social services and public amenities will greatly strengthen any government's efforts to ensure a level playing field for development.

This section, therefore, briefly outlines a number of possible approaches to the spatial management of public spending and where a sample of MENA economies stand.

To manage the spatial incidence of public expenditure, the PEM system has to be capable of

- *Monitoring* the spatial incidence of public expenditure, (measuring what is spent where), and measuring its impact

- *Controlling* the spatial incidence of public expenditure (directing resources to political priority locations)

Controlling the spatial incidence of spending depends upon monitoring it, which depends, in turn, upon expenditures being apportioned geographically in the public accounts. This is where the challenges begin. The location of public expenditure at subnational administrative levels is, of course, automatically traceable to a specific location. In MENA, however, the share of subnational expenditures is very low compared with the OECD average of 17 percent. This comparison then raises the question of how to estimate the apportionment of central government spending between different locations.

- One option is to classify central government expenditure or revenue items or both with a location (zip) code (Jacobs, Hélis, and Bouley 2008). This classification can be done for budgeted expenditure,

actual expenditures, or both. Because of the high level of policy interest in spatial allocations of public spending, many countries ensure
that some form of geographical classification is applied when they
modernize their chart of accounts (e.g., Zambia's Activity-Based
Budgeting [ABB] system, the Dominican Republic's 2002 manual of
budget classifiers, and Mozambique's Budget Framework Law).
Often, it is national parliaments that require expenditures to be classified by location (Schiavo-Campo and Tommasi 1999), which is to
be expected, given the spatial nature of parliamentary representation.

• Another approach—used, for example, in the United Kingdom—is
to ask central spending departments to state, after the end of the
budget year, what proportion of actual spending benefited the population of specific regions, estimating the shares according to guidelines specified by the finance ministry. This disaggregation of central
expenditures is then added to subnational government expenditure to
give the spatial breakdown of spending. The government of the
United Kingdom estimates that about 83 percent of total managed
expenditure (TME) can be apportioned geographically in this way,
and that the other 17 percent benefits the population of the country
as a whole (HM Treasury 2009). The advantage of this approach is
that it does not require an overhaul of the chart of accounts. The disadvantage is that it relies on the objectivity and neutrality of public
servants and could be open to challenge, undermining its credibility.

• A third option is to use administrative data on service outputs to appor-
tion central government expenditures by location. In Madagascar, for
example, investment expenditures were managed centrally, as in most
MENA economies. So there was no statistical record of spending on
school and health facility construction by administrative division; however, it was possible to reconstruct an estimate of how education and
health spending was apportioned between districts, by checking when
new facilities appeared in the administrative records (World Bank
2004a).

Tunisian policy makers have access to data on the allocation of central
government spending by governorate. These data show a tendency for
public investment per capita to be higher than average in some, but not
all, poorer governorates (figure 4.3).

However, most MENA economies' public financial management systems currently do not support analysis of the spatial incidence of expenditure. Not only are subnational expenditures a small share of total
expenditures, but also data on the geographical apportionment of central government spending are often lacking, incomplete, or given limited circulation.

FIGURE 4.3

**Public Investment and per capita Household
Expenditure by Governorate in Tunisia**

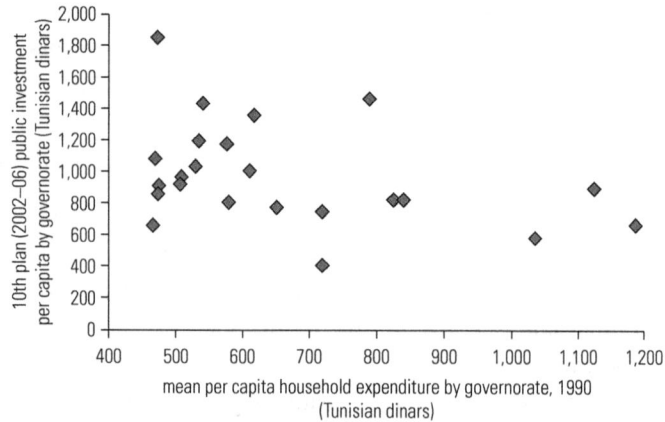

Sources: Département de l'Aménagement du Territoire; INS (2000).

Note: Each diamond represents a governorate.

In countries where the government lacks information on the spatial incidence of public spending, there is a risk that spatial development policies
explicitly targeting lagging areas are being undermined by an allocation of
mainstream spending implicitly skewed toward leading areas. For example,
one of the major findings of the Sapir Report (Sapir 2003) was that the
European Union's regional policy was being nullified by the concentration
of agricultural production subsidies in richer areas. The application of one
or several of the methodologies previously discussed could remedy
MENA's lack of information on the geography of public expenditure and
thus could produce valuable insights for policy makers and citizens.

For the moment, therefore, we can analyze only the spatial incidence
of subnational public spending, and we must do so in the knowledge that
it represents only a fragment of the whole picture. A useful indicator of
whether subnational public spending is mitigating or sustaining spatial
disparities is to be found in the allocation of transfers from the center to
local governments. These so-called "equalization transfers" are usually
intended to improve the spatial equity of public expenditure (Shah 2007),
helping local administrations in poorer areas to compensate for their relatively weak tax base and greater human development needs. They
finance about 60 percent of subnational expenditures in developing and
transition economies, and about 30 percent in OECD countries.

It is, therefore, interesting to ask whether intragovernmental fiscal
transfers from the center to local governments are indeed serving this
purpose in MENA.

Table 4.5 describes the systems for the allocation of transfers in six MENA economies. It was also possible to obtain quantitative data on transfers for three MENA countries: Egypt, the Islamic Republic of Iran, and Jordan. Taken together, they suggest that transfers could be playing more of an equalization role. In most of the six economies described in table 4.5, the allocation procedures tend to be either ad hoc (Egypt, the Islamic Republic of Iran, the West Bank and Gaza) or based upon an area's revenue-generating capacity (Jordan, Tunisia), neither of which would reliably serve an equalization function. The Republic of Yemen,

TABLE 4.5

Transfer Characteristics and Allocation Rules in Six MENA Economies

	Transfer characteristics	Source	Allocation rules
Egypt, Arab Rep.	General development grants: mutual plus earmarked (service and development, land, housing, cleanliness, road)	National budget	No rule-based allocation nor formula; discretionary grants and donations
Iran, Islamic Rep.	Transfers to urban local governments appear to be negligible, particularly in the larger cities. Development transfers: 60–70% earmarked, 30–40% discretionary.	Oil revenues	No formula; allocations decided annually by Parliament
Jordan	Transfers to all municipalities from central government's fuel tax collections.	Fuel taxes	6% of fuel tax generated within the municipality
Tunisia	Earmarked: operating grants through Local Government Common Fund; development grants managed by Fund for Loan and Support for Local Government; sector-based transfers; Regional Development transfers.	National budget	Formula based—10% flat rate, 45% size of local government, 45% according to average property tax
West Bank and Gaza	Current transfers and grants for transport fees are not earmarked; discretionary and emergency transfers that are channeled to specific projects	Transport fees and a separate account assigned for discretionary and emergency transfers	A formula for the pool and distribution of transport fees exists on paper (1997 Local Government Law). (Yet, the formula is only partially applied. Discretionary and emergency transfers are ad hoc.)
Yemen, Rep.	30% of grants from extra-budgetary funds that are earmarked; other nonearmarked funds	Shared revenues from 28 taxes, mainly Zakat[a]	No formula. (Council of Ministers uses nonbinding guidelines—population density, financing gap, degree of deprivation, performance in revenue collection.)

Source: Tosun and Yilmaz 2009.

Note: a. Religiously ordained charitable giving.

however, does have nonbinding guidelines intended to steer resources toward poorer areas.

The allocation of transfers to subnational administrations was analyzed for three economies for which data were available: Egypt, the Islamic Republic of Iran, and Jordan.

Arab Republic of Egypt. Most subnational expenditure in Egypt is executed by governorates. Governors are appointed by the president, and the governorates are deconcentrated administrations without policy-making power over sectoral issues. Although the governor of Alexandria was able to translate his city's robust economic base into a significant fiscal resource (World Bank 2005c), governorates' own resources are usually slight. Therefore, most governorates are dependent for investment resources upon their share of the block grant transfers administered by the Ministry of Local Development. These transfers have the potential to reduce disparities between governorates, by giving the highest transfers to governorates with the weakest economic base; however, the data from fiscal year 2002/03 (figure 4.4) suggest that resource transfers and governorate GDP per capita were not correlated. It should be noted, however, that the arrangements for block grants allocations to governorates are under review.

Islamic Republic of Iran. Transfers from the central to local governments in the Islamic Republic of Iran show a contrasting picture. The subnational administration is organized primarily at the provincial (ostan)

FIGURE 4.4

Transfers from the Center to Governorates Are Not Reducing Spatial Disparities in the Arab Republic of Egypt

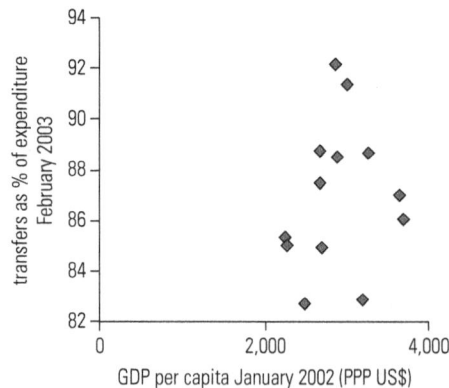

Source: World Bank 2006b.

Note: PPP = purchasing power parity. Each diamond represents a governorate.

level. The apportionment of transfers from the central government to ostans does give priority to lagging areas. On a per capita basis, the transfers ranged in 2002 from 1.2 million rials for Ilam to under 0.1 million rials for Qazvin and Tehran (figure 4.5). An ostan's level of development does not explain all of this wide variation, but it does explain an important part of it. The correlation coefficient between per capita transfers and ostans' Human Development Index was –0.42. With a Life Expectancy Index, it was –0.53; with an Income Index, it was –0.46.

Jordan. Municipalities in Jordan, like Egypt's governorates, have limited financial independence: local government expenditures are only 6 percent of total government spending (FEMISE 2005); however, there are significant variations in public expenditures per capita among municipalities, both between and within regions (figure 4.6). These differences are seemingly not associated with spatial disparities.

It is clear from the previous discussion that most MENA economies can make public financial management a more powerful tool for their spatial development policy: first, by putting in place systems to monitor the spatial incidence of public expenditure; and second, by moving toward a more rules- and needs-based system for intragovernmental fiscal transfers.

FIGURE 4.5

Much Variation, but a Tendency for the Intergovernmental Transfers to Favor Lagging Ostans in the Islamic Republic of Iran

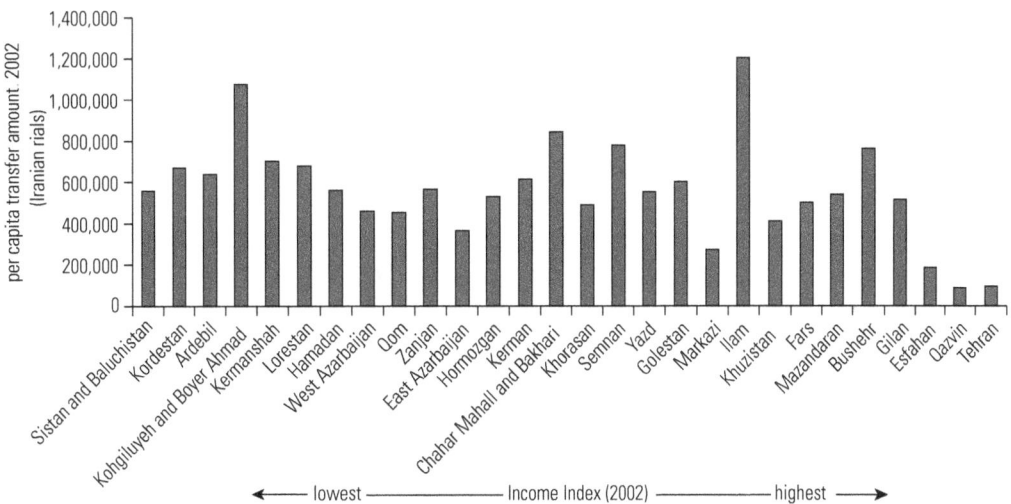

Source: World Bank 2005d.

FIGURE 4.6

Variation in per Capita Expenditure of Local Government by Governorate in Jordan

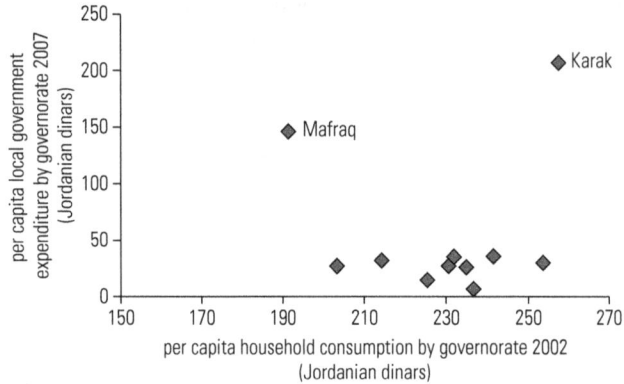

Sources: http://www.moma.gov.jo/municipalDB/landuse.aspx, accessed August 24, 2009; 2002 national household survey.

Note: Amman is not shown in the figure. The data for Amman governorate excluded Amman municipality. Separate data on Amman municipality were not available. Each diamond represents a governorate.

How to Correct Spatial Disparities in Public Education Systems

"In spite of the relative improvement of transportation, I knew that my children could not do better than me if we remained in the same area; therefore it was necessary to go down [from the mountain] to the city for the children's education."

—A parent from Kasserine, a lagging area town in Tunisia

Education, as we have seen, is critical to many pathways for the reduction of spatial disparities. First, convergence in educational attainment leads to convergence in human capital and in earnings. Second, educated people are more mobile and can participate in the redistribution of the population from lagging to leading areas. Third, the education of women unlocks the economic potential of 50 percent of the population and helps close the spatial disparities in fertility that have contributed to the current spatial disparities in well-being. Fourth, today's children in lagging areas are tomorrow's parents, and they will pass their learning on to the next generation. Closing the spatial gap in education is, therefore, a win-win-win-win strategy.

This section puts the spotlight on education by asking three questions:

- What are the spatial disparities in educational access and attainment in MENA?

- To what extent are spatial disparities in education attributable to disparities in service provision?

- What are MENA governments doing to narrow spatial disparities in education, and what is the way forward?

The analysis of spatial disparities in education draws on country case studies of Egypt, the Islamic Republic of Iran, Jordan, Morocco, and the Republic of Yemen.

There Are Significant Spatial Disparities in Enrollment, Attainment, and Achievement

Rural-urban disparities in primary and secondary enrollment rates are an obvious feature of MENA's education indicators (table 4.6). The nonpoor and students living in urban areas tend to have higher access to education than the poor and those who live in rural areas (World Bank 2008a).

There are also notable differences in educational attainment between rural and urban in Egypt, Jordan, and Morocco. Regarding the completion of primary education, the disparity between rural and urban has been narrowing in Egypt and Jordan, while a discernible spatial difference remains in Morocco (figure 4.7). In Morocco, boys' grade repetition rates in rural primary schools are much higher (17 percent) than those of urban girls (10 percent) (World Bank 2007b). Regarding completion rates, spatial differences are higher for secondary and tertiary education than for primary education in Egypt and Morocco (figures 4.7 and 4.8).

The Trends in International Mathematics and Science Study (TIMSS) allows us to gauge spatial disparities in achievement.

TABLE 4.6

Lower Enrollment Rates for Rural Children, Especially the Poor
(Percent)

			Urban		Rural	
			Poor	Nonpoor	Poor	Nonpoor
Algeria	1995	Primary	96.0	95.0	89.0	89.0
		Secondary	77.0	82.0	59.0	66.0
Egypt, Arab Rep.	1999	6–15	95.8	98.5	93.5	96.7
		15–19	72.4	84.9	64.7	72.9
Iran, Islamic Rep.	2001	6–10	99.0	100.0	98.0	98.0
		11–13	92.0	97.0	76.0	84.0
Morocco	1998	7–15	69.4	87.2	36.4	49.8
Tunisia	2000	6–18	79.4	82.2	67.0	70.7
Yemen, Rep.	1998	10–14	83.0	92.1	59.6	62.0

Source: World Bank 2008a.

FIGURE 4.7

**Percentage of Adults Older Than Age 25 Who Completed
Primary Education**

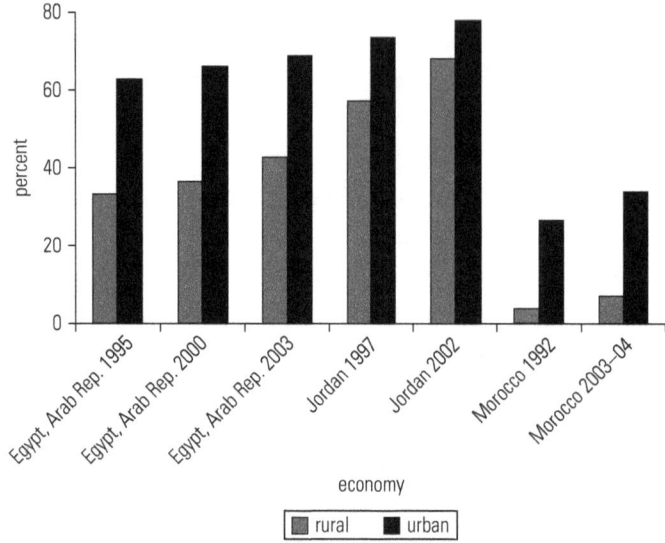

Source: EdStats, World Bank.

FIGURE 4.8

**Percentage of Adults Older Than Age 25 Who Completed
Secondary Education**

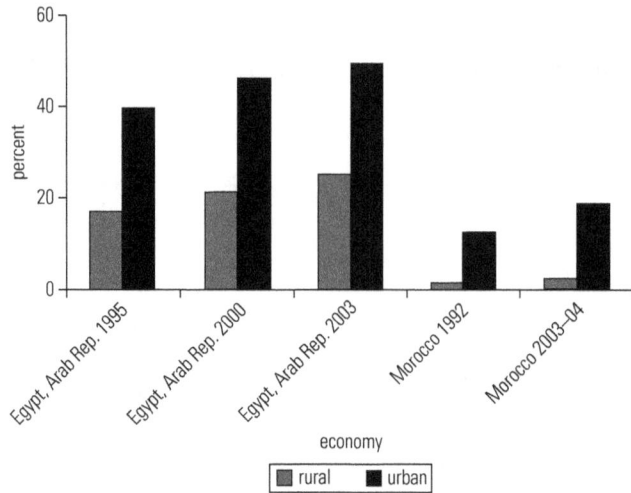

Source: EdStats, World Bank.

MENA economies show rural-urban disparities in mathematics scores, with statistically a significant gap in Egypt, the Islamic Republic of Iran, Jordan, Lebanon, and Tunisia. The Islamic Republic of Iran's rural-urban disparity in the mathematics score is particularly striking. Moreover, the findings of the Program for International Student Assessment (PISA) suggest that being at a rural school is more problematic for low-achieving students than for high-achieving students in Jordan (World Bank 2008b).

Gender gaps in literacy are often widest in lagging areas. In Morocco, the urban literacy rate is 75 percent for women, while it is 14.2 percent for rural women. Being male in a nonrural setting increases the probability of completing primary education by 7 percent, while being male in rural areas increases it by 16 percent. The primary completion urban and rural gender gaps are 5 percent and 9 percent, respectively, in Jordan.

Most Spatial Disparities in Educational Attainment (Completion of School) Are Attributable to the Household Characteristics of the Rural Population[3]

If children in rural areas receive less schooling (figure 4.9) than do their urban counterparts, the next question to ask is to what extent is this lack due to spatial disparities in children's socioeconomic status (demand-side

FIGURE 4.9

Percentage of Adults Older Than Age 25 Who Completed Tertiary Education

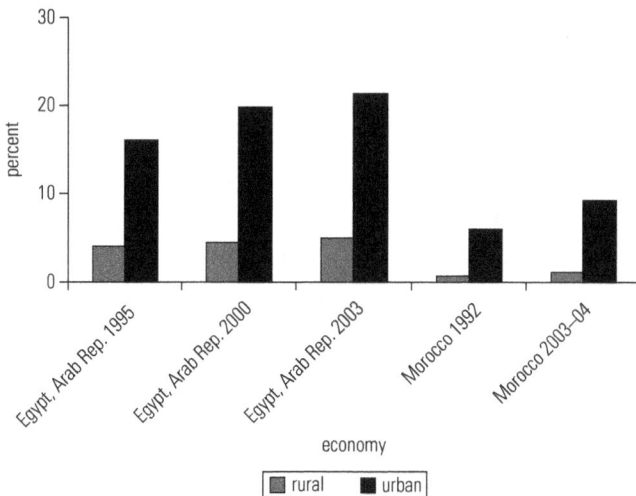

Source: EdStats, World Bank.

factors) and how much is due to spatial disparities in education services (supply-side factors). The appropriate policy response will depend on the answer to this question. Where some or most of the rural-urban disparity can be attributed to inequalities in access to quality educational services, then the case for improving education provision in lagging areas is strongest.

This study examined the determinants of educational attainment in one country with high spatial disparities in attainment (Morocco) and another with low disparities (Jordan).

Morocco. For Morocco, our study (Katayama 2009) used data from the Population and Family Health Survey to examine what determines who completes primary education. The rural-urban difference was 33 percentage points, but how much of this gap was because rural children tend to be poorer and would have had worse educational chances wherever they lived? The analysis revealed that a child's household's economic status was the most important factor; being in the lowest wealth quintile reduces the probability of having completed primary school by 42 percentage points compared with someone in the highest wealth quintile. The next most important factor was gender: being female reduces the probability of having completed primary school by 16 percentage points compared with males. After the respondent's age and the household head's level of education were taken into account, the rural-urban factor explained a gap of only 5 percentage points in the probability of having completed primary education.

The analysis was repeated for secondary education completion, for which there is an urban-rural gap of 13 percentage points. This disparity was found to be explained entirely by household characteristics.

Finally, regarding higher education completion, there was a 10–percentage point rural-urban disparity, and the gap was also significantly attributed to household characteristics.

Jordan. In Jordan, urban-rural gaps in educational attainment rates were found to be relatively small: 5 percentage points for primary education and 11 percentage points for secondary. As in Morocco, household economic status was the main factor behind a person's probability of having completed an educational level. Someone from the poorest wealth quintile was 17 percentage points less likely to have completed primary education than someone from the richest quintile. The gender gap effect was next most important, with a 3–percentage point lower probability for girls than for boys, and was bigger in rural areas. After household characteristics were taken into account, the rural-urban gap was insignificant for the probability of having completed both primary and secondary school.

Spatial Disparities in Learning Achievement Are Caused by Inequality in Education Provision

Spatial disparities in learning achievement are largely due to geographic differences in schooling (figure 4.10).

Jordan and the Islamic Republic of Iran. In both Jordan and the Islamic Republic of Iran, 2007 TIMSS test scores are significantly lower in rural areas for both science and mathematics. This gap remains significant even after taking account of rural-urban differences in the student or family characteristics described in the TIMSS data.[4]

Therefore, it is probable that students in rural schools are studying in a less favorable learning environment than those in urban schools. Teachers in rural schools, for example, tend to be younger and less experienced. Jordanian mathematics and science teachers have 1.1 years' and 3.1 years' less experience (respectively) in rural areas than in urban areas. In the Islamic Republic of Iran, the experience gap is 4.5 years and 3.7 years.

The World Bank (World Bank 2008a) noted MENA's spectacular achievements in increasing enrollment: "For good reasons, the region initially focused on establishing mass education systems by building schools, recruiting teachers, producing textbooks and setting the

FIGURE 4.10

Rural-Urban Disparities in Mathematics Learning, 2007 TIMSS Mathematics Scores

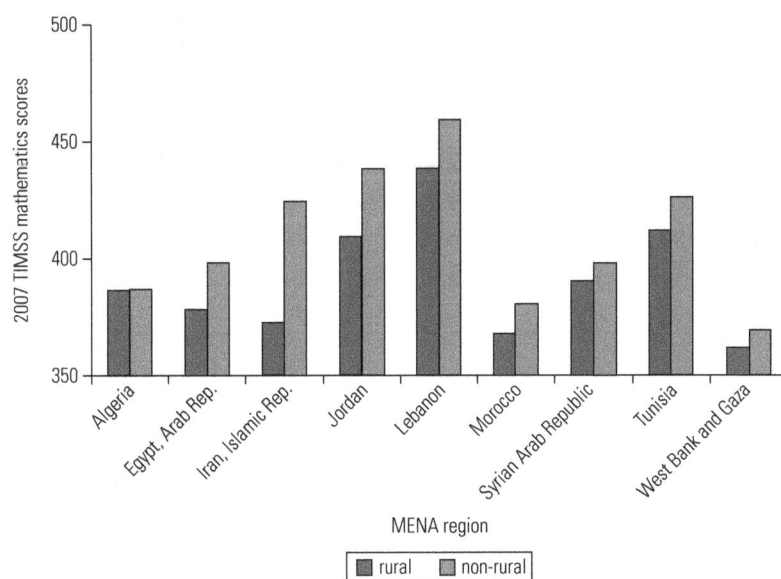

Source: World Bank staff calculation, based on 2007 TIMSS results.

Note: Urban is defined as a location with a population greater than 15,000.

curriculum." Nevertheless, MENA has been less effective than comparator and competitor countries in converting these investments and enrollments into retention and learning (World Bank 2008c, 3): "The educational achievements are compromised in part by high dropout rates, and relatively low scores on international tests. Literacy rates remain low." The idea that spatial disparities in learning achievement might be largely due to geographical differences in the quality of education reflects the same diagnosis.

Policy Implications: Analysis, Demand-Side Interventions, Quality, and a Focus on Girls

These analyses have important implications for MENA policy makers seeking to reduce spatial disparities in education:

Analysis of education spatially. First, on the supply side, there is scope across the region to improve the spatial planning of education infrastructure and to use information technology to bridge physical distances. Spatial analysis of the determinants of educational performance is also critical. Although spatial disparities in educational indicators are glaringly obvious, the causes of these disparities may be subtler. A reactive policy, for example, of school construction in rural areas may be treating the symptoms rather than the cause of the problem if the real bottleneck is on the demand side or related to the quality of education.

Demand-side interventions. Second, spatial disparities in educational attainment—the highest degree of education that a person completes—may have more to do with spatial disparities in households than with the spatial disparities in the availability of educational services per se. Policy interventions to motivate poor households to keep their children in school may, therefore, be a more appropriate response than a focus on educational infrastructure. In Morocco, for example, the government's Conditional Cash Transfer programs will address the costs for poor parents of keeping their children in school (World Bank 2008c).

Quality. Rural children seem to be learning less at school than their urban counterparts, even when they come from similar socioeconomic backgrounds. It is, therefore, critical to address quality issues such as learning environment, teacher training, motivation, and career management in rural areas. School development initiatives and human resource management reforms have the potential to reduce spatial differentials in quality.

A focus on girls. Reducing gender disparities in education, particularly in completion rates, may contribute to reducing spatial disparities in development. This is because girls' education contributes to MENA's demographic transition and because gender disparities in education are wider in lagging areas.

Attacking Spatial Disparities: What MENA Governments Are Doing, and Priority Strategies

On the basis of the considerations discussed earlier, four priority axes can be proposed to combat spatial disparities in education:

- Reducing *spatial disparities in quality* through human resource management innovations and school development initiatives

- *Stimulating the demand* for education in lagging areas

- Reducing *gender disparities* in lagging areas

- Using *spatial planning techniques* to deploy appropriate infrastructure

These priority axes will be illustrated with examples from the country case studies on Egypt, Jordan, Morocco, and the Republic of Yemen.

Reducing Spatial Disparities in Quality through Human Resource Management Innovations and School Development Initiatives

The spatial deployment of teachers and administrators creates inequities in the quality of education. For instance, the TIMSS results of the Islamic Republic of Iran have showed that more experienced teachers deliver better educational outcomes, but the tendency is for rural areas to be allocated the least experienced.

In Morocco, teachers generally move from rural to urban areas as they acquire more experience. A 2007 survey of teachers in Morocco found that difficult living conditions in rural areas led young teachers to seek a change of posting at the first opportunity. This lack of motivation to work in rural schools is reflected in the high level of unexplained absenteeism in rural areas, which in 2007 was the equivalent of 417 teachers being absent all year. The same survey found that underutilization of teachers was particularly acute for small rural lower secondary schools, with teachers working as few as 16 of the legal requirement of 24 hours—already low when compared with international levels (e.g., 37.5 hours in Spain). It is probable that rural principals are less experienced than their urban counterparts, compounding the motivational problems of young teachers.

In Jordan, teaching posts are allocated on the principle of queuing; those who have waited longest get the next job in line. In Egypt, as in Morocco, teachers migrate from rural to urban areas as they gain experience. In the Republic of Yemen, teaching placements are somewhat haphazard; a comparison of Annual Education Survey data with payroll found discrepancies for 30,000 teachers. Teachers are hired on the basis of local preference. The relocation subsidy is poorly regulated and often received long after redeployment. In this rather confused environment, an uninfluential school in a lagging area is unlikely to obtain experienced teachers.

Improved human resource management in public education services is, therefore, critically important for the reduction of spatial disparities in education quality.

First, improved incentives are required for teachers to locate in lagging areas. In the Republic of Yemen, for example, living conditions are reported to be extremely harsh and restrictive for female teachers posted away from their place of origin. Incentives may involve improved living conditions and housing, monetary payments, or improved career prospects. Box 4.4 describes how Algeria has used salary incentives to meet skills shortages in lagging areas. Motivating first-rate principals to accept postings in lagging areas is a key step toward improving education quality, and targeting incentives on such individuals could have a disproportionately positive impact.

Second, more formal, systematic, and needs-based postings procedures are required, to match teachers to vacancies. Where informality and influence characterize posting arrangements, the default outcome will be for disadvantaged areas to be further disadvantaged in teacher allocations. Arrangements for recruiting and training local teachers to

---

BOX 4.4

Algeria Introduces Spatial Salary Incentives, with Mixed Results

The Algerian government provides salary incentives for skilled public sector workers to take up employment in certain lagging areas of the High Plateaus and the South: Djelfa, Laghouat, Naama, El Bayadh, Béchar, Ouargla, Ghardaia, El Oued, and Biskra.

A salary supplement is calculated as a percentage of the employee's basic salary: 10–20 percent for primary school principals and secondary school teachers, 20–50 percent for senior civil service administrators, and 100–120 percent for specialist doctors and university teachers.

The initiative has been most successful for primary school principals, secondary school teachers, and administrators. The targeted regions are now able to fill these posts with relatively little difficulty. Their medical specialist and university teacher vacancies, however, are proving harder to fill, despite the high salary supplementation on offer. Quality of life considerations seem to be the main constraint.

Source: Khelladi 2009.

work in their home communities could help overcome spatial biases in teacher careers, and would have the added benefit of increasing the numbers of female teachers and students (Golnar 1995).

School Development Initiatives (SDIs) are development plans managed at the school level by school boards, teachers, and parents. They have demonstrated great potential as an instrument for improving education quality in targeted geographic areas.

SDIs owe their origin to the Anglo-Saxon and Nordic tradition of school boards or committees, representative of parents and the community, taking an active role in the management of schools. In the United States, for example, many school boards play a part in selecting school principals, teachers, and even books. In developing countries, concerns over the ability of central ministries to manage local expenditures have led to the delegation of spending oversight to parents, teachers, and communities. This change created opportunities for spatially targeted grants to schools with unmet needs.

Of course, the introduction of the SDI approach requires a sound institutional platform. It relies on the capacity and motivation of the local school governance committee. School grant programs require fraud-resistant operational and financial management procedures. SDIs also presuppose that school principals have the skills and motivation to act as leaders in the community, not just as the most senior teacher. The SDI model, therefore, requires pragmatic awareness of the risks involved in countries where school governance remains centralized (for example, Egypt) or subject to the influence of local elites (for example, the Republic of Yemen).

In Jordan, a National School Development Plan (NDSP) has been launched, in line with the SDI approach. Teachers and parents will evaluate their schools, identifying strengths and weaknesses, and draw up development plans incorporating specific measures—new teaching profiles, better equipment, more books, or changes in school activities. They will receive and expend funds, with oversight by parent-teacher associations and community representatives. The goal is also to improve retention. (Currently, 30 percent of students drop out before grade 12.) In Morocco, the School Quality Initiative, which is based on school management committees ("conseils de gestion"), is another exciting development.

Reducing Spatial Disparities through Demand-Side Interventions

As we saw earlier, the low economic status of children in lagging areas may be more of an obstacle to lagging areas' educational attainment than disparities in educational service supply. Poorer households are least able to afford the direct costs of education (fees, uniforms, books, transport, and so on) and the opportunity cost of the child's labor time. One strategy for reducing spatial disparities in education is, therefore, to intervene on the demand side, making it economically more attractive for families to keep their children, and especially their girls, in school.

In conditional cash transfer (CCT) programs, the transfer of a welfare benefit depends upon the receiver's actions. Requirements may involve enrolling children in public education. Unlike many welfare programs, CCTs' impact has been rigorously evaluated through experimental or quasi-experimental methods. There is considerable evidence that CCTs have been an effective way of redistributing income to the poor (Fiszbein and Schady 2009).

CCT programs have potential as an instrument of spatial education policy. Geographic targeting is a common feature (Rawlings and Rubio 2005). Mexico constructs a "marginality index" from census data to identify which communities will participate. In Honduras, beneficiary communities are identified from a census of the height-for-age of first-grade schoolchildren. In Nicaragua, departments and municipalities with the highest poverty incidence are included. In Colombia, the geographic targeting focuses on city status, with cities under 100,000 being selected and department capitals being excluded.

The education components of CCT programs address demand-side obstacles to education by contributing toward the costs of sending a child to school. In Mexico, Honduras, and Turkey, governments have allowed for the opportunity cost of the child's labor as well as the direct cost of fees, school supplies, and travel. In Colombia and Mexico, the grants are higher for secondary-school children than for primary-school children, reflecting the fact that older children are more productive as workers.

CCT programs' positive impacts upon education enrollment have been clear. In Mexico, the program led to an increase in primary-school enrollment ranging from 0.7 to 1.1 percentage points for boys and from 1.0 to 1.5 percentage points for girls. The impacts at secondary level were much bigger, ranging from 3.5 to 5.8 percentage points for boys and from 7.2 to 9.3 percentage points for girls. Colombia's program raised secondary-school enrollment rates by 5.5 percentage points in rural areas and 14 percentage points in urban areas. The Nicaraguan scheme led to improved attendance, with a 30 percent increase in the share of children with fewer than six unexcused absences in a two-month period.

The government of Morocco has launched a pilot CCT to encourage school attendance. It involves 266 rural schools with 88,000 children, serving 49,000 households. The high level of participation is due to the government's strong communications effort. Children's attendance at school is verified through fingerprint recorders. Households receive a check either through their local post office or by postal delivery to the primary school. A mobile team of monitors ("vérificateurs") double-checks attendance. There have been start-up problems: incorrect household registration data, delays in implementation of the Management Information System, and delays in providing the monitors with training and transport. However, these problems are being resolved, and there is already anecdotal evidence that the program is having a positive impact upon the retention of rural girls.

Reducing Gender Disparities in Education in Lagging Areas

"The fact that we don't have a high school in Tanougha has hampered the education of girls, because their parents are not willing to send them, via bus, to the neighbouring village. The girls would indeed have to walk back home after 6 p.m., since the bus is very old and often breaks down."
—Mothers of Ait Hammi (quoted in World Bank 2007a)

As we have seen, the effects of gender disparities and spatial disparities combine to create especially wide gender gaps in lagging areas. In Morocco, for example, the gender gap for literacy is 5 percentage points in urban areas and a staggering 35 percentage points in rural areas. Many causes of the gender gap in education are linked to social constraints on girls' mobility. In low-density rural areas, long distances from home to school and the lack of transportation are known to be a particular impediment to the girls of Algeria, Egypt, the Islamic Republic of Iran, Iraq, and Tunisia. In Upper Egypt, at least half the secondary schools are more than two kilometers from their catchment villages, with a negative impact on girls' attendance. (Upper Egypt accounts for 65 percent of girls dropping out of education.) In the Islamic Republic of Iran, the lack of boarding facilities discourages the enrollment of girls from nomadic families. The absence of upper elementary classes in remote villages has a specific impact on girls, if they are not allowed to continue schooling away from home. Living conditions in lagging areas may be particularly unacceptable to female teachers. The cultural isolation of rural areas and the shortage of educated mothers and other female role models may lead parents to be especially dismissive of the value of girls' education. Children from ethnic minorities in peripheral areas may not be fully familiar with the language of instruction. Finally, the school calendar in many MENA economies matches the rhythm of life in the cities, without reflecting the agricultural cycle and other demands for female labor (Golnar 1995).

Reducing spatial disparities in girls' education will remove one of the causes of spatial disparities in fertility rates. Reducing spatial disparities in fertility rates will, in turn, reduce spatial disparities in dependency ratios, which, as we have seen, are one of the prime causes of spatial dis-parities in well-being.

Figure 4.11 shows how education and location affect women's fertility rates in Egypt. In the poorer governorates of Upper Egypt, such as Assiut, Sohag, Fayoum, and Menia, the difference between illiteracy and secondary-school completion is associated with a reduction in the total fertility rate of 1.5 children per woman. It is also worth noting that the returns to this level of education in terms of fertility reduction (the gap between the top line and the fourth line) is around twice as high in these lagging governorates of Upper Egypt as in the leading governorates of the country.

One can compare the total fertility rate (TFR) of lagging Fayoum in Upper Egypt with better-off Ismailia in Lower Egypt, on the west bank of the Suez Canal. The TFR in Fayoum is 0.96 higher than in Ismailia, meaning that Fayoum's women are expected to have, on average, approx-imately one more child during their lifetime than the women of Ismailia. Using the data in figure 4.11, however, one can estimate that the spatial fertility gap between Ismailia and Fayoum could have been reduced to

FIGURE 4.11

Women's Education Reduces Fertility Rates in the Arab Republic of Egypt

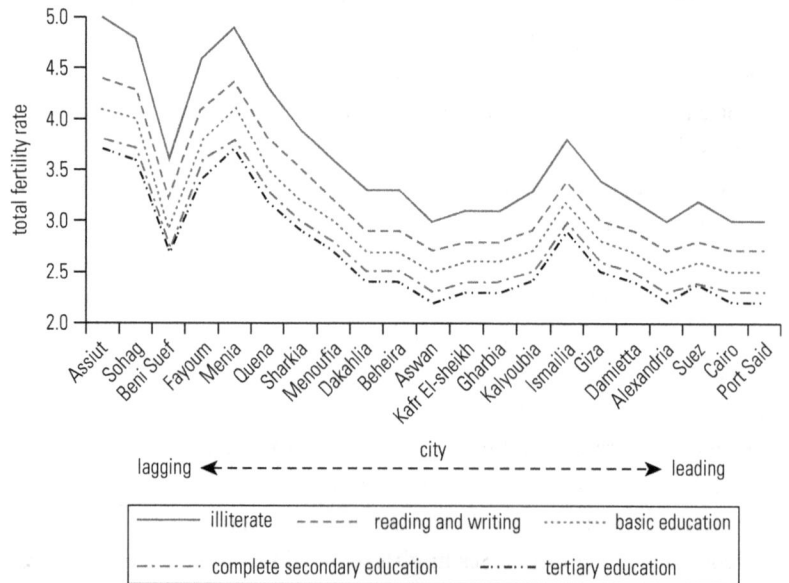

Sources: Goujon, Alkitkat, Lutz, and Prommer 2007; UNDP 2005.

0.65 if Fayoum's women of childbearing age had the same level of education as Ismailia's.

The key policy principle for tackling spatial-cum-gender disparities in education is that any intervention aimed at spatial disparities should be made with girls' distinct needs in mind:

- In the Republic of Yemen, the human resource management agenda is gender-specific: the Girls' Secondary Education Project will subsidize transport costs for woman teachers.

- CCT programs can be designed to provide families with special incentives to keep girls in school. In Mexico, grants at the secondary level are higher for girls, to take account of women's role in passing on human capital to the next generation (Rawlings and Rubio 2005). In the Republic of Yemen, the Girls' Secondary Education Project plans to increase girls' retention rates by providing CCTs to families with girls in grades 4 to 12, inclusive.

- The spatial planning of public investment in education can reflect girls' educational needs. Standard distances between schools and residences should take account of social limitations on girls' mobility. Schools should be provided with adequate water and sanitation, which are a major factor in determining girls' attendance. Information technology can be used to mitigate limitations on the mobility of female students and teachers. Although the evidence suggests that boys tend to monopolize computers in schools at the expense of girls, there are successful examples of computer-based learning programs specifically targeted at girls and women (Huyer, Hafkin, Ertl, and Dryburgh 2005). The Republic of Yemen's Girls Secondary Education Project allows the best women teachers to reach out to selected project schools through videoconferencing and e-mail to provide personal instruction.

Bringing dropped-out girls back into education may require nontraditional approaches. Field studies report the sense of "sadness, anxiety, boredom, and uselessness" felt by girls who have dropped out of education (Golnar 1995). Complementary programs can be designed to help girls who have dropped out of formal education to return to basic education or skills training. In Bangladesh, the nongovernmental organization (NGO) BRAC pioneered this approach, renting houses, courtyards, and storefronts as improvised schools. It has been suggested that women's training annexes could be added to primary schools in the Republic of Yemen, which was the practice in France in the nineteenth and early twentieth centuries. The "Bridge School" approach, which has proved successful in India, creates a pathway for girls to transition back into mainstream public education.

Using Spatial Planning Techniques to Improve the
Spatial Efficiency of Infrastructure

The race to achieve the Millennium Development Goal of full primary-level completion has given strong emphasis to school construction across the MENA region; however, insufficient attention has been given to spatial planning.

- As the goal of universal primary enrollment and completion comes close to being achieved, the focus of attention is shifting from primary to secondary and from lower secondary to upper secondary. Secondary schools are significantly more expensive than primary schools, and they must be in full use for 30 years to amortize their cost. Moreover, secondary schools are fewer in number than primary schools, so distance from home to class has an even greater impact upon enrollments and retention. Therefore, deciding where to put secondary schools is an increasingly important spatial policy issue.

- Population distributions are changing rapidly with urbanization and the spread of the demographic transition from leading to lagging areas. The Republic of Yemen, for example, has the second-highest total fertility rate in the world, the fastest growing city in the world, Sana'a (*Economist* 2005), and a shift in the demographic center of gravity from the highlands toward the coastal cities. The spatial allocation of education assets therefore has to reflect not only the current needs but also the demography of future decades.

- There are powerful and user-friendly Geographical Information Systems (GIS), which enable the optimization of school catchment areas with respect to population trends.

For example, the Republic of Yemen faces a number of spatial imbalances in education. Twenty-five percent of rural schools had fewer teachers than the prescribed minimum, while about 205 urban schools had overcrowded classes in the "unmanageable" range of 70–150 children per class. Only 21 percent of secondary schools met the minimum school size of 180 students specified by the Ministry of Education. Consequently, there were not enough classes for the full range of subjects to be taught; only half the schools had a science stream. Therefore, the government is planning for future needs using GIS. An assessment of all existing first-level schools (grades 1–6) identified their physical condition and the needs for maintenance, renovation, or reconstruction. The survey also identified the potential for building additional classrooms on the current site. The assessment of building requirements took account of projected growth of the population ages 6 to 14, by village. Geo-referenced GIS maps were developed for potential new school sites and for catchment areas, based on the estimated number of children within a 2-kilometer radius of each potential location, and adjusting distances for the difficulty of terrain as measured by slope.

Despite Egypt's high population densities, there are significant spatial inequalities in access to educational infrastructure. A study of mother villages and satellite villages in the governorate of Sohag revealed that while one satellite village had a complete basic education school (grades 1–9), children in another village had to travel 2 kilometers. In the case of one satellite village, the nearest secondary school (grades 10–12) was 5 kilometers away, while it was 10 kilometers away in another. Fortunately, the General Authority for Education Buildings (GAEB) now has the tools to analyze the situation in the form of a georeferenced GIS database of all schools in Egypt. It has the technical capacity to rationalize the catchment areas of upper basic and secondary schools, taking into account population trends, before any major new construction program is undertaken.

Jordan is another illustration of the potential benefits of a spatially based planning approach for education. The country suffers from a serious spatial disequilibrium in the distribution of basic and secondary schools. The current school map results in high maintenance costs and low utilization rates. There is an excess capacity of 172,950 places affecting 59 percent of schools. Many recently constructed schools are located in catchment areas with excess capacity, sometimes within 1 kilometer of another school. At the same time, many schools lack the specialized classrooms and workshops required to deliver instruction in subjects such as science, technology, computing, and the arts. Despite the construction of new facilities, there is a US$36.4 million backlog of expenditure on existing schools, which has led to 42 schools being declared "unsafe." A GIS mapping exercise, along the lines conducted for basic education in the Republic of Yemen, could develop maps of current catchment areas, their "overlap" and likely demographic trends. This exercise would make it possible to identify which schools should be consolidated, which should be expanded, which should be split, and which should be provided with temporary shelter.

Morocco provides a similar example of spatial imbalance in which a GIS map of primary education could provide efficiency savings. While enrollments are mainly concentrated in the 12 northern provinces, many schools in mountainous areas and the south do not have their full complement of students, leaving them with less than the full six primary grades. This lack of students creates problems for families in poorer areas, who may have to split their children between two schools or face long journeys to school. GIS analysis of catchment area populations and travel times could inform decisions on whether to expand, relocate, or consolidate such schools. GIS approaches could also be used to assist decisions on the construction or consolidation of lower secondary schools and "collèges de proximité." GIS could provide a rational basis for deciding whether new education facilities or providing transport to school is the most cost-efficient solution for improving access to secondary education.

Information and communications technology (ICT) has the potential to be a "spatial equalizer," abolishing the handicaps of distance experienced by students in low-density, lagging areas (box 4.5). School principals and teachers can obtain quality, standardized curricula, model lessons, advice, and in-service training. ICT can also deliver exams and standardized tests with integrity and efficiency.

BOX 4.5

Leveling Spatial Disparities in Education: Nine Ideas for Policy Makers

- Closing the spatial gap in education is a paramount strategy for reducing spatial disparities in development.

- Analyzing subnational education indicators to diagnose the causes of spatial disparities in education. Building more schools in lagging areas is not always the answer. Many existing facilities in low-density areas are underused. The quality of teaching and demand-side issues might be more of a problem for lagging areas than the number of schools.

- Using spatially targeted conditional cash transfers to encourage lagging-area parents to keep their children in school.

- Systematizing the arrangements for teacher postings so that more good, experienced teachers go to lagging-area schools.

- Identifying why experienced teachers do not want postings in lagging areas and putting incentives in place—for example, salary supplementation, career advantages, housing, and transport.

- Recruiting teachers locally for lagging areas.

- Making girls and women teachers a priority in all strategies to address spatial disparities in education.

- Using GIS technology and population projections to improve the spatial efficiency of school infrastructure.

- Using ICT to improve teaching and curriculum quality in lagging area schools.

Source: Study Team.

- In Egypt, the Ministries of Education (MoE) and Communications and Information Technology (MCIT) have launched the Egyptian Education Initiative (EEI). The EEI is a public-private partnership between government, the World Economic Forum's ICT member community, and various multinational corporations. It has two "tracks." The pre-university track aims to build capacity of administrators and teachers and improve the delivery of teaching materials. The MCIT plans to use fiber optics and high-speed satellite connections to address locational disadvantages by bringing these services into mother and satellite villages. The higher education track goes one step further, creating electronic content for students in English, information technology, the sciences, and "survival skills" (personal health, basic finance, and statistics). The higher education track also encompasses the development of new management information systems (accreditation and evaluation, personnel management, program budgeting, and infrastructure management).

- The Jordan Education Initiative (JEI) is a similar public-private partnership, involving Cisco and Intel and the networking of schools and universities. The JEI aims to deploy a new outcomes-based grade 1–12 curriculum, supported by online capacity building for teachers and principals.

- In March 2005, the Moroccan Ministry of Education adopted a strategy of generalizing ICT to all public schools by 2008, with the aim of improving the quality of teaching. ICT is to be used to deliver teacher training and improved curricula. The program includes the creation of a national laboratory for curriculum development and a national education Internet portal. The portal will offer teachers access to educational resources, a virtual library, discussion forums, a search engine, and e-mail. The overall program comes at a total cost of around $11 million.

Health: Correcting Spatial Disparities in Access to Care

Geographical differences in health status are both direct and indirect concerns for policy makers: MENA13 governments are spending an average of 3.3 percent of GDP on health services, and the impact of this spending in terms of health status should not depend on where a person lives. But spatial disparities in health also have important indirect policy significance. They can encourage migration from peripheral areas to towns in search of better health and social services (Lall, Timmins, and Yu 2009).

In addition, poor access to health services in lagging areas can contribute to high fertility rates, and thus to high dependency ratios and poverty.

Moreover, the performance of health systems in the MENA region will increasingly be measured in terms of their ability to reduce disparities. As the coverage levels for basic health services approach 100 percent, it will be possible to raise national health indicators only by targeting the worst off.

Health Services and Health Outcomes in Poor Places

There are large spatial disparities within MENA economies in terms of (1) their distribution of *resources* for health care, (2) their populations' *access* to and use of health services, and (3) health *outcomes* (see table 4.7).

There is a concentration of health care personnel in urban areas, predominately in capital cities. Metropolitan areas are likely to offer higher wages, better living conditions, and greater opportunities for professional development than rural areas. In Libya, there are 340 physicians per 100,000 people in the capital city of Tripoli, compared to 96 per 100,000 in the rest of the country as a whole, or a mere 54 per 100,000 in the district of Joufara.[5] In Lebanon, the density of physicians in Beirut is three times higher than that of the Beqaa province.[6] Of Djibouti the World Health Organization reports, "[M]ost doctors and state-accredited or senior health technicians reside in the capital . . . which exacerbates the disparities in health services between the city and inland districts."[7] In the Republic of Yemen, 16 percent of health personnel service Aden City, and 15 percent service the capital Sana'a, while these governorates represent only 3 percent and 8 percent of the total population, respectively.[8] The concentration of physicians in Iraq ranges from 93 per 100,000 people in the capital of Baghdad to 67 in the large city of Basra to 31 in the smaller city of Nassiriya.[9]

The distribution of health care facilities, however, tends to follow the opposite pattern: there are more facilities per capita in low-density areas. This pattern may be due to policy makers' desire to make facilities geographically accessible to all citizens. Data from 2001 indicate that in Jordan, the number of hospital beds per capita ranged from 5 per 10,000 persons in the capital of Amman to 12 in the sparsely populated rural governorate of Ma'an.[10] The distribution of primary health centers in Libya follows a similar pattern, with the lowest numbers per capita in the biggest cities of Tripoli and Benghazi.[11]

Putting these two trends together, one would be right to suppose that rural facilities have fewer staff members and are less used than those in cities. For instance, Tunisia has achieved a fairly even geographic distribution of primary health centers (PHCs), but the individual facilities demonstrate striking differences in productivity. Facilities in the southeast region of the country record an annual average of about two-thirds fewer visits than those in the capital of Tunis.[12] In other cases, rural facilities may not be able to offer certain services at all. In Morocco, most of the primary health facilities (known there as *établissements de soins de santé de base*—ESSBs) are not staffed by physicians, and more than 10 percent of those that were on the books in 2004 closed because of a lack of any trained personnel at all.[13] Data from 2002 in Morocco indicate that public health centers in the urban regions achieved 0.6 consultations per capita per annum, compared to just 0.3 in rural areas.[14] In the Republic of Yemen, while geographic access to health facilities is reported to have improved slightly since 1990, access to a *functioning* facility is thought to be much lower because of chronic shortages of resources and a lack of trained personnel in rural facilities.[15] There, the 8 percent of national health expenditure contributed by donors is used almost exclusively for capital projects, which may further aggravate the imbalance between structures and the personnel and equipment needed to make them function.[16]

A number of demand-side constraints reduce use of health services in poor areas—notably, limited insurance coverage. MENA's health insurance systems tend to focus on wealthier urban residents. In Egypt, where health insurance coverage exhibits a strong association with income (80 percent of insured women are in the two wealthiest quintiles, and the ratio of the number of insured in the wealthiest quintile to the poorest is greater than 100 to 1), the prevalence of coverage is about two times as high in urban areas as it is in rural ones.[17] The more urbanized *mohafazas* (administrative units) in Lebanon—Beirut and Mount Lebanon—report insurance coverage of 60 percent and 54 percent, respectively, while the other *mohafazas* hover at around 34 percent coverage.[18]

Of course, indicators of utilization do not take into account possible differences in the underlying burden of disease and, therefore, cannot serve alone as a measure of satisfied need. For this, we must look at spatial disparities on services for which there is a consistent need in different places, such as the availability of clean drinking water and effective sanitation facilities, and the proportion of births preceded by appropriate antenatal care and delivered by skilled attendants. These variables have been documented extensively in national surveys across the majority of the countries in the MENA region.

- Rural-urban disparities in access to improved potable *water* supplies usually fall with higher levels of national income. MENA's rural-urban water supply gaps tend to be low by world standards, but Morocco and Iraq have anomalously large gaps for their level of development (figure 4.12). Yemen has a very high sanitation gap (figure 4.13).

FIGURE 4.12

Unusually High Urban-Rural Gaps in Access to Potable Water in Morocco and Iraq

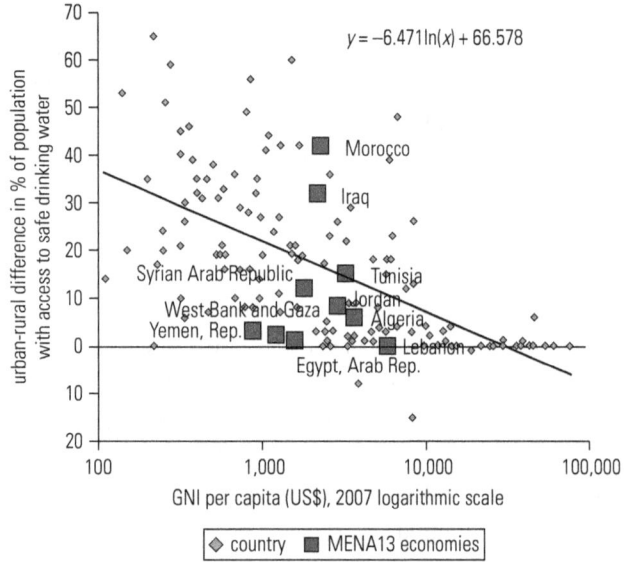

Source: WDI; UNICEF 2009.

- In terms of utilization of key services to protect child health, such as antenatal care, skilled attendance during delivery, and immunization against infectious disease, there are significant disparities between urban and rural populations across the MENA economies. There is a general pattern of diminishing inequality at higher levels of national income, although Morocco and Egypt both exhibit dispro- portionate inequalities compared with other countries of their level of GDP. The Islamic Republic of Iran is an outlier in the other direc- tion, having reduced the number of women who give birth without skilled attendance 3.5-fold between the late 1990s and the 2000s, with a particularly profound effect on the rural areas (Movahedi and others 2009). Disparities in the proportion of children who are fully vaccinated are typically smaller than those for antenatal care or skilled birth attendance, which may be a result of strong international support for immunization activities and a particular focus on rural areas. In the Republic of Yemen, where such disparities do exist, three-quarters of parents with unvaccinated children reported that distance prevented them from reaching the necessary services.[19]

- MENA economies' rural-urban gap in infant mortality rates (IMRs) fall in the same range as those exhibited by rural and urban populations

FIGURE 4.13

Rural-Urban Disparities in Sanitation Coverage

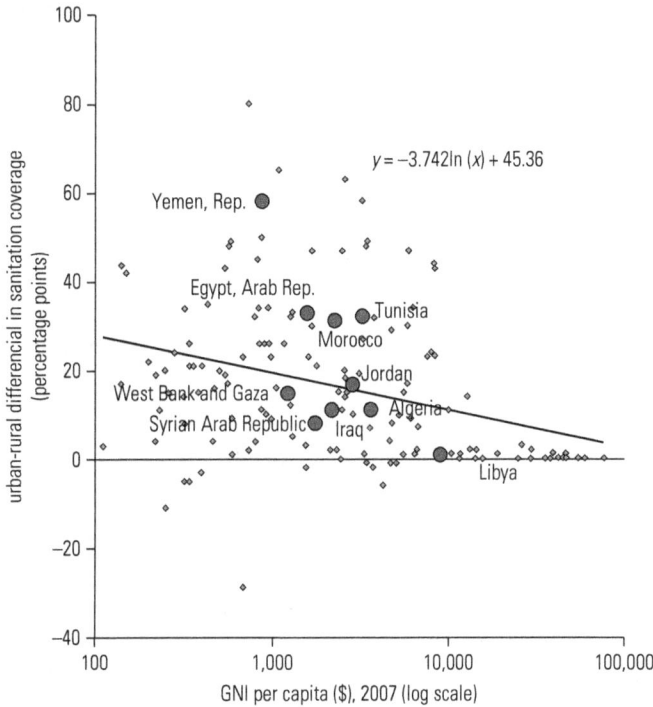

Source: WDI.

Note: GNI = gross national income.

in other countries of similar size and economic status, such as Colombia, Peru, Ukraine, and the Philippines. Most striking, however, is the large absolute difference in infant and maternal mortality rates between the urban and rural populations of Morocco. Judging from the limited amount of longitudinal data available, urban-rural disparities have not been reduced significantly during the past 20 years. In Morocco, although IMR has fallen in both rural and urban populations, the absolute disparity between them has remained largely the same. In Jordan, the disparity widened in the early 1990s and narrowed again after 2000. In the Republic of Yemen, the disparity has grown, doubling in size between 1990 and 2006. Egypt is the exception, having narrowed the gap between IMR in urban and rural populations from more than 50 deaths per 1,000 live births to less than 15.

- In some countries, pockets of bad health indicators are very localized. In Lebanon, 80 percent of infants in Beirut were immunized with the measles, mumps, and rubella (MMR) vaccine, but only 27 percent in the Bekaa. In Tunisia, Kasserine and Sidi Bouzid have not shared in the rest of the country's increased rate of skilled deliveries. In Jordan, under-five mortality rates are 10 percent in Zarqa and 39 percent in Karak. In Morocco, the reduction of the rural-urban gap in maternal mortality between 2000 and 2006 was mostly due to gains in rural areas bordering the Atlantic, while many rural and mountainous regions in west-central Morocco continue to lag behind (Ministère de la Santé 2003, 2007).

Bringing Better Health to Lagging Areas: Not More of the Same

What can MENA governments do to reduce the health status divide between leading and lagging areas?

It is important to recognize the limits of a "copy and paste" strategy based upon the replication of health facility infrastructure. Health facilities in low-density areas often already have low utilization rates and suffer from a lack of qualified personnel and nonstaff recurrent funding. Therefore, the key is to improve the quality of health service delivery. To achieve this means finding service-delivery mechanisms that fit the specific needs of poor or low-density areas (see box 4.6).

When it comes to strengthening public health delivery facilities in lagging areas, successful interventions have focused on *staff incentives and nonstaff recurrent funding*. It is critical to ensure that health personnel are motivated to provide quality services in lagging areas despite the better professional opportunities and quality of life in richer places. Morocco's Integrated Management of Childhood Illnesses (IMCI) program, for example, explicitly focused on the question of staff motivation, with training and free housing for personnel in lagging areas. An evaluation of IMCI found that it had doubled the number of correct antibiotic pre-scriptions, with similar results found in Egypt, Tanzania, Uganda, and Brazil (WHO and DFID 2003). The Social Priorities Program Basic Health Project in Morocco, which targeted facility, equipment, and medication supply rehabilitation and the establishment of lodging facilities for health personnel in the 14 most disadvantaged and least urbanized provinces, was associated with a 150 percent higher rate of medically assisted deliveries over approximately five years (18.5 to 47 percent) (World Bank 2004b).

Spatially adapted delivery systems have proved their cost-effectiveness for low-density areas. The Islamic Republic of Iran has trained local *behvarz* (health workers) to provide family planning and reproductive health care (Sadrizadeh 2004). As a result, service coverage in rural areas has increased from nearly 40 to 90 percent in 15 years (1985–2001). In the Republic of Yemen, community empowerment strategies in early childhood development have proved particularly cost-effective in tackling nutrition in children under five. The Child Development Project (2000–05) involved the organization and mobilization of community-level committees to oversee health training, water distribution, and educational access, and was associated with an improved enrollment rate for primary school girls by 20 percentage points and an increase in access to safe drinking water by 17 percent over five years (World Bank 2006c).

With spatially adapted delivery systems for potable water and sanitation, serving low-density areas does not have to be expensive and institutionally complex. The Egyptian government's Integrated Sanitation and Sewerage and Infrastructure Project (ISSIP) recognized the limitations of extending the urban network architecture into rural areas. Client villages were, therefore, clustered around hydraulic subbasins instead of administrative boundaries, natural dilution was substituted for secondary treatment and decentralized or on-site systems replaced centralized systems, allowing the project to provide connections at a low average capital cost of $140 per inhabitant (Soliman and others 2009). In rural areas of the Republic of Yemen, community ownership and management of piped water services has led to an increase in connection rates and increased consumer satisfaction (Dasgupta, Meisner, Makokha, and Pollard 2009).

Understanding and addressing the demand-side constraints on health service use in poor areas can assist the design of interventions. As for education, a multitude of nonhealth demand-side factors may be limiting the expansion of health services in lagging areas. In the Islamic Republic of Iran, household economic status and mothers' education together explain more than half the variation in the infant mortality rate. Strategies that aim to expand education, transportation, nutrition, water, sanitation, and incomes in lagging areas may have a bigger payoff in terms of spatial disparities in health outcomes than a simple emphasis on the stock of health facilities (CSDH 2008). International evidence sheds light on the important role that improved educational level, social status, and women's welfare have played in countries as disparate as Singapore (World Bank 2009a), Sri Lanka, Costa Rica, and the United Kingdom.[20] Demand-side interventions, therefore, have helped improve the health status of lagging areas' populations.

Successful demand-side interventions have focused on the two pillars of demand: awareness and affordability.

On the awareness side, Egypt's World Bank–funded Population Project managed to expand the provision of family planning services through demand-creation; Social Change Agents raised women's confidence and awareness; and income-generation activities empowered women with their own resources to attend family planning services. The project targeted the lagging area of Upper Egypt, and its demand-side approach succeeded in raising the contraceptive prevalence rate from 18 percent to 37 percent in five years in the target zone, quadrupling attendance at family planning clinics (World Bank 2005h). This was no small-scale pilot project: the Social Change Agents made 3.5 million visits to 230,000 women during the life of the project (Georgetown University 2007). The women saw the Social Change Agents as a "picture of success and respect," which encouraged them to attend health education, public meetings, and adult education. Similarly, the Islamic Republic of Iran's *behvarz* community midwives have helped close rural-urban health disparities by encouraging women to seek formal health services (Aghajanian, Mehryar, Ahmadnia, and Kazemipour 2008).

On the affordability side, expanding insurance schemes into poor areas encourages public and private providers to deliver appropriate forms of care by stimulating demand. In the Islamic Republic of Iran during the past decade, the government has extended insurance to both the urban and rural uninsured. The result of this policy has been to raise rural insurance coverage from 33 percent to more than 76 percent between 2001 and 2006, eliminating what had been a large disparity between the prevalence of coverage in urban and rural areas.[21]

Improved management information systems help health departments to ensure an efficient spatial targeting of resources. The Islamic Republic of Iran's "master plan" approach to health care planning, involving infrastructure development by assessing the number and locations of all levels of health facilities at the district level, has improved the distribution of resources as well as the monitoring of health status progress geographically. In the West Bank and Gaza, the unification of information systems from the Governmental Health Insurance bureaus resulted in a more accessible and transparent beneficiary registry. Together with quality improvement standards and guideline development, these improved information technology systems were associated with an increased procurement, delivery, and availability of pharmaceuticals in lagging areas; an increase of 30 percent in the utilization rates of rehabilitated facilities; and a nearly sevenfold improvement in diabetes management indicators (World Bank 2005g).

The Better Social Safety Nets Are Targeted, the Better Spatial Disparities Are Mitigated

Social Safety Net programs can have a spatial significance. Where spatial pockets of poverty exist, these programs, if well targeted, can be a weapon

---

BOX 4.6

Leveling Spatial Disparities in Health: Four Ideas for Policy Makers

- Analyzing the causes of spatial disparities in health outcomes, to find out whether the root cause lies in socioeconomic inequalities, the quality of service, or physical access to health facilities.

- Implementing information systems for the monitoring of health care activities and the efficient spatial allocation of resources.

- Designing packages of staff incentives and nonstaff recurrent funding for health facilities in lagging areas.

- Investigating nonconventional models for the delivery of health care, potable water, and sanitation services in low-density lagging areas.

Source: Study Team.

---

in government armories to reduce spatial disparities (see box 4.7). If they are poorly targeted, however, they can reinforce the rift between rich and poor places.

Social Safety Nets Are an Instrument of Spatial Policy— For Better or for Worse

Many MENA economies have some kind of Social Safety Net (SSN) program: an arrangement for resource transfers intended to improve social welfare (table 4.8). SSNs can play an important role in reducing poverty and vulnerability to shocks.

SSN approaches range from direct cash and in-kind transfers, food distribution programs, public works, and conditional cash transfers (CCTs) to commodity subsidies, which are usually applied to energy and food. SSNs can be categorized into direct and indirect transfers. Direct transfers include cash transfers (conditional and nonconditional), in-kind transfers, as well as social (noncontributory) pensions, and public works programs. Indirect transfers include commodity subsidies as well as assistance and waiver programs. Social safety nets have multiple goals that differ by program and political motivation. In times of crisis, they aim

TABLE 4.7

Indicators of Rural-Urban Disparities in Health

	Algeria	Djibouti	Egypt, Arab Rep.	Iran, Islamic Rep.	Iraq	Jordan	Lebanon	Libya	Morocco	West Bank and Gaza	Syrian Arab Republic	Tunisia	Yemen, Rep.
Total health expenditure (% of GDP)	3.60%	6.70%	6.30%	7.80%	3.80%	9.90%	8.90%	2.90%	5.10%	—	3.90%	5.30%	4.60%
Government expenditure on health (% of GDP 2004)	2.60%	4.40%	2.20%	3.20%	—	4.70%	3.20%	2.80%	1.70%	7.80%	2.20%	2.80%	2.20%
Private expenditure on health (% of total)	23%	25%	59%	44%	28%	58%	53%	30%	64%	—	52%	56%	54%
Contraceptive prevalence modern methods (% urban)	52%	18%	60%	55%	36%	43%	—	54%	56%	—	48%	53%	34%
Contraceptive prevalence modern methods (% rural)	52%	4%	54%	57%	27%	36%	—	46%	53%	—	35%	54%	13%
Total fertility rate (urban)	2.19	4.1	2.7	1.8	4	3.6	—	3.8	2.1	4.4	3.4	2.46	4.5
Total fertility rate (rural)	2.38	4.9	3.4	2.4	5.1	3.7	—	4.9	3	4.4	4.4	3.29	6.7
Access to improved drinking water (% urban)	88%	98%	99%	97%	92%	98%	100%	98%	98%	91%	94%	99%	74%
Access to improved drinking water (% rural)	82%	54%	97%	86%	57%	94%	100%	99%	57%	90%	80%	84%	52%
Access to improved sanitation (% urban)	98%	70%	85%	86%	98%	92%	100%	99%	98%	100%	100%	96%	92%
Access to improved sanitation (% rural)	87%	19%	52%	78%	82%	76%	87%	98%	58%	93%	94%	64%	34%

Indicator													
Utilization of antenatal care (% urban)	94%	82%	82%	96%	90%	99%	—	—	68%	99%	90%	75%	69%
Utilization of antenatal care (% rural)	85%	41%	62%	88%	75%	98%	—	—	48%	99%	78%	55%	38%
Utilization of skilled birth attendant (% urban)	98%	95%	89%	96%	86%	99%	—	96%	85%	99%	98%	98%	62%
Utilization of skilled birth attendant (% rural)	92%	40%	65%	90%	71%	97%	—	99%	40%	98%	88%	89%	26%
Children fully vaccinated by two years (% urban)	85%	—	89%	—	62%	94%	—	—	94%	95%	89%	96%	58%
Children fully vaccinated by two years (% rural)	89%	—	89%	—	41%	91%	—	—	84%	97%	87%	94%	29%
Infant mortality rate (urban)	33	68	31.7	27.7	35	20	—	21.4	33	26.8	16	16	55.3
Infant mortality rate (rural)	44	54	45.2	30.2	35	23	—	31.4	55	26.6	20	30	73.3
Stunting (% urban)	10%	32%	16%	11%	19%	12%	—	4%	13%	11%	22%	4%	44%
Stunting (% rural)	12%	44%	18%	22%	24%	13%	—	6%	24%	9%	23%	10%	56%
Under-five mortality rate (urban)	40	95	39.1	36.8	41	22	—	27.5	38	29.7	19	—	56.7
Under-five mortality rate (rural)	56	73	56.1	34.6	41	27	—	36.3	69	29.9	23	—	86.1

Sources: See Appendix.
Note: — = not available.

TABLE 4.8

Social Resource Transfers in MENA

	Direct transfers			Indirect transfers		
	Cash and in-kind transfers	Public works programs	Food distribution	Conditional cash transfers	Food subsidies	Energy subsidies
Djibouti	x					
Egypt, Arab Rep.	x	x	x		x	x
Iran, Islamic Rep.	x				x	x
Iraq	x	x	x			
Jordan	x				x	x
Lebanon			x		x	x
Morocco		x		x	x	x
Syrian Arab Republic		x			x	x
Tunisia	x	x	x		x	x
West Bank and Gaza	x	x	x	x		
Yemen, Rep.	x	x	x			

Source: Study Team, based on World Bank 2005a, 2005b, 2007c, 2007d. Countries included the Arab Republic of Egypt, Morocco, the Republic of Yemen, Jordan, the Syrian Arab Republic, the West Bank and Gaza, Iraq, the Islamic Republic of Iran, Djibouti, Tunisia, and Lebanon.

mainly at protecting poor households from economic shocks and, in particular, from decisions that may cause irreversible loss of human capital, such as malnutrition and dropping out of school. SSNs help reduce inequality and extreme poverty, enable households to make better decisions for the future, and help governments manage the social impacts of beneficial reforms (World Bank 2008d).

Commodity subsidies are by far the major SSN in MENA (figure 4.14). In the Republic of Yemen, energy and food subsidies account for almost 8 percent of GDP and are as high as the country's spending on health and education. Energy subsidies are the major subsidy expenditure item. Across the MENA region overall (including GCC economies) energy subsidies were averaging 7.1 percent of GDP (World Bank 2009b), even before the fuel price increases of 2008. For the MENA13, they ranged from Tunisia's 1.5 percent of GDP or 6 percent of government spending, to 12–18 percent of GDP and 30–50 percent of government spending in Algeria, Egypt, the Islamic Republic of Iran, Iraq, and the Syrian Arab Republic (World Bank 2009b).

There are, of course, several problems with SSNs that consist mainly of energy subsidies. They encourage the overuse and inefficient use of energy. They also amplify the impact of worldmarket price fluctuations on the balance of payments and the budget.

For policy makers concerned with spatial disparities, however, a major drawback of energy subsidies is that they are "regressive." This finding

FIGURE 4.14

Commodity Subsidies: A Big Slice of MENA's GDP

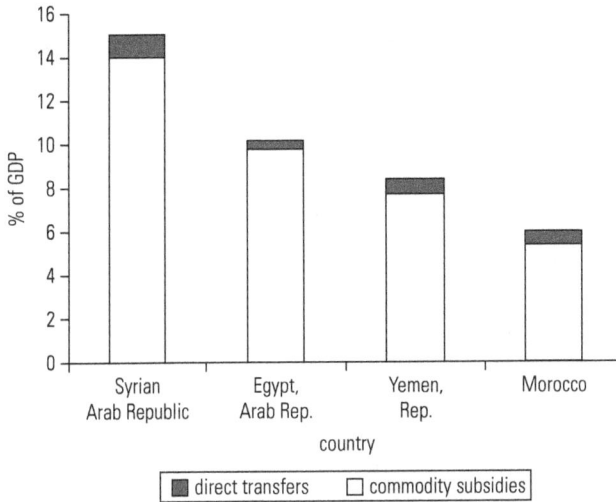

Source: World Bank 2009b.

means that the people who consume the most, the nonpoor, receive the lion's share of the subsidy.

- In Jordan, for example, only 7 percent of fuel subsidies reached the poorest quintile, while 44 percent went to the richest quintile (World Bank 2007d).

- Map 4.1 shows how the regressivity of fuel subsidies helps to widen spatial disparities, taking the example of Iraq. The residents of the low-poverty governorates of Baghdad and the north receive high per capita transfers through the subsidy mechanism, while the worse-off citizens of Kirkuk, Diala, Wasit, Missan, Thi-Qar, Basra, Karbala, An-Najaf, Al-Qadisiya, Babil, and Salahuddin receive a fraction of these amounts.

- Similarly in Egypt, where more than 6 percent of GDP is spent on fuel subsidies, the leading area city of Cairo alone has 58 percent of the country's private cars and, therefore, captures a disproportionate share of the benefits. The lagging governorates of Siwa, Assuit, and Menya, in contrast, have 16 percent of the population but only 3 percent of Egypt's cars between them (IDSC 2007).

Social security systems mostly consisting of mandatory pension and health insurance systems have a low coverage and tend to be focused on

MAP 4.1

Petroleum Product Subsidies Exacerbating Spatial Disparities in Iraq
(thousands of Iraqi dinars per person per month)

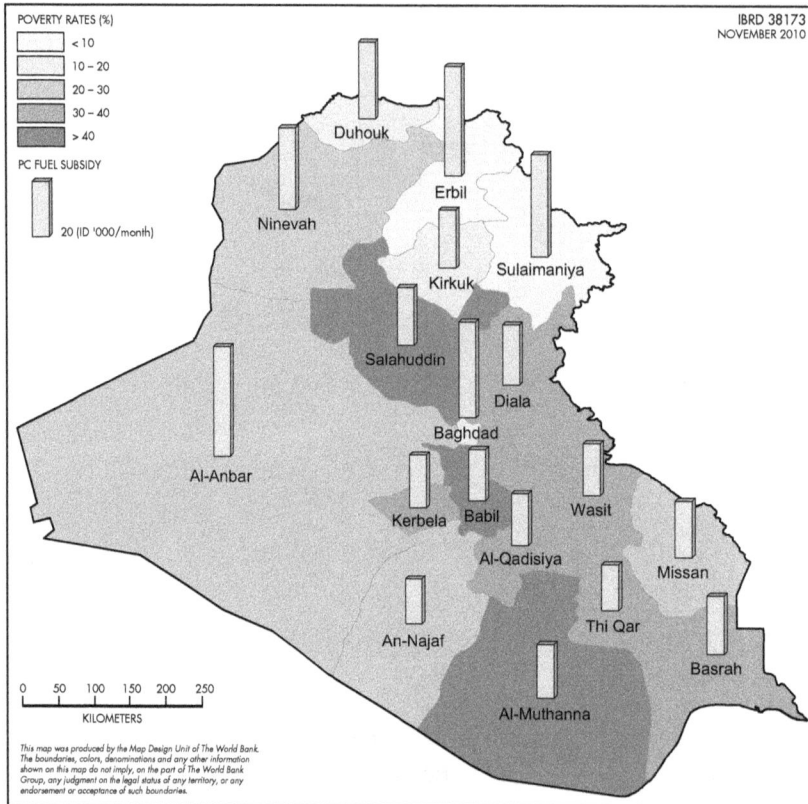

Source: Authors' calculations based on Iraq Household Socioeconomic Survey 2006–07 and World Bank 2009b.

Note: Calculations assume that the percentage of per capita fuel expenditure subsidized is constant across governorates.

high-income and public sector workers in metropolitan and urban areas. For MENA as a whole, they cover a modest 33 percent of the workforce, including a large share of public sector workers. They have very little redistributive effect and leave out vulnerable groups, in particular big shares of the rural population, the informal economy (which predominates in rural and lagging areas), and the elderly (who represent a higher share of the population in rural and lagging areas). In addition, no economy in the region offers genuine unemployment insurance.

Some transfer programs have, on the contrary, a proven positive effect on spatial disparities. Evidence indicates that *social funds* have the ability to target lagging areas effectively (table 4.9). These funds enable communities to identify and implement local investments, which could be in

TABLE 4.9

Most Social Funds Target Lagging Areas Well

Geographic Distribution of Social Fund Resources (%), 1991–99

Decile	Armenia	Bolivia	Honduras	Nicaragua	Peru	Zambia
1 (poorest)	10.7	10.8	14.5	14.7	25.3	9.8
2	13.2	13.6	10.7	14.4	21.2	10.6
3	12.4	15.2	11.4	12.8	19.2	14.9
4	12.0	13.0	9.0	11.4	12.3	8.6
5	9.4	11.0	10.0	10.6	8.3	8.6
6	5.7	11.9	10.4	10.7	4.9	13.5
7	5.7	8.0	8.0	8.3	3.2	8.4
8	6.9	7.6	5.0	6.9	3.0	10.6
9	10.1	6.0	15.1	5.5	1.9	6.4
10 (richest)	13.9	2.8	6.0	4.7	0.7	8.6

Source: Rawlings, Sherburne-Benz, and van Domelen 2004.

TABLE 4.10

Conditional Cash Transfers that Are Proven to Reduce Poverty

Poverty measure		Colombia		Honduras		Mexico			Nicaragua		
		2002	2006	2000	2002	1998	Jun-99	Oct-99	2000	2001	2002
Headcount	Control	0.95	0.9	0.88	0.91	0.89	0.93	0.94	0.84	0.91	0.9
Index	Impact	A	−0.03*	A	B	0.02**	−0.01**	0.00	A	−0.07**	−0.05**
Poverty Gap	Control	0.58	0.54	0.49	0.54	0.47	0.55	0.56	0.43	0.50	0.50
	Impact	A	−0.07**	A	−0.02*	0.01*	−0.03**	−0.02*	A	−0.03**	−0.09**
Squared Poverty	Control	0.53	0.43	0.30	0.36	0.28	0.35	0.36	0.26	0.32	0.32
Gap	Impact	A	−0.02**	A	−0.02*	B	−0.09**	−0.03*	A	−0.12	−0.09**

Source: Fiszbein and Schady 2009.

Note: A = Baseline, before households in CCT treatment groups received transfers; B = No significant impact on poverty measure; * = Significant at the 10 percent level; ** = Significant at the 5 percent level.

the field of health, education, infrastructure, or income-generating activities. Spatially targeted social funds in MENA include Morocco's Initiative Nationale de Développement Humain (INDH) and Egypt's 1,000 Villages program.

Conditional cash transfers (CCTs) are acquiring a successful track record (see table 4.10), confirming their potential as an instrument of spatial policy. They provide cash assistance to poor families, dependent on their behavior, such as keeping children in school or having them vaccinated. The cash reduces poverty directly, and indirectly improves human development by compensating beneficiaries for investing in their education and health. In several countries, CCTs were accompanied by detailed poverty maps, which facilitated high-resolution geographic targeting (Fiszbein and Schady 2009).

But in MENA, these positive examples of transfer programs are by no means prevalent. Effective SSNs fall short of the needs. CCT pilots have been put in place only in Morocco and the West Bank and Gaza (plans exist in the Syrian Arab Republic). Today, most transfer programs in MENA use categorical targeting approaches. This finding means that a household or individual is entitled to benefits if it falls into an eligible category, such as single mothers, widows, the unemployed, the elderly, the disabled, and so forth. Often, these categories are not synonymous with being poor and vulnerable. So many existing programs could contribute more to reducing spatial disparities if better targeted.

In the Republic of Yemen in 2005, for example, the Social Welfare Fund cash transfer program was reaching only 13 percent of the poor population. Of those who did receive cash transfers, 70 percent were not in the target group (Blomquist 2008). Figure 4.15 illustrates the spatial incidence of the recently introduced cash transfer program in Iraq. It is categorically targeted at certain groups of society, including the unemployed, the disabled, orphaned children, divorced or widowed women, and married male university students. Under this plan, household heads must initiate their own registration and provide their own documentation proving that they are poor enough to qualify. When one observes the spatial impact of the program, the correlation between governorates' poverty rates and SSN assistance rates is rather weak. For example, in Najaf, where the 23 percent poverty rate is slightly below the national average, 3.6 percent of the population is benefiting from the subsidy, while in Muthanna, where nearly half the inhabitants

FIGURE 4.15

Spatial Incidence of Cash Transfer Program, Iraq

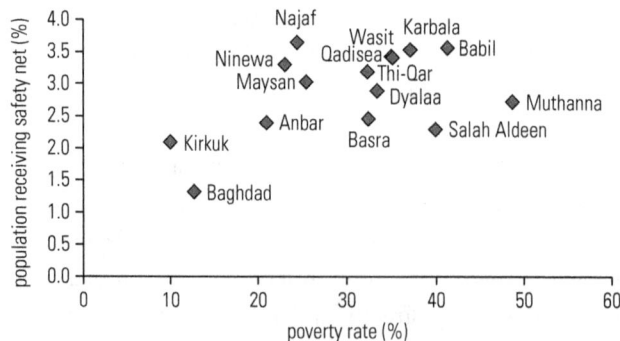

Source: Shlash 2009.

are below the poverty line, just 2.7 percent receive the cash transfer. The lower enrollment rates in Kirkuk and Baghdad, however, do reflect those governorates' lower poverty incidence.

Jordan's National Aid Fund (NAF) enforces its categorical targeting through home visits by NAF officers to verify eligibility, as well as reviewing the statements and documents provided (World Bank 2007d). Under this design, the geographic distribution of social transfers maps more closely onto the spatial distribution of poverty. Per capita income under the category "other government transfers" (i.e., not social security benefits or pensions) was JD 402 in 2006 in rural areas of Jordan compared with JD 248 in urban areas. Residents of the Amman governorate received JD 194, significantly less than the urban average.[22]

Tunisia's Fund of National Solidarity (FSN[23]) shows how needs-based targeting serves as spatial targeting. The FSN was created in 1992 to finance projects too small to fit into sector ministries' normal service packages. A national committee used objective criteria to select 1,811 project zones, and local administrations identified projects. The result is that most FSN expenditure takes place in the country's lagging western and southern areas. Someone's chance of living in an FSN zone is 13 to 17 times higher than the national average in the lagging regions of Le Kef and Gabès.

Targeting Is Key

Better targeting and coverage will therefore make MENA's SSN programs more powerful instruments for the reduction of spatial disparities.

A number of approaches could improve coverage and targeting and enhance programs' contribution to spatial convergence in living standards. If measuring people's incomes directly ("means testing") is difficult and costly, there are proven alternative targeting approaches.

- *Geographical targeting* distributes benefits to people who are identified as likely to be poor or vulnerable on the basis of where they live. This targeting mechanism is cheap and administratively simple, and especially efficient when poverty is highly concentrated and correlated spatially with observable social indicators. The smaller the geographical unit of measurement, the lower the risk of including the nonpoor or excluding the poor. In the Syrian Arab Republic, for example, targeting a transfer by governorate might reduce the national poverty rate by 1.8 percentage points, whereas targeting the same budget by region would only achieve a reduction of 0.6 percentage points. Poverty mapping is, therefore, frequently used to identify target areas. A simulation of geographical targeting using Morocco's poverty map illustrated the higher efficiency of fine geographic targeting. Targeting at district level could achieve the same poverty-reduction impact as targeting at regional level for 36 percent of the cost (Douidich, Ezzrari, and Lanjouw 2008). Refining spatially disaggregated indicators therefore goes hand in hand with improving the exactness of spatial targeting.

- *Proxy means testing* (PMT) is a targeting approach that uses easily observed household indicators, such as ownership of assets and household size, to predict household income with a fair degree of accuracy. It is gaining popularity in the developing world. Chile was the first country to introduce PMT in 1980, followed by Colombia and Mexico, Armenia since 1994, and Turkey since 2002. By 2004, Argentina, Costa Rica, Ecuador, Jamaica, Honduras, and Nicaragua were putting PMT arrangements in place, and the Russian Federation, Egypt, Zimbabwe, and Sri Lanka were running pilot programs (Coady, Grosh, and Hoddinott 2004). Simulations of proxy means testing in the Syrian Arab Republic suggest that it could reduce the poverty rate by close to 2 percentage points more than a universal lump sum transfer of equal budget size. In Egypt, a shift from the current SSN program to proxy means testing plus geographic targeting could produce a 3 percentage point drop in the poverty rate with an unchanged budget (World Bank 2005a). Similar results apply to low-income countries such as the Republic of Yemen, with the difference that the improvements are seen as people becoming less poor (i.e., less depth and severity of poverty) rather than rising above the poverty line altogether.

Below are two simulations of the spatial impact of SSNs.

The first experiment simulates a program in the Syrian Arab Republic, with a budget of US$260 million, or about 1.2 percent of GDP. Map 4.2a shows the spatial distribution of poverty in the Syrian Arab Republic before the program begins, with the highest poverty rates in the far north and the far south.

Under the first variant of a SSN program, the budget available is simply allocated to each of the Syrian Arab Republic's 14 governorates in proportion to the number of poor. Aleppo, therefore, receives more than a third of the program budget (US$96 million), while Damascus capital governorate receives only 5 percent (US$13 million). The governorate allocations are then shared out equally within each governorate. This is a very crude, low-resolution, form of geographical targeting. Map 4.2b shows the impact: a drop in the poverty rate of up to 4.5 percent across the country, with the poorest areas tending to have the greatest decrease in the poverty rate. For example, in the poor governorate of Aleppo, the

MAP 4.2

Poverty Incidence and Poverty Gaps in the Syrian Arab Republic

(a) Poverty Incidence by Governorate, Syrian Arab Republic; (b) Change in Poverty Incidence, with Geographic Targeting; (c) Change in Poverty Incidence, with Geotargeting and PMT; (d) Change in Poverty Gaps, with Geographic Targeting; (e) Change in Poverty Gaps, with Geotargeting and PMT

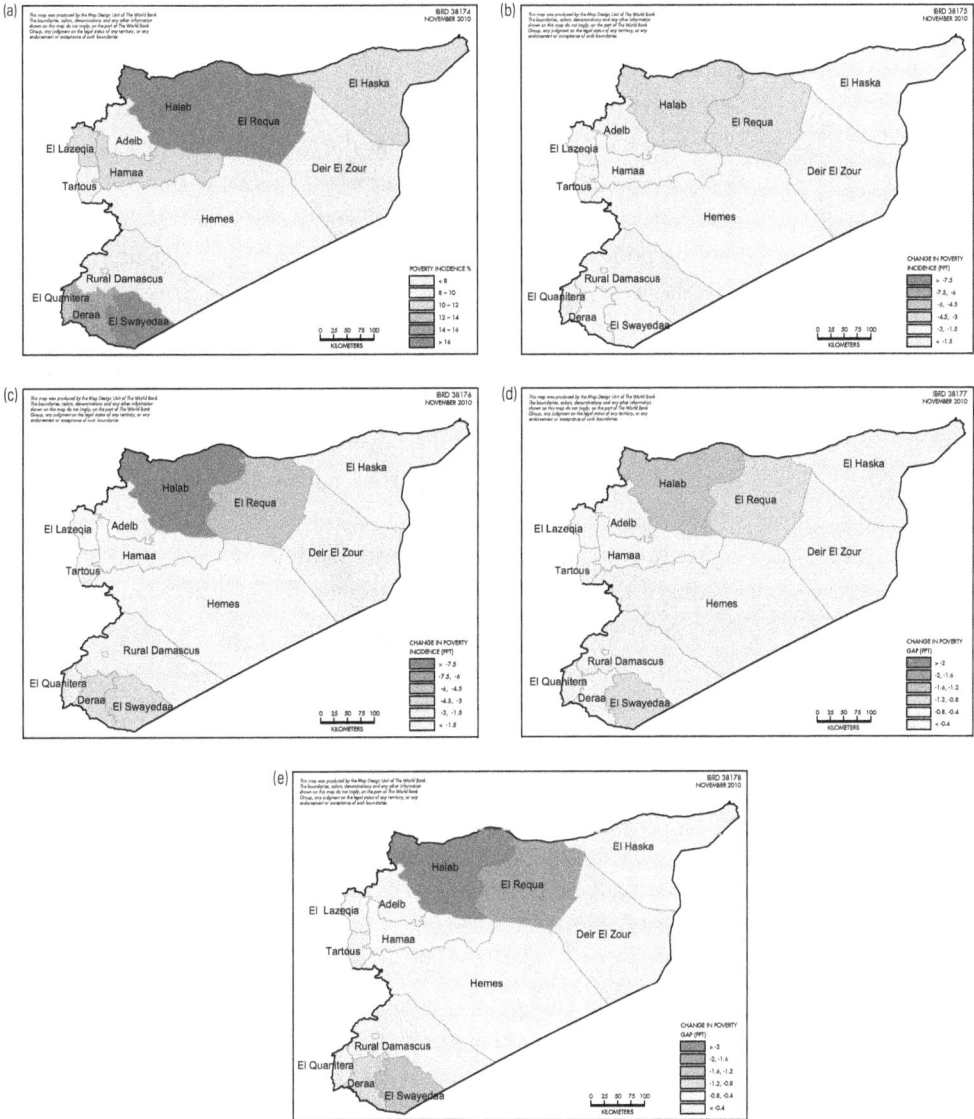

Sources: Authors' simulations using 2003–04 Household Income and Expenditure Database; work by John Blomquist and Nader Kabbani (2007).

Note: Geographic targeting allocates budget to governorates on the basis of the proportion of poor individuals residing in that governorate and then gives each person within that governorate an equal share of the governorate's resources. Administrative cost for targeting assumed to be SL 0.95 million.

Geographical + proxy means first allocates budget to governorates proportionally to poverty and then provides the governorate per capita transfer level to each eligible individual under the proxy-means test. Proxy-means targeting provides the national per capita transfer level to each eligible individual under the proxy means test. Administrative cost for targeting is assumed to be SL 1.24 million.

poverty rate drops from close to 20 percent down to 15.5 percent. Map 4.2c shows what happens if the geographical targeting is complemented by proxy means testing: the leveling of spatial disparities is even more pronounced. Poverty rates in Aleppo and El Swayedaa fall by nearly 8 and 4 percentage points, respectively. The enhanced poverty impact of the combination of PMT and spatial targeting is reflected at the national level: from a starting point of a 11.5 percent poverty rate, a universal lump-sum transfer would reduce the rate to 9.9 percent, the low-resolution geographic targeting to 9.6 percent, and the geotargeting with proxy means testing to 8.2 percent—assuming equal budgets for each option.

A second simulation shows that the spatial impacts of targeted social safety net plans can be even clearer when looking at the depth of poverty. The depth of poverty ("poverty gap") measures how far below the poverty line the poor lie, on average. A transfer might not actually bring a poor household above the poverty line, and thus will not necessarily reduce the poverty rate, but it will always bring it closer to the poverty line and thus will reduce the poverty gap. As the targeting of the social safety net becomes progressively more needs-based (map 4.2d and e), the spatial distribution of the impact on the poverty gap maps more closely onto the spatial distribution of poverty, thus narrowing spatial disparities more effectively.

A simulation for Egypt (World Bank 2005a) compared the spatial impact of the country's existing social safety net plan with that of low-resolution (governorate-level) geographical targeting. The gap between the poverty rates of Upper Rural and Lower Urban Egypt was 31 percentage points in 2005. Distributing LE 3 billion per year (0.6 percent of 2005 GDP) under geographical targeting would reduce the gap to 28 percentage points, and geographical targeting plus a proxy means test would further reduce the gap to 22 percentage points (World Bank 2005a).

In the Republic of Yemen, poverty rates are high, averaging 35 percent nationally and exceeding 50 percent in the poorest governorates. A simulated social safety net with a total budget equivalent to that in the Syrian example (US$194 million, or 1.24 percent of GDP) did not have a significant impact on the poverty rate, because many of the poor fell too far below the poverty line to be lifted above it.

However, as the targeting of the simulated social safety net becomes more precise with the use of geographic and PMT methodologies, the spatial incidence of its impact on the poverty gap (map 4.3b and c) maps more and more closely onto the poverty map (map 4.3a). The governorates with the greatest poverty incidence—Amran, Shabwah, Mareb, Hajja, and Abyan—are those with the greatest decrease in the depth of poverty.

These simulations confirm the potential role of targeted SSN programs as components of strategies to reduce spatial disparities. It is part

MAP 4.3

Poverty Gaps in the Republic of Yemen

(a) Poverty Gaps by Governorate, Republic of Yemen; (b) Change in Poverty Gap, with Geographic Targeting; (c) Change in Poverty Gap, with Geotargeting and PMT

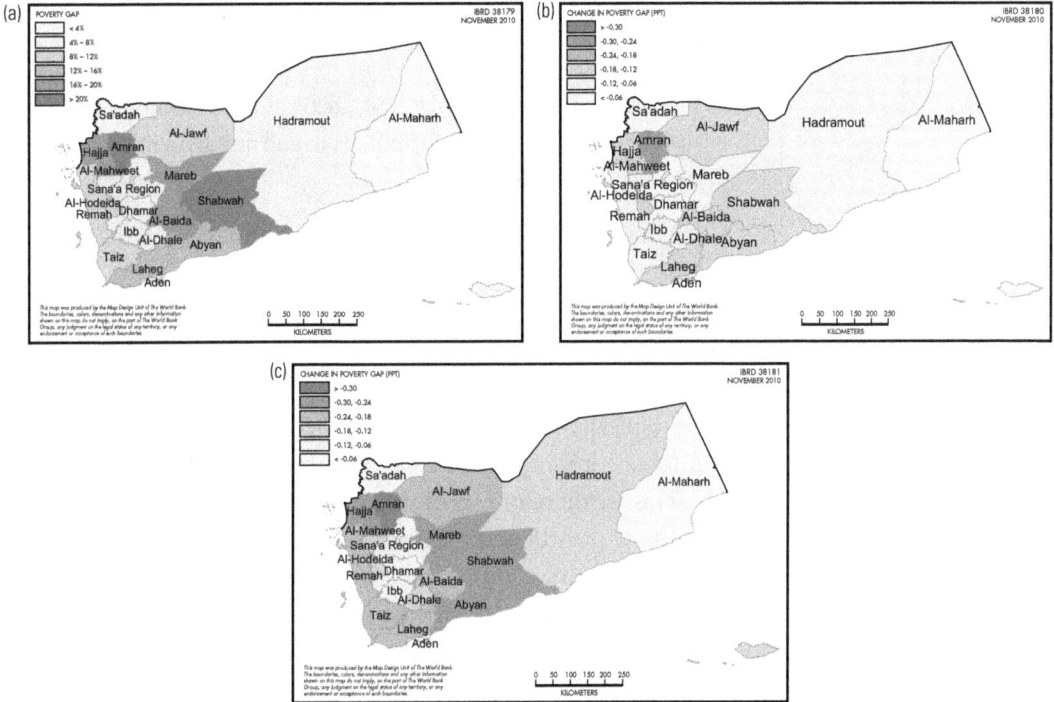

Sources: Authors' simulations using 2005–06 Household Budget Survey; work by John Blomquist and Nader Kabbani (2007).

Note: Geographic targeting allocates budget to governorates on the basis of proportion of poor individuals residing in that governorate and then gives each person within the governorate an equal share of resources. Administrative cost for targeting is assumed to be YR 1.65 million.

Geographical with proxy means first allocates budget to governorates proportionally to poverty and then provides the governorate per capita transfer level to each eligible individual under the proxy means test. Proxy-means targeting provides the national per capita transfer level to each eligible individual under the proxy means test. Administrative cost is assumed to be YR 2.36 million.

of the broader theme that the best way to support disadvantaged places is often to support the disadvantaged people who live in them (see box 4.7).

Smoothing the Path for City Growth

Urbanization helps to reduce spatial disparities. Smoothing the path for urbanization is a recipe for spatial convergence in living standards. First, as we have seen in our discussion of lagging-area diagnostics, poor

---

BOX 4.7

Harnessing Social Safety Nets to Lagging-Areas Policy: Three Ideas for Policy Makers

- Working out whether the spatial incidence of existing resource transfers and subsidies is coherent with national spatial development policies

- Involvement of ministries and institutions responsible for social programs in the formulation and implementation of lagging-areas policies

- Piloting/rolling out needs-based targeting of Social Safety Net programs

Source: Study Team.

---

places are typically held back by large households and low land-labor ratios. Allowing leading urban areas to grow and absorb migrants from lagging areas is, therefore, critical to improving lagging areas' living standards. City growth and rural-urban migration mean more competition for jobs in cities and less in lagging areas, which will help close the wage gap between rich and poor places. Second, artificial limits on city expansion reveal themselves as high rents for urban land and buildings. If people need factories, offices, or accommodation in the city to be close to their work or customers, and the supply of land is limited, rents and real estate prices will rise. In this situation, access to urban land is like a monopoly. The urban population captures an income premium thanks to the choking-off of land supply, thus entrenching the urban-rural incomes gap. Third, the redistribution of population out of lagging areas reduces the spatial component of total inequality.

But fear of urbanization and of spatial disparities has led governments around the world to adopt anti-urbanization policies. These policies come in two varieties:

- Regulatory blocks on urbanization and city growth. Administrations have set limits on land utilization and conversion, rents, migration, private titling, the provision of services to in-migrants, and density (World Bank 2009a, 204).

- Rural economic development programs, designed to (among other things) reduce the economic incentive for people to migrate to the cities.

Urbanization is proceeding apace in MENA13; the average rate of growth of the urban population is 3.3 percent per year, compared with

2.6 percent for national populations (table 4.11). Both urban growth and slum growth in MENA are essentially driven by national population growth and the economics of agglomeration, as figure 4.16 illustrates. (A reasonably precise rule of thumb is that a MENA economies' annual urban population growth rate is the national population growth rate plus 0.7.)

The question, therefore, is not how to slow down city growth, but rather how policy makers can ensure that MENA's city growth is as smooth as possible, involving the minimum of sociopolitical friction and economic distortion. The choice is between the urbanization of planned construction, provision of services to new arrivals, and social integration on the one hand, and the urbanization characterized by slums, haphazard zoning, poor human development, and social dislocation on the other.

A discussion of "smooth city growth" must address three topics: land markets, urban public services, and institutional frameworks. Whether city growth is smooth or painful will depend on how these three issues are resolved. We will look briefly at each in turn, fully recognizing that a few examples cannot do justice to the urban development agenda.

Land Markets that Support Smooth Urban Growth

Well-functioning land markets are critical for smooth urban development. They need to provide urban housing and commercial and industrial

TABLE 4.11

Urban and Slum Growth in MENA, 1990–2001
thousands of people

Country	Total population (1990)	Urban population (1990)	Slum population (1990)	Total population (2001)	Urban population (2001)	Slum population (2001)
Algeria	24,855	12,776	1,508	30,841	17,801	2,101
Djibouti	504	408	n.a.	644	542	n.a.
Egypt, Arab Rep.	56,223	24,999	14,087	69,080	29,475	11,762
Iran, Islamic Rep.	58,435	32,917	17,094	71,369	46,204	20,406
Iraq	17,271	12,027	6,825	23,584	15,907	9,026
Jordan	3,254	2,350	388	5,051	3,979	623
Lebanon	2,713	2,284	1,142	3,556	3,203	1,602
Libya	4,311	3,528	1,242	5,408	4,757	1,674
Morocco	24,624	11,917	4,457	30,430	17,082	5,579
Syrian Arab Republic	12,386	6,061	629	16,610	8,596	892
Tunisia	8,156	4,726	425	9,562	6,329	234
West Bank and Gaza	2,154	1,379	n.a.	3,311	2,222	1,333
Yemen, Rep.	11,590	2,648	1,787	19,114	4,778	3,110

Source: UN Habitat 2006.
Note: n.a. = not applicable.

FIGURE 4.16

National Population Growth Underlies Urban and Slum Population Growth in the Arab Republic of Egypt and Tunisia

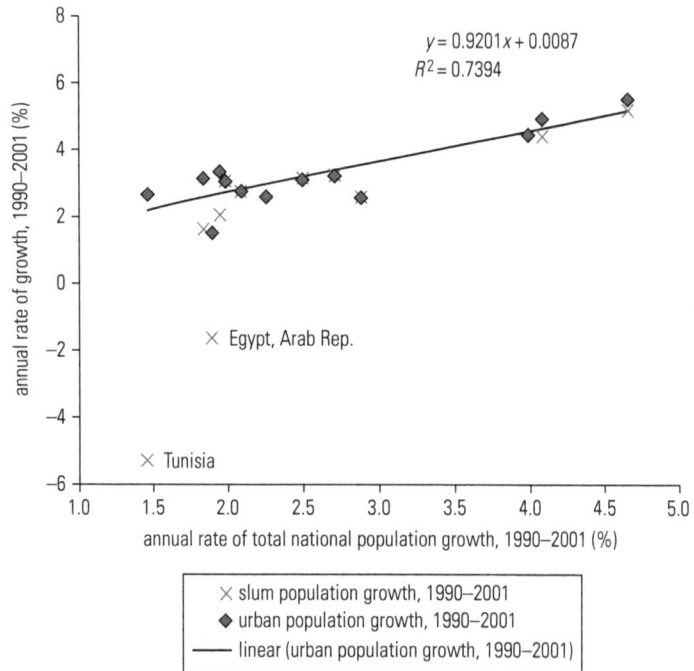

$$y = 0.9201x + 0.0087$$
$$R^2 = 0.7394$$

annual rate of growth, 1990–2001 (%)

✕ Egypt, Arab Rep.

✕ Tunisia

annual rate of total national population growth, 1990–2001 (%)

✕ slum population growth, 1990–2001
◆ urban population growth, 1990–2001
— linear (urban population growth, 1990–2001)

Source: UN Habitat 2006.

sites, and to facilitate the consolidation of agricultural holdings. In MENA, however, there are signs that land markets could be performing better.

Land for housing. The supply of housing in MENA economies does compare well with that of other economies at a similar level of development (World Bank 2005e). The per capita availability of floor space serviced with both water and sanitation is similar to that of comparator economies, with Jordan and the Islamic Republic of Iran faring slightly better than the trend and the Republic of Yemen, Morocco, Algeria, and Tunisia slightly below it. Note that these figures exclude any housing, including slums, without water or sanitation.

However, there are problems of affordability and utilization of the housing stock.

MENA's housing is expensive. In a typical OECD economy, the ratio of house prices to income is around 5 or below. In MENA, however, only Egypt and Tunisia come close to this ratio; Morocco, Lebanon, Jordan, Algeria, Lebanon, and the Islamic Republic of Iran are significantly above it, in the range 6.5–17 (table 4.12). The affordability problem is most acute for low-income households (World Bank 2005e), and anecdotal evidence suggests that it has been worsening over the past decade.

Housing subsidies are sometimes massive but not necessarily reaching those who need them. Interest-rate subsidies, tax benefits, and land subsidies for house purchase and construction are found in Algeria, Egypt, the Islamic Republic of Iran, Jordan, Morocco, Tunisia, and the Republic of Yemen. The cumulative cost of these subsidies can be considerable, and is estimated at 5 percent of GDP for Morocco in 2002 and 7.5 percent of GDP in the Islamic Republic of Iran. Low-income households may have difficulty making the investments that give them access to these subsidies. In Algeria, for example, the poorest 25 percent of urban households were estimated as only receiving 14 percent of all public housing assistance (World Bank 2002).

This is not to say that governments cannot act effectively to provide affordable housing for low-income households. The Iranian and Tunisian governments have a record of success in this area. The key feature was the existence of a dedicated institutional setup with a clear focus on the low-income segment rather than a broad-brush subsidization of the market (box 4.8).

Underutilization is a characteristic of MENA's housing stock. In Morocco, according to the 2001 Housing Survey, 500,000 urban units were vacant. In Egypt, about 1.8 million housing units were vacant in 1996, of which 800,000 to 1 million units were in Cairo, where the vacancy rate was 14.5 percent. Lebanon also suffers from a vacancy rate

TABLE 4.12

Housing Supply Indicators for Eight MENA Economies

Country	Floor area serviced with water and sanitation per person (square meters)	House price to income ratio
Algeria	8.5 (1993)	8.1 (2002 est.)
Egypt, Arab Rep.	12 (1993)	4.9 (1998)
Iran, Islamic Rep.	21 (2002)	9 (2002)
Jordan	10 (1993)	6.5 (1998)
Lebanon	10–12 (2003)	9 (2002)
Morocco	6 (1993)	9.2 (1998)
Tunisia	6.5 (1993)	5.2 (1998)
Yemen, Rep.	4	10–17 (2000)

Source: World Bank 2005e.

Note: Floor area per person = median usable living space per person. House price to income ratio = ratio of the free market price of a dwelling unit to the median annual household income.

BOX 4.8

Stories of Low-Income Housing Provision: Tunisia and the Islamic Republic of Iran

One of the main objectives of the post-1979 revolutionary government in the Islamic Republic of Iran was to improve the supply of low-income housing. In the 10 years to 1989, 856 square kilometers of urban land were acquired by the Urban Land Organization (ULO), roughly half from the government and half by confiscation from the private sector according to the interpretation of Islamic Law that private ownership could not exist for *mavat* (undeveloped) land. The ULO engaged private contractors to provide this land with utilities and thus provided land to some 423,000 families, approximately 27 percent of housing units produced in the country. A criticism of the program is that much of the land acquired by the ULO was not allocated for development. This was in order to regulate migration flows to the larger cities, especially Tehran.

The Tunisian government created the Urban Upgrading and Renovation Agency in 1981. By means of partnerships with municipalities and private developers, the agency managed to reduce the stock of slum housing from 24 percent of the total housing stock to 2 percent from 1974 to 1993. From 1975 to 1994, the percentage of household expenditure devoted to housing went from 22 percent to 28 percent, despite the country's urbanization. The slum population halved between 1990 and 2001. These improvements have had a particularly beneficial impact on the quality of life and productivity of women. Key factors in Tunisia's success were:

- The shift in the 1970s from slum eradication with relocation to slum regularization and upgrading

- The creation in 1981 of the Agence de Réhabilitation et de Rénovation Urbaine as an execution agency for municipalities

- The division of labor between the state (providing infrastructure and connections) and the residents (upgrading housing at their own pace), as exemplified by the upgrading of Kram West in the outskirts of Tunis

Sources: Keivani, Mattingly, and Majedi 2008; Cities Alliance 2003; UN Habitat, 2006; Kraiem 2009.

of 17 percent. These low utilization rates may be partly due to rent controls in the three countries, which discourage owners from renting out and maintaining their properties (World Bank 2005e).

The high cost of urban housing and underutilization of the housing stock act as a brake on rural-urban migration. They, therefore, deny people in migrant-sending areas a key developmental pathway.

Land for business. Surveys of MENA entrepreneurs indicate that they find difficulties in accessing land to be one of their main obstacles to competitiveness. The World Bank's investment climate assessments found that the percentage of firms citing access to land as a "major" or "very severe" constraint was around 40 percent in Morocco, 35 percent in the Republic of Yemen, 35 percent in Algeria, 35 percent in Syria and 20 percent in Egypt (World Bank 2005f). Even when titled land has been identified, the purchase transaction itself is often burdensome. Table 4.13 shows the time and expense of purchasing a property that already has a registered and undisputed title. The MENA13 economies perform well on the time criterion, but worse than any region of the world except Sub-Saharan Africa in terms of the cost, with transactions costing more than 5 percent of the value of the property in Algeria, the Islamic Republic of Iran, Jordan, Syria, Lebanon, Djibouti, and Tunisia.

Algeria's 2002 Investment Climate Assessment highlighted how weak land markets impede competitiveness. Land access ranked as firms' third-biggest complaint. Indeed, 37 percent of firms surveyed said that they were currently searching for land, and they had been doing so for an average of five years. The key problems were inadequate titling and property rights; less than half of industrial land was titled, and business-people stated that corruption was affecting the allocation of government

TABLE 4.13

The Time and Cost Required to Purchase Property: How the MENA13 Match Up against Other Regions

	Days	Cost (% of property value)
Algeria	51.0	7.5
Egypt, Arab Rep.	72.0	0.9
Iran, Islamic Rep.	36.0	10.0
Iraq	8.0	6.5
Jordan	22.0	10.0
Libya	n.a.	n.a.
Morocco	47.0	4.9
Syrian Arab Republic	19.0	28.0
West Bank and Gaza	63.0	0.9
Yemen, Rep.	19.0	3.8
Lebanon	25.0	5.9
Djibouti	40.0	13.2
Tunisia	39.0	6.1
Average MENA13	**36.8**	**8.1**
East Asia and the Pacific	99.0	4.1
Eastern Europe and Central Asia	72.1	1.9
Latin America and the Caribbean	71.4	6.0
OECD	30.3	4.7
South Asia	106.0	5.9
Sub-Saharan Africa	95.6	10.5

Source: http://www.doingbusiness.org/ExploreTopics/RegisteringProperty/, accessed August 26, 2009.

land. Yet at the same time, half of serviced industrial land was lying idle because of administrative controls and the lack of a secondary market (World Bank and IFC 2002).

Land for the rural transition. We have seen that MENA economies' transition of the workforce out of agriculture and into services and manufacturing has been slower than one would expect for their level of development. Efficient agricultural land markets will be important to facilitate the shift of labor out of agriculture in the future, and to increase the earnings of those who remain in farming. Secure and transferable title over farmland enables farmers to consolidate landholdings, to mobilize agricultural finance, and to minimize the inefficiency of absentee ownership when landowners migrate.

A key obstacle to the smooth functioning of MENA's agricultural land markets is the gap between the theory and the practice of land registration. Legislation in economies as diverse as Tunisia and the Republic of Yemen stipulates that only registered land confers ownership rights under the formal judicial system. However, it is often difficult in practice for landowners to obtain and maintain registration; procedures are onerous, the capacity of land registries is limited, and Islamic inheritance rules require subdivision. The result is that the actual pattern of recognized ownership is not reflected in the official record. In the Republic of Yemen, only 13 percent of land held actually has a registered title (World Bank 2009c). Even with a concerted effort, the Tunisian government managed to raise the share of land with a registered title from 25 percent in the 1960s to 50 percent by 2001 (World Bank 2006a). The Egyptian government mandated a land registration system in 1923, but had achieved only 54 percent registration by 1994 (Hanigan and Ibrahim 1994).

The widespread existence of unregistered land is not considered an impediment to day-to-day farming activities. The right to use the land can be confirmed by registration with customary authorities, as in the Republic of Yemen, or by the recognition of the community; however, the gap between the reality of ownership on the ground and the official register can create difficulties in accessing credit or consolidating fragmented landholdings.

Some MENA governments are concerned that agricultural land resources are being consumed by conversion for urban use. The situation varies considerably from country to country. While the ratio of land within urban extents to *agricultural* land is relatively high in Egypt (68 percent), the West Bank and Gaza (57 percent), Lebanon (55 percent), and Jordan (30 percent), it is 10 percent or less for all other economies of the MENA13.[25] In most MENA13 economies, therefore, urban growth is unlikely severely to compromise the agricultural land base.

Moreover, efforts to regulate against the development of farmland can harm the efficiency of land use. Figure 4.17 illustrates this point by the

FIGURE 4.17

Some of Cairo's Most Valuable Land Is Reserved for Agriculture

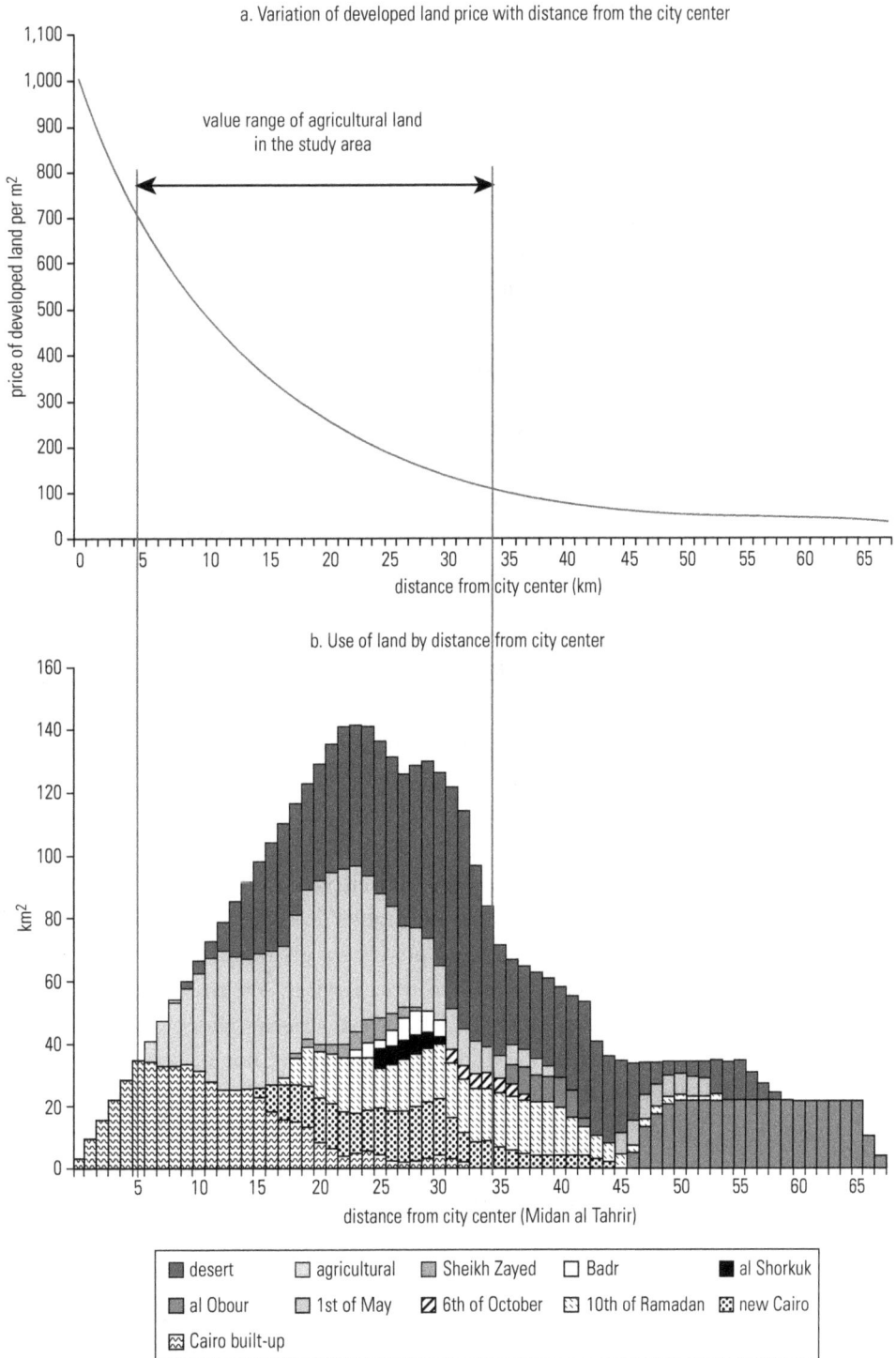

a. Variation of developed land price with distance from the city center

value range of agricultural land
in the study area

price of developed land per m²

distance from city center (km)

b. Use of land by distance from city center

km²

distance from city center (Midan al Tahrir)

desert   agricultural   Sheikh Zayed   Badr   al Shorkuk
al Obour   1st of May   6th of October   10th of Ramadan   new Cairo
Cairo built-up

Source: Presentation to the government of Arab Republic of Egypt by Alain Bertaud, December 2007, personal communication.

distribution of land use in the city of Cairo. A sizeable area of land between 5 and 35 kilometers distant from the city center has been reserved for farming. Land in this zone potentially has a high market value, reflecting the fact that locations near the center of a major agglomeration exhibit high productivity for residential and commercial uses. Its reservation for agriculture is, therefore, a significant loss of value to the economy.

A more efficient and effective approach to land conservation would be to relax regulatory limits on density that force many cities to sprawl outward. Rather than preventing peri-urban agricultural land from achieving higher value by being developed, governments can allow city-center land to achieve higher value by being densified.

Services for Smooth Urban Growth

The integration of new arrivals into the fabric of the city depends critically upon their ability to access public and private services: water and sanitation, power, solid waste collection and disposal, and urban transportation. If public authorities do not provide services to new arrivals, this absence does not slow down the pace of urbanization. On the contrary, it makes urbanization unnecessarily painful, with the emergence of slums, social exclusion, and a potential for political disaffection.

It is not possible or appropriate to set out MENA's entire agenda for urban service development here, but it is useful to illustrate a few key principles with examples from the region.

Planning ahead, rather than reacting to in-migration. There is sometimes a tendency for public authorities to delay the provision of services to new informal settlements. The delay might be because informal settlements are seen as temporary and unwelcome additions to the urban fabric. Or it might be because administrative procedures (e.g., planning, obtaining rights of way) are not adapted to informal settlements.

However, the earlier that services for emerging settlements are planned, the more efficient investments in road, power, water, and sanitation networks will be. But once an ad hoc pattern of settlement has been established, it can be difficult for utilities to provide services cost-effectively or to use their existing administrative procedures. The experience of providing water and sanitation services to illegal peri-urban settlements in Morocco is a case in point (Chauvot de Beauchêne and Mantovani 2009). Many of difficulties encountered in bringing services to these slums were because the utilities were coming in at the end of the settlement process. Peri-urban areas were not included in the service areas of water and sanitation operators, lack of formal title made it difficult for them to obtain the rights of way needed to install services, and unplanned construction made access difficult for their workers. This finding contrasts with the experience of new informal settlements in the Islamic Republic of Iran, where the government seems to have made significant investments in services at an earlier stage (Alaedini, Deichmann, and Shahriari 2007).

With global warming, MENA cities' vulnerability to sea-level rise gives the region a special reason to care that urban growth should be planned. Of all world regions, MENA (including GCC economies) will have the highest share of its population (53 percent) living in coastal areas that are vulnerable to storm surges (Dasgupta, Laplante, Murray, and Wheeler 2009). Urban planning can both minimize construction in vulnerable areas and ensure investment in protective infrastructure, thus reducing future costs of catastrophic flooding.

The risk of pre-servicing urban residential land, however, is that it becomes overpriced and captured by elite groups at the expense of low-income people—who will occupy unplanned areas elsewhere. It is, therefore, important for the authorities to mandate the levels of density required for housing to be truly low-cost.

Responding to the "spatial flow" of market-led city growth. It is also unrealistic to hope that government can reshape the geography of urban growth. As elsewhere in the world, MENA governments have sometimes attempted to limit the development of major cities by creating new serviced settlements in less agglomerated areas. The general lesson is that service-provision and new town creation should follow people's settlement preferences, rather than attempting to lead them. Informal settlements should, therefore, be seen as "part of the housing solution rather than a problem" (World Bank 2005e).

The Islamic Republic of Iran has created 18 new towns since the Revolution, with the aim of protecting farmland and preventing informal settlements around major cities (Ziari 2006). The new towns were constructed at considerable distance from their parent cities, an average of 40 kilometers for the four new towns under construction around Tehran and an average of 35 kilometers for the three around Isfahan. These new towns, however, became dormitory communities for salaried employees of the mother city, without any economic base of their own. The new towns' total population has only reached 5 percent of the target. Significantly, the only exception was Baharestan; its closeness to Isfahan (15 kilometers) made it the most successful new town, and it accounts for 35 percent of the residential units under construction in the entire program. Meanwhile, the main growth in Tehran is in informal peri-urban settlements, where 60 percent of new inhabitants are long-term urban residents unable to find a place to live in the formal areas (Zebardast 2006) The authorities have, therefore, refocused their attention away from new towns and toward increasing the supply of formal housing within the metropolis itself (box 4.8).

The Egyptian government's 1969 Greater Cairo Region Master Scheme called for satellite cities in the desert around Cairo. President Sadat in 1974 called for a "new population map of Egypt." The new ring road around Cairo was intended to limit the city's growth. The 10th of Ramadan City, Sadat City, and 6th of October City were constructed in 1977, 1978, and 1981, respectively. As in the Iranian case, they were built distant (an average of 60 kilometers) from the parent city. Unlike the new Iranian towns, however, these satellite cities in the desert attracted significant levels of business thanks to incentives, including a 10-year tax holiday and free zone status. The problem, however, was that people chose not to live in them because of the difficulties in finding affordable housing, transportation, water, social facilities, schools, shops, and other services, as well as communities and social networks (Stewart 1996). A pattern of reverse commuting, therefore, evolved, with firms busing in their workforces from Cairo. By 2005, the building completion rate in residential subdivisions of 6th of October City ranged from 2 percent to 20 percent (World Bank 2008e).

Meanwhile, however, the forces of agglomeration were accelerating the growth of Cairo's metropolis; established areas such as Mohandessine, Zamalek, Maadi, and Madinat Nasr were growing vertically and densifying, and adjacent informal settlements were expanding laterally. About 60 percent of Cairo's population was probably in informal settlements, and 81 percent of those were on agricultural land (World Bank 2008e). By the early 1990s, therefore, the government was refocusing its efforts on using services to improve the quality of growth in the metropolis rather than to create a "new population map" of alternative agglomerations. The emphasis was now on slum upgrading, the integration of Cairo's adjacent suburbs into the metropolis, and the creation of smaller industrial sites within existing agglomerations such as Basatin, Helwan, and Shubra El Kheima (Sutton and Fahmi 2001).

El-Batran and Arandel make the distinction between Egypt's satellite new towns of the 1970s and 1980s and the "new settlements" approach of the 1990s.

> The new settlements' objective is to learn from informal settlements and emulate them on public desert land. The new settlements rely more heavily on the concept of sites and services than the new towns and incorporate core housing schemes. The target population is the people currently occupying spontaneous settlements, namely low- and middle-income dwellers who are excluded from the formal housing market. New settlements are located in close proximity to Cairo and allow easy access to the city. (El-Batran and Arandel 1998)

In both the Iranian and Egyptian cases, therefore, the authorities seem to have shifted their approach. Both recognized the futility of re-directing metropolitan growth into less agglomerated areas. The efforts of both are now instead concentrated on using service provision to improve the *quality* of metropolitan agglomeration.

Institutional Arrangements for Smooth Urban Growth

If the quality of planning, regulation, and service provision determine whether urbanization is smooth or traumatic, it is the institutional frame-work for municipalities that largely determines the quality of planning, regulation, and service-provision. MENA's high administrative and fiscal centralization makes it hard for municipalities to coordinate and finance urban growth. Decentralization, organizational consolidation, financial management, and capacity building are key issues for strengthening MENA municipalities' ability to respond to the challenge of urban growth (box 4.9). Examples of initiatives in the MENA region are listed in table 4.14.

Can It Work?

How long will the stresses of urbanization last? Today's wealthy cities, such as Paris, Melbourne, London, New York, Shanghai, Stockholm, and Helsinki, were not always so elegant. During the rapid urbanization of the nineteenth and early twentieth centuries, they were infested with slums, filth, and infection (World Bank 2009a, 69). Many decades elapsed between the initial burst of slum growth and the integration of slum populations into the fabric of the city. Do MENA's cities have to wait so long?

Fortunately, we now have examples of quicker transitions. Cities such as Seoul; Singapore; Hong Kong SAR, China; and San José (Costa Rica) are proving that good policies really can smooth the path for urban growth and can shorten the period of painful transition.

- *Institutional arrangements for smooth urban growth.* Costa Rica and the Republic of Korea's regional government boundaries and institu-tional mandates were reconfigured at an early stage of city growth to serve the need for integrated city management.

- *Land transactions.* In Costa Rica, 80 percent of property owners possess registered titles. In Hong Kong SAR, China, flexible land markets were crucial in balancing the demands of residential and commercial real estate.

- *Investing in people.* Costa Rica invests 20 percent of its budget in edu-cation, enabling the social mobility that discourages the emergence

---

BOX 4.9

Facilitating Smoother Urbanization: Six Ideas for Policy Makers

1. Simplifying land development regulations and basing zoning regulations on considerations of environmental impacts, connectivity, and amenity values rather than as an
attempt to slow down urban development. Inappropriate standards, sometimes bor-
rowed from more developed countries, prohibit the construction of affordable housing. For example, minimum plot sizes in Morocco and Jordan are beyond the budgets
of most people there (World Bank 2005e).

2. Shifting public finance away from subsidies for construction and purchase, toward
public-private partnerships for affordable housing.

3. Simplifying titling and registration systems and integrating informal arrangements
into formal legislation. Tunisia's Certificat de Possession and the Arab Republic of
Egypt's Hekr System and Hand Claim with Property Taxes, for example, are practical ways of granting defined rights to rural and urban land occupants without formal
written title.[25] The Islamic Republic of Iran's informal "Promissory Notes" are now
the main form of tenure in Tehran's fringe settlements (Zebardast 2006).

4. Releasing government-owned urban land into the market, where it represents a pool
of underused real estate and is doing so transparently. This approach could apply to
Egypt, Algeria, and the Islamic Republic of Iran.

5. Cutting the red tape and bureaucracy associated with land sales.

6. Planning the provision of urban services in a way that supports the spatial "flow" of
city growth: in other words, slum upgrading, incorporation of informal areas into
service networks, and regulations facilitating densification of established areas.

Source: Study Team.

---

of an urban underclass. Seoul's period of rapid urbanization,
1960–90, coincided with a 120 percent increase in the Korean workforce's average years of education.

- *Connectivity makes it unnecessary for migrants to crowd near places of
employment and allows slum dwellers to integrate into the urban economy.* San
José, Costa Rica, has good affordable bus services within the city, to suburbs, and to neighboring cities. Seoul's radial transport links, including
a subway and a beltway, kept pace with growth in the urban extent.

- *Wisely targeted housing expenditure.* Costa Rica's housing subsidies were
means tested, so they were not received by the better off. Eighty-six
percent of Singapore's population lives in privately owned but publicly
built units. During 1960–80, the government in Hong Kong SAR,

Table 4.14

How MENA Is Upgrading the Institutional Environment for Urban Growth

Approach	What MENA governments are doing
Establishing spatially integrated planning institutions	Cairo's boundaries as a spatial entity now extend well beyond Cairo governorate into adjoining jurisdictions: since 2008 Greater Cairo has included Cairo, Giza, Helwan, and 6th of October governorates. Law no. 119/2008 aims to address this fragmentation, calling for a National Higher Council for Urban Planning and Development.
Matching resources and mandates	The problem of unfunded municipal mandates occurs frequently across the region. Tunisia's 10th Development Plan estimated that around half the country's municipalities were in a "weak" or "vulnerable" financial condition.[a] The government therefore set the target of doubling the share of municipalities collecting the TCL, a tax on industrial, commercial, and professional entities.
Improving access to finance for capital investment	If central governments are wary of the financial risk of municipal borrowing on the open market, other mechanisms may be developed. Morocco's Fonds d'Equipement Communal acts as the central government's banker toward municipalities. Its loans for municipal investments were around MAD 7.5 billion at the end of 2008.[b] Jordan's Cities and Villages Development Bank fulfills a similar role. Tunisia has the Caisse des Prêts et de Soutien des Collectivités Locales. Another option, currently pursued under the Arab Republic of Egypt's Affordable Mortgage Finance program, is to ease low-income households' access to housing loans.
Strengthening managerial capacity at municipal level	In 2001, the Jordanian government responded to a crisis in municipal finances and services by overhauling the structure of municipal government. Under the so-called Amalgamation, the number of councils was reduced from 190 to 99, 762 technical and senior administrative staff were recruited, a management information system was set up, intensive training was provided to staff, and a permanent municipal training center was created.[c]

Source: Study Team, from World Bank project documents and http://www.fec.ma.
Note: a. Project Appraisal Document for World Bank Municipal Development III Project.
b. See http://www.fec.ma.
c. Project Appraisal Document for World Bank Regional and Municipal Development Project.

China contracted out urban development to a specialist organization dominated by private sector interests.

No successful city has avoided the growing pains of urbanization altogether. But international experience does show that the transition can be smoother and quicker if institutions have adequate mandates, if land markets work, if the workforce is educated and mobile, and if public housing expenditure targets affordability for the poor.

Endnotes

1. The sign of the coefficient on trade openness depended on the choice of independent variable: growth of the main city, the urbanization rate, or the agglomeration index.

2. At the beginning of the twentieth century, large swathes of the Middle East were still under Ottoman rule, as part of a global empire that had existed for roughly 400 years. The Ottoman Empire included extensive territories known today as the Syrian Arab Republic, Iraq, Lebanon, Jordan, the Republic of Yemen, Israel, and Palestine, in addition to important footholds in Libya, although its other North African dominions had already been lost to the French (Tunisia and Algeria) and to the British (the Arab Republic of Egypt) (Owen 1992, 8).

3. This analysis uses linear and probit econometric models. Although it is difficult to separate the impacts of different variables, the robustness of the analysis and the low degree of correlation among independent variables are adequate to identify the determinants of spatial disparities. See Katayama (2009) for details.

4. In the analysis of TIMSS 2007, "rural" is defined as a school location in which 15,000 people or fewer reside.

5. World Bank. 2009. "Improving Health Services for All in Libya." In *Libya Public Expenditure Review*. Washington, DC: World Bank Group, p. 142.

6. Regional Health Systems Observatory, World Health Organization (WHO). 2006. *Lebanon: Health Systems Profile*. Cairo: WHO Regional Office for the Eastern Mediterranean, p. 38.

7. Regional Health Systems Observatory, WHO. 2006. *Djibouti: Health Systems Profile*. Cairo: WHO Regional Office for the Eastern Mediterranean, p. 87.

8. Regional Health Systems Observatory, World Health Organization (WHO). 2006. *Yemen: Health Systems Profile*. Cairo: WHO Regional Office for the Eastern Mediterranean, p. 51.

9. Regional Health Systems Observatory, WHO. 2006. *Iraq: Health Systems Profile*. Cairo: WHO Regional Office for the Eastern Mediterranean, p. 35.

10. Department of Statistics [Jordan] and Macro International Inc. "Jordan Population and Family Health Survey 2007." Calverton, MD: Macro International Inc., p. 33.

11. World Bank. 2009. "Improving Health Services for All in Libya." In *Libya Public Expenditure Review*. Washington, DC: World Bank Group.

12. El-Saharty, Sameh and others. 2006. *Tunisia Health Sector Study*. Washington, DC: MNSHD, World Bank Group, p. 44.

13. World Bank. 2009. *Kingdom of Morocco—Health Policy Note*. Washington, DC: World Bank, p. 15.

14. Regional Health Systems Observatory, WHO. 2006. *Morocco: Health Systems Profile*. Cairo: WHO Regional Office for the Eastern Mediterranean, p. 34.

15. Regional Health Systems Observatory, WHO. 2006. *Yemen: Health Systems Profile*. Cairo: WHO Regional Office for the Eastern Mediterranean, p. 3.

16. National Health Accounts Team, Republic of Yemen, and Partners for Health Reform Plus. 2006. *Yemen National Health Accounts: Estimate for 2003*. Bethesda, MD: Partners for Health Reform Plus Project, Abt Associates Inc., p. xv.

17. El-Zanaty, Fatma, and Ann Way. 2006. *Egypt Demographic and Health Survey 2005*. Cairo: Ministry of Health and Population, National Population Council, El-Zanaty and Associates, and ORC Macro, p. 209.

18. Salti, N., and J. Chaaban. 2008. "Health Equity in Lebanon: A Microeconomic Analysis." Unpublished, p. 28.

19. Regional Health Systems Observatory, WHO. 2006. *Yemen: Health Systems Profile*. Cairo: WHO Regional Office for the Eastern Mediterranean, p. 69.

20. Marmot, M. G. and others. 1991. "Health Inequalities among British Civil Servants: The Whitehall II Study." *Lancet* 337: 1387–93.

21. Salehi-Isfahani, D., S. Fesharaki, and M. Majbouri. 2006. "Analysis of Health and Education Expenditures in Iran." Unpublished, p. 9.
22. "2006 Household Expenditures and Income Survey." Hashemite Kingdom of Jordan, Department of Statistics, Amman.
23. Nicknamed "26-26," after the bank account to which citizens make voluntary contributions.
24. GRUMP database and World Bank World Development Indicators. Consistent data are not available for Morocco; the GRUMP database aggregates Morocco with Western Sahara, while the World Bank WDI does not.
25. See http://www.habitat.org/gov/suppdocs/chapter4_strategies_that_improve_tenure_security.pdf, accessed August 27, 2009; and World Bank 2005e.

References

Ades, A., and E. L. Glaeser. 1995. "Trade and Circuses: Explaining Urban Giants." *Quarterly Journal of Economics* 110 (1): 195–227.

Aghajanian, A., A. H. Mehryar, S. Ahmadnia, and S. Kazemipour. 2008. "Impact of the Rural Health Development Programme in the Islamic Republic of Iran on Rural-Urban Disparities in Health Indicators." *World Hospitals and Health Services* 44 (3): 10.

Alaedini, P., U. Deichmann, and H. Shahriari. 2007. *Land Markets and Housing Dynamics in Low Income Settlements in Iran: Examining Data from Three Cities.* http://www.worldbank.org/urban/symposium2007/papers/alaedini.pdf.

Ayubi, N. 1988. "Arab Bureaucracies: Expanding Size, Changing Roles." In *Beyond Coercion: The Durability of the Arab State*, ed. I. Zartman and A. Dawisan. London: Croom Helm.

———. 2008. *Overstating the Arab State.* London: I. B. Tauris.

Beblawi, H., and G. Luciani. 1987. *The Rentier State.* New York: Croom Helm.

Bengio, Ofra, and Gabriel Ben-Dor, eds. 1999. *Minorities and the State in the Arab World.* Boulder, CO: Lynne Rienner.

Blomquist, J. 2008. "Social Safety Nets and the Response to Food, Fuel, and Other Price Shocks in the Middle East and North Africa Region." Unpublished.

Blomquist, J., and N. Kabbani. 2007. "Providing Income Support to the Poor in Syria: Simulating Targeting Options." Unpublished draft report. February.

Brown, C. 1997. *Imperial Legacy: The Ottoman Imprint on the Balkans and the Middle East.* New York: Columbia University Press.

Chauvot de Beauchêne, X., and P. Mantovani. 2009. "Subsidies for the Poor: An Innovative Output-Based Approach. Providing Basic Services to Poor Periurban Neighborhoods in Morocco." In *Water in the Arab World. Management Perspectives and Innovations*, ed. V. Jagannathan, A. M. Shawky, and A. Kremer, 335–53. Washington, DC: World Bank.

Cities Alliance. 2003. "2003 Annual Report." World Bank, Washington, DC.

Cleveland, William L. 1999. *A History of the Modern Middle East*. Boulder, CO: Westview Press.

Coady, D., M. Grosh, and J. Hoddinott. 2004. *Targeting of Transfers in Developing Countries: Review of Lessons and Experience*. Washington, DC: World Bank.

CSDH (Commission on Social Determinants of Health). 2008. *Closing the Gap in a Generation: Health Equity through Action on the Social Determinants of Health*. Geneva: World Health Organization.

Dasgupta, S., B. Laplante, S. Murray, and D. Wheeler. 2009. *Climate Change and the Future Impacts of Storm-Surge Disasters in Developing Countries*. Washington, DC: Center for Global Development.

Dasgupta, S., C. Meisner, A. Makokha, and R. Pollard. 2009. "Community Management of Rural Water Supply: Evaluation of User Satisfaction in Yemen." In *Water in the Arab World: Management Perspectives and Innovations*, ed. V. Jagannathan, A. Shawky, and A. Kremer, 383–99. Washington, DC: World Bank.

Dollar, D., M. Hallward-Driemeier, and T. Mengistae. 2005. "Investment Climate and Firm Performance in Developing Countries." *Economic Development and Cultural Change* 54 (1): 1–31.

Douidich, M., A. Ezzrari, A., and P. Lanjouw. 2008. *Simulating the Impact of Geographic Targeting on Poverty Alleviation in Morocco*. Washington, DC: World Bank.

Economist. 2005. *The Economist Pocket World in Figures 2005*. London.

Eickleman, D. 1976. *Moroccan Islam: Tradition and Society in a Pilgrimage Center*. Austin: University of Texas Press.

El-Batran, M., and C. Arandel. 1998. "A Shelter of Their Own: Informal Settlement Expansion in Greater Cairo and Government Responses." *Environment and Urbanization* 10 (1): 217–32.

FEMISE. 2005. *Jordan Country Profile: The Road Ahead for Jordan.* Cairo: Economic Research Forum and Institut de la Méditerranée.

Findlay, C. 1980. *Bureaucratic Reform in the Ottoman Empire: The Sublime Porte, 1789–1922.* Princeton, NJ: Princeton University Press.

———. 1997. "The Ottoman Administrative Legacy and the Middle East." In *Imperial Legacy: the Ottoman Imprint on the Balkans and the Middle East,* ed. C. Brown. New York: Columbia University Press.

Fiszbein, A., and M. Schady. 2009. *Conditional Cash Transfers: Reducing Present and Future Poverty.* Washington, DC: World Bank.

Freedom House. 2009. "Freedom in the World." http://www.freedom house.org.

Georgetown University. 2007. *Engagement of Social Change Agents in Improving Women's Health in the Arab Republic of Egypt: Developing a Framework for Evaluation and Research.* Washington, DC: Georgetown University, School of Nursing and Health Studies.

Golnar, M. 1995. *Girls' Drop-out from Primary Schooling in the Middle East and North Africa: Challenges and Alternatives.* Amman: UNICEF.

Goujon, A., H. Alkitkat, W. Lutz, and I. Prommer. 2007. *Population and Human Capital Growth in Egypt: Projections for Governorates to 2051.* Luxenburg: International Institute for Applied Systems Analysis.

Hanigan, F. L., and M. M. Ibrahim. 1994. "Completing Egypt's Agricultural Cadaster." *MN GIS/LIS News* (St. Paul), 422–33.

Henry, C. M. 2004. "Algeria's Agonies: Oil Rent Effects in a Bunker State." *Journal of North African Studies* 9 (2): 68–81.

HM Treasury. 2009. "Analysis of Public Expenditure by Country and Region." http://www.hm-treasury.gov.uk/d/10(1).pdf.

Huyer, S., N. Hafkin, H. Ertl, and H. Dryburgh. 2005. "Women in the Information Society." In *From the Digital Divide to Digital Opportunities: Measuring Infostates for Development,* ed. G. Sciadis, chapter 6. Montreal: Orbicom.

IDSC (Information and Decision Support Center). 2007. *Cars in Egypt.* Cairo: IDSC.

INS (Institut National de la Statistique). 2000. *Enquête Nationale sur le Budget. La Consommation et le Niveau de Vie des Ménages.* Tunis: INS.

Jacobs, D., J.-L. Hélis, and D. Bouley. 2008. *Budget Classification.* Washington, DC: International Monetary Fund.

Karaman, K. K. 2009. "Decentralized Coercion and Self-Restraint in Provincial Taxation: The Ottoman Empire, 15th–16th Centuries." *Journal of Economic Behavior and Organization* 71 (3): 690–703.

Katayama, H. 2009. "Geographical Disparities in Enrollment, Attainment and Learning Achievements in the MENA Region." Unpublished.

Kaufman, D., A. Kraay, and M. Mastruzzi. 2009. *Governance Matters VIII. Aggregate and Individual Governance Indicators 1996–2008.* Washington, DC: World Bank.

Keivani, R., M. Mattingly, and H. Majedi. 2008. "Public Management of Urban Land, Enabling Markets, and Low-Income Housing Provision: The Overlooked Experience of Iran." *Urban Studies* 45: 1825–53.

Khelladi, M. 2009. "Inégalités spatiales en Algérie: tendances et politiques publiques." Unpublished background paper for this report.

Korany, B. 1987. "Alien and Besieged Yet Here to Stay: The Contradiction of the Arab Territorial State." In *The Foundations of the Arab State,* ed. G. Salamé, 47–74. London: Croom Helm.

Kraiem, F. 2009. "Tunisia Slum Upgrading Note." Unpublished.

Kuran, T. 2004. "Why the Middle East Is Economically Underdeveloped: Historical Mechanisms of Institutional Stagnation." *Journal of Economic Perspectives* 18: 71–90.

Lall, S. V., and T. Mengistae. 2005. *The Impact of Business Environment and Economic Geography on Plant-Level Productivity: An Analysis of Indian Industry.* Washington, DC: World Bank.

Lall, S., C. Timmins, and S. Yu. 2009. *Connecting Lagging and Leading Regions: The Role of Labor Mobility.* Washington, DC: World Bank.

Leite, P. 2008. "Implementing a Proxy Means-Test to Identify the Poorest in Yemen on the Basis of the Household Budget Survey 05/06 (HBS)." Unpublished.

Luciani, G. 1989. *The Arab State.* Berkeley: University of California Press.

Mengistae, T., and F. Thompson. 2006. "Unbundling Location Effects in Productivity: The Case of Manufacturing Plants in Morocco."

Center for the Study of African Economies. http://www.csae.ox.ac.uk/
conferences/2006-EOI-RPI/papers/csae/Thompson-Mengistae.pdf.

Ministère de la Santé. 2003, 2007. *Santé en Chiffres.* Rabat.

Ministry of Planning and Development Cooperation. 2009. Iraq Household Socio-Economic Survey. Baghdad, Iraq.

Movahedi, M., B. Hajarizadeh, A. Rahimi, M. Arshinehi, K. Amirhos-
seini, and A. A. Hadhgoost. 2009. "Trends and Geographical Inequalities of the Main Health Indicators for Rural Iran." *Health Policy and
Planning* 24: 229–37.

North, D. 1990. *Institutions, Institutional Change, and Economic Performance.* New York: Cambridge University Press.

Owen, R. 1992. *State, Power, and Politics in the Making of the Modern Middle East.* London: Routledge.

Ozbudun, E. 1997. "The Continuing Ottoman Legacy: The State Tradition in the Middle East." In *Imperial Legacy: the Ottoman Imprint on
the Balkans and the Middle East,* ed. C. Brown, 133–57. New York:
Columbia University Press.

Pennell, C. R. 2001. *Morocco since 1830: A History.* London: Hurst.

Political Instability Task Force: M. Marshall and G. Cole. 2009. "Global
Report on Conflict, Governance, and State Fragility." George Mason
University, Fairfax, Virginia.

Rawlings, L. B., and G. M. Rubio. 2005. "Evaluating the Impact of
Conditional Cash Transfer Programs." *World Bank Research Observer*
20 (1): 29–55.

Rawlings, L., L. Sherburne-Benz, and J. van Domelen. 2004. *Evaluating
Social Funds—A Cross-Country Analysis of Community Investments.*
Washington, DC: World Bank.

Richards, A., and J. Waterbury. 1990. *A Political Economy of the Middle East:
State, Class, and Economic Development.* Boulder, CO: Westview Press.

Sadrizadeh, B. 2004. "Strengthening Primary Health Care in the Islamic
Republic of Iran." In *Public Health in the Middle East and North Africa,*
ed. A. M. Pierre-Louis, F. A. Akala, and H. Karam, 115–25. Washington, DC: World Bank Institute.

Sapir, A. 2003. "An Agenda for a Growing Europe: Making the EU Economic System Deliver." Report of an Independent High-Level Study

Group Established on the Initiative of the President of the European Commission.

Schiavo-Campo, S., and D. Tommasi. 1999. *Managing Public Expenditure*. Manila: Asian Development Bank.

Shah, A. 2007. "A Practitioner's Guide to Intergovernmental Fiscal Transfers." In *Intergovernmental Fiscal Transfers: Principles and Practice*, ed. R. Boadway and A. Shah, 1–54. Washington, DC: World Bank.

Shlash, A. 2009. "Iraq High Committee for Strategy Reduction. Draft Strategy Review Presentation." June. Amman.

Soliman, A., A. Shawky, M. Hamed, W. Wakeman, and M. Mehany. 2009. "Rural Sanitation within an IWRM Framework: Case Study of Application in the Delta Region, Egypt." In *Water in the Arab World: Management Perspectives and Innovations*, ed. V. Jagannathan, A. Shawky, and A. Kremer, 401–20. Washington, DC: World Bank.

Stern, N. 2002. *A Strategy for Development*. Washington, DC: World Bank.

Stewart, D. J. 1996. "Cities in the Desert: The Egyptian New-Town Program." *Annals of the American Association of Geographers* 86 (3): 459–80.

Sutton, K., and W. Fahmi. 2001. "Cairo's Urban Growth and Strategic Master Plans in the Light of Egypt's 1996 Population Census Results." *Cities* 18 (3): 135–49.

Thomas, M. 2005. *The French Empire between the Wars: Imperialism, Politics, and Society*. Manchester: Manchester University Press.

Tosun, M. S., and S. Yilmaz. 2008. *Centralization, Decentralization, and Conflict in the Middle East and North Africa*. Washington, DC: World Bank.

———. 2009. "Decentralization and Spatial Dimension of Public Expenditures in MENA Countries." Unpublished background paper for this report.

UN Habitat. 2006. *State of the World's Cities 2006/7: The Millennium Development Goals and Urban Sustainability*. Nairobi: United Nations Human Settlements Program.

UNDP (United Nations Development Programme). 2005. *Egypt Human Development Report 2005*. New York.

UNICEF (United Nations Children's Fund). 2009. *The State of the World's Children 2009: Maternal and Newborn Health. Annual Report*. New York: UNICEF.

WHO (World Health Organization) and DFID (Department for International Development). 2003. *The Analytic Review of the Integrated Management of Childhood Illness Strategy: Final Report.* Geneva: WHO.

World Bank. 2002. *Algeria Low Income Housing Project. Midterm Review Mission Report.* Washington, DC: World Bank.

———. 2004a. *The Geographical Dimension of Public Expenditures and Its Link to Poverty: The Case of Madagascar.* Retrieved August 24, 2009, from http://siteresources.worldbank.org/INTPGI/Resources/342674-1092157888460/Galasso.GeographicalMadagascar.pdf.

———. 2004b. *Implementation Completion Report, Morocco: Social Priorities Program Basic Health Project.* Report No. 28390-MOR. Washington, DC: World Bank.

———. 2005a. *Egypt—Toward a More Effective Social Policy: Subsidies and Social Safety Nets.* Washington, DC: World Bank.

———. 2005b. *Iraq—Social Protection in Transition: Labor Policy, Safety Nets and Pensions.* Washington, DC: World Bank.

———. 2005c. *Local Administration, Fiscal Intergovernmental Arrangements, and Fiscal Decentralization in Egypt.* Washington, DC: World Bank.

———. 2005d. *Decentralization and the Intergovernmental System in Iran.* Washington, DC: World Bank.

———. 2005e. *The Macroeconomic and Sectoral Performance of Housing Supply Policies in Selected MENA Countries: A Comparative Analysis.* Washington, DC: World Bank.

———. 2005f. "Forum on Investment Climate, Egypt." Retrieved August 27, 2009, from http://siteresources.worldbank.org/INTMNAREGTOPPRVSEC/Resources/Land.pdf.

———. 2005g. *Implementation Completion Report, West Bank and Gaza: Health System Development Project.* Report No. 33572. Washington, DC: World Bank.

———. 2005h. *Implementation Completion Report on a Credit in the Amount of US$17.2 Million to the Arab Republic of Egypt for a Population Project.* Report No. 28300-IDA. Washington, DC: World Bank.

———. 2006a. *Tunisia: Agricultural Policy Review.* Washington, DC: World Bank.

———. 2006b. *Upper Egypt: Challenges and Priorities for Rural Development.* Washington, DC: World Bank.

————. 2006c. *Implementation Completion Report, Yemen: Child Development Project*. Report 35003. Washington, DC: World Bank.

————. 2007a. *Kingdom of Morocco: Moving out of Poverty in Morocco*. Washington, DC: World Bank.

————. 2007b. *Morocco Skills Development and Social Protection within an Integrated Strategy for Employment Creation*. Washington, DC: World Bank.

————. 2007c. *Syria Arab Republic: Toward a Social Protection Strategy for a Social Market Economy*. Washington, DC: World Bank.

————. 2007d. *Hashemite Kingdom of Jordan: A Note on Strategy on Modernization of the Social Safety Nets*. Washington, DC: World Bank.

————. 2008a. *The Road Not Traveled. Education Reform in the Middle East and North Africa*. Washington, DC: World Bank.

————. 2008b. *Using PISA to Understand the Determinants of Learning in the Middle East and North Africa*. Washington, DC: World Bank.

————. 2008c. *Kingdom of Morocco Policy Notes: Conditions for Higher and Inclusive Growth*. Washington, DC: World Bank.

————. 2008d. *For Protection and Promotion: The Design and Implementation of Effective Safety Nets*. Washington, DC: World Bank.

————. 2008e. *Arab Republic of Egypt. Towards an Urban Sector Strategy*. Washington, DC: World Bank.

————. 2009a. *World Development Report 2009: Reshaping Economic Geography*. Washington DC: World Bank.

————. 2009b. *Tapping a Hidden Resource: Energy Efficiency in the Middle East and North Africa*. Washington, DC: World Bank.

————. 2009c. "Yemen Synthesis Rural Land Tenure." Unpublished.

————. 2009d. *From Privilege to Competition: Unlocking Private-led Growth in the Middle East and North Africa*. Washington, DC: World Bank.

World Bank and IFC (International Finance Corporation). 2002. *Algeria Investment Climate Assessment*. Washington, DC: World Bank and IFC.

Zebardast, E. 2006. "Marginalization of the Urban Poor and the Expansion of the Spontaneous Settlements on the Tehran Metropolitan Fringe." *Cities* 23 (6): 439–54.

Ziari, K. 2006. "The Planning and Functioning of New Towns in Iran." *Cities* 23 (6): 412–22.

CHAPTER 5

Policy Package 2. Connecting Poor Places to the Poles of Development

Policy Package 2 (Adapted from table 2.3)

Package 2. Connecting poor places to the poles of development.	"Infrastructure" ("spatially connective policies")	For growth to spillover from economic poles into lagging areas, they have to be connected.	Lagging areas close enough to density [and with enough economic density] to benefit	Beware of thinning-out effect in low-potential areas.

The Power of Spillovers

> spillover **A.** *n.* That which spills over; the process of spilling over; (an) incidental development; a consequence, a repercussion, a by-product.
>
> —Oxford English Dictionary

Economic development spills out from leading areas into the areas around them. In terms of economic geography, the agglomeration economics from being close to an economic hub are second only to those of being within the hub itself. The "belt" around an agglomeration can sell its crops and its manufactured goods to the agglomeration without having to subtract long-distance haulage charges from its profit margin. Its workers can commute to the agglomeration and use the agglomeration's markets and health facilities. Its employers can use the agglomeration's financial institutions, shop around for the best deal there for inputs (and not have to worry about transport costs and delivery delays), do business face-to-face with suppliers and clients—and drop into a senior official's office if necessary. Waldo Tobler's first law of geography sums it up: "everything is related to everything else, but near things are more related than distant things" (Tobler 1970).

Spillovers from agglomerations into their peripheries are therefore one of the most powerful forces in spatial development. A key predictor of how prosperous a place becomes is how prosperous the neighboring places are; this is true whether one is talking about the countries of Africa and the Middle East (Parent and Zouache 2008), the provinces of Indonesia (McCulloch and Sjahrir 2008), or the regions of Algeria (Belarbi and Zouache 2009). In the Arab Republic of Egypt, the city governorates of Cairo, Alexandria, and Port Said had (unweighted) average per capita household expenditures of LE 4,813 per annum in 2005. For the governorates that bordered these metro areas,[1] average per capita household expenditures were LE 3,260. For the other governorates, the average was LE 2,632.

Spillover effects, therefore, have the potential to reduce spatial disparities if they yoke lagging areas to the growth of leading regions.

According to the principles of economic geography, to benefit most from these spillover effects, a lagging area must meet two criteria (World Bank 2009a, 76, 246):

- Proximity to a leading area agglomeration

- Population density, so that economies of agglomeration can build up within the lagging area

A Geographical Information System (GIS) can give us an idea of where MENA's lagging areas fit these criteria. MENA has approximately 55 cities of 500,000 inhabitants or more. Using road maps, relief maps, and assumptions about the speed of road travel, the travel time from every location in MENA13 to a city of 500,000 or more inhabitants was calculated. Of course, these estimates are necessarily approximate. Digital data on minor roads and on road quality are not available, and the distribution of population within administrative divisions has to be derived from satellite images of nighttime lighting. But they still give us a rough overview of MENA's connectivity situation (which is shown in map 5.1).

The analysis tells us that MENA has a proximity advantage (table 5.1): most of its population live in cities or close to them. It is estimated that 59 percent of MENA's population live within two hours of one of these cities and 72 percent within three hours (unweighted country average). Only in Algeria does more than half the population appear to live more than three hours away from a city.

And some lagging areas benefit from proximity. Map 3.5 shows where they are. In Morocco, the area from Fès moving northwest toward the sea is lagging, has a dense population, and is close to the hub of Rabat. In Algeria, the lagging *wilaya* of Mascara lies just inland from Oran; Médéa and Aïn Defla are situated just inland from the greater Algiers

MAP 5.1

Trunk Road Connectivity Is Good Where the People Are: Travel Time in Hours to a City of More Than 500,000 Inhabitants, with Closed Borders

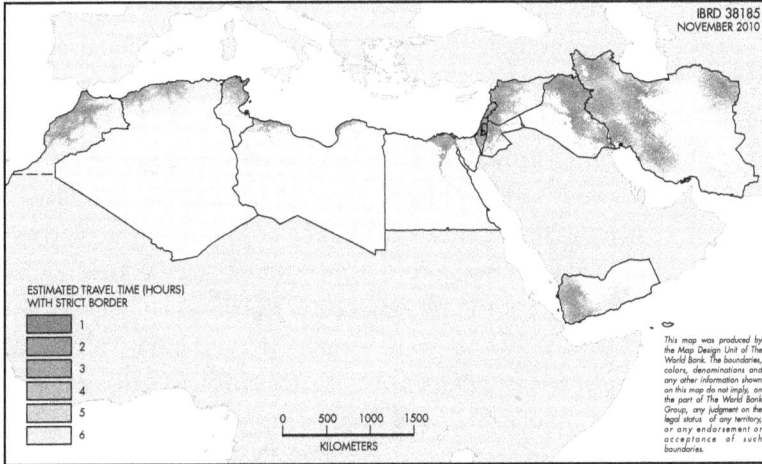

Source: Staff GIS analysis; sources detailed in appendix.

TABLE 5.1

Most of MENA's Population Live Close to Agglomerations

Travel time by hours to a city of 500,000 or more

Country	1	2	3	4	5	6
	% of population					
Algeria	18	13	12	12	13	32
Egypt, Arab Rep.	45	28	7	3	7	10
Iran, Islamic Rep.	37	12	15	16	9	11
Iraq	60	23	12	4	1	0
Jordan	64	28	4	2	1	1
Lebanon	67	27	5	1	0	0
Libya	41	21	13	3	5	16
Morocco	40	14	12	12	12	9
Syrian Arab Republic	52	20	9	4	5	10
Tunisia	28	19	21	12	13	7
West Bank and Gaza	85	13	0	0	2	0
Yemen, Rep.	17	14	37	17	8	7
Total	40	19	13	9	8	11

Sources: Staff calculations using GIS algorithms; Oak Ridge National Laboratory 2005; Nelson 2008.

agglomeration; and Guelma abuts Annaba. In Tunisia, lagging, dense Béja and Kairouan are close to Tunis. In Libya, lagging, dense Al Khums province adjoins Tripoli itself. In Egypt, governorates with poverty rates greater than 20 percent (Beheira and Sharkeyya [UNDP 2008]) are close to the Cairo metropolis. In Iraq, Babil abuts Baghdad. In the Republic of Yemen, Amran lies just to the north of the cluster of leading governorates around Sana'a. In the Islamic Republic of Iran, the ostan of Qom lies just to the south of Tehran. There will be many other lagging areas with the potential to benefit from spillovers, which could be picked up by higher-detail country-level analysis.

But for a lagging area to benefit from proximity to a leading area, it has to be well connected by infrastructure. In Indonesia, it has been shown that the spillover effect extends for 60 kilometers when roads are good and only 25 kilometers when they are poor (World Bank 2009a, 76). The growth of low-income areas around Jakarta in Indonesia, Seoul in the Republic of Korea, and São Paulo in Brazil followed the path of major transport axes (World Bank 2009a, 77). But the same could apply, on a smaller scale, to the agricultural track between a hamlet and the nearest weekly village market, or the dirt road between a village and the nearest market town. Investment in rural infrastructure, including rural roads, was found to be one of the main factors that determined how well a region of India fared in reducing poverty (Datt and Ravallion 1998). About a sixth of the Lao People's Democratic Republic's poverty reduction from 1997–98 to 2002–03 was attributable to rural roads (Warr 2005).

"Spillover connectivity" is different from long-distance connectivity. Spillover connectivity integrates a place into its nearest economic hub so that it can build economic links and share economies of agglomeration. The impact of spillover connectivity is, therefore, unambiguously positive. Long-distance connectivity, in contrast, allows finished goods to be sold in distant markets. Improving long-distance connectivity in lagging areas can therefore be either positive or negative for lagging areas. On the positive side, it improves their access to markets. But on the negative side, it exposes their existing home markets to competition from more efficient producers in agglomerated areas. It is, therefore, very complex to predict whether the impact of better road connectivity will be positive or negative, but international evidence (Mu and Van de Walle 2007; OECD 2009) suggests that short-distance connectivity has a more positive impact than long-distance connectivity.

The question, then, is this: how can the Middle East and North Africa (MENA) connect its lagging areas to agglomeration hubs so that they benefit from spillover effects as much as possible?

This chapter will deal with two kinds of connectivity: physical and virtual. It will begin with an examination of transport connectivity. But it will then go on to discuss how MENA can use information and communications technology (ICT) to bring some of the benefits of proximity to all locations, whether they be near to or distant from the economic hubs.

Road Transport: An Extensive Long-Distance Network but an Underdeveloped Short-Distance Connectivity

MENA's transport infrastructure is basically road-based. There is some rail connectivity, but railways represent only a twelfth of investment needs (Fay and Yepes 2003). Within-country sea and air transportation are of minor importance.

Intercity (i.e., long-distance) connectivity in MENA is generally adequate, thanks to an extensive primary road network. The extent of the paved network naturally varies according to country size, with the Islamic Republic of Iran, Algeria, and Egypt having the largest paved networks (126,000 km, 76,000 km, and 75,000 km, respectively), while Lebanon, West Bank and Gaza, and Djibouti have the smallest networks (6,200 km, 5,200 km, and 1,200 km, respectively). The layout of the region's road network provides a good coverage of population centers (see table 5.1). Other measures of road network coverage, particularly the network density (per area of arable land and per population), also show that MENA generally performs well in comparison with other developing economies (figure 5.1).

MENA's trunk road network fits the region's agglomerated pattern of population distribution. Map 5.1 shows how long it takes for people across the region to travel to a city of at least half a million people, based upon a model that reflects road speeds according to the class of road and the hilliness of the landscape. It is estimated that 72 percent of the MENA13 region's population (excepting Djibouti) live within three hours of such a city (table 5.2).

However, the population coverage of road connectivity varies by country. In Lebanon, the West Bank and Gaza, Jordan, and Iraq, the share of the population living more than three hours from a city is 5 percent or less. At the other extreme, it is greater than 30 percent for the Republic of Yemen, Tunisia, Morocco, and the Islamic Republic of Iran. Algeria is an outlier, with more than half the population estimated to be living more than three hours away from a city of half a million inhabitants.

As one would expect, lagging areas' populations are less likely to be well connected to cities. For the MENA13 economies (minus Djibouti), someone living in a lagging area is 77 percent more likely to be more than three hours from a major city than someone in a nonlagging area. Overall, however, 61 percent of MENA's lagging area populations *do* live within three hours of a city. Moreover, only 14 percent of MENA13's population live *both* in a lagging area *and* at least three hours away from

FIGURE 5.1

Paved Roads Density: MENA Compares Well with Other Middle-Income Countries

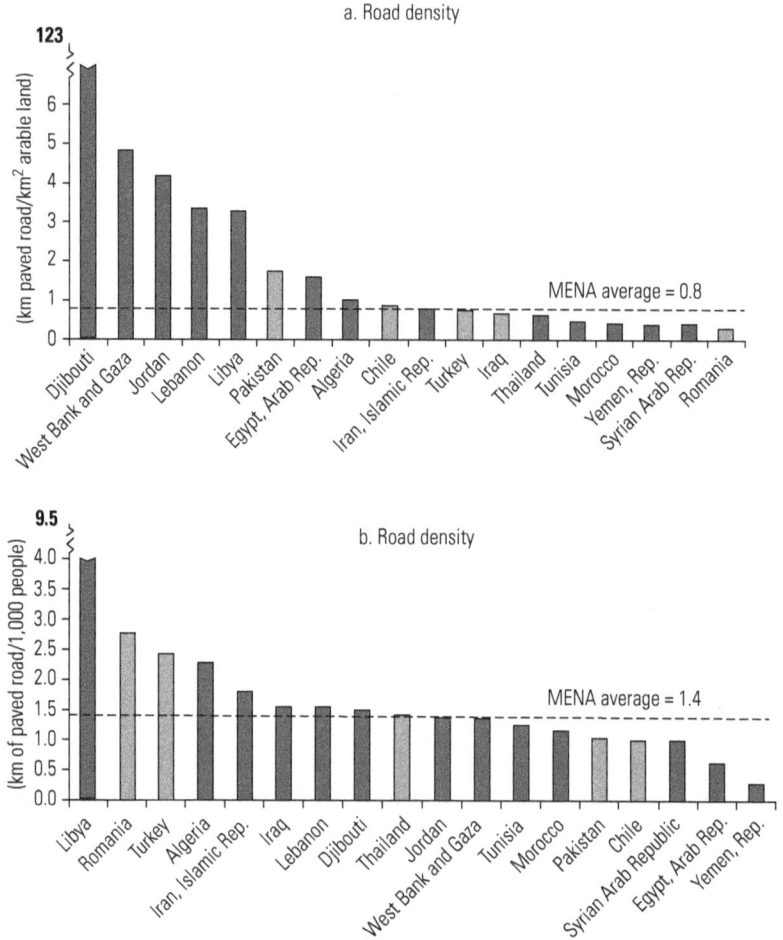

Sources: CIA 2006 (or latest available year); World Bank WDI 2003, 2006.

Note: Paved road data for 2006 are available for most MENA13 economies. Where 2006 data are not available, the latest available data are used, assuming that there have not been significant variations in paved road length between the latest year available and 2006. WDI data is for 2006 for all economies, except for Libya where it is 2003.

a city of half a million people. This suggests that MENA economies should not necessarily assume that long-distance connectivity is a major component of the lagging areas' problem.

But the good picture on long-distance connectivity masks a problem: there is a predisposition toward expanding higher-class roads in MENA at the expense of other key transport expenditures. The paved network represents around 60 percent of the total road network in MENA (figure 5.2). This is quite high for developing countries. The tendency

TABLE 5.2

Percentage of Population Living More Than Three Hours' Road Travel from a City of at Least Half a Million Inhabitants

	% of nationwide population	% of lagging areas* population	% of nationwide population
Lebanon	1	3	1
West Bank and Gaza	2	5	2
Jordan	4	5	2
Iraq	5	11	3
Syrian Arab Republic	18	12	4
Egypt, Arab Rep.	20	43	19
Libya	25	41	16
Yemen, Rep.	31	36	10
Tunisia	32	53	11
Morocco	34	53	12
Iran, Islamic Rep.	37	44	17
Algeria	57	63	19
Total	**28**	**39**	**14**

Source: Staff calculations from data sources in appendix.

Note: *Lagging areas are defined as the two quintiles of administrative divisions with the lowest household poverty or consumption indicators, according to data availability.

FIGURE 5.2

MENA Region Concentrates on Paved Roads More Than in Comparator Economies

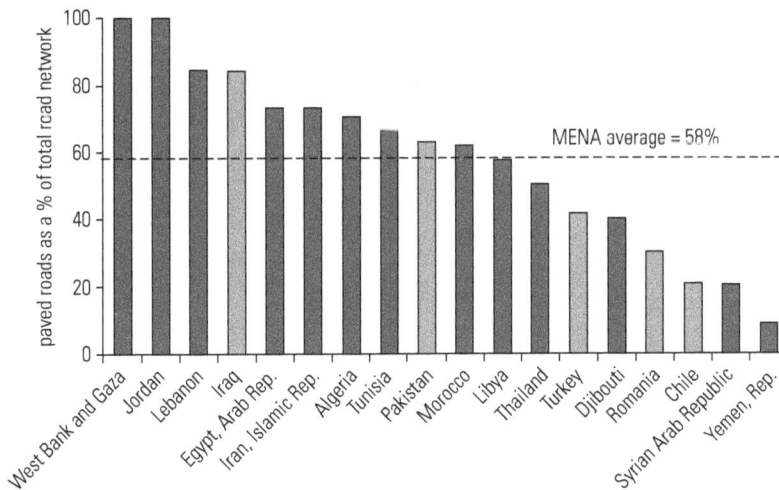

Sources: CIA 2006 (or latest available year); World Bank WDI 2003, 2006.

Note: Paved road data for 2006 are available for most MENA13 economies. Where 2006 data are not available, the latest available data are used, assuming that there have not been significant variations in paved road length between the latest year available and 2006. WDI data is for 2006 for all economies, except for Libya where it is 2003.

toward higher-class paved roads can be partially explained by the spatial concentration of the population and the resulting high traffic levels. However, it may also result from the centralization of road planning and management, the administrative complexity of managing many small secondary road projects for a centralized department, and the undervaluation of rural connectivity.

Table 5.3 summarizes what country transport sector reviews by the European Union, the World Bank, and other institutions have identified as MENA's main problems in ensuring connectivity. The degradation of road surfaces, congestion, poor road safety, the low quality of passenger and freight services, and poor border procedures and facilities emerge as the main constraints. The following pages will discuss each of these in a little more detail.

Degradation of Road Surfaces

The drive toward the expansion of the network is taking place at the expense of road maintenance expenditures. The quality of the road

TABLE 5.3

Road Connectivity Problems in MENA, as Highlighted in EuroMed and World Bank Sector Reviews

	Algeria	Djibouti	Egypt, Arab Rep.	Iran, Islamic Rep.	Iraq	Jordan	Lebanon	Libya	Morocco	Tunisia	Total
Quality of the network											
Deteriorated surfaces of paved roads	X		X	X	X			X			5
Traffic											
Intense traffic on main arteries	X	X	X	X		X	X	X			7
Severe congestion in major cities	X		X	X		X	X	X	X	X	8
Safety											
Poor road safety	X	X	X	X	X	X	X	X			8
Transport services (passengers)											
Low quality of passenger transport services	X	X	X	X			X				5
Transport services (freight)											
Low quality of freight transport services	X		X			X	X		X	X	6
Old trucking fleet			X	X	X	X	X		X		6
Logistics											
Underdeveloped logistics facilities	X	X		X		X	X		X	X	7
Border-crossing											
Cumbersome customs procedures			X	X	X	X		X		X	6
Insufficient harmonization of procedures with neighbors	X	X		X	X	X	X		X	X	8

Source: Study Team from World Bank and EuroMed transport sector reviews, various years.

Note: Empty cell = not reported as problem.

network in MENA is, therefore, deteriorating. World Bank studies identified road deterioration as a major problem in Algeria, Egypt, the Islamic Republic of Iran, Iraq, Libya, and West Bank and Gaza. About 30 percent of the paved network in Egypt and Algeria is in bad condition, and up to 50 percent in West Bank and Gaza. No accurate measures are available for other economies in the region since they generally lack an effective asset management system—another indication of the neglect of road maintenance. Meanwhile, few exact figures exist on the quality of the unpaved road network, although it is generally accepted among professionals that it is in worse shape than that of the paved network. In Algeria, for example, 70 percent of communal roads were only in poor or fair condition, compared with 46 percent of national roads (World Bank 2007a). Djibouti keeps about 70 percent of its paved roads in fair to very good condition, thanks to the use of high-quality construction materials and favorable geological and climatic conditions. A large share of Djibouti's unsurfaced roads, however, is deteriorating due to lack of maintenance (World Bank 2005a).

Roads maintenance often suffers from underfunding. During the 15 years up to 2007, Algeria was allocating only 0.2 percent of GDP to road maintenance, compared with an international norm of 0.5–1 percent (World Bank 2007a). In 2004, Egypt was allocating only 0.05 percent of GDP, despite having an adequate roads network in terms of coverage (World Bank 2007b). High axle loads aggravate the lack of maintenance. In Jordan, annual spending on road maintenance averaged only US$12.8 million per year during 1998–2003, whereas estimated needs were double that figure (World Bank 2004). Libya spends most of its 0.8 percent of GDP roads budget on new construction and very little on maintenance.

The resulting maintenance backlogs across MENA's roads sector entail severe economic losses, both for the government and for the road user. The South African government has estimated that repair costs are multiplied by a factor of 6 after three years of neglect and by 18 after five years of neglect (World Bank 2007a). And it is reported that a $1 reduction in road maintenance expenditure can increase the cost of vehicle operation by $2 to $3 (World Bank 1989).

Rural Connectivity Deficits

Another contrast to the efforts to expand the trunk (long-distance) network is the comparative neglect of rural accessibility, despite some recent improvements. The rural index indicator for MENA, defined as the percentage of rural population with access to an all-season road, was estimated at about 60 percent in 2004 (figure 5.3), which is one of the lowest values in the world (outperforming only Sub-Saharan Africa and

FIGURE 5.3

Rural Access: MENA versus Comparator Regions

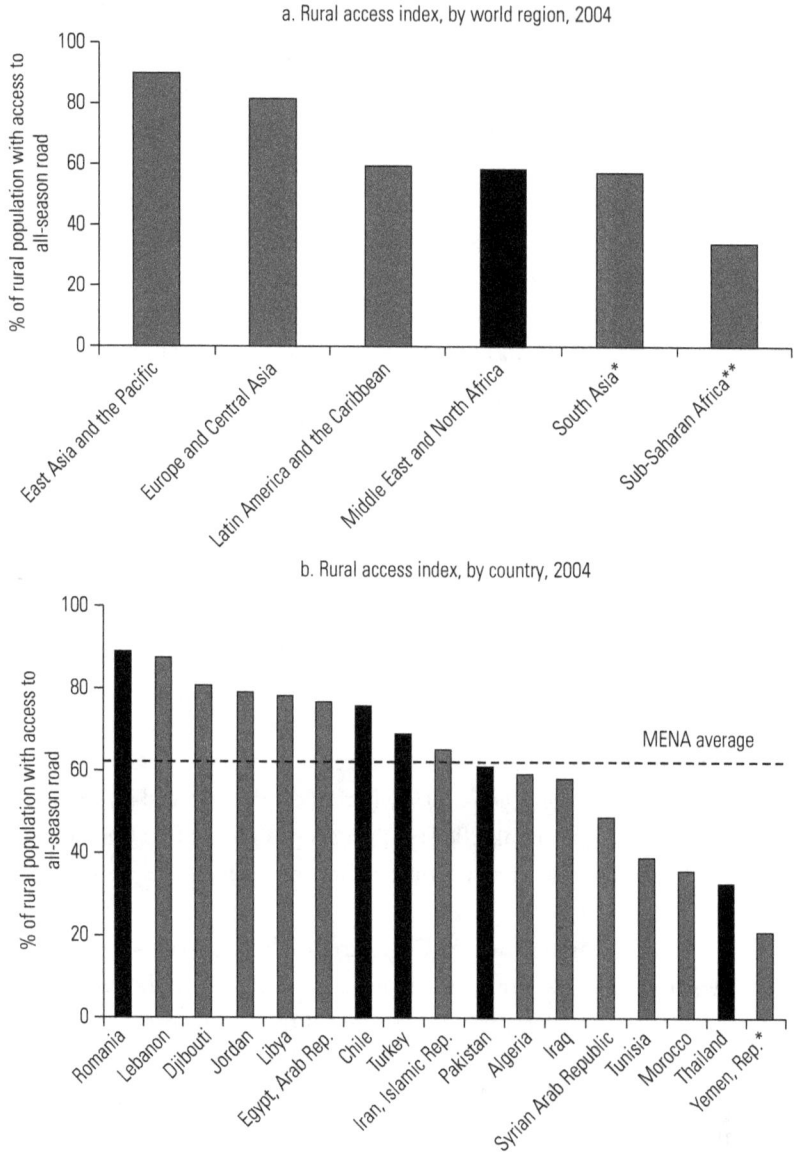

a. Rural access index, by world region, 2004

b. Rural access index, by country, 2004

Source: Roberts, Shyan, and Cordula 2006.
Note: *Top:* * Data for 2003–04, ** data for 1999–2004. *Bottom:* * Data for 1999.

South Asia). The Republic of Yemen, Morocco, Tunisia, and the Syrian Arab Republic had the lowest indicators in MENA at respectively about 20, 38, 40, and 50 percent in 2004.

However, significant improvements have been recently noted, particularly in the Republic of Yemen and Morocco. Morocco launched its National Rural Roads Program (NRRP) in 1994. During the following

10 years, the government constructed or improved more than 10,000 kilometers of rural roads. Many positive impacts were observed: increased frequency of public transport, a shift toward higher-value crops, doubled enrollment in private education, increased teacher retention rates, and more use of health facilities. Nonetheless, only 43 percent of the rural population was estimated to have "easy access" to roads by 2004. The government therefore launched its NRRP-2 for 2005–10. An important change is that the old plan set targets in terms of kilometers of road constructed whereas the NRRP-2 focused on maximizing the number of people served (Levy 2004).

Despite the high headline costs of large-scale rural roads programs, they are actually quite cost-effective on a per capita basis. Even in the Republic of Yemen's mountainous landscape, the Rural Access Program is estimated to bring surfaced road connectivity at a cost of around $100 per rural inhabitant (World Bank 2009e). The Moroccan National Rural Roads Program (NRRP2) set a threshold criterion for connectivity of $490 per beneficiary. The first phase of the NRRP2 is establishing rural road connections at a cost of around $350 per person (2.1 million beneficiaries for DH 5.6 billion). However, unit costs will rise steeply as rural connectivity rates improve and only the most isolated communities are left to connect.

Urban Congestion: Too Many Private Cars

MENA's urban road systems are seizing up. A sharp increase in motorization rates and the lack of public space for further infrastructure development are suffocating MENA's agglomerations. Excessive congestion is therefore constraining connectivity in most MENA cities, particularly Tehran, Cairo, Alexandria, Casablanca, and Beirut, with the associated increase in travel time, energy inefficiency, and poor air quality.

Urban congestion has an economic and a human cost. In 1989, the average speed of Cairo traffic during the rush hour was 8.1 kilometers per hour in peak periods. Since then the vehicle fleet may have quadrupled (El Araby 2002). On the urban expressways, which were constructed in order to decongest the city, average speeds were found in 2000 to be as low as 10 kilometers per hour and traffic queues often extended 2 to 3 kilometers (World Bank 2000). Egypt's National Research Center found that the average noise level in Cairo from 7 a.m. until 10 p.m. was 85 decibels, equivalent to a freight train passing 5 meters away (Slackman 2008)! One estimate (Shokri 2005) is that Tehranis spend a total of 4.5 million hours per day waiting in traffic and that the space required to park the city's cars increases by 5 hectares per day. In Algiers, average journey times are reported to be as high as 80 minutes each day (World Bank

2007a). Traffic speeds in Beirut are as low as 12 kilometers per hour for much of the day (World Bank 2006a). Particulate matter concentrations in MENA[2] cities are around 85 grams per cubic meter, compared with 60 grams for the world as a whole, and cost MENA about 0.9 percent of gross national income in terms of impaired health (World Bank 2009b), compared with 0.5 percent worldwide. Moreover, motorization rates are set to increase with economic growth.

The problem is that motorization in MENA leans toward private cars at the expense of public transportation. Higher-income economies in MENA have a significantly higher share of cars in their fleets, indicating a consumer preference for personal car ownership, when income levels permit, to meet transportation needs and to compensate for the lack of public transportation and the poor quality of available services. The result is that buses' share of the total vehicle fleet is more than twice as high in comparator economies with similar levels of income (Chile, Turkey, Pakistan, and Romania) as in the MENA region: 5 percent versus 2 percent. In Tehran and Isfahan, around 30 percent of all urban trips are made in private cars, which is unusually high for a country at this level of development (World Bank 2005b); and in Lebanon 68 percent of motorized trips are made by private car (World Bank 2006a). In 2006 the rate of private car ownership in Damascus was similar to that of Ireland (World Bank 2008). This model of urban transportation development in MENA, focused on private cars and low-quality bus services, is becoming unsustainable.

The building blocks for an efficient (bus-based) urban public transportation system are well known and tested:

- The establishment of a public transport regulatory authority

- Integrated urban transport planning

- Route planning and procurement of services by the public authority

- Provision of services by several private operators

- Performance monitoring and enforcement by the public authority

- Allocation of some road space dedicated for public transport

As this sequence suggests, a city region's ability to mobilize public transportation for spillover connectivity will depend critically upon the establishment of an empowered regulatory authority.

Difficulties faced by women in using public transportation hinder their participation in the workforce. As low female labor force participation is part of the lagging area problem in MENA, it will be important to consider female-only transport services or other culturally acceptable transport modes, particularly in conservative areas.

Some MENA cities lack adequate bypass roads for long-distance freight traffic, which worsens urban congestion. This situation occurs in Algiers, Beirut, and Amman. Despite the extensive spread of MENA's trunk road network, some countries also have a few critical stretches of intercity road where congestion is particularly high due to inadequate road quality and capacity. These roads include segments of Algeria's east-west northern axis and the International Corridor from the port of Djibouti to the Ethiopian border.

Road Safety

MENA's road safety record is bad and worsening. Road safety appeared as a major issue in all eight of the MENA13 economies for which the World Bank has conducted recent transport sector reviews. The region's average rate of road crash fatalities is currently one of the highest in the world, be it measured per capita or per registered vehicles (10 people killed per 100,000 people and 25 people killed per 100,000 vehicles per year; see figure 5.4). The situation is particularly worrisome in Morocco, Jordan, and the Islamic Republic of Iran (figure 5.5). In the Islamic Republic of Iran, the fatality rate of 50 deaths per 10,000 vehicles per year is 20 times the norm for developed countries, and road accidents have been estimated to cost 3 percent of GDP (Ayati and Behnood 2007). The causes of poor road safety in the Islamic Republic of Iran include poor driver training, slack enforcement of traffic rules (World Bank 2005b), dangerous intersections, lack of warning signs, worn pavement markings, bad quality road surfaces, and inadequate maintenance.

FIGURE 5.4

MENA Is a Region of Dangerous Roads

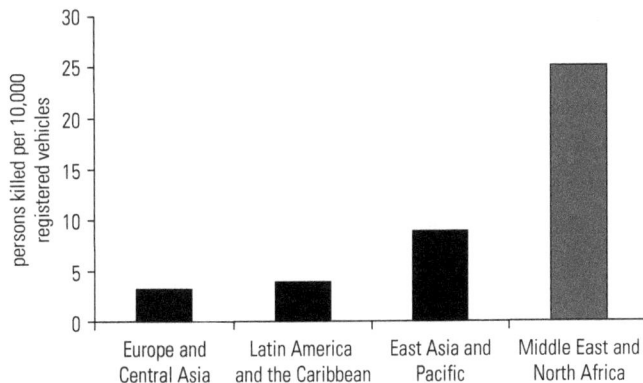

Source: International Road Federation 2008.

FIGURE 5.5

Average Rates of Road Crash Fatalities per Capita and Registered Vehicles in MENA Region and in Comparator Countries

Road fatalities in MENA

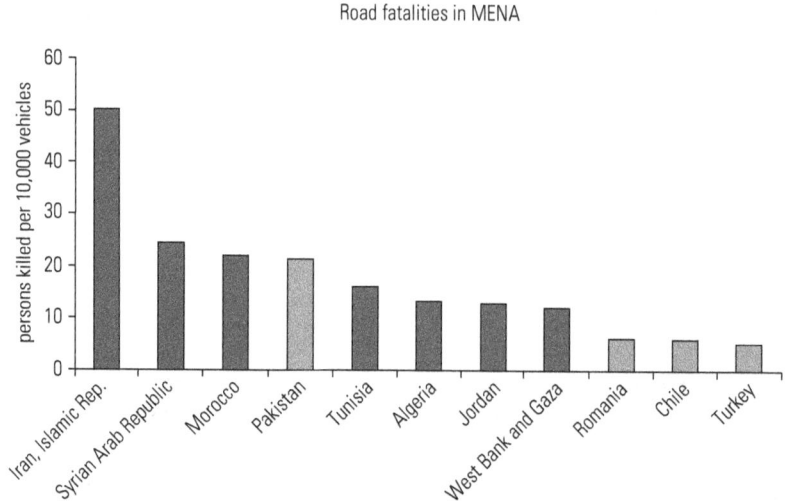

Sources: For Iran: World Bank. "Technical Assistance Project for Road Safety. Concept Note." For all other countries, team calculations based on International Road Federation 2008.

In 2002, about 5 percent of health loss in MENA, measured in terms of Disability-Adjusted Life Years (DALYs), was due to road crashes. This is higher than any other region and makes road crashes the third leading cause for health loss in MENA. In 2030, road crashes are expected to become the leading cause for health loss in MENA, accounting for about 8 percent of total health loss in the region.

Low Efficiency of Road Use

The return on MENA's new road investment is currently being undermined by inappropriate regulation of the commercial operators who use them. The third key challenge facing MENA's roads sector is, therefore, to create a favorable business environment for transportation.

While it is easy to criticize road sector regulation, it has proved extremely difficult for MENA economies to achieve a satisfactory middle way between overregulation, which raises prices and restricts supply, and underregulation, which leads to poor service quality. Egypt, the Islamic Republic of Iran, Iraq, and Jordan are examples of overregulation keeping costs up. Algeria, Lebanon, and Tunisia are examples of the combination of low costs and low service quality in the transport sector that results from underregulation (box 5.1).

BOX 5.1

Seeking the Balance between Underregulation and Overregulation of Freight and Passenger Transportation

- In *the Arab Republic of Egypt*, the privatization of the roads sector has been under way since the early 1990s; however, the largest companies remain state-owned, are inefficient, and offer low service quality (Euro Med Transport Project 2004b). Regulations and duties on the import of trucks (especially refrigerated trucks) and spare parts help keep the operating costs for trucks 30–50 percent higher than in Lebanon and Jordan (World Bank 2006c). Road sector institutional responsibilities are fragmented between three ministries (World Bank 2007i).

- In the *Islamic Republic of Iran*, the formal passenger transport sector is largely under state control, and the low quality of services provided exacerbates reliance on private cars and informal collective taxis (World Bank 2005b).

- In postwar *Iraq*, the trucking sector was essentially monopolized by government-controlled firms. The emphasis was placed on volumes rather than service quality. Truck maintenance was insufficient and the vehicle fleet was aging (United Nations and World Bank 2003).

- In *Jordan*, the "turn system" is the main bottleneck affecting the trucking industry. Private operators cannot approach and negotiate with customers directly, but must go through UCOLT, a state-owned company, which allocates jobs among contractors. This rigid system leads to an oversupply of trucks and long waiting periods. Operators do not have an incentive to offer better services and their returns are low, while prices are high (Euro Med Transport Project 2004c).

- In *Algeria*, freight transport was completely liberalized in 1988, and the private sector is now dominant for both passenger (90 percent) and freight (95 percent) transport. However, a lack of adequate regulation of private operators initially led to fragmentation and a poor quality of service. More recently, entry regulations have been enforced, incentives for operators to group have been introduced, and the situation has improved somewhat (Euro Med Transport Project 2004a).

- *Lebanon's* complete absence of entry regulations in the passenger transport sector since 1996 has led to the emergence of myriad small operators, 70 percent of whom use private cars, which contribute to congestion concerns. Oversupply has led to price-cutting at the expense of vehicle maintenance, service quality, and safety (World Bank 2006a).

- *Morocco's* freight transport sector is another instance of atomization, with 90 percent of operators owning just one or two trucks, a predominance of informal carriers (70–75 percent), a lack of specialized vehicles such as refrigerated trucks, and an antiquated vehicle fleet (on average 13 years) (World Bank 2006b).

- *Tunisia's* freight transport has been completely liberalized, ensuring low tariffs (Euro Med Transport Project 2004d).

Regional Trade Facilitation Matters Crucially for Lagging Areas

Land borders can create artificial lagging areas. Put simply, if it is diffi-cult for freight and people to cross a land border, the areas on either side of it are cut off from part of their economic hinterland. Even in the highly integrated European Union (EU), border regions are twice as likely to be lagging regions than are nonborder regions (Van Well 2006, 80). In MENA, there are several lagging border areas that could benefit from their proximity to major cities in neighboring countries if travel across borders were as easy as within borders. There is also a tendency for governments to underinvest in transborder road and rail links, maybe because part of the benefits of such investment will go to another coun-try or simply because of a lack of coordination between each country's transport planners (Puga 2008).

Cross-border trade within MENA is low. The Maghreb (Algeria, Libya, Mauritania, Morocco, and Tunisia) has one of the lowest figures for intraregional trade integration of any region in the world: regional trade represents only 1.3 percent of total Maghreb trade with the world. The Mashreq region is somewhat more integrated. The intraregional share of their total trade, at about 17 percent, is much less than the 65 percent plus of the two largest trading blocks (North American Free Trade Agreement [NAFTA] and EU), rather less than that of Association of Southeast Asian Nations (ASEAN) (26 percent) and rather more than the Southern Cone Common Market (Mercado Común del Sur) (Mercosur) (16 percent) and the Arab League countries as a whole (11 percent) (World Bank 2009d).

A comparison of map 5.2 with map 5.1 shows how zones of economic proximity can spill across national boundaries to benefit lagging areas in some countries. The far northeast of Morocco benefits from proximity to Oran in Algeria. The lagging far northeast of Algeria benefits from proximity to Tunis. The poor northern tip of Lebanon benefits from proximity to Syria's Damascus-Aleppo axis. The disadvantaged region of northern Syria gains from proximity to Gaziantep, one of the most developed provinces of southeast Turkey, and Diyarbakir. Finally, the lagging ostan of Khuzistan in the southwest of the Islamic Republic of Iran gains from proximity to Basra in Iraq.

The construction of transborder connections and the easing of border crossings are therefore not only trade promotion policies; they can also be spatial development strategies.

A measure of the room for progress is the World Bank's Logistics Per-formance Index (LPI), which measures the ease of doing trade across bor-ders.[3] Table 5.4 compares nine MENA13 economies' trade logistics with those from other parts of the world. Of the countries surveyed, Tunisia and

MAP 5.2

Smooth Border Crossings Would Give Lagging Border Regions a Better Chance of Benefiting from Spillover Connectivity: Travel Time in Hours to a City of More Than 500,000 Inhabitants, with Zero-Hour Border Crossings

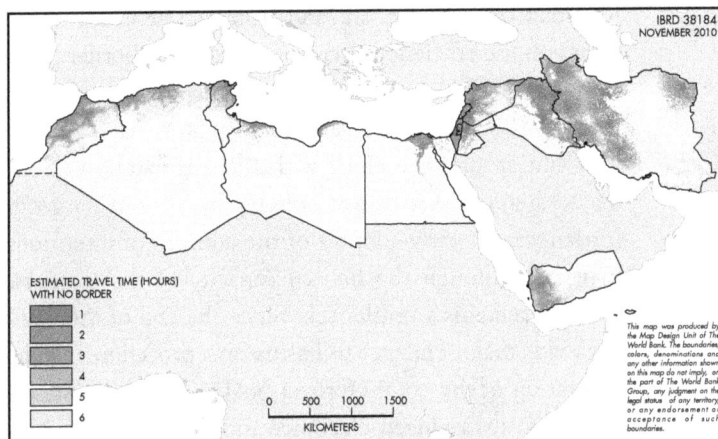

Source: Staff GIS analysis; sources detailed in appendix.

TABLE 5.4

MENA's 2006–08 Logistics Performance Index (LPI) Benchmarked

	Overall LPI	Efficiency of customs and other border procedures	Quality of transport and IT infrastructures	Logistics competence	Domestic transportation costs
Djibouti	1.94	1.92	1.64	2.00	2.80
Algeria	2.06	1.83	1.60	1.92	3.17
Syrian Arab Republic	2.09	2.17	1.91	1.80	2.89
Yemen, Rep.	2.29	2.18	2.08	2.22	2.67
Sub-Saharan Africa average	**2.35**	**2.21**	**2.11**	**2.33**	**2.98**
Egypt, Arab Rep.	2.37	2.00	2.08	2.38	2.83
Lebanon	2.37	2.14	2.17	2.40	3.40
Morocco	2.38	2.20	2.33	2.13	2.38
Lower-middle-income average	**2.46**	**2.26**	**2.30**	**2.38**	**3.04**
Iran, Islamic Rep.	2.51	2.44	2.50	2.69	2.93
Latin America and the Caribbean average	**2.57**	**2.38**	**2.38**	**2.52**	**2.97**
Tunisia	2.76	2.83	2.83	2.43	3.20
Upper-middle-income average	**2.76**	**2.60**	**2.55**	**2.72**	**2.90**
Jordan	2.89	2.62	2.62	3.00	2.92

Source: http://info.worldbank.org/etools/tracksurvey, accessed March 2009.

Jordan measured up against the average performance rating for the upper-middle-income country peer group. Morocco, Lebanon, and Egypt were very close to the Sub-Saharan African average. Djibouti, Algeria, Syria, and the Republic of Yemen achieved a significantly lower score than the average for Sub-Saharan Africa. Breaking the LPI down, only the Islamic Republic of Iran, Jordan, and Tunisia rated higher than Sub-Saharan Africa on the efficiency of customs and other border procedures.

Some MENA economies' customs performance has improved in recent years. Algeria's customs procedures have been streamlined, and now run around the clock with the introduction of the SIGAD automated system. As a transit country because of its geographic location, Jordan was an early adopter of the concept of intermodal transport and logistics, although the limited capacity of the main customs depot in Amman remains a bottleneck. Since the end of the Civil War, Lebanon has made major changes to its customs procedures, including the implementation of the computerized NAJM customs system. Morocco's customs reforms reduced clearance times from 5.5 to 2 days by the early 2000s, by means of the simplification of procedures and forms, the use of information technology, and measures to reduce corruption (World Bank 2002). Tunisia has introduced the electronic SINDA customs management system. In 2002, Syria, Lebanon, and Jordan adopted a common set of customs procedures to facilitate border crossings.

However, despite the improvements in customs procedures, the shortage of modern logistics platforms and infrastructure remains a handicap to international trade regionwide. Whereas a survey of enterprises in 2001 found tariffs to be the top obstacle to cross-border trade, by 2008 infrastructure services and red tape had overtaken tariffs (Hoekman and Zarrouk 2009). The infrastructural aspect of logistics emerges in sector reviews as a top priority issue in Morocco and Tunisia, where progress has already been made on the procedural side of cross-border trade.

Priorities for Improving Spillover Connectivity

First, MENA's *broad pattern of public expenditure* in transport could benefit from rebalancing. The earlier analysis suggests that MENA economies should consider reallocating resources away from expansion of the domestic trunk road network toward (a) maintenance of the existing network, (b) improving rural access, (c) trans-border networks, and (d) improving traffic management.

Second, *urban and peri-urban mass transit systems* are critical if people from lagging areas are to benefit from agglomerations' demand for labor. In Morocco, for example, the recent investments in peri-urban rail links have enabled workers to commute into the prime cities of Rabat and Casablanca from Salé, Kenitra, and Mohammedia (Er-Rouch 2009). As cities grow, so do commuting distances; in Egypt, the average time spent commuting increased by about a third between 1988 and 1998 (Assaad and Arntz 2005). While rarely justified on a purely financial basis and therefore requiring substantial public contributions, mass transit investments support smooth urban expansion (chapter 4) and yield significant economic benefits.

Many MENA cities will need new approaches to urban mass transit. At present, it is common for mass transit to consist largely of low-quality publicly owned bus services, and unaffordable public investment in light rail is seen as the only alternative. However, there are other potential strategies:

- First, many MENA economies have informal urban shared taxi sectors, providing low-quality services. However, they often lack private bus services of high enough quality to compete with private cars for the middle-class market. Lifting barriers to private investment in urban transport can encourage the development of formal, high-quality private bus services.

- Second, bus rapid transport (BRT) is proving itself a lower-cost alternative to light rail for high-volume mass transit. At its peak, Bogotá's TransMillenio system can move 25,000 people per hour across a single point in space. It is estimated that dedicated bus lanes can handle 40 to 60 vehicles per hour (Levinson, Zimmerman, Clinger, and Rutherford 2002), competing with private cars for speed, comfort, and cost. The BRT model also permits the relatively simple participation of multiple operators on the network, some of which may be private.

- Third, improving *transborder connectivity* will be particularly important in ensuring that lagging areas harness spillover connectivity benefits. A strategy to improve cross-border connectivity could contain the following components:

  - An analysis of the main obstacles to cross-border connectivity: procedures, regulations, the lack of regional logistics services, and missing infrastructure links (roads, railways, multimodal facilities, border infrastructure, and logistical platforms). The Transport and Trade Facilitation Audit (TTFA) is an established methodology for identifying such bottlenecks.

  - Concrete international cooperation in areas such as data, training, and information systems

  - Spatial planning to capture economies of scale and match investments to transport flows

  – Bilateral and regional agreements on road and rail transport

  – A transit regime for long-distance trade (e.g., the TIR [Transports Internationaux Routiers] system)

• Fourth, making MENA's road infrastructure more productive will depend on finding the *appropriate mix of liberalization and regulation* in the passenger and freight transportation sectors. According to the country experiences in box 5.1, key elements of a good regulatory and institutional approach include the following:

  – Creation of integrated and empowered municipal authorities for urban transport, to ensure a coordinated approach to urban transport planning (defining the roles of public and private operators) and to public transportation across administrative jurisdictions.

  – Open access to private operators and withdrawal of the public sector from freight transportation. Freight transportation is a sector par excellence in which the private sector's dynamism and responsiveness are essential.

  – Gradual and strict regulation of vehicles' safety standards and axle weights. Progressive implementation will give operators time to adapt and to avoid the disruption of services for low-income passengers.

  – Liberalization of importation of commercial vehicles and parts, including specialized vehicles such as refrigerated trucks.

  – Accepting that the fragmentation of the road freight sector is normal. Even in developed countries, around 80 percent of road haulers operate one or two vehicles. If larger road freight companies are not emerging in MENA, this may be because of an unfavorable general business environment for large formal companies or because of a lack of large, consolidated shipments in a fragmented goods market. *Atomization of the transportation sector does not mean that it needs additional regulation.* (See box 5.2.)

Electronic Proximity: New Tool for the Integration of Lagging Areas

Isolation from information and relationships is a key part of the lagging area problem. It puts the populations of lagging areas at a disadvantage when it comes to interacting with bureaucracies and markets.

Information and communication technology[4] (ICT), therefore, give policy makers a whole new set of options for attacking spatial disparities. They make it possible to create virtual proximity where physical

---

BOX 5.2

Enhancing Spillover Connectivity in MENA: Four Ideas for Policy Makers

- Identify lagging areas that are dense and close enough to agglomerations to benefit from spillover connectivity, including transborder connectivity.

- Identify the constraints on spillover connectivity in these areas, paying specific attention to infrastructure maintenance, short-distance urban and rural connections, and the efficiency of freight and passenger transport operators.

- Work out which institutional arrangements are needed to underpin the integrated planning of connections within a city and its hinterland.

- Within a territorial development framework, prepare a plan integrating the institutional, regulatory, and investment actions required to connect a city and its hinterland.

Source: Study Team.

---

proximity is impossible. Of course, electronic connectivity can never compensate lagging areas for high transport costs to agglomerations, but it can help mitigate the informational and relational penalties of distance (table 5.5).

ICT Can Help Lagging Areas

Mobile phones have a special potential in rural areas in developing countries; the next billion mobile subscribers will consist mainly of the rural poor (World Bank 2009c). Three-quarters of all mobile handsets are now used in developing countries (*Economist* 2008). Mobile phones are now the world's largest distribution platform, offering applications such as m-health, m-education, and m-banking.

However, ICT infrastructure can be weak in lagging areas. In many rural parts of the world, such problems can be very basic: aging copper-based telephone lines, or local monopolies of telecommunication corporations over exchanges and "last mile" infrastructure, with little incentive to open up to alternative providers.

For every 10-percentage-point increase in broadband penetration in developing countries, there is a 1.4-percentage-point growth benefit, but the penetration of broadband connectivity into developing countries' rural areas has been slow. Less than 5 percent of low-income countries' populations were connected to broadband networks in 2007, and that was mostly in urban centers (World Bank 2009h). For digital subscriber

TABLE 5.5

How ICT Can Benefit Lagging Areas

Individuals	Businesses	Government
Making transactions with businesses and government quicker and cheaper, e.g., by saving a trip to check school exam scores	Making transactions with consumers or government quicker and cheaper	Delivering time savings and reduction of costs in transacting with citizens or businesses
Improving access to public services through e-government, e-health, and e-education, if offered	Improving access to new markets; connecting to economic opportunities and integration at the national and international levels	Enhancing community development
Increasing employment opportunities	Stimulating development and facilitating business services needed by SMEs and home businesses	Emergency or disaster support
Improving access to financial services, such as banking, payments or remittances and money transfers	Improving the investment climate in lagging areas	Reducing tax collection costs
Relieving the need to migrate to urban centers	Increasing productivity	New sources of income
Access to knowledge, skills, and networks to increase opportunities	Access to knowledge, skills, and networks to increase opportunities	Improved ability to deliver public services
Improving access to information services		Developing the local private sector and lessening migration to the cities

Source: Study Team.

Note: SMEs = small and medium enterprises.

line (DSL) technologies, which are the most popular platform for broadband services worldwide, there is a particular problem of attenuation of signal with distance. This means that quality is lower and costs are higher in low-density areas. In the absence of a universal service obligation (USO) relating to broadband Internet, its provision is subject to market forces, which do not favor areas of dispersed population because of the high investment and low demand (Warren 2007). There is, therefore, a danger that nonusers of the Internet and mobile telephony in lagging areas will become disenfranchised. As ICT becomes progressively regarded as the default communication medium, those without access to it become gradually marginalized (Warren 2007).

Table 5.5 summarizes how ICTs can benefit lagging areas. Examples abound of successful pilots demonstrating how ICTs have overcome problems of geographical isolation that were once thought to be insurmountable.

- The high cost of setting up bank branches used to be considered a barrier to providing formal banking services to rural and semirural areas of Brazil. At the end of 2000, 71 percent of Brazil's 5,636 municipalities had bank services. But three years later, all of them did. The difference was the explosion of banking correspondents: small retailers such as kiosks or pharmacies equipped with a point-of-sale (POS) device, a keypad or maybe a personal computer, for customers to enter their personal identity numbers. The POS device might be as simple as a mobile phone. By the end of 2005, 90,000 banking correspondents were in action. They had become the core of retail financial services in the lagging areas of the north and northeast, where 51 and 42 percent of municipalities, respectively, were now served exclusively by correspondents (CGAP 2006a; CGAP 2006b).

- There are many examples worldwide of SMS (Short Message Service) alert systems giving farmers, fisherfolk, and traders real-time information on market prices in different locations.

- The Egyptian Education Initiative (EEI) has established information technology clubs nationwide, with a focus on rural areas. By pooling hardware, software, and connections, these clubs help reduce usage costs to about US$0.20 an hour, overcoming the financial barrier to Internet access in low-income areas (MCIT 2008).

- Egypt's Ministry of Communications and Information Technology has also deployed public-private partnerships to set up information technology (IT) clubs across the country. The majority of the 1,427 clubs are in low-income and rural areas, with the highest per capita coverage in lagging Upper Egypt and the frontier governorates. Local small enterprises are using the IT clubs to leverage scarce computing power.

- Tunisia has established cyberparks for remote labor in 16 provincial towns. They host 395 enterprises (MCT 2009). However, information is not available on their impact in lagging areas or on their cost-effectiveness in terms of jobs created.

- National Research and Education Networks (NRENs) can pool information resources (electronic library access) among universities to reduce disparities in resources. An example is the Egyptian Universities Network (EUN: http://www.eun.eg), which was an early example of a regional NREN and which now links with NRENs in Europe and North America.

- An innovative new project, supported by the UN World Food Programme (WFP), uses mobile phones to deliver food vouchers to Iraqi refugees living in the country. This system enables them to buy a wider range of food, including fish and eggs, rather than being dependent on government-run food shops. Significantly, the WFP reports that mobile ownership among refugees is almost universal, even though other assets might be in short supply.

- In a context of movement restrictions, mobile phones and the Internet are widely used in the West Bank and Gaza to facilitate remittances and to stay in touch with family members. The West Bank and Gaza leads in the rural adoption of new ICTs: more than a quarter of rural households own a computer and more than a tenth have Internet access.

- Tunisia's remote medicine investments allow outlying hospitals to take advantage of remote pathology, consultation, and conference services.

MENA's Rural ICT: A Strong Legacy of Fixed Lines, but Lagging Access to Mobile Telephony and the Internet

Comparing MENA's rural areas with those of other regions, the good news is that MENA has a comparatively high rate of access to electricity (figure 5.6). MENA's rural areas, however, have much poorer access to

FIGURE 5.6

The Spatial Coverage of ICT in Developing Regions' Rural Areas

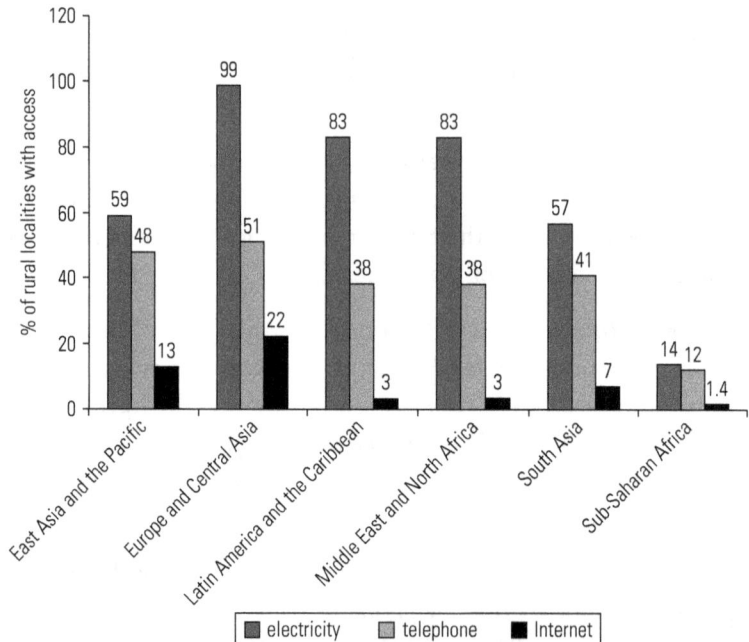

Source: ITU 2008.

Note: Based on data between 2000 and 2006 using simple averages.

telephone and Internet services than their counterparts in South Asia and East Asia, as well as Europe and Central Asia. Mobile telephony's comparative advantage over fixed telephony is strongest in low-density areas, where the cost per household of installing and maintaining cable connections is highest. However, the shift in rural areas from fixed-line to mobile telephony has been less pronounced in MENA than in other parts of the world. In all the other regions, the rate of rural mobile usage has overtaken that of fixed lines. In MENA, however, 37 percent of households have fixed lines and 26 percent have mobile lines. A probable reason is that MENA made significant early investments in extending fixed-line telephony to rural areas, achieving high rural usage rates compared with East Asia and the Pacific (10 percent), Latin America and the Caribbean (13 percent), South Asia (11 percent), and Sub-Saharan Africa (1 percent). Only Europe and Central Asia (46 percent) have higher rates of rural household fixed-line connections than MENA (ITU 2008).

Expansion of ICT Use in Lagging Areas

When designing strategies to extend ICTs to lagging areas, it is useful to break the task down into two components: (a) the market efficiency gap and (b) the access gap (Navas-Sabater and Dymond 2002). The market efficiency gap is the difference between the current level of service penetration and the level achievable in a liberalized and stable regulatory environment. The access gap relates to the gap between leading and lagging areas that would remain under efficient market conditions because the lagging population cannot afford the market prices at which the service is offered.

Sector reform will help close the market efficiency gap by increasing competition, reducing tariffs, and increasing supply. As can be seen in Table 5.6, fixed-line liberalization still has a way to go in MENA.

The present and planned liberalization of the fixed-line and data markets in some MENA economies should enhance infrastructure-based competition in these countries. Allowing for international connectivity competition in most MENA economies will also lower international bandwidth costs, which will allow the Internet and data providers to start offering more advanced services at cost-based rates, and hence much lower rates, across the country (Arab Advisors Group 2008).

Figure 5.7 compares the spread of communications technology in MENA economies with global trends around 2007–08. In 2007, Jordan was ahead of the global trend for cellular subscriptions, with Egypt, the Islamic Republic of Iran, Libya, Lebanon, and Syria lagging behind. In 2008, most MENA economies' monthly cellular tariffs were below the global trend, but not Morocco's and Lebanon's. Broadband connections have been slow to grow in Libya and Syria.

TABLE 5.6

Fixed-Line and Internet Market Status (According to Operational Licenses) in MENA

Country	Fixed lines	Internet	Cellular operators
Algeria	Duopoly	Competitive	3
Egypt, Arab Rep.	Monopoly	Competitive	3
Iraq	Monopoly	Competitive	5
Jordan	Competitive	Competitive	4
Lebanon	Monopoly	Competitive	3
Morocco	Competitive	Competitive	3
West Bank and Gaza	Monopoly	Competitive	2
Syrian Arab Republic	Monopoly	Competitive	2
Tunisia	Monopoly	Competitive	3
Yemen, Rep.	Monopoly	Duopoly	4

Sources: Arab Advisors Group 2008; Internet search for cellular operators.

To close the access gap, governments need to use a mix of approaches, including regulatory incentives to attract investors, smart subsidies, and a universal access fund (Navas-Sabater and Dymond 2002). Telecommunications sector liberalization will increase total service supply and reduce rates. However, policy makers should be aware that increased competition and reduced tariffs can discourage operators from investing in low-density areas where the cost of infrastructure per subscriber is higher. Governments may wish to set up specific incentives for ICT operators to expand into poorer areas. The economic rationale for such measures would be that information-related services create positive externalities of social integration and efficient markets. It is, therefore, important to identify incentives that encourage operators to meet the government's spatial objectives without distorting or stunting the overall growth of the sector.

The traditional solution to spatial disparities in ICT access has been simple: instructing state-owned fixed-line monopolies to expand into rural areas, as in many MENA economies. This is a high-cost solution, as publicly owned fixed-line technologies are the least efficient technology in low-density areas. Another disadvantage of the fixed-line monopoly approach to expanding lagging area coverage is that operators can use their social mandate as a cover for their suboptimal financial performance; once a state-owned monopoly has such a noncommercial objective, it is very difficult for the government to distinguish the costs of the social provision from the costs of inefficiency.

FIGURE 5.7

Telecommunications: Who Is Ahead and Who Is Behind the International Trend?

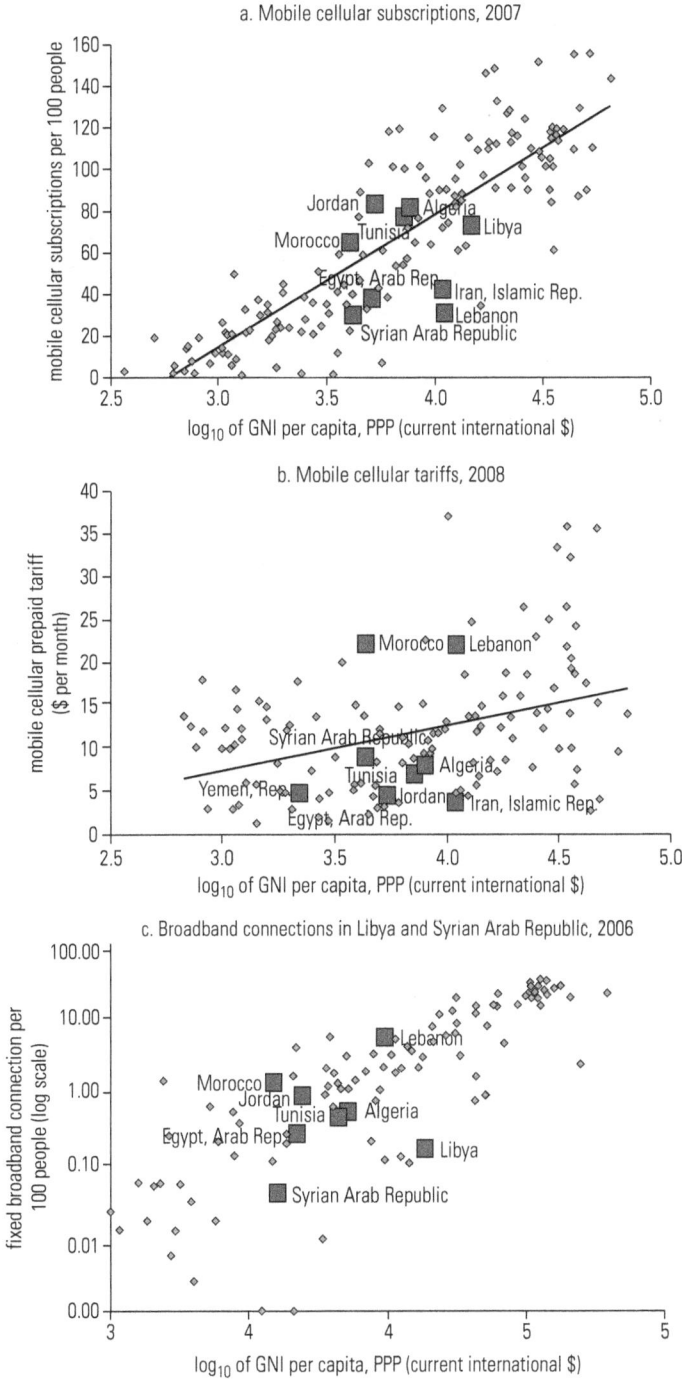

a. Mobile cellular subscriptions, 2007

b. Mobile cellular tariffs, 2008

c. Broadband connections in Libya and Syrian Arab Republic, 2006

Source: International Telecommunications (ITU) database.

BOX 5.3

Bringing ICT Connectivity to Lagging Areas: Two Ideas for Policy Makers

- Shifting from a telecoms policy for lagging areas based on monopolies' and oligopolies' "social mandates" to an approach founded on the market-based allocation of spatial incentives to competing private operators.

- Implementing public-private partnerships for ICT-enabled services to lagging areas—for example, financial services, Internet clubs, distance education, and market information.

Source: Study Team.

A second solution has been for governments to levy fees on telecom operators in order to fund social ICT programs (see box 5.3). Morocco, for example, has adopted levies to finance the GENIE program (computers in schools), and levies on operators have subsidized the Smart Village Technopark, a public-private partnership in the outskirts of Cairo. But this approach carries some risks. First, it is difficult for special social programs to reach a broad range of disadvantaged people. Second, the fact that operators are transferring a part of their oligopoly rents to government may strengthen their bargaining power in opposing the entry of new operators.

A more attractive example of the incentives approach was to be found in Chile, an early telecoms reformer. In 1994, the government established a Telecommunications Development Fund, financed by the national budget, to catalyze *private* investment in pay phone service in low-income areas. Between 1995 and 2000, the fund supported the provision of pay phone service to more than 6,000 rural localities with about 2.2 million inhabitants, thereby reducing the proportion of Chile's population living in places without access to basic voice communication from 15 percent in 1994 to 1 percent in 2002. In addition, some 25,000 individual rural telephone lines were provided. The subsidies cost the government *less than 0.3 percent* of total telecommunications sector revenue during the funding period, and fund administration costs about 3 percent of the monies granted. The fund's success and efficiency was largely due to extensive reliance on market forces to determine and allocate subsidies, minimal regulatory intervention, simple and relatively expeditious processing, and effective government leadership. Competition among operators for the rural market and subsidies led to substantial reductions in cost (Wellenius 2002).

Endnotes

1. Giza, Gharbeyya, Suez, Ismailiya, Kalyoubiya, Sharkiya, Matrouh, and Beheira.

2. Including the Gulf Cooperation Council (GCC).

3. The Logistics Performance Index (LPI) reflects the overall perception of a country's logistics based on over 1,000 responses to a survey of logistics performance evaluated in seven key subcategories. These categories include efficiency of customs and other border procedures, quality of transport and IT infrastructures, international and domestic transportation costs, ease of shipments and logistics competence, and tracking ability and timeliness of shipments. The value of the index ranges from 1 to 5, with a higher score representing a better performance.

4. For present purposes, ICT comprises the following subsectors: telecommunications services (fixed and mobile), telecom hardware, computer hardware, software, networking, ICT-enabled services (ITES), IT applications, and advanced media. The broadcasting and postal sectors, which are also considered part of the ICT sector by some countries, are not treated.

References

Arab Advisors Group. 2008. *ADSL Rates in the Arab World: A Regional Comparison.* Amman: Arab Advisors Group.

Assaad, R., and M. Arntz. 2005. "Constrained Geographical Mobility and Gendered Labor Market Outcomes under Structural Adjustment: Evidence from Egypt." *World Development* 33 (3): 431–54.

Ayati, E., and H. R. Behnood. 2007. "The Burden of Fatalities Resulting from Road Accidents: An Epidemiological Study of Iran." Paper presented at the 14th International Conference, "Road Safety on Four Continents," Bangkok.

Belarbi, Y., and A. Zouache. 2009. *Regional Employment Growth and Spatial Dependence in Algeria, 1998–2005.* Cairo: Economic Research Forum.

CGAP (Consultative Group to Assist the Poor). 2006a. *FocusNote: Using Technology to Build Inclusive Financial Systems.* Washington, DC: CGAP.

———. 2006b. *Mobile Phones for Microfinance.* Washington, DC: CGAP.

CIA (Central Intelligence Agency). 2006-present. *The World Factbook. Field Listing: Roadways.* Washington, DC: CIA.

Datt, G., and M. Ravallion. 1998. "Why Have Some Indian States Done Better than Others at Reducing Rural Poverty? *Economica* 65 (257): 17–38.

Economist. 2008. "Halfway There: How to Promote the Spread of Mobile Technologies among the World's Poorest." May 29.

El Araby, M. (2002). "Urban Growth and Environmental Degradation: The Case of Cairo, Egypt." *Cities* 19 (6): 389–400.

Er-Rouch, O. 2009. "Train Commuting: A Necessary Pain." June 24, Agence Maghreb Arabe Presse. http://www.map.ma/eng/sections/general/train_commuting__a_n/view.

Euro Med Transport Project. 2004a. *Algeria Diagnostic Study.*

———. 2004b. *Egypt Diagnostic Study.*

———. 2004c. *Jordan Diagnostic Study.*

———. 2004d. *Tunisia Diagnostic Study.*

Fay, M., and T. Yepes. 2003. *Investing in Infrastructure: What Is Needed from 2000 to 2010.* Washington, DC: World Bank.

Hoekman, B., and J. Zarrouk. 2009. "An Assessment of the Changes in Cross-Border Trade Costs in the Pan-Arab Free Trade Area, 2001–2008." *MNA Knowledge and Learning Fast Brief 30.* World Bank, Washington, DC.

IRF (International Road Federation). 2008. "World Road Statistics." IRF, Geneva.

ITU (International Telecommunications Union). 2008. *Measuring Information and Communication Technology Availabilty in Villages and Rural Areas.* Geneva: ITU.

Levinson, H., S. Zimmerman, J. Clinger, and S. Rutherford. 2002. "Bus Rapid Transit: An Overview." *Journal of Public Transportation* 5 (2): 1–29.

Levy, H. 2004. "Rural Roads and Poverty Alleviation in Morocco." Paper presented at Scaling Up Poverty Reduction: A Global Learning Process and Conference, Shanghai, May 25–27. World Bank, Washington, DC.

McCulloch, N., and B. S. Sjahrir. 2008. *Evaluating the Determinants of Subnational Growth in Decentralized Indonesia.* Washington, DC: World Bank.

MCIT (Ministry of Communications and Information Technology, Egypt). 2008. *The Egyptian Education Initiative: Keys to Success.* Cairo: MCIT.

MCT (Ministry of Communication Technologies, Tunisia). 2009. "ICT in Tunisia: National Strategy, Main Achievements and Future Prospects." http://www.infocom.tn/index.php?id=199.

Mu, R., and D. Van de Walle. 2007. *Rural Roads and Local Market Development in Vietnam.* Washington, DC: World Bank.

Navas-Sabater, J., and A. Dymond. 2002. *Telecommunications and Information Services for the Poor: Toward a Strategy for Universal Access.* Washington, DC: World Bank.

Nelson, A. 2008. *Travel Time to Major Cities: A Global Map of Accessibility.* Ispra, Italy: Global Environment Monitoring Unit—Joint Research Centre of the European Commission. http://gem.jrc.ec.europa.eu/.

Oak Ridge National Laboratory. 2005. *Landscan Global Population Database.* http://www.ornl.gov/landscan.

OECD (Organisation for Economic Co-operation and Development). 2009. *How Regions Grow: Trends and Analysis.* Paris: OECD.

Parent, O., and A. Zouache. 2008. "Determinants of Growth in Africa and Middle East: How to Implement Geographical Features and Institutional Factors?" Paper presented at Economic Research Forum 15th Annual Conference, Cairo.

Puga, D. 2008. "Agglomeration and Cross-Border Infrastructure." *European Investment Bank Papers* 13 (2): 102–24.

Roberts, Peter, K. C. Shyan, and Rastogi Cordula. 2006. "Rural Access Index: A Key Development Indicator." Transport Papers, March. World Bank, Washington, DC.

Shokri, F. 2005. "Congestion, Pollution Still Plague Tehran." *Iran Daily,* January 13.

Slackman, M. 2008. "A City Where You Can't Hear Yourself Scream." *New York Times,* April 14.

Tobler, W. 1970. "A Computer Movie Simulating Urban Growth in the Detroit Region." *Economic Geography* 46 (suppl.): 234–40.

UNDP (United Nations Development Program). 2008. *Poverty, Growth, and Income Distribution in Lebanon.* Beirut: UNDP.

United Nations and World Bank. 2003. *Iraq Joint Needs Assessment. Transport and Telecommunications.* Baghdad: United Nations and World Bank.

Van Well, L. 2006. *ESPON Project 1.1.3. Enlargement of the European Union and the Wider European Perspective as Regards Its Polycentric Spatial Structure. Part 1. Summary.* Esch-sur-Alzette, Luxembourg: European Spatial Planning Observation Network.

Warr, P. 2005. *Road Development and Poverty Reduction: The Case of Lao PDR*. Manila: Asian Development Bank Institute.

Warren, J. 2007. "The Digital Vicious Cycle: Links between Social Disadvantage." *Telecommunications Policy* 13: 374–88.

Wellenius, B. 2002. *Closing the Gap in Access to Rural Telecommunications: Chile, 1995–2002*. Washington, DC: World Bank.

World Bank. 1989. *Road Deterioration in Developing Countries: Causes and Remedies*. Washington, DC: World Bank.

———. 2000. *Cairo Urban Transport Note*. Washington, DC: World Bank.

———. 2002. *Best Practices in Customs Reform—Lessons from Morocco*. Washington, DC: World Bank.

———. 2004. *Hashemite Kingdom of Jordan. Amman Development Corridor Project Appraisal Document*. Washington, DC: World Bank.

———. 2005a. *Djibouti Transport Sector Review*. Washington, DC: World Bank.

———. 2005b. *Islamic Republic of Iran Transport Sector Review and Strategy Note*. Washington, DC: World Bank.

———. 2006a. *Lebanon Urban Transport Development Project. Project Appraisal Document*. Washington, DC: World Bank.

———. 2006b. *La Logistique du Commerce et la Competitivité du Maroc*. Washington, DC: World Bank.

———. 2006c. *Upper Egypt: Challenges and Priorities for Rural Development*. Washington, DC: World Bank.

———. 2007a. *People's Democratic Republic of Algeria: A Public Expenditure Review. Volumes I and II*. Washington, DC: World Bank.

———. 2007b. *Arab Republic of Egypt. Enhancing the Performance of the Road Sector*. Washington, DC: World Bank.

———. 2008. *Syrian Arab Republic. Technical Assistance to the Transport Sector. Concept Note*. Washington, DC: World Bank.

———. 2009a. *World Development Report 2009: Reshaping Economic Geography*. Washington DC: World Bank.

———. 2009b. *Tapping a Hidden Resource: Energy Efficiency in the Middle East and North Africa*. Washington, DC: World Bank.

————. 2009c. *Information and Communications for Development: Extending Reach and Increasing Impact.* Washington, DC: World Bank.

————. 2009d. *Regional Cross-Border Trade Facilitation and Infrastructure Study for Mashreq Countries.* Washington, DC: World Bank.

————. 2009e. "Project Paper: Yemen Second Rural Access Project." World Bank, Washington, DC.

CHAPTER 6

Policy Package 3.
Underpin Private Sector
Interest in Nonleading Areas

Policy Package 3 (adapted from table 2.3)

Package 3. Underpin private sector interest in nonleading areas	"Incentives" ("spatially focused policies")	Sometimes non-leading areas *do* move ahead to leading-area status (e.g., Tunisia's center-east, Morocco's Tanger-Tétouan)	Areas where the private sector sees unrealized growth potential	Beware of incentives and induce-ments to locate businesses in lagging areas

Our first policy package was aimed at leveling the playing field for development. It was applicable to all lagging areas. The second policy package was about helping lagging areas to benefit from spillover connectivity, and only places close enough to growth poles stood to gain. Now we will look at the third policy package, where the aim is to realize a lagging area's economic potential.

Regional economic development strategies have a poor track record and should not be entered into lightly. If the lagging-area problem is likely to resolve itself in an acceptable time frame through out-migration, a targeted regional economic development approach will be redundant. If the lagging area in question lacks the human and natural resource base to attract private investment, a targeted regional economic development approach will be unsuccessful. Investing in people and leveling the playing field for development (Policy Package 1) should, therefore, *always* be the foundation of a lagging-area strategy.

However, sometimes it does make sense to layer a targeted regional development approach on top of Policy Package 1. It makes sense where out-migration is not going to solve the lagging-area problem and where there is a genuine prospect of competitive private cluster development.

Although most economically lagging areas remain lagging areas because of the forces of agglomeration, a few do catch up:

- In 1980, *Tunisia's* center-east region's mean per capita household consumption was 63 percent of that of Tunis. Since then, living standards have risen rapidly and converged, reaching 91 percent of the level of Tunis by 2000. But the south and the northeast, which had approximately the same level of consumption as the center-east in 1980, got left behind; their levels of consumption were 61 and 68 percent (respectively) of Tunis's in 2000.

- The Tanger-Tétouan region in *Morocco* had a mean per capita household consumption in 1998 that was 60 percent of Greater Casablanca's. It ranked eighth out of Morocco's 15 regions in terms of per capita household consumption, alongside Fès-Boulemane. As of the latest (2008) household income and expenditure survey, however, Tanger-Tétouan's mean per capita household consumption was 8 percent higher than Casablanca's, bringing Tanger-Tétouan to the number-two spot, behind the Rabat-Salé-Zemmour-Zaer capital region itself. Between 1994 and 2004, Tanger-Tétouan received 110,000 net in-migrants, equivalent to 4.5 percent of its 2004 population. Fès-Boulemane, however, is now right at the bottom of the ranking.

- The *Islamic Republic of Iran* saw an overall reduction in intergovernorate disparities between the pre- and post-Revolutionary period and 1985; the unweighted coefficient of variation of governorates' mean per capita household consumption fell from 0.27 to 0.22 during 1976–2005. But within that overall convergence, some individual lagging governorates made some remarkable progress. Bushehr, Ilam, and Mazandaran all rose at least 10 places in the governorate rankings, raising their per capita household consumption from 32–48 percent to 63–85 percent of Tehran's. These three provinces are far apart—Bushehr is on the Gulf, Ilam on the Iraqi border, and Mazandaran on the Caspian Sea—so each has capitalized on a different latent competitive advantage to play catch-up.

- *Looking beyond MENA:* In the United States, the states in the southeast and the south—such as the Carolinas, Georgia, Louisiana, and Mississippi—have reversed their status as senders of migrants from Reconstruction until the mid-20th century (World Bank 2009a) to become net receivers of internal migration (Suchan and others 2007; Perry 2006). Ireland was the second-poorest country in the European Union (EU) in 1995, in terms of purchasing-power-adjusted GDP per capita, but by 2002 it was the second-richest country.

So lagging area catch-ups, though rare, can happen. The question for this chapter is: what role can governments play to facilitate the process?

There is reason to believe that governments *can* facilitate the growth of agglomeration economies in lagging areas (World Bank 2009a). The Sapir Report on EU economic policy (Sapir 2003) was noncommittal on the impact of European Union regional and cohesion investments on lagging areas, but it came to the firm conclusion that national government had a strong role to play in determining a lagging area's economic prospects by establishing a favorable investment climate and a level of administrative competence. Examples of successful programs for realizing the potential for locational competitiveness include Chile's Corporacion de Fomento, which focused on fruit exports; the Republic of Korea's Specialized Economic Zones (1972–81); and Ireland's promotion of high-technology investments nationwide (Dillinger 2007). The multisectoral South-West China Area Development Program found that the program investments, 43 percent of which were targeted at agricultural production, managed to steer the poorest villages of the region onto a sustained higher growth path (Jalan and Ravallion 1996).

We will, therefore, start by looking at the performance of regional economic development policies in lagging areas around the world. We will show that these policies have generally failed because they have tried to fight against economies of agglomeration with spatially targeted public expenditures. The problem is that the economies of agglomeration are extremely powerful. So either public financial incentives are insufficient to direct economic activity sustainably toward lagging areas, or they do so at a fiscal cost that is disproportionate to the benefits.

We will then briefly describe regional economic development policies targeting lagging areas in the MENA13 economies. It will become apparent that the focus of these policies has also been on spatially targeted public expenditures, the formula that has proven unsuccessful elsewhere in the world.

The chapter will then describe alternative approaches to regional economic development that are based not upon the distortion of economic forces but upon the realization of a lagging area's economic potential. In this model, the government's role is that of coordinating public and private players rather than that of using the public purse to influence the private sector's location decisions. In short, the old approach tries to combat agglomeration economies, but the new one tries to create coordination economies.

Finally, we will ask how the new approach could be applied to a core sector for many lagging areas: agriculture.

Difficulty and Expense of Using Public Money to Lure Development to Lagging Areas

The impact of spatially targeted public expenditure is notoriously difficult to evaluate. There are so many factors affecting a lagging area's development and so few similar regions to use for comparison that it is hard to work out what would have happened without the government's targeted spending. The Organisation for Economic Co-operation and Development (OECD) comments that "objective difficulties of evaluating cross-sectoral policies, especially in quantitative terms, leave little material for research into the success or failures of policy" (OECD 2006a). Estimates of the impact of the United States's biggest regional development program, the Appalachian Regional Commission (ARC), vary from massive to negligible, depending on how comparator counties are selected (Glaeser and Gottlieb 2009).

However, the available literature certainly has little positive to say about the potential of public expenditure to incentivize economic growth in lagging areas.

One traditional approach has been to focus public infrastructural investment on lagging areas; however, a number of econometric studies indicate that the returns to public investment are indeed highest in leading areas where they benefit from economies of agglomeration. Algeria's public investment into lagging areas since the end of the Civil War has had no apparent impact upon employment growth; the regions that grow fastest are those with rich neighbors (Belarbi and Zouache 2009). Infrastructure investment in the United States did not explain convergence between states (Lall and Yilmaz 2000). An econometric estimation of firms' location choices in Uganda showed that upgrading roads in a lagging province would increase its share of the food and beverage sector by only 0.3 or 0.4 percentage points, whereas a province adjoining the capital would benefit to the tune of 4.7 percentage points (Lall, Schroeder, and Schmidt 2009). A review of the literature (Eberts 1990) found evidence that public infrastructure investment *did* support spatial economic convergence in the United States, Mexico, and Japan in certain circumstances: the investment had to be in a nonlagging (intermediate) area with some potential. Brakman and others (2005) show that the European Union's approach of connecting lagging areas to leading areas through improved infrastructure might actually have increased the leading-lagging divide by making it easier for leading areas to sell their products in lagging areas.

Governments have also attempted to direct or steer corporate investment toward lagging areas, with similarly poor results. Despite massive public expenditures, Italy's Mezzogiorno's wages only briefly converged toward northern Italian levels—during the 1960s—and development subsidies stimulated rent-seeking behavior and corruption (Boltho, Carlin, and Scaramozzino 1997). In its time, the Soviet Union used to locate industrial plants in outlying areas for political or strategic reasons. Many of those factory towns are no longer viable in a market economy because of their distance from suppliers and consumers. The migration of workers back to denser areas is sometimes the best solution to their high unemployment rates (Bogetic 2008). The German government's use of spatially targeted investment subsidies to stimulate growth in the East German Länder in the 1990s distorted investment toward buildings and capital-intensive industries, despite the fact that capital was less productive in those lagging areas (Quehenberger 2000). In Brazil, a bidding war between the states of Bahia and Rio Grande do Sul for a Ford Motor Company investment left the taxpayer carrying a bill of $172,000 per job created, five times the cost of a job in Tennessee (Calmon 2003). The cost per job of the United Kingdom's Enterprise Zones has been estimated at $125,000 in 2007 prices, and that of the United States's Empowerment Zones was similarly high (Glaeser and Gottlieb 2009).

Even where spatially targeted incentives have induced firms to invest in lagging areas, the gains have often been unsustainable. Brazil's subsidies for investment in the northeast were outweighed by national firms' preference for siting plants near their headquarters in the south (Carvalho, Lall, and Timmins 2006). Tunisia's experience of spatial investment subsidies was that it created a north-south "median band" of investment, as firms located as close as they could to the east coast without losing the subsidy. A notorious example in the United Kingdom is Nissan's assembly plant in Sunderland, in England's lagging northeast, whose survival has been perennially insecure and dependent upon government subsidies (Castle 2001).

MENA's Focus on Using Public Resources to Override Economies of Agglomeration

So the global experience of using financial incentives to steer economic activity toward lagging areas has been negative. But in MENA, spatially targeted financial incentives are still widespread. Investment promotion law in most countries divides the national territory into different zones and establishes priority areas with preferential investment conditions. They consist primarily of tax exemptions and investment grants aimed at guiding private sector investments toward poorer locations. Table 6.1 summarizes the range of spatial incentives available in MENA.

TABLE 6.1

Spatially Targeted Incentives for Business Are Prevalent in MENA

	ALG	EGY	JOR	IRN	IRQ	LEB	LIB	MOR	SYR	TUN	WBG	YEM
Fiscal incentives												
Extended corporate tax holidays	✓	✓	✓	✓	✓	✓	✓	✓	✓	✓	✓	✓
Personal income tax holiday									✓	✓		
Exemption on social security contributions										✓		
Exemptions on duties, customs, and indirect taxes	✓		✓	✓	✓	✓	✓	✓	✓	✓	✓	
Financial incentives												
General investment grant		✓								✓		
Discounted or free land		✓	✓	✓				✓	✓	✓		
Subsidized infrastructure costs		✓	✓					✓	✓	✓	✓	
Employment grants		✓										
Technical assistance and training grants		✓						✓				

Source: Study Team survey of World Bank reports and Web documents.

Note: Some incentives may not have been covered in the available documentation. Djibouti is not covered. ALG = Algeria, EGY = Egypt, Arab Rep., JOR = Jordan, IRN = Iran, Islamic Rep., IRQ = Iraq, LEB = Lebanon, LIB = Libya, MOR = Morocco, SYR = Syrian Arab Republic, TUN = Tunisia, WBG = West Bank and Gaza, YEM = Yemen, Rep.

Location-specific exemptions from corporate taxation and duties customs and indirect taxes are found throughout MENA (box 6.1). Partial or full corporate income tax holidays are granted to firms locating in the lesser-developed regions of virtually all economies in the MENA region. These holidays are often extensions of 5 to 10 years added to the general exemptions granted to investments in nonpriority locations. In the case of the Arab Republic of Egypt, corporate tax exemptions are granted for up to 20 years in the least-developed areas. Exemptions are usually extended to reinvested profits. Other fiscal incentives include the exemption of personal income taxes and social security contributions for employees. Spatial exemptions on customs duties and other indirect taxes on the purchase of machinery, materials, and other items are also very common in the MENA region (Algeria, Jordan, Iraq, Lebanon, Libya, Morocco, Tunisia, and the West Bank and Gaza). Many countries also offer subsidies to investors in target areas. Investment grants cover a portion of the initial investment costs of a project and are often aimed at compensating for the lack physical infrastructure or human capital in remote areas. In Tunisia, the state allocates investment grants of up to 30 percent for projects locating in the priority investment zones. In Morocco, investment grants are offered to cover part of external infrastructure costs as well as professional training costs for projects

---

BOX 6.1

Tax Breaks for Lagging Areas in MENA

In *Morocco*, firms that locate in areas with low levels of economic activity benefit from a preferential fiscal treatment consisting of a 50 percent cut in corporate tax or income tax for five years. These preferences cover Morocco's periphery: the Mediterranean coast and the Rif in the north, the provinces close to the Algerian border in the east, and the far south (Source: Investment Charter, Morocco-ANPME).

Tunisia offers tax incentives in the 140 "Zones de Développement Régional" (ZDR), in the western region and along the north-south central axis. Specifically, industry, crafts, and certain services are exempt from corporate tax and a personal income tax for their first 10 years and benefit from a 50 percent tax holiday for the following 10 years. Reinvested profits benefit from a complete tax deduction. Businesses are exempted from the Social Housing Promotion Fund for five years.

In *Jordan*, projects initiated in Class C development areas, where economic activity is lowest, are granted a 75 percent corporate tax holiday for the first 10 years. Incentives in the more developed Class B and Class A development areas are 50 and 25 percent, respectively.

In the Arab Republic of Egypt, firms located in remote areas benefit from a 10-year tax holiday (as opposed to the standard five-year period) for all investments. The exemption is 20 years outside the Old Valley (World Bank 2008c).

In *Lebanon*, investments in the poorer areas of northeast and southeast Lebanon, defined as Zone C, benefit from a complete exemption for a period of 10 years on income tax and taxes on dividends—as opposed to 50 percent for five years in Zone B areas and a maximum of two years in Zone A.

In *Libya*, law no. 5 of 1997 on the promotion of investment of foreign capital allows projects constructed in "regional development areas" to receive an additional period of exemption by decision of the Libyan General People's Committee.

In *Algeria*, law no. 1/2003 grants a 10-year exemption on various business taxes in the high plateaus and the south. Investments in underdeveloped areas also benefit from a real estate tax exemption and reduced duties on imports relevant to the investment (Khelladi 2009).

In the *Islamic Republic of Iran*, the tax code grants a complete income tax exemption for a period of four years for extractive activities undertaken in "less developed regions," as opposed to the regular 80 percent exemption.

In *Iraq*, investment law no. 13/2006 allows for an extension in the period of tax and fee exemption granted to all projects (from 10 years to a maximum of 15), depending on a project's geographical location.

In the *Republic of Yemen*, projects in Investment Zone B benefit from an additional two years of profit taxes compared to projects in Zone A.

(box continues on the following page.)

In the *West Bank and Gaza*, the law of 1998 grants extended tax exemptions for investments in remote areas or for areas under the threat of settlement.

In the *Syrian Arab Republic*, an extended two years of income tax exemption is granted for agricultural and industrial projects set up in developing governorates.

Source: Study team, from Web sites and publications of national investment promotion bureaus.

initiated in lagging areas. Technical assistance and training grants for investment in remote areas are also offered in Egypt.

Some investment incentives are specifically aimed at facilitating access to land for investors in priority development areas. In Morocco, an additional investment grant is offered covering 20 percent of land costs for projects started in less-developed regions. The Egyptian government grants land freely for investments in Upper Egypt and some areas of Middle Egypt. Access to land at particularly competitive prices is offered within special development zones in Jordan, the Islamic Republic of Iran, Morocco, and Tunisia. Other incentives support employment in lagging areas. In Egypt, a grant is offered for each person employed in Upper Egypt and certain areas of Middle Egypt for investments of a certain size.

Special economic zones (SEZs) are often located in lagging areas as an instrument of regional economic development policy. This is the case of zones located in the oriental, northern, and southern regions of Morocco, in the inland governorate of Gafsa in Tunisia, and those in the southeast and northeastern regions of the Islamic Republic of Iran, where population is scarce and economic activity is, therefore, low (map 6.1). On top of fiscal exemptions and investment grants, SEZs usually offer streamlined business services, such as one-stop shops and simplified bureaucratic procedures. The physical infrastructure and the services provided reduce start-up costs for investors and to attract enterprises of similar types, thereby favoring industrial clustering.

Financial Incentives to Steer the Spatial Pattern of Development Have Not Been Successful

Despite the prevalence of spatially targeted financial incentives in MENA economies, there is no clear evidence of their effectiveness.

MAP 6.1

The Islamic Republic of Iran's Placement of Economic Zones in Low-Density Areas

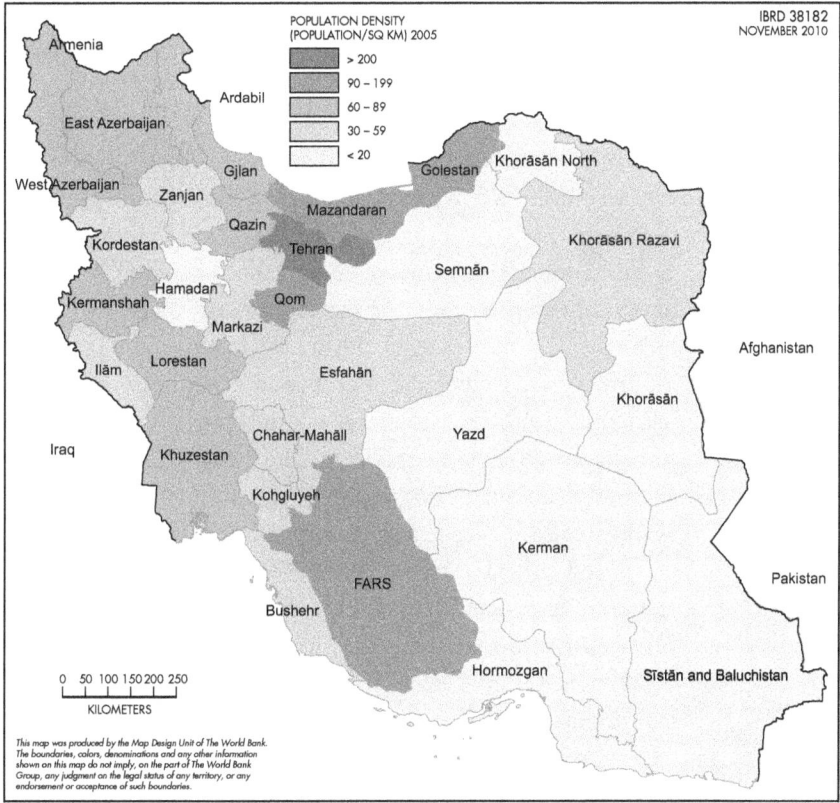

Source: World Bank 2009b.

Note: SEZ = special economic zone, FTZ = free trade zone.

For a financial incentive program to be deemed a success, it would have to pass three tests:

- *The response test.* Investors would have to be observed to locate in the targeted area; if they don't, the incentive did not work.

- *The sustainability test.* Businesses would have to remain in the targeted area once the incentive is withdrawn; if they don't, the incentive's impact was only temporary.

- *The economic efficiency test.* If businesses need a special incentive to locate in a target area, it must be because there is a profitability disadvantage to locating there. So the incentive must be at least as big as the profitability disadvantage for businesses to locate in the target area.

Therefore the incentive is encouraging inefficient production, thus creating an economic efficiency loss for the economy. However, if enterprises in the target area eventually achieve economies of scale and agglomeration, then the target area's profitability disadvantage will be reduced, and the incentive will no longer be necessary. So the economic efficiency test is that growth in the target area eventually becomes self-sustaining.

What little information is available suggests that MENA's spatial financial incentives have been no more successful than those in other parts of the world.

From the 1960s onward, Algeria implemented regional economic development programs for priority areas. These programs included investment in state-owned industries. The strategy involved spreading industrial activity beyond Algiers and Oran with the creation of new industrial poles in peripheral coastal sites: Arzew in the west and Annaba and Skikda in the east. The 1968 program for the Amazigh (Berber)-speaking Aurès region in eastern Algeria, for example, envisaged expansion of a textile factory, a brick and tile plant, a tannery, a powdered milk factory, a furniture factory, mines, data processing centers, and large-scale artisanal units. However, the continued polarization in Algiers remained (Sutton 1976), both for public and private investments. Between 1966 and 1972, 1,116 out of 1,821 private investment projects submitted for state approval were for Algiers *wilaya* provinces alone. The second-place *wilaya* (oasis) attracted only 144 applications. In short, spatial financial incentives in Algeria did not pass the impact test.

The Syrian Arab Republic also experienced difficulties during the 1990s in using industrial zones as incentives to locate businesses in lagging areas. Although the main vocation of the country's industrial zones was to ensure the appropriate zoning of industrial activity, to minimize pollution, and to preserve the residential environment, they were also used to encourage economic activity in lagging rural areas. The director of Syria's Private Industrial Sector (Shahin 1999) describes how the government provided land in rural industrial zones at "symbolic prices" with the aim of "limiting migration and lessening the pressure on services in large cities." Rural areas benefited from concessional loans, tax exemptions, and assistance with inputs and marketing. The government also deliberately located large public industrial enterprises in rural areas with the aim of reducing the cost of raw materials for the private sector there. Despite these efforts, economies of agglomeration prevailed: the private sector persisted in locating in urban areas because of the availability of inputs and services. The rural areas remained competitive only in traditional handicraft activities, which depended on rural skills and creativity. Again, the spatial financial incentives failed the impact test.

In Tunisia, until 2007, the government offered investment grants of 25 percent for firms locating in the "Zones de Développement Régional" (ZDR). The aim was to steer investments westward, away from the coast. This policy initially led to the concentration of investments along the very eastern strip of the ZDR area, as opposed to being evenly spread out across the underdeveloped areas. In other words, the incentives passed the impact test but probably failed the sustainability and efficiency tests, because businesses were clearly still seeking to locate as far east as possible. Recognizing the situation and wishing to counter it, the government reclassified the ZDRs into three groups according to employment rates and human development levels. Today, the areas closer to the coast receive an investment grant of 8 percent and the central axis 15 percent; the areas defined as "Zones de Développement Prioritaires"—mainly the western regions—receive an investment grant of 25–30 percent (see map 6.2). These incentives seem to be passing the impact test, at least; Tunisian officials cite a number of major investors moving west, including the Italian clothing company, United

MAP 6.2

Tunisia's Priority Development Zones

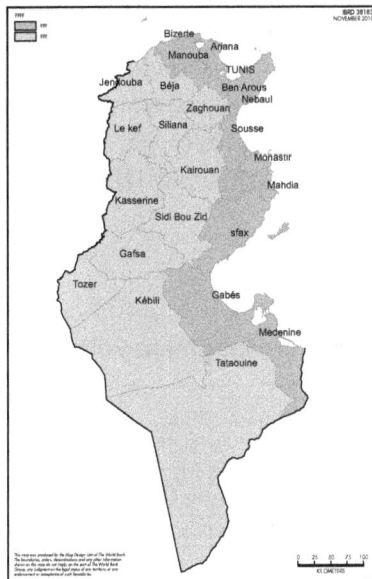

Source: Tunisia-API.

Note: The grey areas are Priority Development Zones.

Colors of Benetton. It is too early yet to say whether they pass the sustainability and efficiency tests. As map 6.2 shows, some of the subsidized zones are very close to the booming east coast, and the fact that some businesses choose to locate there could be due more to spillover effects from agglomerated areas than to the financial incentives.

New Paradigm of Regional Economic Development Policy

Because financial incentives for regional economic development have such a poor track record, governments in developed countries are adopting a new approach to regional economic development policy. This approach accepts that the forces of agglomeration are too strong to be overridden by public money. So it goes with the flow of the market, helping lagging areas to capitalize on genuine competitive advantages. Rejecting centralized and top-down approaches to planning, it emphasizes the need for local ownership of initiatives and consistent involvement of the private sector. The role of the government becomes one of facilitator: building links among (a) the private sector, (b) central government departments, (c) local administrations, and (d) education and research institutions (see table 6.2). It may be impossible to overpower the forces of agglomeration, the thinking goes, but there is no reason governments cannot help overcome diseconomies of coordination.

We will now look at the elements of the new paradigm as they appear in the global literature, much of it by the OECD.

Infrastructure is effective only in combination with education. A recent study (OECD 2009, 82) modeled the relationship between road infrastructure (kilometers of roadway per capita) and subnational growth rates (gross regional domestic product, or GRDP) across developed countries

TABLE 6.2

Old and New Paradigms of Regional Economic Development Policy

	Old paradigm	New paradigm
Objectives	Trying to compensate for locational disadvantages of lagging regions	Tapping underused potential to enhance regional competitiveness
Unit of intervention	Administrative units	Functional economic areas
Strategies	Sectoral approach	Integrated approach
Tools	Subsidies and state aids	Mix of soft and hard capital (capital stock, labor market, business environment, social capital, and networks)
Actors	Central government	Different levels of government (with private sector)

Source: OECD 2009.

between 1995 and 2005. It found that infrastructural investment influences growth only when combined with human capital and innovation. This relationship held in several model specifications at both territorial and subterritorial (TL3 and TL2) levels of spatial aggregation when controlling for a number of other factors. Looking at panel data, analysts found a lagged effect of infrastructure three years after the investment, but only in the presence of "innovation" (represented by patenting activity). Using another model, they found a five-year effect, but only in the presence of "human capital" (measured by primary and tertiary education attainment rates). The main caveats were that the definition of infrastructure was very narrow (excluding communications, energy, and so on) and that the analysis also ignores private stocks of capital.

The study cautioned that a lagging area that invests exclusively in infrastructure may fall victim to the "leaking by linking" phenomenon (Hirschman 1958), as businesses continue to agglomerate in previously vital areas but now use the new trunk connectivity networks to crowd out local producers who before were protected by their inaccessibility (OECD 2009, 38). The construction of motorways into Poland's lagging eastern regions will, for example, expose their producers' home markets to competition from more efficient areas (OECD 2008).

The need to combine infrastructure with human capital is particularly stark when the aim is to facilitate ICT-enabled growth poles, which are clusters of high-tech firms that benefit from synergies of collocation. Examples of planned growth poles in MENA include the Smart Village on the outskirts of Cairo[1] and the Sidi Abdallah Technopole 30 kilometers south of Algiers.

Conversely, raising levels of higher education without providing connectivity and employment may have little effect on economic performance. The city of Ostrava in the Czech Republic has a large number of higher educational institutions, but its growth is hampered by its dismal access to the main highway network (OECD 2004).

If regional development is to be based on genuine local potential, regions need a decentralized, bottom-up approach to policy design and implementation. Though decisions arrived at by top-down approaches may be coherent with other national policies and priorities, regional actors are able to make better use of information about local capacities and local needs than are central authorities. Local actors are also more likely to embrace projects and support their implementation when they feel that they personally have been a part of the projects' design.

Mobilizing local stakeholders may require both decentralization and a structured dialogue between the different levels of government. An example of this is the European Union's LEADER Community Initiative, which has figured prominently in the EU's rural development

strategies since the early 1990s. The program aims to promote endogenous growth within a finite territory through decentralized local action
groups, which craft development plans and manage projects. The model
has made important impacts on both development and local governance
(OECD 2006b, 90). In Mexico, one of the pillars of rural development
policy is the government's bottom-up territorial perspective, exemplified
by its creation of Rural Development Councils. Through these organs,
municipalities decide on the acceptability of locally proposed projects
within the broader framework of the state's rural development strategy
(OECD 2007, 86). The Netherlands demonstrates a flexible approach
with its *Agenda for a Vital Countryside*, a document published in 2004 to
define rural policy. Although the *Agenda for a Vital Countryside* articu-
lates national priorities and targets, it devolves much of the responsibility
over translating these policies into action to the communities involved
(OECD 2006b, 83).

*The public-private interface is a key source of regional productivity growth
and innovation.* So the policy maker's role is not to "pick winners" but to
facilitate interaction between public agencies, private firms, and other
institutions. This advice draws on the observation that regional growth
and productivity increases are driven by the formation of clusters: "geographically proximate group[s] of interconnected companies and associated institutions in a particular field, linked by commonalities and
complementarities" (Porter 2000). Clustered firms create direct and
indirect employment, generate spillovers and stimulate productivity,
and diversify regional economies through innovation (Hotz-Hart 2000).

As the Asian experience illustrated, it is "devilishly hard" to deliberately generate clusters—and, therefore, foolhardy to make that an
explicit goal (Yusuf 2008). But policy makers can still play an important
role in fomenting interchanges between regional actors and assembling
the links on which clusters are built. They can promote informal networks and formal trade associations where appropriate. They can also
ensure that public educational institutions cultivate stronger ties with
the private sector. The dynamic relationship between government and
industry can be thought of as a "discovery process," one that is "as
much about eliciting information from the private sector on significant
externalities and their remedies as it is about implementing appropriate
policies" (Rodrik 2004, 4).

Italy's ERVET (Regional Institution for Territorial Economic Development) is an excellent example of this. Created in the 1970s to support
regional development in the region of Emilia-Romagna, it has a share-
holding structure that engages the local public sector, credit and financial
institutions, and entrepreneurial organizations, among others. Through
its extensive network, ERVET has supported the small and medium

enterprises (SMEs) that dominate the core of the economy there (Cooke and Morgan 1995). The Republic of Korea is often cited as an example of the vital role of private sector leadership for regional development. In the 1960s, and 1970s, the Korean government created New Industrial Cities under the guidance of the private sector, and they have flourished in subsequent decades (Park 2009).

Closer to home, Morocco's 1996 *Le Maroc Compétitif* initiative identified four sectors as candidates for cluster development: tourism, sea products, electronics and Internet technology, and textiles and apparel. *Le Maroc Compétitif* fostered a continuous dialogue between public and private institutions aimed at identifying and coordinating the investments and regulatory reforms that were critical for cluster growth. It is impossible to separate the impacts of *Le Maroc Compétitif* from other drivers of growth in the targeted sectors. After all, they were selected for *Le Maroc Compétitif* precisely because of their potential. However, in terms of the political economy of reform, *Le Maroc Compétitif* was part of the growth of a durable partnership between the state and the organized private sector in the formulation of economic and industrial policy (Cammett 2007). Although *Le Maroc Compétitif* did not have spatial development objectives, its diagnosis-through-dialogue approach could well prove applicable to MENA's lagging areas.

Because cluster-driven growth is multisectoral, policy makers need to shift increasingly to a territorial perspective rather than a sectoral one. For example, Chile's National Innovation Council found it difficult to identify the synergies and spillovers that would achieve the necessary buy-in from local stakeholders by means of a sectoral approach (OECD 2009, 76). The developed countries' rural policy record is another case in point. In general, the focus of their strategies for rural development has been the subsidization of agriculture, which represents a mere 10 percent of the total rural workforce (OECD 2006b, 13). Governments were slow to identify other potential sources of rural growth because they conceptualized rural areas as solely agricultural. Recently, however, developed-country governments have broadened their sectoral focus. In Italy, the Territorial Pacts initiative promotes the grouping of rural municipalities to achieve a critical mass for attracting investment (Johnston 2005). The Mexican Micro-Regions Strategy is also applauded for its territorial perspective. This strategy addresses the needs of the most marginalized rural populations by coordinating development strategy with them in a participatory manner within a geographic framework, providing a package of 11 basic services through decentralized Strategic Community Centers.[2] What all these approaches share in common is the impetus to mobilize local assets through interinstitutional coordination.

Governments must, therefore, consider the best governance arrangements for territorial coordination. The choice of structures will depend upon the existing administrative culture and systems. Writing of Australia, one author described the challenge: "to coordinat[e] a multitude of autonomous agents with different, often competing interests, agendas and views . . . without formal power or actual possibility to force others into acting according to one's own agenda and without full information" (Huber 2005). The final chapter of this report explores the institutional dimension of spatial development and describes various options for coordination.

Realizing Agricultural Potential through Clusters

Although rural households often draw their livelihoods from diverse sources, agriculture is still central to MENA's rural economies and is a cornerstone of employment in many of MENA's lagging areas. In the Islamic Republic of Iran in 1996, where 21 percent of the population was employed in agriculture, 30 percent of the population in the six ostans with the lowest per capita consumption were defined as "skilled agricultural and fishery workers." In Morocco, 43 percent of employment in 2007 was in agriculture, rising to 58 percent in the six regions with the lowest per capita household consumption (Haut Commissariat du Plan 2007). The association between agricultural employment and lagging areas is, of course, only to be expected because both are less likely to be metropolitan.

Any increase in the returns to farmwork can be broken down into the following components:

- An increase in the ratio of land to labor

- An increase in the productivity of land in terms of crop and livestock yields

- A shift in the product mix toward higher-value products

- An increase in the unit value of a given product

We will look at each of these sources of growth in turn. The conclusion will be that resource availability and domestic markets place limits on productivist strategies, but that a combination of high-value products and raising the unit value of output is the best bet for MENA's lagging areas.

Increasing the ratio of land to labor, as table 3.2 illustrated, has to be a major source of agricultural labor productivity increases in MENA.

Significant increases in the area of agricultural land, however, are not feasible. The area of arable land in the MENA13 increased by 0.2 percent per year over 1970–2005, while the number of people employed in agriculture increased by 0.8 percent per year (gross domestic income, or GDI). We saw in chapter 3 that MENA's agricultural workforce growth is far greater than it would normally be for countries at this level of development. Furthermore, it is widely recognized that the expansion of MENA's agricultural land area in recent years has been into marginal, environmentally fragile areas and has contributed to land degradation in the region's semi-arid areas. Increases in the ratio of agricultural land to agricultural labor, therefore, have to come from a shift in employment out of farming. At present, two MENA13 countries, Iraq and Lebanon, have begun to see a reduction in the absolute number of people employed in agriculture (GDI).

Productivity-based strategies also have their limits. Most MENA economies' ministries of agriculture see their main role as promoting an increase in the productivity of land in terms of crop and livestock yields. Higher productivity has the added benefit of reducing MENA economies' dependence on food imports, a major political concern, particularly after the leap in food prices in 2007–08.

The MENA13 economies have achieved excellent yield increases over recent decades, including a 2.1 percent average annual increase in cereals yields between 1970 and 2005. However, much of agriculture's yield gains have been thanks to its increased drawdown of the region's scarce water resources. In Syria, for example, 66 percent of the average increase in wheat yields from 1985–89 to 2001–05 stemmed from an increase in the area of wheat under irrigation (World Bank 2008b). The region's statistics show a rapid increase in the share of cropped land under irrigation: over 1970–2000, it increased by 20 percent in Morocco; 50 percent in Lebanon; 60 percent in the Republic of Yemen; and 100 percent or more in Algeria, Iraq, Libya, and Syria (GDI). The current situation is one in which agriculture is consuming the lion's share of water withdrawals (see table 6.3), while demographic and economic growth are driving up nonagricultural water demand, all MENA economies are overexploiting water resources in some localities, some (Egypt, Jordan, and the Republic of Yemen) are surviving on nonrenewable resources at the national level, and climate change is already reducing water supply.

A second generation of irrigation investments is, therefore, appearing in MENA, where the aim is not to divert more water onto more land but to raise the productivity of water. The basic components of such a strategy include the pressurization of water delivery systems; the conversion of on-farm irrigation systems from flood to drip or

TABLE 6.3

Agriculture Is Straining Water Resources in MENA

Country	Agricultural water withdrawals (m³ x 10⁹, 2002)	Total water withdrawals (m³ x 10⁹, 2002)	Total renewable water resources as % of total water use
Algeria	3.9	6.1	236
Djibouti	0.0	0.02	1579
Egypt, Arab Rep.	59.0	68.3	85
Iran, Islamic Rep.	66.2	72.9	189
Jordan	0.8	1.0	87
Lebanon	0.9	1.4	n.a.
Morocco	11.0	12.6	230
Syrian Arab Republic	18.9	20.0	132
Tunisia	2.2	2.6	174
Yemen, Rep.	6.3	6.6	62

Source: World Bank 2007, 160–92.

Note: n.a. = not applicable.

sprinkler; the mobilization of Water Users' Associations (WUAs) to manage water distribution, operations, and maintenance; and links to extension and marketing arrangements. Tunisia was an early adopter of the irrigation efficiency approach in MENA, and Morocco, Egypt, the Islamic Republic of Iran, and Syria are all committed to scaling it up (Jagannathan, Mohamed, and Kremer 2009, 170, 433). Some countries, notably Egypt and Iraq, can increase yields through improved drainage, as waterlogging has led to salinification and land degradation.

Agronomic and husbandry improvements will continue to produce modest yield growth. This change includes improvements in cultivars and breeds, farming practices and use of equipment, and purchased inputs. However, the biological capacity of MENA's crop and animal species to deliver higher yields is critically dependent upon water availability. Farmers are often well aware of the technical possibilities being offered, but they lack access to credit or (especially in rainfed areas) are wary of the associated risk.

The shift to high-value agricultural products—fruit and vegetables—looks like one of the main sources of growth for MENA's agricultural sector. Although fruits and vegetables occupy only 7 percent as much land as cereals (FAOSTAT), their area has been growing by 2.1 percent per year since 1970, compared with 0.2 percent per year for cereals. Fruit and vegetables use water much more cost-effectively than alternative products; the economic return to water use for vegetables is 6.3 times higher than for wheat and 10 times higher than for beef cattle (World Bank 2003).

But the size of the domestic market sets another limit on high-value cropping. For cereals, the market is not a problem because increased MENA production will substitute for imports. But the problem with increasing the supply of other farm products, such as fruit and vegetables, is that when farmers produce more, the increase in supply drives prices down so far that farmers' incomes fall instead of rise. Table 6.4 shows how the farmgate prices for fruit and vegetables have tended to fall over recent years: 50 of the 72 country-product prices dropped over the period. The greater the increase in farmers' production, therefore, the higher the risk of a drop in their incomes.

An increase in the unit values of agricultural output, however, seems to be a promising potential source of growth for MENA's agriculture sectors. Improving the quality and marketing of food products is critical. MENA's growing urban middle class, increased female labor force participation, the tourism industry, and the explosion of supermarket retailing, are all drivers of demand for higher-quality—and higher-priced—food products. Participation in modern, quality-focused supply chains can boost farmers' income in middle-income countries by 10–100 percent (Flores, Reardon, and Hernandez 2006); however, the requirement for quality and standardization can easily exclude smaller or capital-scarce farming operations (World Bank 2008a, 126–28).

Developing export markets for MENA's fruit and vegetables is one way of raising unit values. The prices achieved by those who

TABLE 6.4

Price Decreases Were the Rule for MENA's Fruit and Vegetable Farmers, 1995–2007

	Price decrease 1995–2007 (%)							
	Apples	Apricots	Beans, green	Cucumbers and gherkins	Eggplants (aubergines)	Onions, dry	Peaches and nectarines	Tomatoes
Algeria	−31	−18	−27	−29	−39	16	−16	−3
Egypt, Arab Rep.	−27	−27	31	−48	−29	14	−27	−21
Iran, Islamic Rep.	5	19	−19	−15	2	−21	11	−44
Jordan	−44	9	−43	29	45	−28	−51	26
Lebanon	−27	−35	−68	−44	−51	5	−41	−46
Morocco	35	60	−45	−42	−42	−33	60	−42
West Bank and Gaza	36	−52	−11	14	11	21	−29	80
Tunisia	−27	−41	−20	−40	−37	−37	−48	−24
Yemen, Rep.	37	−62	82	−62	−44	−56	−52	−48

Sources: FAOSTAT; World Development Indicators Database, accessed October 13, 2009.

Note: Figures for the West Bank and Gaza and some for the Republic of Yemen are for 2000–07.

penetrate export markets can be orders of magnitude higher than those available on the domestic market (World Bank 2006b, 42–44). MENA economies have a fourfold trade competitiveness advantage when it comes to high-value cropping. First, the southern Mediterranean countries are a natural agro-ecological home for the multitude of food plants that originated in the Middle East. Second, MENA economies are extremely cost-competitive in fruit and vegetables, as demonstrated, for example, by domestic resource cost calculations for Syria and Tunisia (World Bank 2008b; World Bank 2006a). Third, they are close to the importing countries of the EU, the Gulf Cooperation Council (GCC), or both. Fourth, MENA's climate allows it to sell into the off-season for EU producers, when import restrictions are fewer and retail prices are higher. The catch is that high-income export markets' demands for quality and standardization are even more rigorous than those of high-end national markets, and the demands include the added challenges of phytosanitary compliance and traceability.

Successful quality-based supply chains depend on the links among a range of private and institutional actors:

• The farmers themselves

• Private operators involved in finance, collection, sorting, packing and refrigeration, transport, and marketing

• Agricultural input and equipment suppliers (for their knowledge and experience as well as for their products)

• Extension and farmer education services

• National public institutions responsible for phytosanitary certification and export formalities

• Public institutions responsible for water and transport infrastructure

So agricultural growth is cluster-driven too. As in OECD countries, the main thrust of agricultural policy in most MENA economies has long been productivism: public spending on water diversion for agriculture and on price subsidies (for energy, irrigation water, applied inputs, and producer prices). A subsidy and productivism policy stance brings a mixture of benefits and costs. It helps countries to reduce dependence on international markets for staple foods. But it has a significant fiscal cost and reduces agriculture's contribution to the economy by distorting farmers' production choices.

Production subsidies can either exacerbate or mitigate spatial inequality. Although they transfer resources from urban to rural areas, often the better-off rural areas receive a disproportionate share of the production subsidy because they are involved in a disproportionate share of agricultural production. But the small part of subsidies that goes to smaller farms or poorer areas can also make a critical contribution to farm incomes there. In Tunisia, for example, it is the well-watered wheat-growing areas that have received the lion's share of wheat price support and water tariff discounts (see table 6.5), but it is the lagging rural areas of Le Kef and Béja in the northwest that would suffer the greatest percentage decrease in incomes if output markets were to be liberalized (Ideaconsult 2006). In Syria, the cotton-based economy of irrigated areas in the lagging northeast is entirely dependent on subsidies (World Bank 2008b), and Lebanon's tobacco subsidy primarily benefits the lagging southern provinces.

On the basis of the previous discussion, however, it would appear that the main potential engine of agricultural growth in MENA's lagging areas is cluster development around quality-driven supply chains. Production subsidies can support farm incomes as long as they are in place, but they cannot be a source of sustained growth.

MENA provides several excellent examples of the cluster and supply-chain approach being applied to lagging-area agriculture.

- The Agricultural Exports and Rural Income (AERI) project in the lagging area of Upper Egypt built links among farmers, SME processors, financial institutions, farm advisers, the Assiut Business Association, private vets, dairy processors, and input suppliers. Its approach was based upon a market assessment of unmet demand for quality products in urban centers and Upper Egypt's potential cost competitiveness advantage. The project's outcomes were positive. For example, at a cost of about $180 per farmer, its livestock component raised

TABLE 6.5

Forms of Subsidization of Agriculture, 2005

	EGY	IRN	IRQ	LEB	MOR	SYR	TUN	WBG
Applied inputs price subsidy	X	X	X	X		X		
Producer price support for some commodities	X	X	X	X	X	X	X	
User charge for public irrigation schemes below operating and maintenance cost	X	X	X	X	X		X (Wheat)	
Major fuel subsidy	X	X	X			X		

Source: World Bank 2007.

Note: EGY = Egypt, Arab Rep., IRN = Iran, Islamic Rep., IRQ = Iraq, LEB = Lebanon, MOR = Morocco, SYR = Syrian Arab Republic, TUN = Tunisia, WBG = West Bank and Gaza.

buffalo and cow milk production by 63 and 153 percent, respectively, and increased net incomes by 20 percent within a target group of 50,000 farmers (ACDI/VOCA).

- Exports of Tunisia's high-value olive oil took off after the removal of the public sector monopoly in 1994. Nearly the entire product is exported unbranded and in bulk. However, there is a rapidly growing number of virgin bottled oil brands, which command far higher prices. The emergence of high-value olive oil products depends on farmers' ability to supply quality raw materials, processor access to finance and modern equipment, market information supplied by producer groupings, and state-run testing and certification facilities (World Bank 2006a).

- Morocco's agricultural development strategy, *Plan Maroc Vert*, will test several key principles of the new paradigm for regional economic development. *Plan Maroc Vert's* model of agricultural development is cluster or supply-chain driven, and the government has assigned itself the role of facilitating links among farmers, trader-processors (*aggrégateurs*), service organizations, research institutions, and local administrations. The institutional framework for *Plan Maroc Vert* is decentralized to the regional level so it can ease the coordination among local public and private institutions. By the same logic, responsibility for the ORMVAs (*Offices Régionales des Mise en Valeur Agricole*) has been transferred from the Ministry of Agriculture's headquarters to its deconcentrated offices in the regions.

The purpose of this brief discussion has been to illustrate how cluster-based, private sector–driven model of regional economic development can be applied to agriculture. As the previous examples show, the starting point is potential investor interest, and the key role for government is that of coordinator and provider of information.

Conclusion

Leveling the playing field (Policy Package 1) is the foundation for lagging-area development, but sometimes it is appropriate to add the targeted economic development package. Spatially targeted economic development strategies are relevant where out-migration is not a solution and where there is a genuine prospect of private sector–led growth.

This chapter has argued that public financial incentives for regional economic development do not work; their impacts are insufficient, too costly, or unsustainable. MENA economies, like the developed world, have nonetheless focused on them. Using the state's convening power to facilitate cluster-driven development makes more sense.

Active investor participation in the formulation of regional development plans is the critical test. Private sector leadership is the sign that a lagging area has genuine competitive potential. Without private sector involvement in the process, however, a government risks targeting expenditures on areas where there is no genuine prospect of cluster-driven growth.

Endnotes

1. http://www.smart-villages.com.
2. OECD 2006a (OECD Rural Policy Reviews: Mexico).

References

ACDI/VOCA. "Egypt—Agricultural Exports and Rural Incomes: Dairy and Livestock." http://www.acdivoca.org/acdivoca/portalhub.nsf/ID/egyptAERI.

Belarbi, Y., and A. Zouache. 2009. *Regional Employment Growth and Spatial Dependence in Algeria, 1998–2005.* Cairo: Economic Research Forum.

Bogetic, Z. 2008. "Advancing Regional Development in Russia." In *The World Bank's Experience with Regional and Territorial Development: Proceedings from the World Bank Session of the European Commission's Open Days,* Brussels, October 8. Washington, DC: World Bank.

Boltho, A., W. Carlin, and P. Scaramozzino. 1997. "Will East Germany Become a New Mezzogiorno?" *Journal of Comparative Economics* 112 (4): 241–64.

Brakman, S., H. Garretsen, J. Gorter, A. Van der Horst, and M. Schramm. 2005. *New Economic Geography, Empirics, and Regional Policy.* The Hague: CPB Netherlands Bureau for Economic Policy Analysis.

Calmon, P. C. 2003. *Evaluation of Subsidies in Brazil.* Washington, DC: World Bank.

Cammett, M. 2007. "Business–Government Relations and Industrial Change: The Politics of Upgrading in Morocco and Tunisia." *World Development* 35 (11): 1889–903.

Carvalho, A., S. Lall, and C. Timmins. 2006. *Regional Subsidies and Industrial Prospects of Lagging Regions.* Washington, DC: World Bank.

Castle, S. 2001. "Nissan Poised to Make Micra Decision as Sunderland Wins GBP 40 Million in Subsidies." *Independent* (London), January 18.

Cooke, P., and K. Morgan. 1995. "Growth Regions under Duress: Renewal Strategies in Baden Wurttemberg and Emilia-Romagna." In *Globalization, Institutions, and Regional Development in Europe,* eds. A. Amin and T. Nigel, 91–117. Oxford, U.K.: Oxford University Press.

Dillinger, W. 2007. *Poverty and Regional Development in Eastern Europe and Central Asia.* Europe and Central Asia Chief Economist's Regional Working Paper Series. Washington, DC: World Bank.

Eberts, R. W. 1990. "Public Infrastructure and Regional Economic Development." *Federal Reserve Bank of Cleveland Economic Review* (Q1): 15–27.

Flores, L., T. Reardon, and R. Hernandez. 2006. *Supermarkets, New-Generation Wholesalers, Farmers Organizations, Contract Farming, and Lettuce in Guatemala: Participation by and Effects on Small Farmers.* East Lansing: Michigan State University, Department of Agricultural Economics.

Glaeser, E. L., and J. D. Gottlieb. 2009. *The Economics of Place-Making Policies.* Washington, DC: National Bureau of Economic Research.

Haut Commissariat du Plan. 2007. *Activité, Emploi et Chômage.* Rabat, Morocco: Direction de la Statistique.

Hirschman, A. O. 1958. *The Strategy of Development.* New Haven, CT: Yale University Press.

Hotz-Hart, B. 2000. "Innovation Networks, Regions, and Globalization." In *Oxford Handbook of Economic Geography,* ed. G. Clark, M. Gertler, and M. Feldman, 432–50. Oxford, U.K.: Oxford University Press.

Huber, W. 2005. "Federal Co-ordination in Australia." In *New Approaches to Rural Policy: Lessons from around the World,* ed. OECD, 61–67. Paris: Organisation for Economic Co-operation and Development.

Ideaconsult. 2006. *République Tunisienne: Ministère de l'Agriculture et des Ressources Hydrauliques. Actualisation de l'étude de la compétitivité de la production agricole.* Tunis.

Jagannathan, N. V., A. S. Mohamed, and A. Kremer. 2009. *Water in the Arab World: Management Perspectives and Innovations.* Washington, DC: World Bank.

Jalan, J., and M. Ravallion. 1996. "Are There Dynamic Gains from a Poor Area Development Program?" Policy Research Working Paper 1695. World Bank, Washington, DC.

Johnston, D. 2005. "The New Economic Imperative in Rural Regions." In *New Approaches to Rural Policy: Lessons from Around the World,* ed. OECD, 15–20. Paris: Organisation for Economic Co-operation and Development.

Khelladi, M. 2009. *Inégalités spatiales en Algérie: tendances et politiques publiques.* Unpublished background paper for this report.

Lall, S., and S. Yilmaz. 2000. "Regional Economic Convergence: Do Policy Instruments Make a Difference?" *Annals of Regional Science* 35 (1): 153–66.

Lall, S., E. Schroeder, and E. Schmidt. 2009. *Identifying Spatial Efficiency-Equity Trade-offs from Territorial Development Policies: Evidence from Uganda.* Washington, DC: World Bank.

OECD (Organisation for Economic Co-operation and Development). 2004. *OECD Territorial Reviews: Czech Republic.* Paris: OECD.

———. 2006a. *Reinventing Rural Policy.* Paris: OECD.

———. 2006b. *OECD Rural Policy Reviews: The New Rural Paradigm— Policies and Governance.* Paris: OECD.

———. 2007. *OECD Rural Policy Reviews: Mexico.* Paris: OECD.

———. 2008. *OECD Territorial Review of Poland.* Paris: OECD.

———. 2009. "Investing for Growth. Building Innovative Regions." Policy Report. Meeting of the Territorial Development Policy Committee (TDPC) at the Ministerial Level.

Park, S. O. 2009. "A History of the Republic of Korea's Industrial Structural Transformation and Spatial Development." In *Reshaping Economic Geography in East Asia,* eds. Y. Huang and A. M. Bocchi, 320–36. Washington, DC: World Bank.

Perry, M. 2006. *Domestic Net Migration in the United States: 2000 to 2004.* Washington, DC: U.S. Census Bureau.

Porter, M. E. 2000. "Location, Clusters, and Company Strategy." In *Oxford Handbook of Economic Geography*, ed. G. Clark, M. Gertler, and M. Feldman, 253–74. Oxford, U.K.: Oxford University Press.

Quehenberger, M. 2000. "Ten Years After: Eastern Germany's Convergence at a Halt?" *EIB Papers* 5 (7): 117–36.

Rodrik, D. 2004. *Industrial Policy for the Twenty-first Century.* Cambridge, MA: John F. Kennedy School of Government.

Sapir, A. 2003. "An Agenda for a Growing Europe: Making the EU Economic System Deliver." Report of an Independent High-Level Study Group Established on the Initiative of the President of the European Commission.

Shahin, B. 1999. "Industrial Sites in Syria." *Journal of Economic Cooperation among Islamic Countries 20* (1): 71–84.

Suchan, T., M. Perry, J. Fitzsimmons, A. Juhn, A. Tait, and C. Brewer. 2007. *Census Atlas of the United States.* Washington, DC: U.S. Census Bureau.

Sutton, K. 1976. "Industrialisation and Regional Development in a Centrally Planned Economy—The Case of Algeria. *Tijdschrift voor Econ. en Soc. Geografie* 67: 83–94.

World Bank. 2003. *Trade, Investment, and Development in the Middle East and North Africa: Engaging with the World.* Washington, DC: World Bank.

———. 2006a. *Tunisia: Agricultural Policy Review.* Washington, DC: World Bank.

———. 2006b. *West Bank and Gaza Country Economic Memorandum. Growth in West Bank and Gaza: Opportunities and Constraints. Volume II.* Washington, DC: World Bank.

———. 2007. *Making the Most of Scarcity: Accountability for Better Water Management in the Middle East and North Africa.* Washington, DC: World Bank.

———. 2008a. *Agriculture for Development: World Development Report 2008.* Washington, DC: World Bank.

———. 2008b. *Syrian Agriculture: Towards the Social Market.* Washington, DC: World Bank.

————. 2008c. "Government PSD Policies and Industrial Strategy in Egypt." Unpublished Background Note to the World Bank MENA Flagship Report on Private Sector Development.

————. 2009a. *World Development Report 2009: Reshaping Economic Geography*. Washington DC: World Bank.

————2009b. *Iran—Employment Dynamics and Job Creation in Iran's Special Zones: Evidence from an Employers' Survey*. Washington, DC: World Bank.

Yusuf, S. 2008. "Can Clusters Be Made to Order?" In S. Yusuf, K. Nabeshima, and S. Yamashita, *Growing Industrial Clusters in Asia*, 1–39. Washington, DC: World Bank.

CHAPTER 7

Proximity for All: Public Institutions for Spatial Policies

This final chapter of the report draws the threads together. It asks one last question: how can governments organize themselves to address the spatial dimension of development?

The title of this final chapter is "Proximity for All." Some of the benefits of development traditionally have been reserved for people who live close to the center—close to the center of government and to national institutions. This proximity has led to the perception that citizens are included or excluded from the fruits of development according to where they live. These perceptions of spatially differentiated treatment, in turn, fuel political anxiety about spatial disparities. So this section is about how administrative reforms can ensure that even those who live many kilometers from the capital can share the benefits of proximity to decision making.

Spatial Disparities: A Big Task for the State

To recap, this report began with the iron laws of economic geography. The forces of agglomeration draw economic activity and workers into areas of high density. Investments in agglomerated areas give higher returns than those in lagging areas. So there is a trade-off between the objective of raising national growth and that of spreading growth geographically.

We saw that people living in agglomerated areas are better off in terms of just about any indicator of development: monetary consumption, poverty rates, health, and education.

This report then described how the spatial dimension heated the politics of inequality. A sense of place affects how people identify themselves and how they define their relationship with the state. Political organization and representation are geographical phenomena. When ethnicity and religious affiliation map onto geography, the spatial aspect of politics becomes even more potent.

Spatial disparities have, therefore, become a politically charged issue in MENA. As elsewhere in the world, they are seen as an injustice. A government's political success depends upon it being able to demonstrate that its citizens share the benefits of development, irrespective of the accident of where they live.

So the critical policy question is that of how MENA governments can reduce spatial disparities without losing the economic benefits of agglomeration.

This report's analysis showed that MENA governments, fortunately, have three opportunities:

- *Opportunity number 1.* Governments can raise people's living standards in lagging areas without distorting market forces. The key is investing in people and leveling the playing field for development.

- *Opportunity number 2.* Lagging areas near major agglomerations can "hitch a ride" on their growth, provided that the required connectivity is in place.

- *Opportunity number 3.* There are cases—in MENA and elsewhere—of areas outside the main agglomerations moving up the rankings by mobilizing their unrealized economic potential.

So there are three policy packages: one that can apply to any lagging area, a second that requires proximity to growth centers, and a third that requires some form of unrealized economic potential. Before one weighs in with a policy response, therefore, it is important to diagnose what kind of lagging-area problem a place is suffering from. The study showed how lagging areas come in several varieties: high- and low-density, connected and isolated.

But we saw that lagging-area problems are not always as serious as they first appear. Statistics have a way of concealing the concentrations of human deprivation in leading areas. Also, some of the difference in living standards between rich places and poor places is due to household characteristics rather than spatial disparities in economic opportunity. The high fertility rates in lagging areas have conferred a legacy of high dependency ratios, and internal migration rates are too low to redistribute population toward leading areas. Indeed, in some countries, nearly all the gap between leading and lagging provinces are based on household characteristics.

Low accountability indicators worldwide are usually associated with high agglomeration. MENA's history since the 19th century has bequeathed a legacy of political and administrative centralization. The outcome was a spatially unequal climate for development in which metropolitan areas fared better than the periphery. MENA leaders are now striving to undo this inheritance. This report has given a glimpse of what MENA governments are doing and might do to level the playing field for development in the domains of public finance, the business environment, urban development, education, health, and social safety nets. A special place is given to girls' education in lagging areas, which is the key policy for reducing spatial disparities.

Lagging areas can take advantage of spillover connectivity if they are close enough to economic agglomeration to benefit from it. MENA's connectivity infrastructure (essentially the road network) suffers from an imbalance between high spending on upper-grade trunk roads on the one hand and shortfalls in maintenance, rural roads, urban public transportation, and border infrastructure on the other. Improving lagging areas' spillover connectivity will involve addressing these transport sector deficits. Governments can now also encourage the innovative use of new information and communication technologies to give peripheral areas at least some of the benefits of proximity to economic density.

Some nonleading areas have caught up with leading areas by cashing in on their economic potential. The question is how governments can encourage spatial catch-up. Most governments around the world have focused their efforts on using distortionary financial incentives to push private investment toward lagging areas. But the evidence is that the incentive-push approach almost always fails; it is disproportionately expensive, ineffective, and unsustainable. So now governments around the world are adopting an alternative regional economic development model in which the role of the state is to facilitate private investment by coordinating public and private actors around emerging clusters. This approach is particularly applicable to MENA's agribusiness sector, which has the potential to drive development in many lagging areas.

But this all seems pretty daunting. It sounds as though any government wishing to address spatial disparities must activate the entire machinery of the state: ministries of finance, education, health, social affairs, municipalities, transport, telecommunications, industry, agriculture, and public works, not to mention local administrations and the research community.

Therefore, the next question is how the state can best organize and mobilize itself to address the spatial dimension of development. What institutional frameworks can tie so many strands into a manageable whole?

How States Organize and Mobilize to Address the Spatial Dimension of Policy

Perhaps because of their common historical legacy, many MENA countries and economies have similar government structures (World Bank 2007). Figure 7.1 is a stylized and simplified illustration of the structure of the state in MENA. Most of the business of government has traditionally been conducted by the central government. Deconcentrated offices of the sector ministries have performed their mandates in the provinces, accountable to the ministerial hierarchy in the capital city. Appointed governors—reporting to the internal security ministry—have represented the government in the provinces. Advised by an appointed executive council, they have overseen the activities of local administrations; however, governors and local governments have had limited direct influence over the planning and implementation of sectoral development (box 7.1). They have depended upon indirect and sometimes ad hoc relationships with the deconcentrated line ministries.

Managing local development within such a centralized structure is clearly a massive challenge. On the one hand, the institutions with the power and resources—the sector ministries—are centrally accountable

FIGURE 7.1

A Stylized Portrait of the Multilevel State in the MENA Region

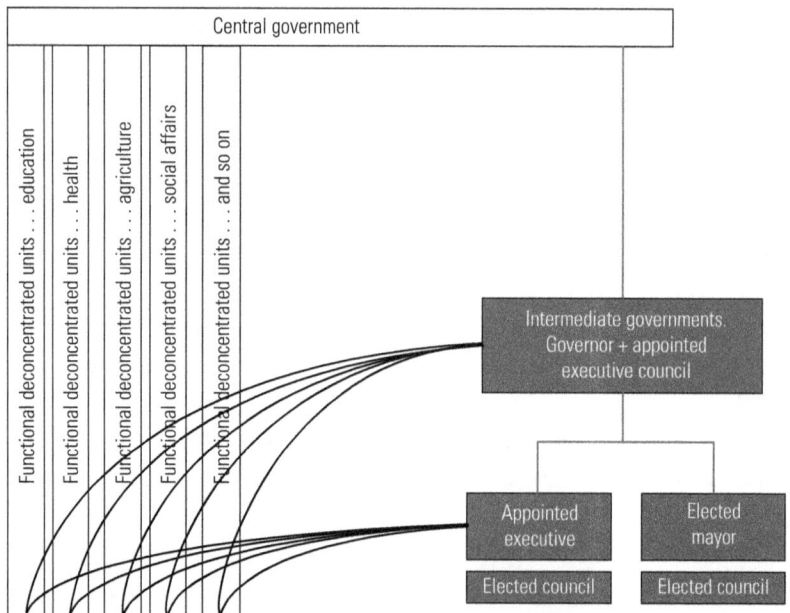

Source: Adapted from World Bank (2007), and based on the Arab Republic of Egypt, the Islamic Republic of Iran, Jordan, Lebanon, Morocco, Tunisia, the Republic of Yemen, and the West Bank and Gaza.

BOX 7.1

Examples of Appointed Provincial and Elected Municipal Local Administration in MENA

- In *Jordan*, 12 governorates have governors appointed by the Ministry of Interior. There are then 51 districts and 89 subdistricts, of which the head is also nominated by the center. At the lower level, 93 municipalities are governed by mayors and local councils elected directly by the people.

- *Morocco* has 39 provinces and 8 urban prefectures. Their governors are appointed by the king. The administrations of the country's 1,503 communes are accountable to elected councils. Legislation of 1997 envisaged the creation of regional (i.e., multi-province) administrations accountable to elected regional councils. The mandate of the regions is under consideration.

- In *Tunisia*, the governors of the 24 governorates are appointed by the Ministry of Interior and operate under its supervision. Urban areas and rural-urban centers are governed by municipalities with an elected municipal council, which, in turn, elects mayors from within its ranks.

- The *West Bank and Gaza* has a similar system although there is often a mismatch between formal provisions and practice resulting from the particular situation on the ground.

- In the *Islamic Republic of Iran*, provinces, districts, and rural counties are deconcentrated units, for which governors and administrators are appointed from the center. There are then more than 1,000 municipalities and 68,000 rural municipalities. These are not completely decentralized because they are governed jointly by the Ministry of Interior and locally elected councils, and the role of the latter is limited.

- The *Arab Republic of Egypt* and the *Republic of Yemen* do not have decentralized government units. There are elected local councils that operate within the deconcentrated levels of government, but with limited real powers.

Source: Study Team.

---

and vertically organized, making coordination at the local level very difficult. On the other, the institutions with the multisectoral territorial mandate—the subnational administrations—have very limited resources and capacity and sometimes also a restricted geographical coverage.

A review of global experience suggests that there are at least five basic approaches whereby states can integrate the management of the various sectoral strands of spatial policy. These are described, in turn, below: territorial development planning, needs-based spatial allocation of fiscal resources, the program mode, deconcentration, and decentralization.

Territorial Development Planning

Territorial development planning (*aménagement du territoire*) has been associated with the francophone administrative tradition. (In fact, it does not
even have an agreed-upon name in English!) This approach involves a
central institution with the responsibility for monitoring and analyzing
spatial development trends and for feeding spatial orientations into the
national public investment planning process. So the defining characteristic of the *aménagement du territoire* approach is the injection of spatial
analysis into national investment planning.

Of the MENA economies,

- Algeria's 2001 law on *aménagement du territoire*[1] allows for a Territorial Master Plan *(Schéma National d'Aménagement du Territoire—
  SNAT)*, published in 2009, as well as master plans covering specific
  regions, *wilayate*, metropolitan areas, and coastal zones; however,
  for these exercises to become fully operational, the development
  planning process would have to be revised to incorporate them. This
  revision would, in turn, open the wider question of how subnational
  governments—which contribute to the various master plans—would
  participate in national development planning alongside the central
  government (Khelladi 2009, 49).

- In Morocco, arrangements for territorial planning are evolving rapidly,
  driven by the political commitment to regionalization. King
  Mohammed VI's Royal Address of December 12, 2006, restated in
  November 2008, announced the strengthening of regional administrations with responsibility for the territorial development of clusters of
  provinces. A new ministerial department in charge of *aménagement du
  territoire* has been established. A Consultative Commission has been
  created to develop a new approach to regionalization, and it is considering a revision of the current provincial and prefectoral boundaries to
  establish more economically and geographically rational territories.
  Two pilot Regional Spatial Development Plans (for the Tadla-Azilal
  and Meknès-Tafilalet regions) and two pilot Regional Development
  Strategies (for the Fès-Boulemane and the Souss-Massa regions) have
  recently been adopted by the Regional Councils. As in Algeria, however, the question remains of how to integrate territorial planning
  within the national development planning and budgeting process.

- Tunisia is perhaps the country that has taken the *aménagement du territoire* approach to its logical conclusion: the developing planning
  process is conceived as a matrix of "vertical" sectoral plans with "horizontal" area-based plans, all within the framework of a Territorial
  Master Plan (box 7.2).

BOX 7.2

How Tunisia Integrates the Spatial Dimension into National Development Planning

The current territorial planning approach in Tunisia dates from the preparation of the Seventh Plan. In 1985, the government created the Commissariat Général de Développement Régional (CGDR). Its mandate was to integrate the territorial planning approach into the development planning cycle. The Commissariat Général is responsible for

- Preparing a regional development plan

- Disseminating information on the regions

- Designing development programs and coordinating their implementation

The CGDR is represented by a deconcentrated directorate in each governorate. The analytical basis of regional policy is the *Schéma National d'Aménagement du Territoire* (Territorial Master Plan). The Interministerial Committee for Territorial Planning (CIAT) steers its preparation, under the oversight of the Ministry of Development and International Cooperation (MDCI). The drafting is the job of the Territorial Planning Directorate General of the Ministry of Environment, Habitat, and Territorial Planning (MEHAT), which, in turn, draws on data provided by the governorates. A national master plan (*Schéma d'Orientation National*) aggregates the subplans for each economic region, governorate, and municipality.

So the preparation of the five-year plans involves the integration of the regional planning process above with the sectoral planning process led by the line ministries in Tunis. The intersection takes place at the level of the governorate. The Regional Development Directorate, the deconcentrated counterpart of the Ministry of Development at the governorate level, coordinates the regional planning process, liaising with the officers of the sectoral ministries posted to their governorate.

Source: Study Team.

Needs-Based Spatial Allocation

Needs-based spatial allocation of fiscal resources can come in two forms: as untied grants or as tied program funding.

The formula-based approach to the spatial allocation of fiscal grants is common in federal states, where the central government's political credibility depends upon its resource transfers being seen as transparent and equalizing. In Belgium, for example, the "National Solidarity Measure" has transferred since 1990 a sum of €11.6 per inhabitant for each percentage point difference between a lagging region's income tax receipts and the national average (Gérard 2001). The Swiss government has published an "index of fiscal capacity" for each canton since 1959; cantons' transfers depend on their index. Every five years, India's constitution requires the president to establish an independent Finance Commission to recommend the allocation of resources from the center to the states. Assistance is transferred according to the Gadgil formula, a weighted index that is based on states' populations, tax performance, per capita income, and vulnerability to "special problems" such as natural disasters or urban congestion. The European Union's Cohesion Policy now accounts for around a third of the European Community budget. Allocations were decided by the European Council in 2005 for 2007–13 on the basis of objective statistics and a formula known as the "Berlin method." Each member state is allocated a per capita amount so that the poorest receive the most. The amount is then capped so that it cannot exceed a maximum percentage of GDP (European Commission 2007).

In the absence of simple and transparent allocation rules, however, political bargaining is likely to prevail. In Argentina, for example, where 65 percent of provincial expenditures are funded by transfers from the center, the allocation rules are theoretically set out in the *Coparticipatión Federal de Impuestos* (federal tax-sharing agreement). Indeed, there is a general trend for resources to be transferred from richer states to poorer states. There are so many loopholes and exceptions in the rules, however, that provincial politicians have been able to influence the allocations. The outcome is significant variability among the receipts of provinces with similar needs (Saiegh and Tommasi 1999). Intragovernmental bargaining is currently not really an important feature in MENA, because subnational administrations are politically dependent upon the center.

The second way in which a central government steers fiscal resources toward poor areas is as the financier of nationwide schemes in which the level of activity in a given location is based upon need. This approach is common in national programs to improve social services, such as India's *Sarva Shiksa Abhiyan* (Education for All Program) or Reproductive and Child Health Program, where special allocations are made to poor states, and incentives applied for raising human development indicators in tribal areas. In the United States, 89 percent of the federal development budget is spent through some 180 sectoral programs, each with its own allocation mechanism (Drabenstott 2005). In MENA, a number of nationwide human development schemes follow this logic—for example, Morocco's National Human Development Initiative (INDH), and Egypt's 1000 Villages Program, where eligibility is based on spatially disaggregated development indicators. Intergovernmental contracting, whereby funds are transferred across levels of government for the fulfillment of certain predetermined goals, is an option under the scheme approach. In Mexico, these contracts (known as *convenios*) are reported to have contributed to capacity building within subnational governments and to have fostered greater trust across levels of government (OECD 2009, 7).

We saw in chapter 4 that much scope remains in MENA to use needs-based fiscal allocation rules to support lagging areas. Moreover, if decentralization continues and if new centers of power emerge outside the central government, rules-based fiscal allocations will become even more important to prevent the emergence of intragovernmental political bargaining for funds.

The Program Mode

With area-based programs, the approach is to bring the spatial dimension to policy by creating dedicated funds and institutions for specific areas. This approach has the advantage of being quickly implementable without any restructuring of existing administrative structures, but the risk is that they undermine local government by creating parallel systems. The main design issue, therefore, is how to integrate the area-based program with the activities of local governments and the deconcentrated provincial and district departments of line ministries. MENA governments are grappling with the coordination challenge in different ways. The planning (identification) and implementation of activities can be either local or central.

- *Central identification.* The Islamic Republic of Iran's Bureau for Deprived Regions reports directly to the Office of the President. It has its own dedicated departmental budget, which it deploys by earmarking transfers to sector ministries for investments in specific areas. Typical projects include rural electrification and roads. This approach may have the advantage of quick "campaign mode" results—the Bureau reported 1,576 projects completed in 10 days (IRNA 2003). However, it runs the risk of low local ownership of the investments.

- *Decentralized identification and central implementation.* Algeria's 1998 Special Fund for the Development of the Southern Regions was funded by a 1 percent levy on fuel. It funded projects for the environment, infrastructure, renewable energy, and quality of life in border areas. Projects are identified by the *wilayate*, approved by the Ministry of the Interior and the cabinet, and then incorporated into the Plan for the Southern Regions. The budget for 2006 was DA 432 billion, or around US$6 billion (Khelladi 2009).

- *Decentralized identification and deconcentrated implementation.* Egypt's Shrouk program (since 1994) and the World Bank–funded Sohag

Rural Development Project financed small-scale projects, principally in rural areas. The projects were identified by local communities in the form of Village Priority Development Plans. Projects were implemented by the deconcentrated offices of sector ministries at governorate and district levels. In the case of Sohag, sector ministries directly supervised construction for projects of less than US$250,000 and delegated the supervision of larger construction works to consultants. The limited level of delegation from Cairo to the program location created some difficulties: each sector ministry followed its own procurement procedures and microcredit applications took a long time to process (World Bank 2008).

- *A shift toward more deconcentrated identification and implementation.* Tunisia's Office for Forestry and Livestock Development in the northwest (ODESYPANO) was created in 1981, with funding from the European Union, the World Bank, Germany, and the Food and Agriculture Organization. It covered five governorates and its basic approach was to convert scrubland into permanent grazing through the provision of forest protection, livestock breeding, and rural tracks. In its first phase (1981–89), the Ministry of Agriculture initiated and delivered these services directly through its dedicated ODESYPANO office. By 1989, however, it was clear that a lack of community ownership was lowering the project's impacts: projects were unnecessarily costly, the new rangelands were being overgrazed, and the new roads were not being well maintained. ODESYPANO, therefore, invested five years (1989–94) in building communities' capacity to plan and implement investments. The community-led approach—in place since 1994—has brought about lower contract prices and has improved the sustainability of investments. The challenge now is that communities' local development plans call for investments beyond the mandate of the Ministry of Agriculture. ODESYPANO is, therefore, signing protocols with each governor, whereby the *Délégué* (subgovernor) will convene the deconcentrated officials of other sector ministries, along with local NGOs, to implement community development plans.

In the design of area-based programs, therefore, there is a trade-off between the implementation capacity of sector ministries—especially where large investments are concerned—and the need for local ownership. In countries such as Brazil and Spain, regional governments serve as a bridge between the center and local administrations, providing a combination of local ownership and critical institutional mass. A common theme is that long-term investment in local capacity creates the foundation for successful area-based programs.

Deconcentration

Deconcentration brings decision making physically closer to citizens and thus makes central governments more responsive to local needs. In the context of MENA's administrative systems, deconcentration means the delegation of power *within* central ministries from administrative units in the national capital to administrative units in provincial capitals or district towns. Deconcentration, therefore, does not increase formal external accountability, but it does reduce the bureaucratic burden of sending decisions up and down the management hierarchy between the locality and the capital. And deconcentration does bring administrators physically closer to end users, thereby increasing their exposure to citizens' voice. It makes for a more efficient implementation of policies and enhances internal accountability by strengthening internal oversight (World Bank 2003). Another advantage of deconcentration from the policy makers' point of view is that each sectoral ministry can deconcentrate at its own pace by adjusting its own internal administrative procedures. The daunting prospect of a nationally coordinated reform process can, therefore, be avoided.

Deconcentration is on the agenda across the MENA13, with proposals under consideration in Algeria, Egypt, the Islamic Republic of Iran, Iraq, Jordan, Morocco, and Tunisia. Given the similarities of the region's administrative structures and political objectives, there is great scope for MENA's policy makers to learn from each other's experience. Some of the key lessons have been the following:

* Deconcentration involves the delegation of three kinds of decision making—on activities, on finance, and on human resource management (HRM)—and it works best when all three are deconcentrated in parallel. If we take the case of Egypt's Ministry of Agriculture, local governors have authority over field staff. But the governorates' ability to act independently—for example, in the case of a pest invasion—is less than it appears, because the Ministry of Agriculture in Cairo still controls nonstaff budget releases. This arrangement leads to a weak double line of accountability (World Bank 2009b). The Moroccan government is making progress on the delegation of decisions concerning activities and finance (box 7.3). But its HRM remains centralized—to the detriment of performance.

* The central ministry's policy making and oversight functions remain critical when policy execution is deconcentrated. For example, the deconcentration of many of the functions of the Islamic Republic of Iran's Management and Planning Organisation (MPO) to ostan governors' offices in July 2007 may have weakened the organization's capacity to monitor and manage the economy from the center. In

---

BOX 7.3

Morocco's Experimentation with Deconcentration Illustrates the Challenges

Morocco's government has made a strong drive toward deconcentration in recent years though sometimes in an ad hoc and evolutionary manner. Morocco's choices illustrate the practical challenges of deconcentration and how one MENA country is addressing them.

Supraministerial leadership. The monarchy has been a driving and coordinating authority behind deconcentration. The royal decree of December 2, 2005, established common rules for the organization of the central administrations and required central administrations to conduct organizational audits with a view to prepare Deconcentration Master Plans (*Schémas Directeurs de Déconcentration*). Five line ministries, including the Ministry of Agricultural and Maritime Fisheries (MAPM) and the Ministry of Health (MH), prepared their master plans, but the preparation of additional plans has been put on hold since the Palace ordered the production of a National Deconcentration Charter. The charter is to define principles for the deconcentration process with a view to support the regionalization agenda laid out by the Palace in the Royal Statements delivered on December 12, 2006, and November 6, 2008. The question, however, is whether a sufficiently strong leadership and coordination function for deconcentration is emerging within the government itself.

The enabling framework. The Moroccan government is underpinning sectoral deconcentration with cross-cutting financial and HRM reforms. A recent circular by the Ministry of Economy and Finance simplified the procedures for transferring budget credits to deconcentrated units within sector ministries. The government has increased budget management autonomy for the sector ministries and their deconcentrated services by

---

contrast, the Tunisian model of deconcentrated planning retains a leadership role for planning departments in Tunis (box 7.2). And under the Moroccan model, central departments exercise control over decentralized units by means of contract programs (box 7.3).

- It becomes extremely important that the mandates of elected local authorities (municipalities, communes, and so on) are clearly defined when the deconcentrated units of sector ministries are reinforced. A lack of clarity over the demarcation of responsibilities between elected local authorities and appointed ministry officials can cause friction.

- Deconcentration *does* need a strong central champion and coordinator to create a favorable environment for financial and HRM reforms. Morocco and Egypt have both adopted a sector-wide

aggregating budget categories and allowing the *ordonnateurs* and *sous-ordonnateurs* to relocate within these categories without the ex ante approval of the Finance Ministry. The government has also taken steps to reduce HRM constraints on deconcentration: a government-wide Strategic Staffing Frameworks process; draft public service legislation establishing the principles of mobility, secondment, and external assignment; concours procedures that would increase autonomy of the line ministries; and financial incentives for redeployment to remote regions. (However, the legislation has been opposed by employee interests and has been stalled in the Senate since December 5, 2005.)

The oversight function. Deconcentration of responsibilities is being backed by strengthened internal accountability and by the reinforcement of each ministry's headquarters policy and oversight role. The Moroccan government's instrument of choice is the performance-based contract program between central and branch offices. As of mid-2009, these programs existed in the Health, Agriculture, Transport, and Education ministries. Again, the question remains of where strong coordination takes place at the supraministerial level.

The need for mandate clarity. In parallel with deconcentration within ministries, the government is setting up regional (supraprovincial) administrations and is reinforcing the financial and technical capacities of elected local authorities. The government's social and economic program identifies the regions as a key interlocutor in the government's new spatial development strategy and the socioeconomic development of urban and rural territories. The government, therefore, realizes that it is now critical to clarify the mandates and relationships among the three sets of administrative bodies.[2] The Palace has indicated a preference for making the deconcentrated services of the sector ministries accountable to the (appointed) central government representatives at the regional level.

Source: Study Team.

approach to deconcentration, with sector ministries reforming their own internal decision-making rules at their own pace. This approach avoids the political challenge of setting one ministry in a coordination role over the others. However, it has its limits: without a centrally agreed-upon legal and managerial framework for the delegation of financial and HRM responsibilities, subnational units' powers may be more theoretical than real.

Decentralization

Decentralization is not a panacea. It can make spatial disparities either bigger or smaller. What matters for reducing spatial disparities is narrowing the resource and capacity gap between local administrations in leading and lagging areas.

Decentralization is a formal arrangement to improve external accountability at the local level. Through local elections, citizens acquire a direct stake in decision making (World Bank 2003). Decentralization can enhance transparency and discourage corruption (Fisman and Gatti 2000). Another motive for decentralization is the hope that lagging areas' citizens will consider themselves more included in the political process.

Decentralization is not advanced in MENA. Instead, the region's subnational government structures fall into one of two classes:

- In the typical case, the country or economy has a two-tier subnational administrative structure. Intermediate-tier deconcentrated administrative units, appointed by and accountable to the center, have a substantial public service delivery function. Locally elected authorities have a much more limited mandate: to cover road maintenance, solid waste management, recreation services, markets, and so forth (e.g., the Islamic Republic of Iran, Jordan, Tunisia, and the West Bank and Gaza).

- In the alternative case, elected local councils themselves share power with the deconcentrated units of centrally controlled ministries (e.g., Egypt and the Republic of Yemen).

The high level of centralization in MENA's government structures is evidenced by local governments' low share of public spending. Figures for MENA economies are well below those of comparator middle-income countries and the world average (figure 7.2). Moreover, central governments often impinge on local administrations' financial management.

FIGURE 7.2

MENA's Local Governments Spend Far Less Than Those in Comparable Economies

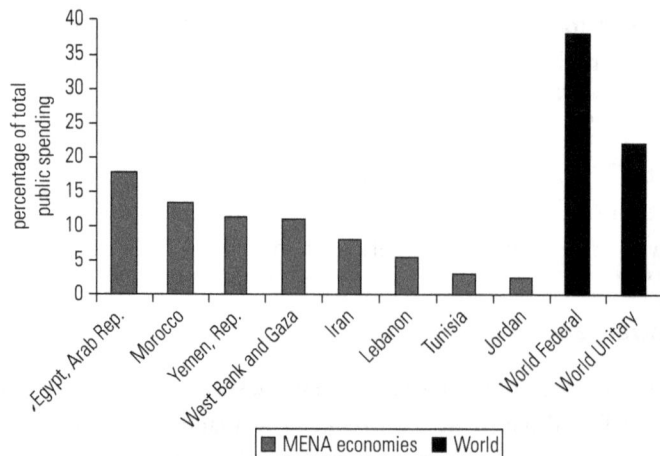

Sources: World Bank 2007; Tosun and Yilmaz 2008.

In some countries, revenues collected at the local level come under partial control of the center (e.g., the West Bank and Gaza, or Egypt). And, as noted in table 4.5, intergovernmental transfer rules are usually ad hoc and unpredictable, a condition that can keep local governments in a permanent state of financial and political dependency and can make it difficult for them to address local development priorities (Shah 1999).

Would more decentralization and fiscal decentralization reduce spatial disparities in MENA? Maybe, but maybe not.

There is a vast literature to the effect that the transfer of power and resources to lower levels of government helps match resources to needs (Rodriguez-Pose, Tijmstra, and Bwire 2009). If, as suggested earlier, MENA's lagging areas have suffered from a lack of political voice, surely decentralization can help level the playing field for development by giving people in poor places more influence over policy making.

The problem is that fiscal decentralization increases the lagging-area citizens' influence only over the area's local administration's resources, not over the national allocation of resources. It does not address the resource and capacity disparities among local administrations.

Indeed, there is a "dark side" to fiscal decentralization. There is a risk (a) of a mismatch between fiscal responsibilities and spending mandates and (b) of the overloading of subnational governments' limited managerial capacity. Mismatches between roles and resources can lead to deterioration in service quality and the quality of spending. In a sample of middle- and high-income countries, greater fiscal decentralization was associated with a shift in public spending from investment to current expenditures and a slowdown in growth (Rodriguez-Pose, Tijmstra, and Bwire 2009). Decentralization of expenditures in post-1990 Central and Eastern European countries was also linked to lower growth, although decentralization of revenue powers seems to have been more positive (Rodriguez-Pose and Kroijer 2008). Fiscal decentralization is usually a political response to spatial disparities or ethnic division and is often, therefore, implemented without sufficient attention to the potential negative economic consequences (IMF 2009).

Moreover, it is far from fact that decentralization or fiscal decentralization per se is a remedy for spatial disparities (IMF 2009). Decentralization can improve or worsen the quality of local services provided to citizens, depending on the quality of the accountability systems in place. Transferring powers from the center to an unaccountable—and maybe technically and managerially less competent—local elite can lead to worse outcomes. Local authorities' capacity is likely to be weakest in lagging areas, and the power of elites may also be more concentrated (World Bank 2006).

Cross-country analysis (Ezcurra and Rodriguez-Pose 2009) reveals that decentralization in low- and middle-income countries is linked to, if anything, a faster *increase* in spatial disparities over time. This occurence might be because decentralization gives richer territories more political scope to control revenues, resulting in less horizontal redistribution toward poorer administrative divisions. Another possible reason is that less-developed areas—particularly in developing countries—lack the technical and administrative capacity to take advantage of the powers devolved to them (Rodriguez-Pose and Gill 2004). In Argentina, for example, poorer states were unable to take advantage of the decentralization of the education sector because they lacked the resources to do so (World Bank 2006). In Brazil, decentralization burdened poorer regions and municipalities with mandates that they could not fulfill, leading to an increase in health disparities (Baiocchi 2006). In China, spatial disparities in public expenditures increased during the decentralization period of 1978–93 (Lin, Tao, and Liu 2006).

So what is the verdict on decentralization and spatial disparities in MENA? We can sum up the global evidence in three propositions:

- There are good reasons to continue decentralization in MENA: to improve accountability, responsiveness, and service quality, and to democratize local decision making. The empowerment of municipal authorities will strengthen their hand in planning for growing populations (see chapter 4) and public transportation needs (see chapter 5).

- But decentralization will not necessarily reduce spatial disparities, and it may increase them. Decentralizing mandates alone will probably increase spatial disparities by putting extra strain on the limited financial and managerial capacities of local administrations in lagging areas.

- So what matters for spatial disparities is creating transparent and predictable arrangements for equalizing intragovernmental fiscal transfers, and building local governments' capacity in lagging areas (see box 7.4).

In conclusion, although most MENA governments have a strong commitment to the development of lagging areas, few of them have decided what kind of institutional platform is needed for a regional-spatial approach to development policy. Governments in the MENA region have inherited centralized, vertical, sectoral administrative hierarchies. If they are to work spatially, they must be adapted to local, multisectoral policy making and implementation.

Conclusion: Keeping Spatial Development Simple

Spatial development is messy. It respects no sectoral boundaries. It is characterized by the diversity of places and of their inhabitants.

BOX 7.4

Mobilizing Institutions for Spatial Policy Making: Seven Ideas for Policy Makers

- Identify the institutional "home" or "champion" for spatial development—an institution with the influence within government to monitor and coordinate across ministries, and with the planning capacity to develop spatial policy.

- Integrate a territorial planning (*aménagement du territoire*) exercise into the formulation of the national development plan.

- Develop a transparent needs- or formula-based system for intragovernmental fiscal transfers.

- Strengthen the formal role of deconcentrated and decentralized administrations in investment planning.

- Review the "enabling environment" for deconcentration. Is there a strong "champion" monitoring and coordinating the process? Even though activities may have been delegated, do regulations for the management of public finances and staff permit adequate delegation of financial and HRM decision making?

- Review *in an integrated way* the mandates and resourcing of the different levels of government to ensure the overall logic and coherence of the whole.

- Identify the capacity-building needs of decentralized administrations.

Source: Study Team.

Matching Policy Packages to Lagging Areas

Policy packages	World Development Report 2009 terminology	Why?	Where?
Package 1. Level the playing field and the opportunity for human development in lagging areas	"Institutions" ("spatially blind policies")	Spatial disparities in well-being can narrow even while production is agglomerating, so long as policies are appropriate. MENA has a historical legacy of policies' widening disparities.	Applicable to all lagging areas
Package 2. Connect poor places to the poles of development	"Infrastructure" ("spatially connective policies")	For growth to spill over from economic poles into lagging areas, they have to be connected.	Lagging areas close enough to density to benefit
Package 3. Underpin private sector interest in nonleading areas	"Incentives" ("spatially focused policies")	Sometimes nonleading areas *do* move ahead to leading-area status (e.g., Tunisia's center-east, Morocco's Tanger-Tétouan)	Areas where the private sector sees unrealized growth potential

Sources: Study team and World Bank 2009a.

It is full of contrasts between rich and poor, dense and sparse, near and distant. All things are interlinked and interacting: rainfall, economics, fertility, migration, public expenditure, institutional architecture, and politics. Generalizations that work at one spatial level break down when one zooms in to a finer level of disaggregation or zooms out to a broader overview.

It may all seem overwhelmingly complicated. This is probably why development policy institutions—the World Bank included—usually prefer to treat development sectorally rather than spatially. Sectors have neater boundaries, fewer institutions, and fewer relationships to think about.

But MENA governments do not have the luxury of ignoring the spatial dimension of development. Geography is intrinsic to the everyday business of politics from Casablanca to Baluchistan.

The aim of this report has, therefore, been to offer MENA's policy makers a structure within which to arrange the untidy reality of spatial development (table 2.3). It is a framework that begins with diagnosis and ends with three policy packages.

The report has explored how the framework would apply in practice to MENA's specific lagging-area challenges. The findings can be summarized as eight simple axioms for spatial policy making in MENA.

1. *Spatial development begins with clear institutional roles and processes.* Spatial policy making is multisectoral and multi-institutional. The "process platform" for spatial development includes arrangements for monitoring and coordination, resource allocation, planning, and role definition.

2. *Analysis is vital.* MENA needs better spatially disaggregated statistics, especially broken down by gender. It is critical to check that spatial disparities really are a major development issue; very often, they are not as important as politics portrays them. Diagnosing the lagging area will identify the right policy package(s).

3. *Good development is good spatial development.* First and foremost, lagging areas need a level playing field for development. Simply by fulfilling their existing mainstream mandates to provide a positive business environment and services to the poor, sector ministries will be making a full contribution to national spatial development objectives. Girls' education in lagging areas is the top priority for spatial development. Erasing spatial disparities in the business environment should offer a high benefit at a particularly low cost.

4. *Bringing social services to lagging areas* usually means (a) finding the incentives for high-quality personnel to work in underprivileged areas and for poor people to use public services, and (b) tailoring

delivery mechanisms to lower-density areas. Simply building more facilities might not solve the problem.

5. *Commodity subsidies channel a lot of public money to leading areas.* Targeted social protection schemes are more spatially equitable.

6. *A short-distance spillover connection is essential.* Short-distance spillover connectivity between leading and lagging areas is the transportation priority for MENA's lagging areas. Depending on a lagging area's specific geography, this connection could mean investment in rural feeder roads, roads maintenance, intra-urban public transportation, border logistics, or peri-urban radial connections, as well as better regulation of transport operators. Electronic connectivity offers new potential for lagging areas to obtain the benefits of proximity.

7. *The best-practice approach to regional economic development* emphasizes the coordination of multiple actors to facilitate private sector interest in an area's latent potential. Attempts to use financial incentives to shunt private investment toward lagging areas have a very bad track record.

8. Finally, *spatial development is about choices.* Agglomeration may be an inevitable part of growth and development, but governments can choose to welcome the benefits of agglomeration or to discourage them. They can choose between the paths of smooth and disruptive agglomeration. Agglomeration creates spatial disparities in development, but governments can choose between policies that exacerbate them or those that mitigate them.

This report has succeeded if it has shone light on these choices and made their implications clearer, thus helping the Middle East and North Africa to ensure proximity for all.

Endnotes

1. Law no. 01-20 of December 12, 2001 (Government of Algeria 2001).
2. There is a telling parallel with Chile, which created such a system of Regional Development Associations in 2006. The main weaknesses documented thus far include (a) their lack of capacity to conduct a thorough analysis of local needs and capacities, (b) the weak effect that their recommendations have on public investment, and (c) their poorly defined mandate (OECD 2009, 24).

References

Baiocchi, G. 2006. "Inequality and Innovation: Decentralization as an Opportunity Structure in Brazil. In *Decentralisation and Local*

Governance in Developing Countries: A Comparative Perspective, ed. P. Bardhan and D. Mookherjee, 53–80. Cambridge: MIT Press.

Drabenstott, M. 2005. "A Review of the Federal Role in Regional Development." Federal Reserve Bank of Kansas City, Kansas City.

European Commission. 2007. *Growing Regions, Growing Europe: Fourth Report on Economic and Social Cohesion.* Luxembourg: Office for Official Publications of the European Communities.

Ezcurra, R., and A. Rodriguez-Pose. 2009. *Does Decentralization Matter for Regional Disparities: A Cross-Country Analysis.* London: SERC, London School of Economics.

Fisman, R., and R. Gatti. 2000. *Decentralization and Corruption: Evidence across Countries.* Washington, DC: World Bank.

Gérard, M. 2001. "Fiscal Federalism in Belgium." Conference on Fiscal Imbalance, Quebec City, September 13–14.

IMF (International Monetary Fund). 2009. *Macro Policy Lessons for a Sound Design of Fiscal Decentralization.* Washington, DC: IMF.

IRNA (Islamic Republic News Agency). 2003. "Iranian Government to Privatize Printing Houses, Postal Services." February 5. http://www.payvand.com/news/03/feb/1033.html.

Khelladi, M. 2009. "Inégalités spatiales en Algérie: tendances et politiques publiques." Unpublished background paper for this report.

Lin, J., R. Tao, and M. Liu. 2006. "Decentralization and Local Governance in China's Economic Transition." In *Decentralization and Local Governance in Developing Countries: A Comparative Perspective*, eds. P. Bardhan and D. Mookherjee, 305–27. Cambridge: MIT Press.

OECD (Organisation for Economic Co-operation and Development). 2009. *Policy Brief: Regional Innovation in 15 Mexican States.* Paris: OECD.

Rodriguez-Pose, A., and N. Gill. 2004. "Is There a Global Link between Spatial Disparities and Devolution?" *Environment and Planning.* 36: 2097–117.

Rodriguez-Pose, A., and A. Kroijer. 2008. *Fiscal Decentralization and Economic Growth in Central and Eastern Europe.* Madrid: Instituto Madrileño de Estudios Avanzados.

Rodriguez-Pose, A., S. Tijmstra, and A. Bwire. 2009. "Fiscal Decentralization, Efficiency, and Growth." *Environment and Planning.* http://www.envplan.com/abstract.cgi?id=a4087.

Saiegh, S. M., and M. Tommasi. 1999. "Why Is Argentina's Fiscal Federalism So Inefficient? Entering the Labyrinth." *Journal of Applied Economics* 2 (1): 169–209.

Shah, A. 1999. *Balance, Accountability, and Responsiveness: Lessons about Decentralization.* Washington, DC: World Bank.

Tosun, M. S., and S. Yilmaz. 2008. *Centralization, Decentralization and Conflict in the Middle East and North Africa.* Washington, DC: World Bank.

World Bank. 2003. *Better Governance for Development in the Middle East and North Africa: Enhancing Inclusiveness and Accountability.* Washington, DC: World Bank.

———. 2006. *World Development Report 2006: Equity and Development.* Washington, DC: World Bank.

———. 2007. *Decentralization and Local Governance in MENA: A Survey of Policies, Institutions, and Practices.* Washington, DC: World Bank.

———. 2008. *Sohag Rural Development Project: Implementation Completion and Results Report.* Washington, DC: World Bank.

———.2009a. *World Development Report 2009: Reshaping Economic Geography.* Washington, DC: World Bank.

———. 2009b. *Egypt—Linking Funding to Outputs: Expenditures of the Ministry of Agriculture and Land Reclamation.* Washington, DC: World Bank.

Appendix:
MENA Region

ALGERIA

	Country	MENA13[a]	Source
General			
Population (millions), 2007	34	334	WDI Database
GDP per capita, PPP (constant 2005 international dollars), 2008	7,422	6,198[b]	WDI Database
GDP growth (average annual %), 1999–2008	3.8	4.7[b]	WDI Database
Physical geography			
Surface area (1,000 km[2]), 2008	2,381	8,774	WDI Database
Arable land (% of surface area), 2005	3	6	WDI Database
Average precipitation (mm/year), 2008	89	137	FAO AQUASTAT
Renewable water resources per capita (m[3]/inhab/year), 2008	340	1,014	FAO AQUASTAT
Human geography			
Population growth (annual), 2008	1.5	1.9	WDI Database
Labor force participation rate (% of population ages 15–64), 2007	60	52	WDI Database
Population density (people/km[2]), 2008	14	38	WDI Database
Population in cities > 1 million (% of total population), 2007	10	22[c]	WDI Database
Population in largest city (% of urban population), 2007	15	24[d]	WDI Database
Agglomeration index (settlement size: 100,000)	50	63	Uchida and Nelson 2008
Gender parity index for net primary enrollment rate, 2007	0.98	0.98[e]	UNESCO
Structure of the economy			
Agriculture, value added (% of GDP), 2008	9	11[b]	WDI Database
Industry, value added (% of GDP), 2008	69	44[h]	WDI Database
Energy wealth (net energy exports per capita), ktoe, 2007	3.75	1.28[f]	IEA (International Energy Agency)
Governance			
Voice and accountability, 2008 (percentile rank 0–100, 100 = best)	18	23.7	World Bank WGI
Connectivity			
Paved roads (% of total road network), 2004	70	58	CIA Factbook
Road density (km of paved roads/km[2] of arable land), 2004	1	0.8	WDI Database/CIA Factbook
Road density (km of paved roads/1,000 people), 2004	2.3	1.4	WDI Database/CIA Factbook
Travel time to city index (%)	57	28	Author's calculations (source in Appendix)
Rural access index (%), 2004	59	58	Roberts and others 2006
National average distance to capital city (km), 2000	1,108	436	World Bank 2009
Rail density (km of track/km[2] of arable land), 2005	0.06	0.05	WDI Database/Euromed
Rail density (km of track/1,000 people), 2005	0.13	0.09	WDI Database/Euromed

(continued on next page)

ALGERIA (continued)

	Country	MENA13[a]	Source
Mobile cellular subscriptions (per 100 people), 2007	81	58[g]	WDI Database
Population covered by mobile cellular network (%), 2007	82	89	WDI Database
Internet users (per 100 people), 2007	10	18	WDI Database
Spatial disparities			
Mean per capita consumption ratio (capital region/national)	..	1.51[h]	
Mean per capita consumption ratio (urban/rural)	..	1.82[i]	

	Urban	Rural	Source
Population growth (% annual), 2008	2.5	−0.3	WDI Database
Fertility rate (births per woman), 2005	2.7	3.4	MICS3
Poverty rate (based on national poverty line), 1995	14.7	13.3	World Bank 1999
Improved water source (% of population with access), 2005	88	82	MICS3 2005
Improved sanitation (% of population with access), 2005	98	87	MICS3 2005
Stunting (%), 2005	10	12	MICS3 2005
Infant mortality rate, 2000	23	44	MICS2 2000
Under-5 mortality rate, 2000	40	56	MICS2 2000

Geographic character of lagging area population (%)	Country		MENA13	
	Sparse	Dense	Sparse	Dense
Far from major cities	15	48	6[j]	33[j]
Close to major cities	4	33	5[j]	56[j]

Algeria: Spatial Concentration of Economic Activity

Source: G-Econ project, Yale, 2010.

Algeria: Lagging Area Typology

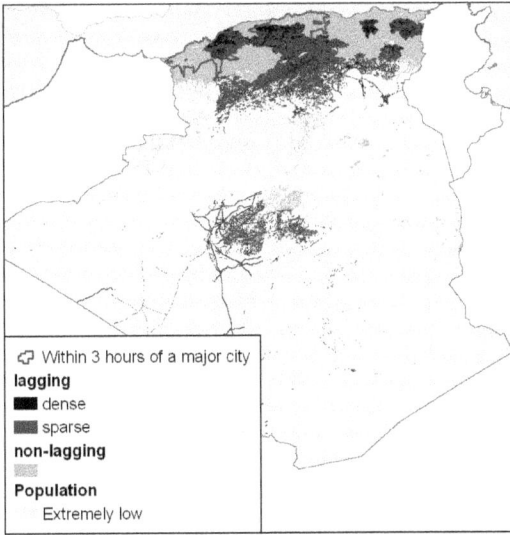

Sources: Elevation, SRTM30 (2000); land cover, GLC2000 (2000); population, Landscan (2005); rail, VMAP0 (1997); rivers, CIA World Data Bank II (1980s); roads, Euro-med (2000) and VMAP0 (1997); slope, in degrees, SRTM30 (2000); urban areas, GPW3-GRUMP (2000); water bodies, Global Lakes and Wetlands Database layer 1 (2004).

Algeria: Spatial Integration Diamond

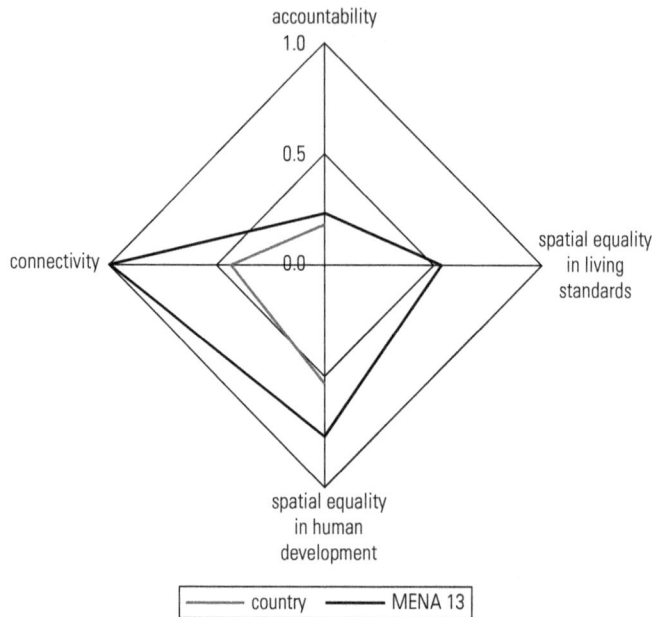

Sources: Accountability: World Bank World Governance Index 2008; spatial equality in human development: Multiple Indicator Cluster Survey2 (MICS2) 2000; connectivity: author's calculation based on Nelson (2008). Sources in Appendix.

Notes: a. Averages are weighted, whenever possible.
b. Data unavailable for Islamic Republic of Iran and the West Bank and Gaza.
c. Data unavailable for Djibouti, Tunisia, and the West Bank and Gaza.
d. Data unavailable for Djibouti, Jordan, Tunisia, and the West Bank and Gaza.
e. Data unavailable for Islamic Republic of Iran, Iraq, Libya, Syrian Arab Republic, and the Republic of Yemen.
 f. Data unavailable for Djibouti and the West Bank and Gaza.
g. Data unavailable for Islamic Republic of Iraq.
h. Data unavailable for Algeria, Libya, and the West Bank and Gaza.
 i. Data unavailable for Algeria, Lebanon, and Libya.
 j. Data unavailable for Djibouti.
.. = not available; MICS = Multiple Indicator Cluster Survey.
Because of missing data, the spatial concentration of economic activity maps are not available for Jordan, Lebanon, and Tunisia, and the West Bank and Gaza, and the lagging area map is not available for the Islamic Republic of Iran.

Definition of Spatial Integration Diamond Indicators:

Accountability: Voice and accountability index, reversed (percentile rank 0–100, 100 = best).

Spatial equality in living standards: rural per capita consumption as percentage of urban per capita consumption (%).

Spatial equality in human development: urban infant mortality as percentage of rural infant mortality (%).

Connectivity: Travel time to city index (% of population). See indicator definitions for more details.

DJIBOUTI

	Country	MENA13[a]	Source
General			
Population (millions), 2008	0.8	334	WDI Database
GDP per capita, PPP (constant 2005 international dollars), 2008	1975	6198[b]	WDI Database
GDP growth (average annual %), 1999–2008	3	4.7[b]	WDI database
Physical geography			
Surface area (1,000 km²), 2008	23	8,774	WDI Database
Arable land (% of surface area), 2005	0	6	WDI Database
Average precipitation (mm/year), 2008	220	137	FAO AQUASTAT
Renewable water resources per capita (m³/inhab/year), 2008 (estimate)	353	1,014	FAO AQUASTAT
Human geography			
Population growth (annual), 2008	0.8	1.9	WDI Database
Labor force participation rate (% of population ages 15–64), 2007	70	52	WDI Database
Population density (people/km²), 2008	37	38	WDI Database
Population in cities > 1 million (% of total population)	..	22[c]	
Population in largest city (% of urban population)	..	24[d]	
Agglomeration index (settlement size: 100,000)	50	63	Uchida and Nelson 2008
Gender parity index for net primary enrollment rate, 2007	0.86	0.98[e]	UNESCO
Structure of the economy			
Agriculture, value added (% of GDP), 2007	4	11[b]	WDI Database
Industry, value added (% of GDP), 2007	17	44[b]	WDI Database
Energy wealth (net energy exports/per capita), ktoe	..	1.28[f]	
Governance			
Voice and accountability, 2008 (percentile rank 0–100, 100 = best)	16.3	23.7	World Bank WGI
Connectivity			
Paved roads (% of total road network), 2006	39	58	World Bank 2006a
Primary road density (km of paved roads/km² of arable land), 2006	122.6	0.8	WDI database/World Bank 2006a
Primary road density (km of paved roads/1,000 people), 2006	1.5	1.4	WDI database/World Bank 2006a
Travel time to city index (%)	0	28	Author's calculations (source in Appendix)
Rural access index (%), 2004	81	58	Roberts and others 2006
National average distance to capital city (km), 2000	85	436	World Bank 2009
Rail density (km of track/km² of arable land), 2006	10.6	0.05	World Bank 2006b
Rail density (km of track/1,000 people), 2006	0.13	0.09	World Bank Railway Database
Mobile cellular subscriptions (per 100 people), 2005	6	58[g]	WDI Database
Population covered by mobile cellular network (%), 2006	75	89	WDI Database
Internet users (per 100 people), 2007	1	18	WDI Database
Spatial disparities			
Mean per capita consumption ratio (capital region/national), 2002	1.24	1.51[h]	Djibouti National HH Survey 2002
Mean per capita consumption ratio (urban/rural), 2002	1.69	1.82[i]	Djibouti National HH Survey 2002
	Urban	**Rural**	**Source**
Population growth (% annual), 2008	2.2	1.0	WDI Database
Fertility rate (births per woman), 2006	2.19	2.38	MICS3 2006
Poverty rate (based on national poverty line)	..	..	
Improved water source (% of population with access), 2006	98	54	MICS3 2006
Improved sanitation (% of population with access), 2006	70	19	MICS3 2006
Stunting (%), 2006	32	44	MICS3 2006
Infant mortality rate, 2006	68	54	MICS3 2006
Under-5 mortality rate, 2006	95	73	MICS3 2006

Geographic character of lagging area population (%)	Country		MENA13	
	Sparse	Dense	Sparse	Dense
Far from major cities	..	..	6 j	33 j
Close to major cities	..	..	5 j	56 j

Djibouti: Spatial Integration Diamond

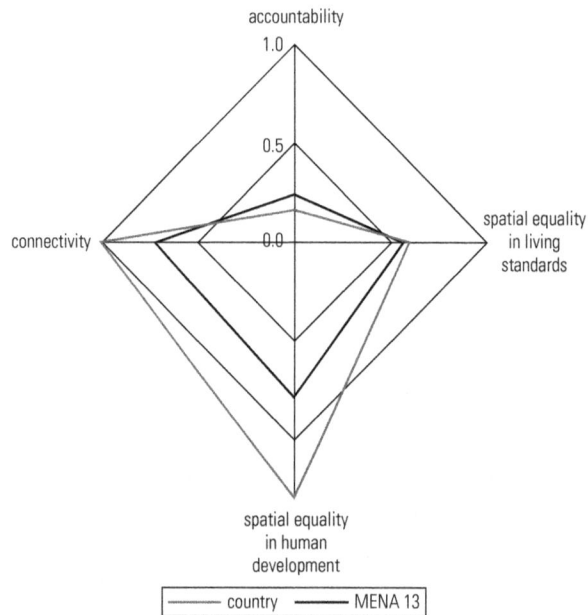

Sources: Accountability: World Bank World Governance Index 2008; spatial equality in living standards: Djibouti National Household Survey 2002; spatial equality in human development: MICS3 2006; connectivity: author's calculation based on Nelson (2008). Sources in Appendix.

Notes: a. Averages are weighted, whenever possible.
b. Data unavailable for Islamic Republic of Iran and the West Bank and Gaza.
c. Data unavailable for Djibouti, Tunisia, and the West Bank and Gaza.
d. Data unavailable for Djibouti, Jordan, Tunisia, and the West Bank and Gaza.
e. Data unavailable for Islamic Republic of Iran, Iraq, Libya, Syrian Arab Republic, and the Republic of Yemen.
f. Data unavailable for Djibouti and the West Bank and Gaza.
g. Data unavailable for Islamic Republic of Iraq.
h. Data unavailable for Algeria, Libya, and the West Bank and Gaza.
i. Data unavailable for Algeria, Lebanon, and Libya.
j. Data unavailable for Djibouti.
.. = not available; MICS = Multiple Indicator Cluster Survey.
Because of missing data, the spatial concentration of economic activity maps are not available for Jordan, Lebanon, and Tunisia, and the West Bank and Gaza, and the lagging area map is not available for the Islamic Republic of Iran.

Definition of Spatial Integration Diamond Indicators:
Accountability: Voice and accountability index, reversed (percentile rank 0–100, 100 = best).

Spatial equality in living standards: rural per capita consumption as percentage of urban per capita consumption (%).

Spatial equality in human development: urban infant mortality as percentage of rural infant mortality (%).

Connectivity: Travel time to city index (% of population). See indicator definitions for more details.

ARAB REPUBLIC OF EGYPT

	Country	MENA13[a]	Source
General			
Population (millions), 2008	82	334	WDI Database
GDP per capita, PPP (constant 2005 international dollars), 2008	5,011	6,198[b]	WDI Database
GDP growth (average annual %), 1999–2008	5	4.7[b]	WDI database
Physical geography			
Surface area (1,000 km[2]), 2008	1,001	8,774	FAO AQUASTAT
Arable land (% of surface area), 2007	3	6	WDI Database
Average precipitation (mm/year), 2008	51	137	FAO AQUASTAT
Renewable water resources per capita (m[3]/inhab/year), 2008	703	1,014	FAO AQUASTAT
Human geography			
Population growth (annual), 2008	1.8	1.9	WDI Database
Labor force participation rate (% of population ages 15–64), 2007	50	52	WDI Database
Population density (people/km[2]), 2008	82	38	WDI Database
Population in cities > 1 million (% of total population), 2007	20	22[c]	WDI Database
Population in largest city (% of urban population), 2007	35	24[d]	WDI Database
Agglomeration index (settlement size: 100,000)	93	63	Uchida and Nelson 2008
Gender parity index for net primary enrollment rate, 2007 (estimate)	0.96	0.98[e]	UNESCO
Structure of the economy			
Agriculture, value added (% of GDP), 2008	14	11[b]	WDI Database
Industry, value added (% of GDP), 2008	36	44[b]	WDI Database
Energy wealth (net energy exports/per capita), ktoe, 2007	0.16	1.28[f]	IEA
Governance			
Voice and accountability, 2008 (percentile rank 0–100, 100 = best)	14.4	23.7	World Bank WGI
Connectivity			
Paved roads (% of total road network), 2009	73	58	CIA Factbook
Primary road density (km of paved roads/km[2] of arable land), 2009	1.6	0.8	WDI Database/CIA Factbook
Primary road density (km of paved roads/1000 people), 2009	0.6	1.4	WDI Database/CIA Factbook
Travel time to city index (%)	20	28	Author's calculations (source in Appendix)
Rural access index (%), 2004	77	58	Roberts and others 2006
National average distance to capital city (km), 2000	558	436	World Bank 2009
Rail density (km of track/km[2] of arable land), 2005	0.17	0.05	WDI/World Bank Railway Database
Rail density (km of track/1,000 people), 2005	0.07	0.09	WDI/World Bank Railway Database
Mobile cellular subscriptions (per 100 people), 2008	51	58[q]	WDI Database
Population covered by mobile cellular network (%), 2007	94	89	WDI Database
Internet users (per 100 people), 2008	15	18	WDI Database
Spatial disparities			
Mean per capita consumption ratio (capital region/national), 2005	1.75	1.51[h]	Demography and Health Survey 2005
Mean per capita consumption ratio (urban/rural), 2005	1.92	1.82[i]	Demography and Health Survey 2005

	Urban	Rural	Source
Population growth (% annual), 2008	1.9	1.7	WDI Database
Fertility rate (births per woman), 2005	2.7	3.4	Demography and Health Survey 2005
Poverty rate (based on national poverty line), 2004 and 2005	10.1	26.8	World Bank 2007
Improved water source (% of population with access), 2005	99	97	Demography and Health Survey 2005
Improved sanitation (% of population with access), 2005	85	52	Demography and Health Survey 2005
Stunting (%), 2005	16	18	Demography and Health Survey 2005

(continued on next page)

ARAB REPUBLIC OF EGYPT (continued)

	Country	MENA13[a]	Source
Infant mortality rate, 2005	32	45	Demography and Health Survey 2005
Under-5 mortality rate, 2005	39	56	Demography and Health Survey 2005

Geographic character of lagging area population (%)	Country		MENA13	
	Sparse	Dense	Sparse	Dense
Far from major cities	0	43	6 [j]	33 [j]
Close to major cities	0	56	5 [j]	56 [j]

Arab Republic of Egypt: Spatial Concentration of Economic Activity

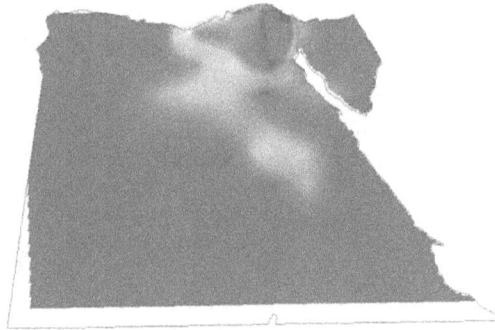

Source: G-Econ project, Yale, 2010.

Arab Republic of Egypt: Lagging Area Typology

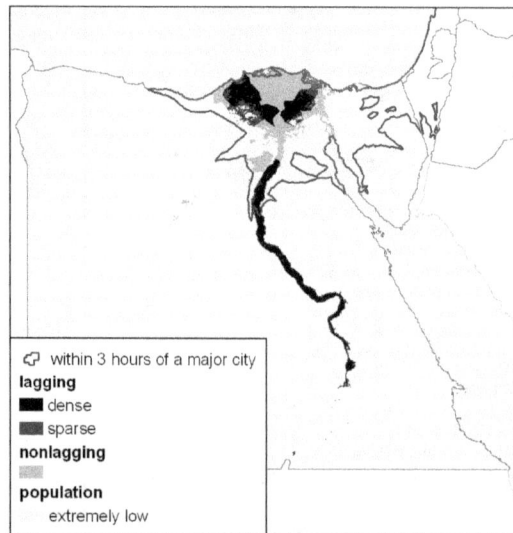

Sources: Elevation, SRTM30 (2000); land cover, GLC2000 (2000); population, Landscan (2005); rail, VMAP0 (1997); rivers, CIA World Data Bank II (1980s); roads, Euro-med (2000) and VMAP0 (1997); slope, in degrees, SRTM30 (2000); urban areas, GPW3-GRUMP (2000); water bodies, Global Lakes and Wetlands Database layer 1 (2004).

Arab Republic of Egypt: Spatial Integration Diamond

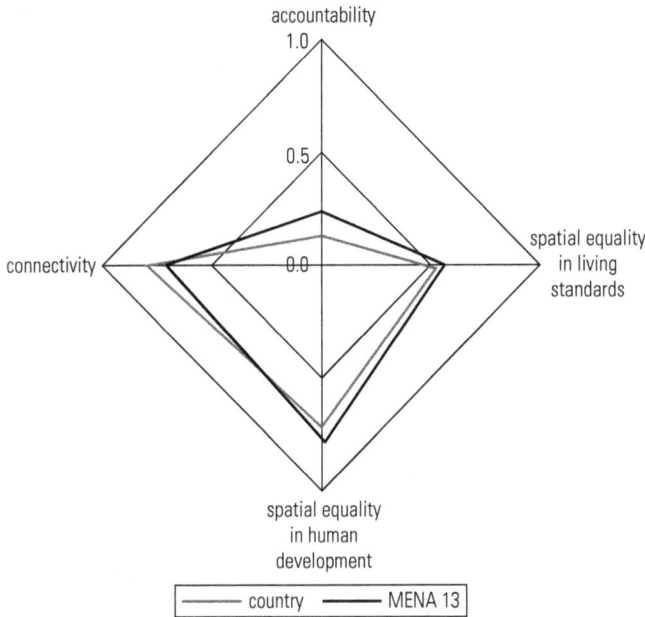

Sources: Accountability: World Bank World Governance Index 2008; spatial equality in living standards: Demographic and Health Survey 2005; spatial equality in human development: Demographic and Health Survey 2005; connectivity: author's calculation based on Nelson (2008). Sources in Appendix.

Notes: a. Averages are weighted, whenever possible.
b. Data unavailable for Islamic Republic of Iran and the West Bank and Gaza.
c. Data unavailable for Djibouti, Tunisia, and the West Bank and Gaza.
d. Data unavailable for Djibouti, Jordan, Tunisia, and the West Bank and Gaza.
e. Data unavailable for Islamic Republic of Iran, Iraq, Libya, Syrian Arab Republic, and the Republic of Yemen.
f. Data unavailable for Djibouti and the West Bank and Gaza.
g. Data unavailable for Islamic Republic of Iraq.
h. Data unavailable for Algeria, Libya, and the West Bank and Gaza.
i. Data unavailable for Algeria, Lebanon, and Libya.
j. Data unavailable for Djibouti.
.. = not available; MICS = Multiple Indicator Cluster Survey.
Because of missing data, the spatial concentration of economic activity maps are not available for Jordan, Lebanon, and Tunisia, and the West Bank and Gaza, and the lagging area map is not available for the Islamic Republic of Iran.

Definition of Spatial Integration Diamond Indicators:

Accountability: Voice and accountability index, reversed (percentile rank 0–100, 100 = best).

Spatial equality in living standards: rural per capita consumption as percentage of urban per capita consumption (%).

Spatial equality in human development: urban infant mortality as percentage of rural infant mortality (%).

Connectivity: Travel time to city index (% of population). See indicator definitions for more details.

ISLAMIC REPUBLIC OF IRAN

	Country	MENA13[a]	Source
General			
Population (millions), 2008	72	334	WDI Database
GDP per capita, PPP (constant 2005 international dollars), 2007	10,346	6,198[b]	WDI Database
GDP growth (average annual %), 1999–2008	5.4	4.7[b]	WDI database
Physical geography			
Surface area (1,000 km²), 2008	1,745	8,774	WDI Database
Arable land (% of surface area), 2005	10	6	WDI Database
Average precipitation (mm/year), 2008	228	137	FAO AQUASTAT
Renewable water resources per capita (m³/inhab/year), 2008	1,876	1,014	FAO AQUASTAT
Human geography			
Population growth (annual), 2008	1.3	1.9	WDI Database
Labor force participation rate (% of population ages 15–64), 2007	55	52	WDI Database
Population density (people/km²), 2008	44	38	WDI Database
Population in cities > 1 million (% of total population), 2007	23	22[c]	WDI Database
Population in largest city (% of urban population), 2007	16	24[d]	WDI Databse
Agglomeration index (settlement size: 100,000)	55	63	Uchida and Nelson 2008
Gender parity index for net primary enrollment rate	..	0.98[e]	
Structure of the economy			
Agriculture, value added (% of GDP), 2008	10	11[b]	WDI Database
Industry, value added (% of GDP), 2008	45	44[b]	WDI Database
Energy wealth (net energy exports/per capita), ktoe	1.89	1.28[f]	IEA
Governance			
Voice and accountability, 2008 (percentile rank 0–100, 100 = best)	8.2	23.7	World Bank WGI
Connectivity			
Paved roads (% of total road network), 2006	73	58	CIA Factbook
Primary road density (km of paved roads/km² of arable land), 2006	0.8	0.8	WDI Database/CIA Factbook
Primary road density (km of paved roads/1,000 people), 2006	1.8	1.4	WDI Database/CIA Factbook
Travel time to city index (%)	37	28	Author's calculations (source in Appendix)
Rural access index (%), 2004	66	58	Roberts and others 2006
National average distance to capital city (km), 2000	654	436	World Bank 2009
Rail density (km of track/km² of arable land), 2005	0.04	0.05	WDI Database/World Bank 2005
Rail density (km of track/1,000 people), 2005	0.11	0.09	WDI Database/World Bank 2005
Mobile cellular subscriptions (per 100 people), 2008	60	58[g]	WDI Database
Population covered by mobile cellular network (%), 2007	95	89	WDI Database
Internet users (per 100 people), 2008	32	18	WDI Database
Spatial disparities			
Mean per capita consumption ratio (capital region/national), 2005	1.54	1.51[h]	Iran Nationa HH Survey, 2005
Mean per capita consumption ratio (urban/rural), 2005	1.87	1.82[i]	Iran Nationa HH Survey, 2005
	Urban	**Rural**	**Source**
Population growth (% annual), 2008	2.1	−0.3	WDI Database
Fertility rate (births per woman), 1998	1.8	2.4	Abbasi-Shavazi and McDonald 2005
Poverty rate (based on national poverty line), 2005	0.8	7.2	World Bank 2008c
Improved water source (% of population with access), 2000	99	86	WHO-UNICEF Joint Monitoring Report
Improved sanitation (% of population with access), 2000	86	78	WHO-UNICEF Joint Monitoring Report
Stunting (%), 2000	11	22	Health Systems Profile: Iran
Infant mortality rate, 2000	28	30	Mehryar 2004
Under-5 mortality rate, 2000	37	35	Mehryar 2004

Geographic character of lagging area population (%)	Country		MENA13	
	Sparse	Dense	Sparse	Dense
Far from major cities	8	36	6[j]	33[j]
Close to major cities	6	50	5[j]	56[j]

Islamic Republic of Iran: Spatial Concentration of Economic Activity

Source: G-Econ project, Yale, 2010.

Islamic Republic of Iran: Spatial Integration Diamond

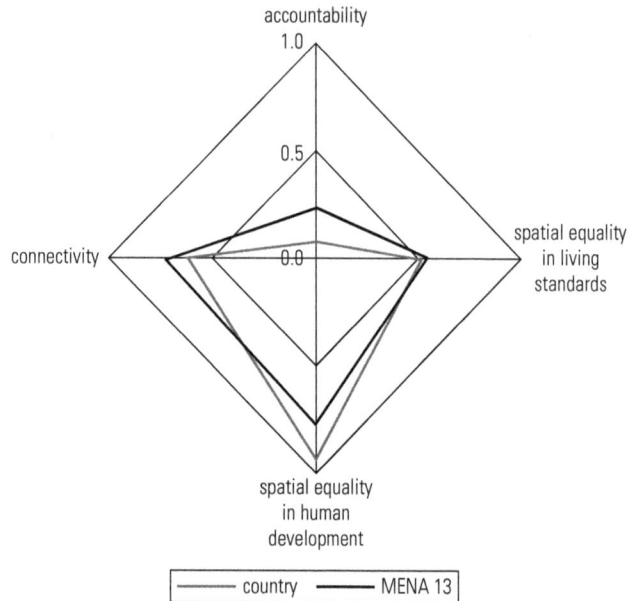

Sources: Accountability: World Bank World Governance Index 2008; spatial equality in living standards: Iran National Household Survey 2005; spatial equality in human development: Mehryar (2004); connectivity: author's calculation based on Nelson (2008). Sources in Appendix.

Notes: a. Averages are weighted, whenever possible.
b. Data unavailable for Islamic Republic of Iran and the West Bank and Gaza.
c. Data unavailable for Djibouti, Tunisia, and the West Bank and Gaza.
d. Data unavailable for Djibouti, Jordan, Tunisia, and the West Bank and Gaza.
e. Data unavailable for Islamic Republic of Iran, Iraq, Libya, Syrian Arab Republic, and the Republic of Yemen.
f. Data unavailable for Djibouti and the West Bank and Gaza.
g. Data unavailable for Islamic Republic of Iraq.
h. Data unavailable for Algeria, Libya, and the West Bank and Gaza.
i. Data unavailable for Algeria, Lebanon, and Libya.
j. Data unavailable for Djibouti.
.. = not available; MICS = Multiple Indicator Cluster Survey.
Because of missing data, the spatial concentration of economic activity maps are not available for Jordan, Lebanon, and Tunisia, and the West Bank and Gaza, and the lagging area map is not available for the Islamic Republic of Iran.

Definition of Spatial Integration Diamond Indicators:
Accountability: Voice and accountability index, reversed (percentile rank 0–100, 100 = best).

Spatial equality in living standards: rural per capita consumption as percentage of urban per capita consumption (%).

Spatial equality in human development: urban infant mortality as percentage of rural infant mortality (%).

Connectivity: Travel time to city index (% of population). See indicator definitions for more details.

IRAQ

	Country	MENA13[a]	Source
General			
Population (millions), 2009 (estimate)	29	334	CIA Factbook
GDP per capita, PPP (constant 2005 dollars), 2009 (estimate)	3,600	6,198[b]	CIA Factbook
GDP growth (average annual %), 1999–2008	..	4.7[b]	WDI database
Physical geography			
Surface area (1,000 km^2), 2008	438	8,774	WDI Database
Arable land (% of surface area), 2005	13	6	WDI Database
Average precipitation (mm/year), 2008	216	137	FAO AQUASTAT
Renewable water resources per capita (m^3/inhab/year), 2008 (estimate)	2,512	1,014	FAO AQUASTAT
Human geography			
Population growth (annual), 2009 (estimate)	2.5	1.9	CIA Factbook
Labor force participation rate (% of population ages 15–64), 2007	43	52	WDI Database/CIA Factbook
Population density (people/km^2), 2008	66	38	CIA Factbook
Population in cities > 1 million (% of total population)	21	22[c]	WDI Database
Population in largest city (% of urban population)	25	24[d]	WDI Database
Agglomeration index (settlement size: 100,000)	71	63	Uchida and Nelson 2008
Gender parity index for net primary enrollment rate	..	0.98[e]	
Structure of the economy			
Agriculture, value added (% of GDP), 2009 (estimate)	10	11[b]	CIA Factbook/WDI Database
Industry, value added (% of GDP), 2009 (estimate)	63	44[b]	CIA Factbook/WDI Database
Energy wealth (net energy exports/per capita), ktoe	2.44	1.28[f]	IEA
Governance			
Voice and accountability, 2008 (percentile rank 0–100, 100 = best)	12	23.7	World Bank WGI
Connectivity			
Paved roads (% of total road network), 2003	84	58	World Bank-UN 2003
Primary road density (km of paved roads/km^2 of arable land), 2003	0.6	0.8	WDI Database/World Bank-UN 2003
Primary road density (km of paved roads/1,000 people), 2003	1.4	1.4	WDI Database/World Bank-UN 2003
Travel time to city index (%)	5	28	Author's calculations (source in Appendix)
Rural access index (%), 2004	58	58	Roberts and others 2006
National average distance to capital city (km), 2000	281	436	World Bank 2009
Rail density (km of track/km^2 of arable land), 2005	0.04	0.05	WDI Database/World Bank-UN 2003
Rail density (km of track/1,000 people), 2005	0.1	0.09	WDI Database/World Bank-UN 2003
Mobile cellular subscriptions (per 100 people)	..	58[g]	
Population covered by mobile cellular network (%), 2006	72	89	WDI Database
Internet users (per 100 people), 2008	1	18	CIA Factbook
Spatial disparities			
Mean per capita consumption ratio (capital region/national), 2007	1.02	1.51[h]	Shlash 2009
Mean per capita consumption ratio (urban/rural), 2007	1.58	1.82[i]	Shlash 2009
	Urban	**Rural**	**Source**
Population growth (% annual)	..	..	
Fertility rate (births per woman), 2006	4	5.1	MICS3 2006
Poverty rate (based on national poverty line), 2007	16.1	31.3	Iraq National HH Survey 2007
Improved water source (% of population with access), 2006	92	57	MICS3 2006
Improved sanitation (% of population with access), 2006	98	82	MICS3 2006
Stunting (%), 2006	19	24	MICS3 2006
Infant mortality rate, 2006	35	35	MICS3 2006
Under-5 mortality rate, 2006	41	41	MICS3 2006

Geographic character of lagging area population (%)	Country		MENA13	
	Sparse	Dense	Sparse	Dense
Far from major cities	2	9	6[j]	33[j]
Close to major cities	9	80	5[j]	56[j]

Iraq: Spatial Concentration of Economic Activity

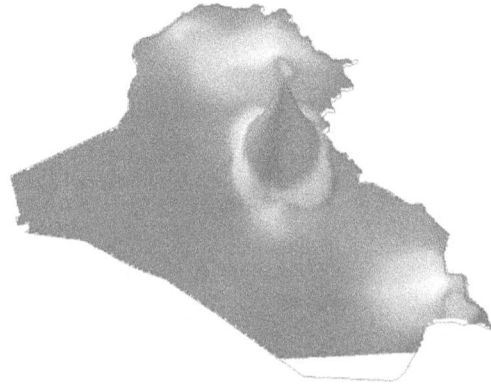

Source: G-Econ project, Yale, 2010.

Iraq: Lagging Area Typology

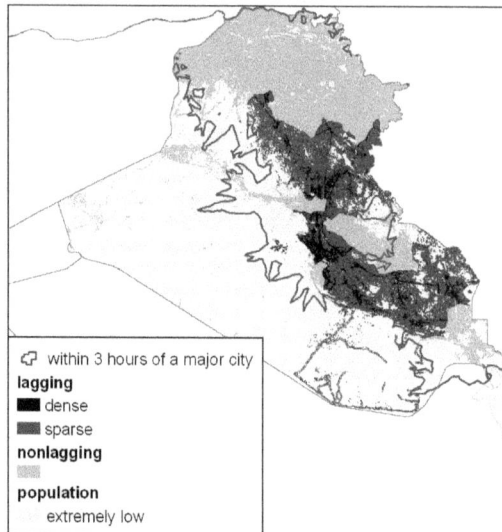

within 3 hours of a major city
lagging
■ dense
■ sparse
nonlagging
▨
population
extremely low

Sources: Elevation, SRTM30 (2000); land cover, GLC2000 (2000); population, Landscan (2005); rail, VMAP0 (1997); rivers, CIA World Data Bank II (1980s); roads, Euro-med (2000) and VMAP0 (1997); slope, in degrees, SRTM30 (2000); urban areas, GPW3-GRUMP (2000); water bodies, Global Lakes and Wetlands Database layer 1 (2004).

Iraq: Spatial Integration Diamond

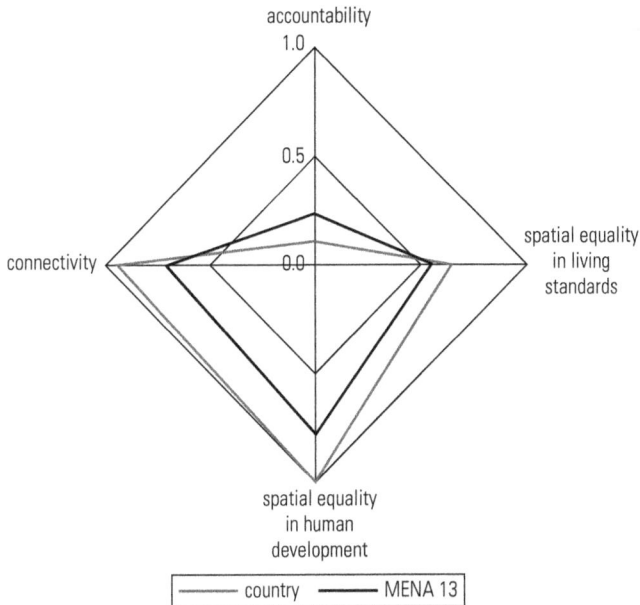

Sources: Accountability: World Bank World Governance Index 2008; spatial equality in living standards: Shlash (2009); spatial equality in human development: MICS3 2006; connectivity: author's calculation based on Nelson (2008). Sources in Appendix.

Notes: a. Averages are weighted, whenever possible.
b. Data unavailable for Islamic Republic of Iran and the West Bank and Gaza.
c. Data unavailable for Djibouti, Tunisia, and the West Bank and Gaza.
d. Data unavailable for Djibouti, Jordan, Tunisia, and the West Bank and Gaza.
e. Data unavailable for Islamic Republic of Iran, Iraq, Libya, Syrian Arab Republic, and the Republic of Yemen.
f. Data unavailable for Djibouti and the West Bank and Gaza.
g. Data unavailable for Islamic Republic of Iraq.
h. Data unavailable for Algeria, Libya, and the West Bank and Gaza.
i. Data unavailable for Algeria, Lebanon, and Libya.
j. Data unavailable for Djibouti.
„ = not available; MICS = Multiple Indicator Cluster Survey.
Because of missing data, the spatial concentration of economic activity maps are not available for Jordan, Lebanon, and Tunisia, and the West Bank and Gaza, and the lagging area map is not available for the Islamic Republic of Iran.

Definition of Spatial Integration Diamond Indicators:

Accountability: Voice and accountability index, reversed (percentile rank 0–100, 100 = best).

Spatial equality in living standards: rural per capita consumption as percentage of urban per capita consumption (%).

Spatial equality in human development: urban infant mortality as percentage of rural infant mortality (%).

Connectivity: Travel time to city index (% of population). See indicator definitions for more details.

JORDAN

	Country	MENA13[a]	Source
General			
Population (millions), 2008	6	334	WDI Database
GDP per capita, PPP (constant 2005 international dollars), 2008	5,055	6,198[b]	WDI Database
GDP growth (average annual %), 1999–2008	5.6	4.7[b]	WDI database
Physical geography			
Surface area (1,000 km²), 2008	89	8,774	WDI Database
Arable land (% of surface area), 2005	2	6	WDI Database
Average precipitation (mm/year), 2008	111	137	FAO AQUASTAT
Renewable water resources per capita (m³/inhab/year), 2008 estimate	153	1,014	FAO AQUASTAT
Human geography			
Population growth (annual), 2008	3.2	1.9	WDI Database
Labor force participation rate (% of population ages 15–64), 2007	47	52	WDI Database
Population density (people/km²), 2008	67	38	WDI Database
Population in cities > 1 million (% of total population), 2007	18	22[c]	WDI Database
Population in largest city (% of urban population), 2005	..	24[d]	
Agglomeration index (settlement size: 100,000)	77	63	Uchida and Nelson 2008
Gender parity index for net primary enrollment rate, 2007	1.02	0.98[e]	UNESCO
Structure of the economy			
Agriculture, value added (% of GDP), 2008	4	11[b]	WDI Database
Industry, value added (% of GDP), 2008	32	44[b]	WDI Database
Energy wealth (net energy exports/per capita), ktoe	−1.22	1.28[f]	IEA
Governance			
Voice and accountability, 2008 (percentile rank 0–100, 100 = best)	26.9	23.7	World Bank WGI
Connectivity			
Paved roads (% of total road network), 2006	100	58	CIA Factbook
Primary road density (km of paved roads/km² of arable land), 2006	4.2	0.8	WDI Database/CIA Factbook
Primary road density (km of paved roads/1,000 people), 2006	1.4	1.4	WDI Database/CIA Factbook
Travel time to city index (%)	4	28	Author's calculations (source in Appendix)
Rural access index (%), 2004	79	58	Roberts and others 2006
National average distance to capital city (km), 2000	171	436	World Bank 2009
Rail density (km of track/km² of arable land), 2005	0.34	0.05	WDI Database/Euromed
Rail density (km of track/1,000 people), 2005	0.11	0.09	WDI Database/Euromed
Mobile cellular subscriptions (per 100 people), 2008	90	58[g]	WDI Database
Population covered by mobile cellular network (%), 2008	99	89	WDI Database
Internet users (per 100 people), 2008	25	18	WDI Database
Spatial disparities			
Mean per capita consumption ratio (capital region/national), 2002	1.54	1.51[h]	Jordan National HH Survey 2002
Mean per capita consumption ratio (urban/rural), 2002	1.32	1.82[i]	Jordan National HH Survey 2002
	Urban	**Rural**	**Source**
Population growth (% annual), 2008	3.3	3.0	WDI Database
Fertility rate (births per woman), 2007	3.6	3.7	Population and Family Health Survey 2007
Poverty rate (based on national poverty line), 2002	12.9	18.7	World Bank 2004
Improved water source (% of population with access), 2007	98	94	Population and Family Health Survey 2007
Improved sanitation (% of population with access), 2007	92	76	Population and Family Health Survey 2007
Stunting (%), 2007	12	13	Population and Family Health Survey 2007

(continued on next page)

JORDAN (continued)

	Country	MENA13[a]	Source
Infant mortality rate, 2007	20	23	Population and Family Health Survey 2007
Under-5 mortality rate, 2007	22	27	Population and Family Health Survey 2007

Geographic character of lagging area population (%)	Country		MENA13	
	Sparse	Dense	Sparse	Dense
Far from major cities	4	1	6[j]	33[j]
Close to major cities	4	91	5[j]	56[j]

Jordan: Lagging Area Typology

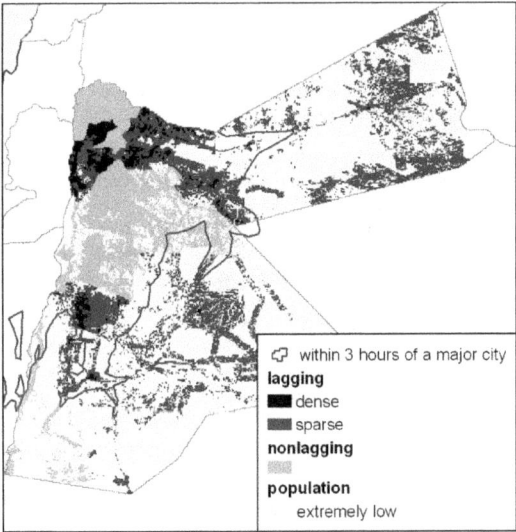

Sources: Elevation, SRTM30 (2000); land cover, GLC2000 (2000); population, Landscan (2005); rail, VMAP0 (1997); rivers, CIA World Data Bank II (1980s); roads, Euro-med (2000) and VMAP0 (1997); slope, in degrees, SRTM30 (2000); urban areas, GPW3-GRUMP (2000); water bodies, Global Lakes and Wetlands Database layer 1 (2004).

Jordan: Spatial Integration Diamond

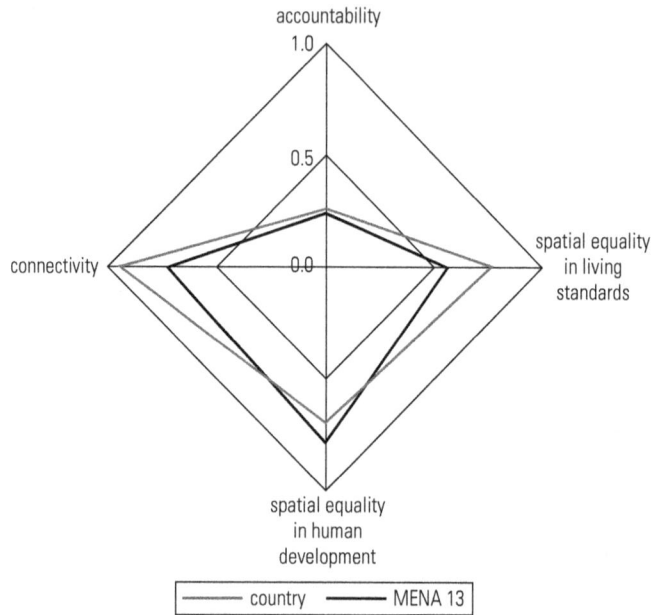

Sources: Accountability: World Bank World Governance Index 2008; spatial equality in living standards: Jordan National Household Survey 2002; spatial equality in human development: Population and Family Health Survey 2007; connectivity: author's calculation based on Nelson (2008). Sources in Appendix.

Notes: a. Averages are weighted, whenever possible.
b. Data unavailable for Islamic Republic of Iran and the West Bank and Gaza.
c. Data unavailable for Djibouti, Tunisia, and the West Bank and Gaza.
d. Data unavailable for Djibouti, Jordan, Tunisia, and the West Bank and Gaza.
e. Data unavailable for Islamic Republic of Iran, Iraq, Libya, Syrian Arab Republic, and the Republic of Yemen.
f. Data unavailable for Djibouti and the West Bank and Gaza.
g. Data unavailable for Islamic Republic of Iraq.
h. Data unavailable for Algeria, Libya, and the West Bank and Gaza.
i. Data unavailable for Algeria, Lebanon, and Libya.
j. Data unavailable for Djibouti.
.. = not available; MICS = Multiple Indicator Cluster Survey.
Because of missing data, the spatial concentration of economic activity maps are not available for Jordan, Lebanon, and Tunisia, and the West Bank and Gaza, and the lagging area map is not available for the Islamic Republic of Iran.

Definition of Spatial Integration Diamond Indicators:
Accountability: Voice and accountability index, reversed (percentile rank 0–100, 100 = best).

Spatial equality in living standards: rural per capita consumption as percentage of urban per capita consumption (%).

Spatial equality in human development: urban infant mortality as percentage of rural infant mortality (%).

Connectivity: Travel time to city index (% of population). See indicator definitions for more details.

LEBANON

	Country	MENA13[a]	Source
General			
Population (millions), 2008	4	334	WDI Database
GDP per capita, PPP (constant 2005 international dollars), 2008	10,877	6,198[b]	WDI Database
GDP growth (average annual %), 1999–2008	3.5	4.7[b]	WDI database
Physical geography			
Surface area (1,000 km²), 2008	10	8774	WDI Database
Arable land (% of surface area), 2005	18	6	WDI Database
Average precipitation (mm/year), 2008	661	137	FAO AQUASTAT
Renewable water resources per capita (m³/inhab/year), 2008	1,074	1,014	FAO AQUASTAT
Human geography			
Population growth (annual), 2008	1.0	1.9	WDI Database
Labor force participation rate (% of population ages 15–64), 2007	54	52	WDI Database
Population density (people/km²), 2008	405	38	WDI Database
Population in cities > 1 million (% of total population), 2007	45	22[c]	WDI Database
Population in largest city (% of urban population), 2007	52	24[d]	WDI Databse
Agglomeration index (settlement size: 100,000)	76	63	Uchida and Nelson 2008
Gender parity index for net primary enrollment rate, 2007	0.99	0.98[e]	UNESCO
Structure of the economy			
Agriculture, value added (% of GDP), 2008	6	11[b]	WDI Database
Industry, value added (% of GDP), 2008	22	44[b]	WDI Database
Energy wealth (net energy exports/per capita), ktoe	−0.98	1.28[f]	IEA
Governance			
Voice and accountability, 2008 (percentile rank 0–100, 100 = best)	35.6	23.7	World Bank WGI
Connectivity			
Paved roads (% of total road network), 2000	85	58	WDI database
Primary road density (km of paved roads/km² of arable land), 2000	3.3	0.8	WDI Database/SESRIC database
Primary road density (km of paved roads/1,000 people), 2000	1.6	1.4	WDI Database/CIA Factbook
Travel time to city index (%)	1	28	Author's calculations (source in Appendix)
Rural access index (%), 2004	87	58	Roberts and others 2006
National average distance to capital city (km), 2000	60	436	World Bank 2009
Rail density (km of track/km² of arable land), 2005	0	0.05	
Rail density (km of track/1,000 people), 2005	0	0.09	
Mobile cellular subscriptions (per 100 people), 2008	35	58[q]	WDI Database
Population covered by mobile cellular network (%), 2006	100	89	WDI Database
Internet users (per 100 people), 2007	38	18	WDI Database
Spatial disparities			
Mean per capita consumption ratio (capital region/national), 2004	1.34	1.51[h]	Lebanon National HH Survey 2004
Mean per capita consumption ratio (urban/rural)	..	1.82[i]	Lebanon National HH Survey 2004
	Urban	**Rural**	**Source**
Population growth (% annual), 2008	1.2	0.1	WDI Database
Fertility rate (births per woman)	..	..	
Poverty rate (based on national poverty line), 1995	8	>25	Haddad 1996
Improved water source (% of population with access), 2006/1999	100	100	WDI Database
Improved sanitation (% of population with access), 2006	100	87	WDI/WHO-UNICEF Joint Monitoring Rep.
Stunting (%), 2005	..	..	
Infant mortality rate, 2005	..	..	
Under-5 mortality rate, 2005	..	..	

Geographic character of lagging area population (%)	Country		MENA13	
	Sparse	Dense	Sparse	Dense
Far from major cities	1	3	6[j]	33[j]
Close to major cities	5	91	5[j]	56[j]

Lebanon: Lagging Area Typology

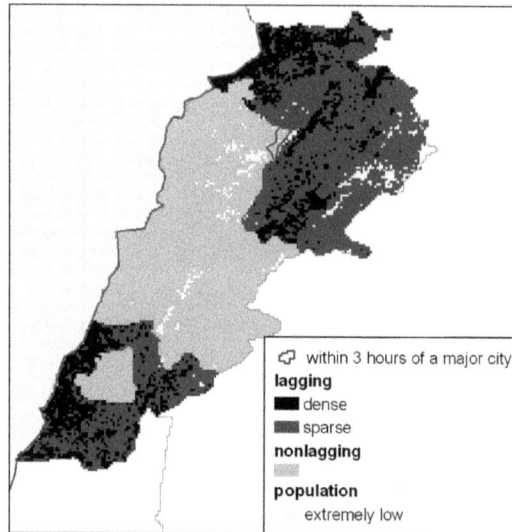

Sources: Elevation, SRTM30 (2000); land cover, GLC2000 (2000); population, Landscan (2005); rail, VMAP0 (1997); rivers, CIA World Data Bank II (1980s); roads, Euro-med (2000) and VMAP0 (1997); slope, in degrees, SRTM30 (2000); urban areas, GPW3-GRUMP (2000); water bodies, Global Lakes and Wetlands Database layer 1 (2004).

Lebanon: Spatial Integration Diamond

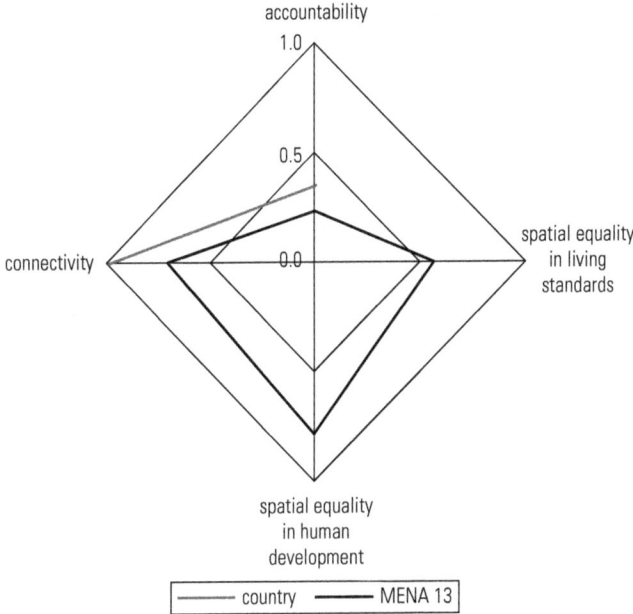

Sources: Accountability: World Bank World Governance Index 2008; connectivity: author's calculation based on Nelson (2008). Sources in Appendix.

Notes: a. Averages are weighted, whenever possible.
b. Data unavailable for Islamic Republic of Iran and the West Bank and Gaza.
c. Data unavailable for Djibouti, Tunisia, and the West Bank and Gaza.
d. Data unavailable for Djibouti, Jordan, Tunisia, and the West Bank and Gaza.
e. Data unavailable for Islamic Republic of Iran, Iraq, Libya, Syrian Arab Republic, and the Republic of Yemen.
f. Data unavailable for Djibouti and the West Bank and Gaza.
g. Data unavailable for Islamic Republic of Iraq.
h. Data unavailable for Algeria, Libya, and the West Bank and Gaza.
i. Data unavailable for Algeria, Lebanon, and Libya.
j. Data unavailable for Djibouti.
.. = not available; MICS = Multiple Indicator Cluster Survey.
Because of missing data, the spatial concentration of economic activity maps are not available for Jordan, Lebanon, and Tunisia, and the West Bank and Gaza, and the lagging area map is not available for the Islamic Republic of Iran.

Definition of Spatial Integration Diamond Indicators:
Accountability: Voice and accountability index, reversed (percentile rank 0–100, 100 = best).

Spatial equality in living standards: rural per capita consumption as percentage of urban per capita consumption (%).

Spatial equality in human development: urban infant mortality as percentage of rural infant mortality (%).

Connectivity: Travel time to city index (% of population). See indicator definitions for more details.

LIBYA

	Country	MENA13[a]	Source
General			
Population (millions), 2008	16	334	WDI Database
GDP per capita, PPP (constant 2005 international dollars), 2008	1,4970	6,198[b]	WDI Database
GDP growth (average annual %), 1999–2008	4	4.7[b]	WDI database
Physical geography			
Surface area (1,000 km²), 2008	1,759	8,774	WDI Database
Arable land (% of surface area), 2005	1	6	WDI Database
Average precipitation (mm/year), 2007	56	137	FAO AQUASTAT
Renewable water resources per capita (m³/inhab/year), 2008 (estimate)	95	1,014	FAO AQUASTAT
Human geography			
Population growth (annual), 2008	1.9	1.9	WDI Database
Labor force participation rate (% of population ages 15–64), 2007	55	52	WDI Database
Population density (people/km²), 2008	4	38	WDI Database
Population in cities > 1 million (% of total population), 2007	55	22[c]	WDI Database
Population in largest city (% of urban population), 2007	46	24[d]	WDI Databse
Agglomeration index (settlement size: 100,000)	77	63	Uchida and Nelson 2008
Gender parity index for net primary enrollment rate	..	0.98[e]	
Structure of the economy			
Agriculture, value added (% of GDP), 2009 (est.)	4	11[b]	CIA Factbook/WDI Database
Industry, value added (% of GDP), 2009 (est.)	78	44[b]	CIA Factbook/WDI Database
Energy wealth (net energy exports/per capita), ktoe	5.22	1.28[f]	IEA
Governance			
Voice and accountability, 2008 (Percentile Rank 0–100, 100 = best)	2.4	23.7	World Bank WGI
Connectivity			
Paved roads (% of total road network), 2003	57	58	CIA Factbook
Primary road density (km of paved roads/km² of arable land), 2003	3.3	0.8	WDI Database/CIA Factbook
Primary road density (km of paved roads/1,000 people), 2003	9.5	1.4	WDI Database/CIA Factbook
Travel time to city index (%)	25	28	Author's calculations (source in Appendix)
Rural access index (%), 2004	78	58	Roberts and others 2006
National average distance to capital city (km), 2000	910	436	World Bank 2009
Rail density (km of track/km² of arable land), 2005	0	0.05	World Bank Railway Database
Rail density (km of track/1,000 people), 2005	0	0.09	World Bank Railway Database
Mobile cellular subscriptions (per 100 people), 2007	73	58[g]	WDI Database
Population covered by mobile cellular network (%), 2006	71	89	WDI Database
Internet users (per 100 people), 2007	5	18	WDI Database
Spatial disparities			
Mean per capita consumption ratio (capital region/national)	..	1.51[h]	
Mean per capita consumption ratio (urban/rural)	..	1.82[i]	

	Urban	Rural	Source
Population growth (% annual), 2008	2.2	1.1	WDI Database
Fertility rate (births per woman), 2001	3.8	4.9	Health Systems Profile: Libya
Poverty rate (based on national poverty line)	..	..	
Improved water source (% of population with access), 1995	98	99	WHO-UNICEF Joint Monitoring Report
Improved sanitation (% of population with access), 1995	99	98	WHO-UNICEF Joint Monitoring Report
Stunting (%), 2001	4	6	Health Systems Profile: Libya
Infant mortality rate, 2001	21	31	Health Systems Profile: Libya
Under-5 mortality rate, 2005	27.5	36.3	Health Systems Profile: Libya

Geographic character of lagging area population (%)	Country		MENA13	
	Sparse	Dense	Sparse	Dense
Far from major cities	4	37	6[j]	33[j]
Close to major cities	5	54	5[j]	56[j]

Libya: Spatial Concentration of Economic Activity

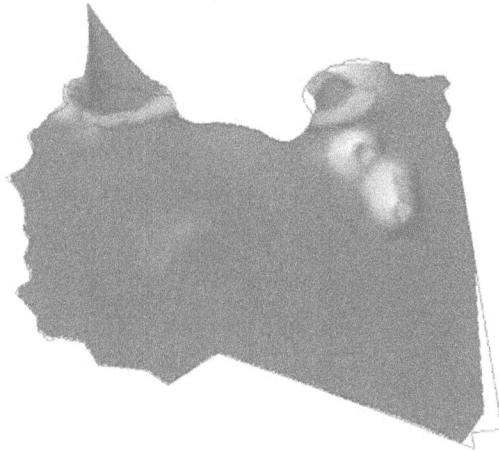

Source: G-Econ project, Yale, 2010.

Libya: Lagging Area Typology

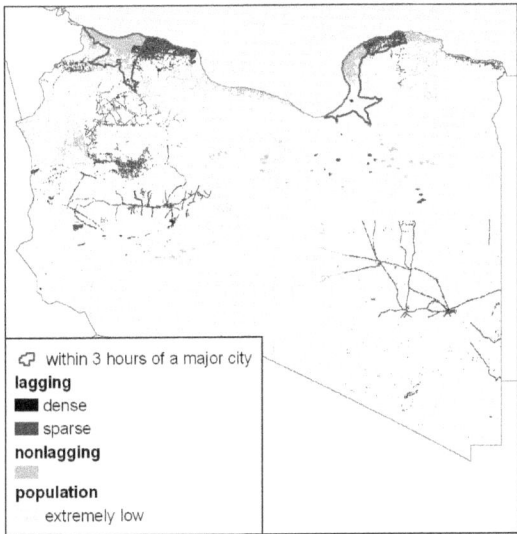

within 3 hours of a major city
lagging
 dense
 sparse
nonlagging
population
 extremely low

Sources: Elevation, SRTM30 (2000); land cover, GLC2000 (2000); population, Landscan (2005); rail, VMAP0 (1997); rivers, CIA World Data Bank II (1980s); roads, Euro-med (2000) and VMAP0 (1997); slope, in degrees, SRTM30 (2000); urban areas, GPW3-GRUMP (2000); water bodies, Global Lakes and Wetlands Database layer 1 (2004).

Libya: Spatial Integration Diamond

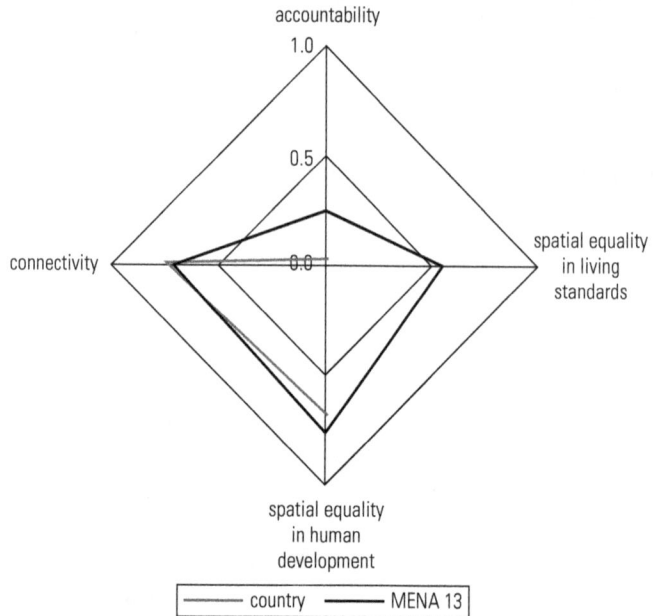

Sources: Accountability: World Bank World Governance Index 2008; spatial equality in human develop-ment: Health Systems Profile: Libya 2007; connectivity: author's calculation based on Nelson (2008). Sources in Appendix.

Notes: a. Averages are weighted, whenever possible.
b. Data unavailable for Islamic Republic of Iran and the West Bank and Gaza.
c. Data unavailable for Djibouti, Tunisia, and the West Bank and Gaza.
d. Data unavailable for Djibouti, Jordan, Tunisia, and the West Bank and Gaza.
e. Data unavailable for Islamic Republic of Iran, Iraq, Libya, Syrian Arab Republic, and the Republic of Yemen.
f. Data unavailable for Djibouti and the West Bank and Gaza.
g. Data unavailable for Islamic Republic of Iraq.
h. Data unavailable for Algeria, Libya, and the West Bank and Gaza.
i. Data unavailable for Algeria, Lebanon, and Libya.
j. Data unavailable for Djibouti.
.. = not available; MICS = Multiple Indicator Cluster Survey.
Because of missing data, the spatial concentration of economic activity maps are not available for Jordan, Lebanon, and Tunisia, and the West Bank and Gaza, and the lagging area map is not available for the Islamic Republic of Iran.

Definition of Spatial Integration Diamond Indicators:
Accountability: Voice and accountability index, reversed (percentile rank 0–100, 100 = best).

Spatial equality in living standards: rural per capita consumption as percentage of urban per capita con-sumption (%).

Spatial equality in human development: urban infant mortality as percentage of rural infant mortality (%).

Connectivity: Travel time to city index (% of population). See indicator definitions for more details.

MOROCCO

	Country	MENA13[a]	Source
General			
Population (millions), 2008	31	334	WDI Database
GDP per capita, PPP (constant 2005 international dollars), 2008	3,938	6,198[b]	WDI Database
GDP growth (average annual %), 1999–2008	4.3	4.7[b]	WDI database
Physical geography			
Surface area (1,000 km^2), 2008	446	8,774	WDI Database
Arable land (% of surface area), 2005	19	6	WDI Database
Average precipitation (mm/year), 2008	346	137	FAO AQUASTAT
Renewable water resources per capita (m^3/inhab/year), 2008 (estimate)	918	1,014	FAO AQUASTAT
Human geography			
Population growth (annual), 2008	1.2	1.9	WDI Database
Labor force participation rate (% of population ages 15–64), 2007	54	52	WDI Database
Population density (people/km^2), 2008	70	38	WDI Database
Population in cities > 1 million (% of total population), 2007	19	22[c]	WDI Database
Population in largest city (% of urban population), 2007	18	24[d]	WDI Databse
Agglomeration index (settlement size: 100,000)	47	63	Uchida and Nelson 2008
Gender parity index for net primary enrollment rate, 2007	0.95	0.98[e]	UNESCO
Structure of the economy			
Agriculture, value added (% of GDP), 2008	16	11[b]	WDI Database
Industry, value added (% of GDP), 2008	20	44[b]	WDI Database
Energy wealth (net energy exports/per capita), ktoe	−0.45	1.28[f]	IEA
Governance			
Voice and accountability, 2008 (percentile rank 0–100, 100 = best)	27.9	23.7	World Bank WGI
Connectivity			
Paved roads (% of total road network), 2006	62	58	CIA Factbook
Primary road density (km of paved roads/km^2 of arable land), 2006	0.4	0.8	WDI Database/CIA Factbook
Primary road density (km of paved roads/1,000 people), 2006	1.2	1.4	WDI Database/CIA Factbook
Travel time to city index (%)	34	28	Author's calculations (source in Appendix)
Rural access index (%), 2004	36	58	Roberts and others 2006
National average distance to capital city (km), 2000	369	436	World Bank 2009
Rail density (km of track/km^2 of arable land), 2005	0.02	0.05	WDI/World Bank Railway Database
Rail density (km of track/1,000 people), 2005	0.06	0.09	WDI/World Bank Railway Database
Mobile cellular subscriptions (per 100 people), 2008	73	58[g]	WDI Database
Population covered by mobile cellular network (%), 2006	98	89	WDI Database
Internet users (per 100 people), 2008	33	18	WDI Database
Spatial disparities			
Mean per capita consumption ratio (capital region/national), 1998	1.16	1.51[h]	Morocco National HH Survey 1998
Mean per capita consumption ratio (urban/rural), 1998	2.17	1.82[i]	Morocco National HH Survey 1998
	Urban	**Rural**	**Source**
Population growth (% annual), 2008	1.8	0.4	WDI Database
Fertility rate (births per woman), 2007	2.1	3	Santé en chiffres 2007
Poverty rate (based on national poverty line), 2007	4.8	14.5	Haut Commissariat au Plan
Improved water source (% of population with access), 2004	98	57	WHO-UNICEF Joint Monitoring Report
Improved sanitation (% of population with access), 2004	98	58	WHO-UNICEF Joint Monitoring Report
Stunting (%), 2003	13	24	EPSF 2003
Infant mortality rate, 2007	33	55	Santé en chiffres 2007
Under-5 mortality rate, 2007	38	69	Santé en chiffres 2007

Geographic character of lagging area population (%)	Country		MENA13	
	Sparse	Dense	Sparse	Dense
Far from major cities	19	34	6 ʲ	33 ʲ
Close to major cities	11	36	5 ʲ	56 ʲ

Morocco: Spatial Concentration of Economic Activity

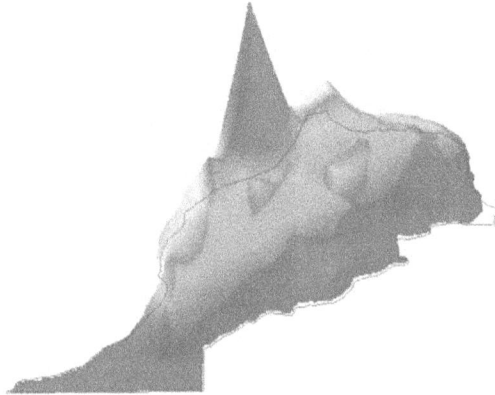

Source: G-Econ project, Yale, 2010.

Morocco: Lagging Area Typology

within 3 hours of a major city
lagging
■ dense
▨ sparse
nonlagging
population
   extremely low

Sources: Elevation, SRTM30 (2000); land cover, GLC2000 (2000); population, Landscan (2005); rail, VMAP0 (1997); rivers, CIA World Data Bank II (1980s); roads, Euro-med (2000) and VMAP0 (1997); slope, in degrees, SRTM30 (2000); urban areas, GPW3-GRUMP (2000); water bodies, Global Lakes and Wetlands Database layer 1 (2004).

Morocco: Spatial Integration Diamond

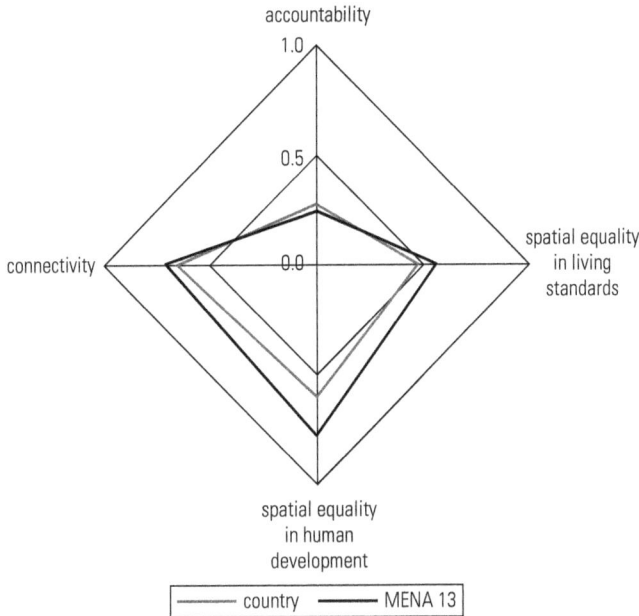

Sources: Accountability: World Bank World Governance Index 2008; spatial equality in living standards: Morocco National Household Survey 1998; spatial equality in human development: Santé en chiffres 2007; connectivity: author's calculation based on Nelson (2008). Sources in Appendix.

Notes: a. Averages are weighted, whenever possible.
b. Data unavailable for Islamic Republic of Iran and the West Bank and Gaza.
c. Data unavailable for Djibouti, Tunisia, and the West Bank and Gaza.
d. Data unavailable for Djibouti, Jordan, Tunisia, and the West Bank and Gaza.
e. Data unavailable for Islamic Republic of Iran, Iraq, Libya, Syrian Arab Republic, and the Republic of Yemen.
f. Data unavailable for Djibouti and the West Bank and Gaza.
g. Data unavailable for Islamic Republic of Iraq.
h. Data unavailable for Algeria, Libya, and the West Bank and Gaza.
i. Data unavailable for Algeria, Lebanon, and Libya.
j. Data unavailable for Djibouti.
.. = not available; MICS = Multiple Indicator Cluster Survey.
Because of missing data, the spatial concentration of economic activity maps are not available for Jordan, Lebanon, and Tunisia, and the West Bank and Gaza, and the lagging area map is not available for the Islamic Republic of Iran.

Definition of Spatial Integration Diamond Indicators:
Accountability: Voice and accountability index, reversed (percentile rank 0–100, 100 = best).

Spatial equality in living standards: rural per capita consumption as percentage of urban per capita consumption (%).

Spatial equality in human development: urban infant mortality as percentage of rural infant mortality (%).

Connectivity: Travel time to city index (% of population). See indicator definitions for more details.

SYRIAN ARAB REPUBLIC

	Country	MENA13[a]	Source
General			
Population (millions), 2008	21	334	WDI Database
GDP per capita, PPP (constant 2005 international dollars), 2008	4,232	6,198[b]	WDI Database
GDP growth (average annual %), 1999–2008	3.5	4.7[b]	WDI database
Physical geography			
Surface area (1,000 km^2), 2008	185	8,774	WDI Database
Arable land (% of surface area), 2005	27	6	WDI Database
Average precipitation (mm/year), 2008	252	137	FAO AQUASTAT
Renewable water resources per capita (m^3/inhab/year), 2008	791	1,014	FAO AQUASTAT
Human geography			
Population growth (annual), 2008	3.5	1.9	WDI Database
Labor force participation rate (% of population ages 15–64), 2007	51	52	WDI Database
Population density (people/km^2), 2008	116	38	WDI Database
Population in cities > 1 million (% of total population), 2007	30	22[c]	WDI Database
Population in largest city (% of urban population), 2007	25	24[d]	WDI Databse
Agglomeration index (settlement size: 100,000)	57	63	Uchida and Nelson 2008
Gender parity index for net primary enrollment rate, 2007	..	0.98[e]	
Structure of the economy			
Agriculture, value added (% of GDP), 2008	20	11[b]	WDI Database
Industry, value added (% of GDP), 2008	35	44[b]	WDI Database
Energy wealth (net energy exports/per capita), ktoe	0.21	1.28[f]	IEA
Governance			
Voice and accountability, 2008 (percentile rank 0–100, 100=best)	4.8	23.7	World Bank WGI
Connectivity			
Paved roads (% of total road network), 2006	20	58	CIA Factbook
Primary road density (km of paved roads/km^2 of arable land), 2006	0.4	0.8	WDI Database/CIA Factbook
Primary road density (km of paved roads/1,000 people), 2006	1	1.4	WDI Database/CIA Factbook
Travel time to city index (%)	18	28	Author's calculations (source in Appendix)
Rural access index (%), 2004	49	58	Roberts and orthers 2006
National average distance to capital city (km), 2000	289	436	World Bank 2009
Rail density (km of track/km2 of arable land), 2005	0.06	0.05	WDI/World Bank Railway Database
Rail density (km of track/1,000 people), 2005	0.14	0.09	WDI/World Bank Railway Database
Mobile cellular subscriptions (per 100 people), 2008	33	58[g]	WDI Database
Population covered by mobile cellular network (%), 2007	96	89	WDI Database
Internet users (per 100 people), 2008	17	18	WDI Database
Spatial Disparities			
Mean per capita consumption ratio (capital region/national), 2004	1.55	1.51[h]	Syria National HH Survey 2004
Mean per capita consumption ratio (urban/rural), 2004	1.52	1.82[i]	Syria National HH Survey 2004

	Urban	Rural	Source
Population growth (% annual), 2008	4.1	2.7	WDI Database
Fertility rate (births per woman), 2007	3.4	4.4	MICS 2007
Poverty rate (based on national poverty line), 2004	7.9	14.5	El Laithy and Abu-Ismail 2005
Improved water source (% of population with access), 2006	94	80	MICS 2007
Improved sanitation (% of population with access), 2006	100	94	MICS 2007
Stunting (%), 2007	22	23	MICS 2007
Infant mortality rate, 2007	16	20	MICS 2007
Under-5 mortality rate, 2007	19	23	MICS 2007

Geographic character of lagging area population (%)	Country		MENA13	
	Sparse	Dense	Sparse	Dense
Far from major cities	4	8	6[j]	33[j]
Close to major cities	8	80	5[j]	56[j]

Syrian Arab Republic: Spatial Concentration of Economic Activity

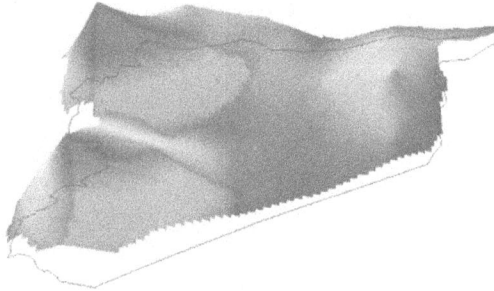

Source: G-Econ project, Yale, 2010.

Syrian Arab Republic: Lagging Area Typology

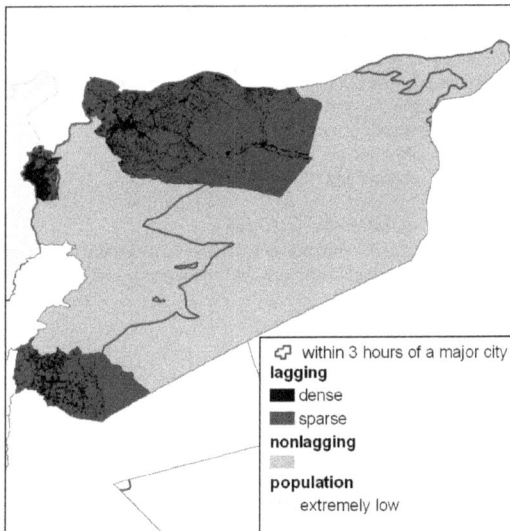

Sources: Elevation, SRTM30 (2000); land cover, GLC2000 (2000); population, Landscan (2005); rail, VMAP0 (1997); rivers, CIA World Data Bank II (1980s); roads, Euro-med (2000) and VMAP0 (1997); slope, in degrees, SRTM30 (2000); urban areas, GPW3-GRUMP (2000); water bodies, Global Lakes and Wetlands Database layer 1 (2004).

Syrian Arab Republic: Spatial Integration Diamond

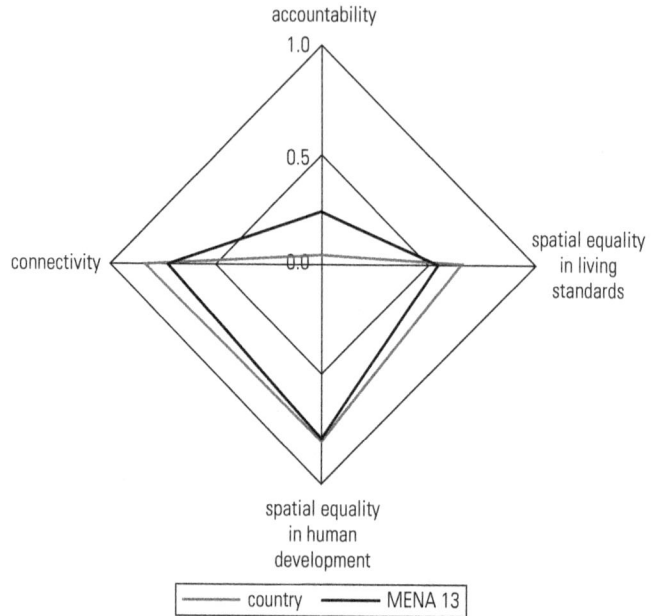

Sources: Accountability: World Bank World Governance Index 2008; spatial equality in living standards: Syria National Household Survey 2004; spatial equality in human development: MICS 2007; connectivity: author's calculation based on Nelson (2008). Sources in Appendix.

Notes: a. Averages are weighted, whenever possible.
b. Data unavailable for Islamic Republic of Iran and the West Bank and Gaza.
c. Data unavailable for Djibouti, Tunisia, and the West Bank and Gaza.
d. Data unavailable for Djibouti, Jordan, Tunisia, and the West Bank and Gaza.
e. Data unavailable for Islamic Republic of Iran, Iraq, Libya, Syrian Arab Republic, and the Republic of Yemen.
f. Data unavailable for Djibouti and the West Bank and Gaza.
g. Data unavailable for Islamic Republic of Iraq.
h. Data unavailable for Algeria, Libya, and the West Bank and Gaza.
i. Data unavailable for Algeria, Lebanon, and Libya.
j. Data unavailable for Djibouti.
.. = not available; MICS = Multiple Indicator Cluster Survey.
Because of missing data, the spatial concentration of economic activity maps are not available for Jordan, Lebanon, and Tunisia, and the West Bank and Gaza, and the lagging area map is not available for the Islamic Republic of Iran.

Definition of Spatial Integration Diamond Indicators:
Accountability: Voice and accountability index, reversed (percentile rank 0–100, 100 = best).

Spatial equality in living standards: rural per capita consumption as percentage of urban per capita consumption (%).

Spatial equality in human development: urban infant mortality as percentage of rural infant mortality (%).

Connectivity: Travel time to city index (% of population). See indicator definitions for more details.

TUNISIA

	Country	MENA13[a]	Source
General			
Population (millions), 2008	10	334	WDI Database
GDP per capita, PPP (constant 2005 international dollars), 2008	7,348	6,198[b]	WDI Database
GDP growth (average annual %), 1999–2008	5	4.7[b]	WDI Database
Physical geography			
Surface area (1,000 km², 2008	163	8,774	WDI Database
Arable land (% of surface area), 2005	18	6	WDI Database
Average precipitation (mm/year), 2008	207	137	FAO AQUASTAT
Renewable water resources per capita (m³/inhab/year), 2008	452	1,014	FAO AQUASTAT
Human geography			
Population growth (annual), 2008	1	1.9	WDI Database
Labor force participation rate (% of population ages 15–64), 2007	51	52	WDI Database
Population density (people/km²), 2008	67	38	WDI Database
Population in cities > 1 million (% of total population)	..	22[c]	
Population in largest city (% of urban population)	..	24[d]	
Agglomeration index (settlement size: 100,000)	39	63	Uchida and Nelson 2008
Gender parity index for net primary enrollment rate, 2007	1.01	0.98[e]	UNESCO
Structure of the economy			
Agriculture, value added (% of GDP), 2008	10	11[b]	WDI Database
Industry, value added (% of GDP), 2008	28	44[b]	WDI Database
Energy wealth (net energy exports/per capita), ktoe	−0.11	1.28[f]	IEA
Governance			
Voice and accountability, 2008 (percentile rank 0–100, 100 = best)	11.5	23.7	World Bank WGI
Connectivity			
Paved roads (% of total road network), 2006	66	58	CIA Factbook
Primary road density (km of paved roads/km² of arable land), 2006	0.5	0.8	WDI Database/CIA Factbook
Primary road density (km of paved roads/1,000 people), 2006	1.3	1.4	WDI Database/CIA Factbook
Travel time to city index (%)	32	28	Author's calculations (source in Appendix)
Rural access index (%), 2004	39	58	Roberts and others 2006
National average distance to capital city (km), 2000	335	436	World Bank 2009
Rail density (km of track/km² of arable land), 2005	0.08	0.05	EU DESTIN Project
Rail density (km of track/1,000 people), 2005	0.22	0.09	EU DESTIN Project
Mobile cellular subscriptions (per 100 people), 2008	83	58[g]	WDI Database
Population covered by mobile cellular network (%), 2007	100	89	WDI Database
Internet users (per 100 people), 2008	27	18	WDI Database
Spatial disparities			
Mean per capita consumption ratio (capital region/national), 2000	1.33	1.51[h]	INS 2000
Mean per capita consumption ratio (urban/rural), 2000	1.86	1.82[i]	INS 2000
	Urban	**Rural**	**Source**
Population growth (% annual), 2008	1.6	−0.2	WDI Database
Fertility rate (births per woman), 2006	2.5	3.3	World Bank 2006c
Poverty rate (based on national poverty line), 2000	1.6	8.3	INS 2000
Improved water source (% of population with access), 2006	99	84	MICS3 2006
Improved sanitation (% of population with access), 2006	96	64	MICS3 2006
Stunting (%), 2006	4	10	MICS3 2006
Infant mortality rate, 2006	16	30	MICS3 2006
Under-5 mortality rate	..	..	

Geographic character of lagging area population (%)	Country		MENA13	
	Sparse	Dense	Sparse	Dense
Far from major cities	16	37	6[j]	33[j]
Close to major cities	13	34	5[j]	56[j]

Tunisia: Lagging Area Typology

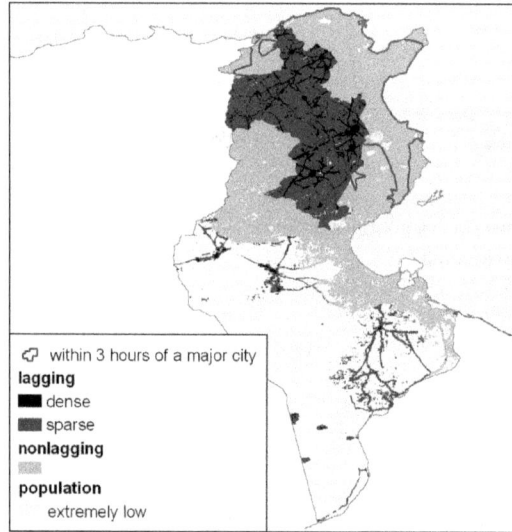

Sources: Elevation, SRTM30 (2000); land cover, GLC2000 (2000); population, Landscan (2005); rail, VMAP0 (1997); rivers, CIA World Data Bank II (1980s); roads, Euro-med (2000) and VMAP0 (1997); slope, in degrees, SRTM30 (2000); urban areas, GPW3-GRUMP (2000); water bodies, Global Lakes and Wetlands Database layer 1 (2004).

Tunisia: Spatial Integration Diamond

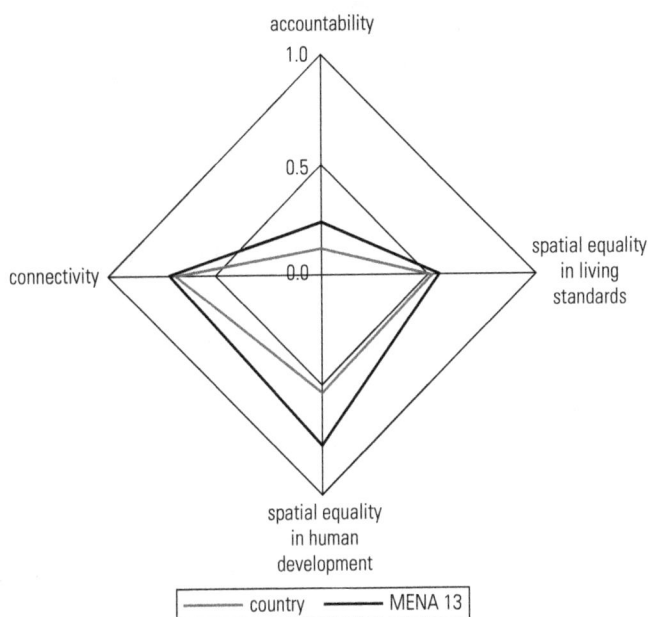

accountability
1.0
0.5
0.0
spatial equality
in living
standards
connectivity
spatial equality
in human
development

country ——— MENA 13

Sources: Accountability: World Bank World Governance Index 2008; spatial equality in living standards: INS 2000; spatial equality in human development: MICS3 2006; connectivity: author's calculation based on Nelson (2008). Sources in Appendix.

Notes: a. Averages are weighted, whenever possible.
b. Data unavailable for Islamic Republic of Iran and the West Bank and Gaza.
c. Data unavailable for Djibouti, Tunisia, and the West Bank and Gaza.
d. Data unavailable for Djibouti, Jordan, Tunisia, and the West Bank and Gaza.
e. Data unavailable for Islamic Republic of Iran, Iraq, Libya, Syrian Arab Republic, and the Republic of Yemen.
f. Data unavailable for Djibouti and the West Bank and Gaza.
g. Data unavailable for Islamic Republic of Iraq.
h. Data unavailable for Algeria, Libya, and the West Bank and Gaza.
i. Data unavailable for Algeria, Lebanon, and Libya.
j. Data unavailable for Djibouti.
.. = not available; MICS = Multiple Indicator Cluster Survey.
Because of missing data, the spatial concentration of economic activity maps are not available for Jordan, Lebanon, and Tunisia, and the West Bank and Gaza, and the lagging area map is not available for the Islamic Republic of Iran.

Definition of Spatial Integration Diamond Indicators:
Accountability: Voice and accountability index, reversed (percentile rank 0–100, 100 = best).

Spatial equality in living standards: rural per capita consumption as percentage of urban per capita consumption (%).

Spatial equality in human development: urban infant mortality as percentage of rural infant mortality (%).

Connectivity: Travel time to city index (% of population). See indicator definitions for more details.

WEST BANK AND GAZA

	Country	MENA13[a]	Source
General			
Population (millions), 2008	4	334	WDI Database
GDP per capita, PPP (2009 $), 2008 (estimate)	2,900	6,198[b]	CIA Factbook
GDP growth (average annual %), 1999–2008	..	4.7[b]	WDI Database
Physical geography			
Surface area (1,000 km^2), 2008	6	8,774	WDI Database
Arable land (% of surface area), 2005	18	6	WDI Database
Average precipitation (mm/year), 2008	402	137	FAO AQUASTAT
Renewable water resources per capita (m^3/inhab/year), 2008	202	1,014	FAO AQUASTAT
Human geography			
Population growth (annual), 2008	3.4	1.9	WDI Database
Labor force participation rate (% of population ages 15–64), 2007	43	52	WDI Database
Population density (people/km^2), 2008	638	38	WDI Database
Population in cities > 1 million (% of total population)	..	22[c]	
Population in largest city (% of urban population)	..	24[d]	
Agglomeration index (settlement size: 100,000)	90	63	Uchida and Nelson 2008
Gender parity index for net primary enrollment rate, 2007	1	0.98[e]	UNESCO
Structure of the economy			
Agriculture, value added (% of GDP), 2008 (estimate)	5	11[b]	CIA Factbook/WDI Database
Industry, value added (% of GDP), 2008 (estimate)	14	44[b]	CIA Factbook/WDI Database
Energy wealth (net energy exports/per capita), ktoe	..	1.28[f]	IEA
Governance			
Voice and accountability, 2008 (percentile rank 0–100, 100 = best)	22.1	23.7	World Bank WGI
Connectivity			
Paved roads (% of total road network), 2006	100	58	CIA Factbook
Primary road density (km of paved roads/km^2 of arable land), 2006	0.4	0.8	WDI Database/CIA Factbook
Primary road density (km of paved roads/1,000 people), 2006	0.3	1.4	WDI Database/CIA Factbook
Travel time to city Index (%)	2	28	Author's calculations (source in Appendix)
Rural access index (%), 2004	..	58	Roberts and others 2006
National average distance to capital city (km)	..	436	World Bank 2009
Rail density (km of track/km^2 of arable land)	0	0.05	
Rail density (km of track/1,000 people)	0	0.09	
Mobile cellular subscriptions (per 100 people), 2007	28	58[g]	WDI Database
Population covered by mobile cellular network (%), 2007	95	89	WDI Database
Internet users (per 100 people), 2007	10	18	WDI Database
Spatial Disparities			
Mean per capita consumption ratio (capital region/national)	..	1.51[h]	
Mean per capita consumption ratio (urban/rural), 2005	1.18	1.82[i]	PCBS 2006

	Urban	Rural	Source
Population growth (% annual), 2008	3.6	3.1	WDI Database
Fertility rate (births per woman), 2006	4.4	4.4	Family Health Survey 2006
Poverty rate (based on national poverty line), 2003	16	15	World Bank 2003
Improved water source (% of population with access), 2006	91	90	Family Health Survey 2006
Improved sanitation (% of population with access), 2006	100	93	Family Health Survey 2006
Stunting (%), 2006	11	9	Family Health Survey 2006
Infant mortality rate, 2006	27	27	Family Health Survey 2006
Under-5 mortality rate, 2006	30	30	Family Health Survey 2006

Geographic character of lagging area population (%)	Country		MENA13	
	Sparse	Dense	Sparse	Dense
Far from major cities	0	5	6[j]	33[j]
Close to major cities	2	93	5[j]	56[j]

West Bank and Gaza: Lagging Area Typology

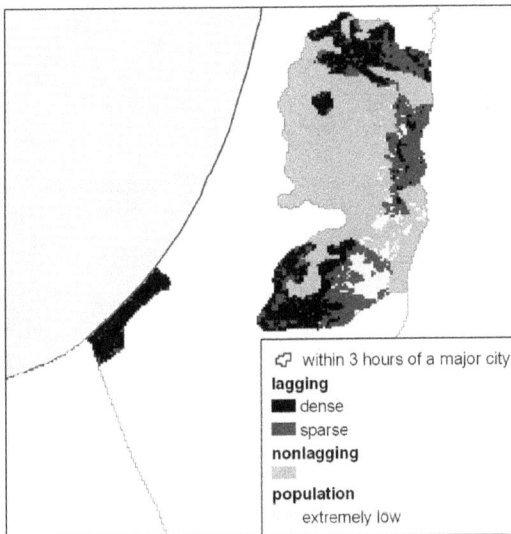

Sources: Elevation, SRTM30 (2000); land cover, GLC2000 (2000); population, Landscan (2005); rail, VMAP0 (1997); rivers, CIA World Data Bank II (1980s); roads, Euro-med (2000) and VMAP0 (1997); slope, in degrees, SRTM30 (2000); urban areas, GPW3-GRUMP (2000); water bodies, Global Lakes and Wetlands Database layer 1 (2004).

West Bank and Gaza: Spatial Integration Diamond

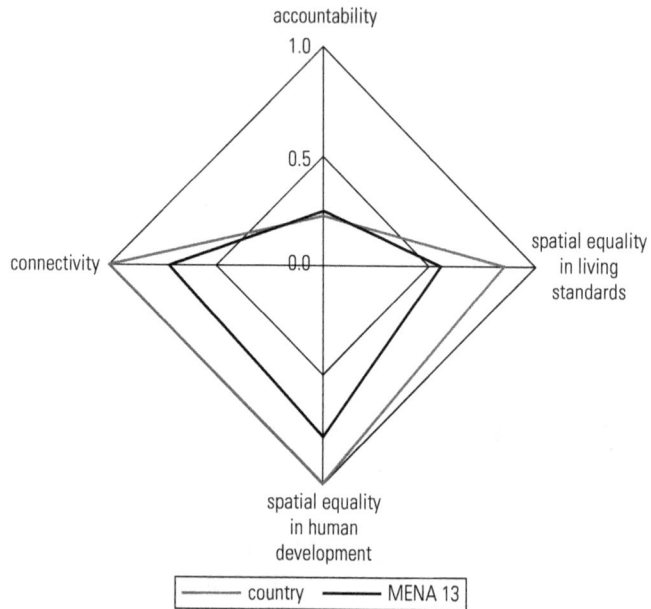

Sources: Accountability: World Bank World Governance Index 2008; spatial equality in living standards: PCBS 2006; spatial equality in human development: Family Health Survey 2006; connectivity: author's calculation based on Nelson (2008). Sources in Appendix.

Notes: a. Averages are weighted, whenever possible.
b. Data unavailable for Islamic Republic of Iran and the West Bank and Gaza.
c. Data unavailable for Djibouti, Tunisia, and the West Bank and Gaza.
d. Data unavailable for Djibouti, Jordan, Tunisia, and the West Bank and Gaza.
e. Data unavailable for Islamic Republic of Iran, Iraq, Libya, Syrian Arab Republic, and the Republic of Yemen.
f. Data unavailable for Djibouti and the West Bank and Gaza.
g. Data unavailable for Islamic Republic of Iraq.
h. Data unavailable for Algeria, Libya, and the West Bank and Gaza.
i. Data unavailable for Algeria, Lebanon, and Libya.
j. Data unavailable for Djibouti.
.. = not available; MICS = Multiple Indicator Cluster Survey.
Because of missing data, the spatial concentration of economic activity maps are not available for Jordan, Lebanon, and Tunisia, and the West Bank and Gaza, and the lagging area map is not available for the Islamic Republic of Iran.

Definition of Spatial Integration Diamond Indicators:

Accountability: Voice and accountability index, reversed (percentile rank 0–100, 100 = best).

Spatial equality in living standards: rural per capita consumption as percentage of urban per capita consumption (%).

Spatial equality in human development: urban infant mortality as percentage of rural infant mortality (%).

Connectivity: Travel time to city index (% of population). See indicator definitions for more details.

REPUBLIC OF YEMEN

	Country	MENA13[a]	Source
General			
Population (millions), 2008	23	334	WDI Database
GDP per capita, PPP (constant 2005 international dollars), 2008	2,232	6,198[b]	WDI Database
GDP growth (average annual %), 1999–2008	3.9	4.7[b]	WDI database
Physical geography			
Surface area (1,000 km^2), 2008	528	8,774	WDI Database
Arable land (% of surface area), 2005	3	6	WDI Database
Average precipitation (mm/year), 2008	167	137	FAO AQUASTAT
Renewable water resources per capita (m^3/inhab/year), 2008 (estimate)	92	1,014	FAO AQUASTAT
Human geography			
Population growth (annual), 2008	3	1.9	WDI Database
Labor force participation rate (% of population ages 15–64), 2007	45	52	WDI Database
Population density (people/km^2), 2008	44	38	WDI Database
Population in cities > 1 million (% of total population), 2007	9	22[c]	WDI Database
Population in largest city (% of urban population), 2007	30	24[d]	WDI Databse
Agglomeration index (settlement size: 100,000)	23	63	Uchida and Nelson 2008
Gender parity index for net primary enrollment rate	..	0.98[e]	
Structure of the economy			
Agriculture, value added (% of GDP), 2009 (estimate)	10	11[b]	CIA Factbook/WDI Database
Industry, value added (% of GDP), 2009 (estimate)	39	44[b]	CIA Factbook/WDI Database
Energy wealth (net energy exports/per capita), ktoe	0.38	1.28[f]	IEA
Governance			
Voice and accountability, 2008 (percentile rank 0–100, 100 = best)	14.9	23.7	World Bank WGI
Connectivity			
Paved roads (% of total road network), 2005	9	58	CIA Factbook
Primary road density (km of paved roads/km^2 of arable land), 2005	0.4	0.8	WDI Database/CIA Factbook
Primary road density (km of paved roads/1,000 people), 2005	0.3	1.4	WDI Database/CIA Factbook
Travel time to city index (%)	31	28	Author's calculations (source in Appendix)
Rural access index (%), 2004	21	58	Roberts and others 2006
National average distance to capital city (km), 2000	406	436	World Bank 2009
Rail density (km of track/km^2 of arable land)	0	0.05	
Rail density (km of track/1,000 people)	0	0.09	
Mobile cellular subscriptions (per 100 people), 2006	14	58[g]	WDI Database
Population covered by mobile cellular network (%), 2006	68	89	WDI Database
Internet users (per 100 people), 2007	1	18	WDI Database
Spatial disparities			
Mean per capita consumption ratio (capital region/national), 2005	1.7	1.51[h]	Yemen National HH Survey 2005
Mean per capita consumption ratio (urban/rural), 2005	1.67	1.82[i]	Yemen National HH Survey 2005
	Urban	**Rural**	**Source**
Population growth (% annual), 2008	4.9	2.1	WDI Database
Fertility rate (births per woman), 2002	4.5	6.7	Family Health Survey (PAPCHILD)
Poverty rate (based on national poverty line), 1998	30.8	45	World Bank 2002
Improved water source (% of population with access), 2006	74	52	MICS 2006
Improved sanitation (% of population with access), 2006	92	34	MICS 2006
Stunting (%), 2006	56	57	MICS 2006
Infant mortality rate, 2006	55	73	MICS 2006
Under-5 mortality rate, 2006	57	86	MICS 2006

Geographic character of lagging area population (%)	Country		MENA13	
	Sparse	Dense	Sparse	Dense
Far from major cities	11	24	6[j]	33[j]
Close to major cities	7	57	5[j]	56[j]

Republic of Yemen: Spatial Concentration of Economic Activity

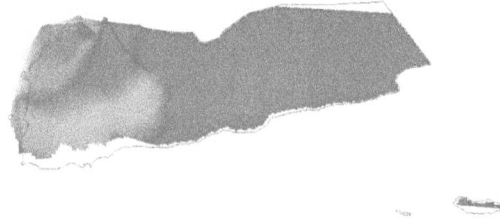

Source: G-Econ project, Yale, 2010.

Republic of Yemen: Lagging Area Typology

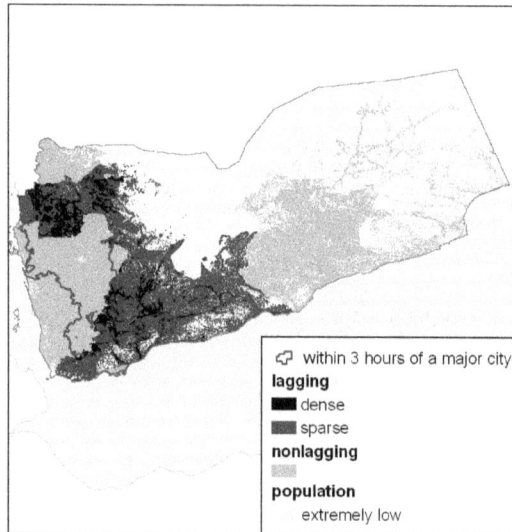

Sources: Elevation, SRTM30 (2000); land cover, GLC2000 (2000); population, Landscan (2005); rail, VMAP0 (1997); rivers, CIA World Data Bank II (1980s); roads, Euro-med (2000) and VMAP0 (1997); slope, in degrees, SRTM30 (2000); urban areas, GPW3-GRUMP (2000); water bodies, Global Lakes and Wetlands Database layer 1 (2004).

Republic of Yemen: Spatial Integration Diamond

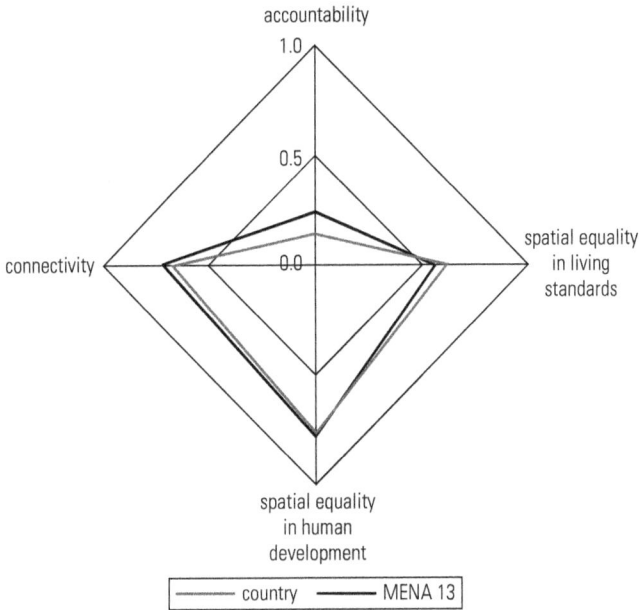

Sources: Accountability: World Bank World Governance Index 2008; spatial equality in living standards: Yemen National Household Survey 2005; spatial equality in human development: MICS 2006; connectivity: author's calculation based on Nelson 2008. Sources in appendix.

Notes: a. Averages are weighted, whenever possible.
b. Data unavailable for Islamic Republic of Iran and the West Bank and Gaza.
c. Data unavailable for Djibouti, Tunisia, and the West Bank and Gaza.
d. Data unavailable for Djibouti, Jordan, Tunisia, and the West Bank and Gaza.
e. Data unavailable for Islamic Republic of Iran, Iraq, Libya, Syrian Arab Republic, and the Republic of Yemen.
f. Data unavailable for Djibouti and the West Bank and Gaza.
g. Data unavailable for Islamic Republic of Iraq.
h. Data unavailable for Algeria, Libya, and the West Bank and Gaza.
i. Data unavailable for Algeria, Lebanon, and Libya.
j. Data unavailable for Djibouti.
.. = not available; MICS = Multiple Indicator Cluster Survey
Because of missing data, the spatial concentration of economic activity maps are not available for Jordan, Lebanon, and Tunisia, and the West Bank and Gaza, and the lagging area map is not available for the Islamic Republic of Iran.

Definition of Spatial Integration Diamond Indicators:
Accountability: Voice and accountability index, reversed (percentile rank 0–100, 100 = best).

Spatial equality in living standards: rural per capita consumption as percentage of urban per capita consumption (%).

Spatial equality in human development: urban infant mortality as percentage of rural infant mortality (%).

Connectivity: Travel time to city index (% of population). See indicator definitions for more details.

Indicator Definitions

Indicator	Source	Notes
Population	WDI Database	Total population is based on the de facto definition of population, which counts all residents regardless of legal status or citizenship, except for refugees not permanently settled in the country of asylum (generally considered part of the population of their country of origin). The values shown are midyear estimates. Source: United Nations Population Division.
GDP per capita, PPP	WDI Database	GDP per capita is based on purchasing power parity (PPP). PPP GDP is gross domestic product converted to international dollars using purchasing power parity rates. An international dollar has the same purchasing power over GDP as the U.S. dollar has in the United States. GDP at purchaser's prices is the sum of gross value added by all resident producers in the economy plus any product taxes and minus any subsidies not included in the value of the products. It is calculated without making deductions for deprecia-tion of fabricated assets or for depletion and degradation of natural resources. Data are in constant 2005 international dollars. Source: World Bank.
GDP growth	WDI Database	Annual percentage growth rate of GDP at market prices is based on constant local currency. Aggregates are based on constant 2000 U.S. dollars. GDP is the sum of gross value added by all resident producers in the economy plus any product taxes and minus any subsidies not included in the value of the products. It is calculated without making deductions for depreciation of fabricated assets or for depletion and degradation of natural resources. Source: World Bank.
Surface area	WDI Database	A country's total area includes areas under inland bodies of water and some coastal waterways. Source: Food and Agriculture Organization.
Arable land	WDI Database	Arable land includes land under temporary crops (double-cropped areas are counted once), temporary meadows for mowing or for pasture, land under market or kitchen gardens, and land tem-porarily fallow. Land abandoned as a result of shifting cultivation is excluded. Source: Food and Agriculture Organization.
Average precipitation	FAO/AQUASTAT	Long-term double average over space and time of the precipitation falling on the country in a year is expressed in depth (mm/year).
Total renewable water resources/ per capita	FAO/AQUASTAT	Sum per capita of internal renewable water resources and external actual renewable water resources take into consideration the quantity of flow reserved to upstream and downstream countries through formal or informal agreements or treaties and possible reduction of external flow because of upstream water abstraction. It corresponds to the maximum theoretical yearly amount of water actually available for a country at a given moment. Source: Food and Agriculture Organization.
Population growth	WDI Database	Annual percentage growth rate of total population is used.
Labor Force Participation Rate	WDI Database	Labor force participation rate is the proportion of the population ages 15 and older that is economically active (all people who supply labor for the production of goods and services during a specified period.) Source: International Labour Organization.

(continued on next page)

Indicator	Source	Notes
Population density	WDI Database	Population density is midyear population divided by land area in square kilometers. Population is based on the de facto definition of population, which counts all residents regardless of legal status or citizenship-except for refugees not permanently settled in the country of asylum. Land area is a country's total area, excluding area under inland water bodies, national claims to continental shelf, and exclusive economic zones. In most cases the definition of inland water bodies includes major rivers and lakes. Sources: FAO and World Bank population estimates.
Population in cities > 1 million	WDI Database	Population in urban agglomerations of more than one million is the percentage of a country's population living in metropolitan areas that in 2000 had a population of more than one million people. Source: United Nations, World Urbanization Prospects.
Population in largest city	WDI Database	Percentage of a country's urban population living in that country's largest metropolitan area is used. Source: United Nations, World Urbanization Prospects.
Agglomeration index	Uchida and Nelson 2008	Percentage of population living in areas with a population density of at least 150 people/km^2 that are no more than an hour's travel time from a city of 100,000 people is used.
Gender parity index for net primary enrollment rate	UNESCO	Quotient of the number of females and the number of males enrolled in a primary education is used. Net enrollment ratio is the ratio of children of official school age based on the International Standard Classification of Education (1997) who are enrolled in school to the population of the corresponding official school age.
Agriculture, value added	WDI Database	Net output of the agricultural sector after adding up all outputs and subtracting intermediate inputs is used. It is calculated without making deductions for depreciation of fabricated assets or depletion and degradation of natural resources. Agriculture includes forestry, hunting, and fishing, as well as cultivation of crops and livestock production. Source: World Bank and OECD.
Industry, value added	WDI Database	Net output of the industrial sector after adding up all outputs and subtracting intermediate inputs is used. It is calculated without making deductions for depreciation of fabricated assets or depletion and degradation of natural resources. Industry comprises value added in mining, manufacturing, construction, electricity, water, and gas. Source: World Bank and OECD.
Energy wealth	IEA Database	Annual difference between a nation's energy exports and energy imports is measured per capita.
Voice and accountability	Worldwide Governance Indicators	Extent to which a country's citizens are able to participate in selecting their government is evaluated as well as freedom of expression, freedom of association, and free media.
Paved roads	CIA Factbook	Roads surfaced with crushed stone (macadam) and hydrocarbon binder or bituminized agents, with concrete, or with cobblestones is measured in length. Source: International Roads Federation.
Road density	CIA Factbook	Length of paved roads (km) (includes crushed stone and hydrocarbon binder or bituminized agents, with concrete, or with cobblestones) is measured per unit area of arable land (km^2) or per thousand people.
Travel time to city index	Authors' calculations	Percentage of population living over 3 hours' road travel away from a city of at least 0.5 million inhabitants is used.

(continued on next page)

Indicator	Source	Notes
Rural access index	Roberts et al. 2006	In practice, the RAI measures the number of rural people who live within two kilometers (typically equivalent to a walk of 20–25 minutes) of an all-season road as a proportion of the total rural population. An "all-season road" is a road that is motorable all year round by the prevailing means of rural transport (typically a pick-up or a truck that does not have four-wheel drive).
National average distance to capital city	World Bank 2009	Population weighted average distance to the capital city is used.
Rail density	WDI Database/ Euromed	Length of railway route available for train service, irrespective of the number of parallel tracks, is measured per area of arable land (km^2) or per thousand people.
Mobile cellular subscriptions	WDI Database	Subscriptions to a public mobile telephone service using cellular technology provide access to the public switched telephone network. Post-paid and prepaid subscriptions are included. Source: International Telecommunications Union and World Bank estimates.
Population covered by mobile cellular network	WDI Database	Percentage of people that live in areas served by a mobile cellular signal regardless of whether they use it is measured. Source: International Telecommunications Union and World Bank estimates.
Internet users	WDI Database	Number of people with access to the worldwide network is used. Source: International Telecommunications Union and World Bank estimates.
Mean per capita consumption	Multiple sources (mainly national household surveys)	Average consumption of goods and services per person is used.
Population growth	WDI Database	Annual population growth rate is used. Population is based on the de facto definition of population, which counts all residents regardless of legal status or citizenship, except for refugees not permanently settled in the country of asylum (generally considered part of the population of the country of origin). Source: United Nations Population Division.
Fertility rate	Multiple sources (mainly national household surveys)	Annual number of births per woman is used.
Poverty rate	Multiple sources (mainly national household surveys)	Percentage of national population living below the national poverty line is used.
Improved water source	Multiple sources (mainly national household surveys)	Percentage of the population with reasonable access to an adequate amount of water from an improved source, such as a household connection, public standpipe, borehole, protected well or spring, and rainwater collection is used. Unimproved sources include vendors, tanker trucks, and unprotected wells and springs. Reasonable access is defined as the availability of at least 20 liters per person a day from a source within one kilometer of the dwelling. Source: World Health Organization and United Nations Children's Fund.
Improved sanitation	Multiple sources (mainly national household surveys)	Percentage of the population with at least adequate access to excreta disposal facilities that can effectively prevent human, animal, and insect contact with excreta is used. Improved facilities range from simple but protected pit latrines to flush toilets with a sewerage connection. For effectiveness, facilities must be correctly constructed and properly maintained. Source: World Health Organization and United Nations Children's Fund.

(continued on next page)

Indicator	Source	Notes
Stunting	Multiple sources (mainly national household surveys)	Percentage of children having a height (or length). more than two standard deviations below the median of the NCHS/WHO growth reference for their age is used. Source: World Health Organization.
Infant mortality rate	Multiple sources (mainly national household surveys)	Number of infants dying before reaching one year of age is measured per 1,000 live births in a given year. Source: Inter-agency Group for Child Mortality Estimation.
Under-5 mortality rate	Multiple sources (mainly national household surveys)	Probability per 1,000 that a newborn baby will die before reaching age five is used if subject to current age-specific mortality rates. Source: Inter-agency Group for Child Mortality Estimation.

References

Abbasi-Shavazi, M. J., and P. McDonald. 2005. "The Fertility Decline in the Islamic Republic of Iran, 1972–2000." *Asian Population Studies*, 2 (3): 217–37.

El Laithy, H., and K. Abu-Ismail. 2005. "Poverty in Syria: 1996–2004." Unpublished.

Haddad, A. 1996. *Poverty in Lebanon*. Beirut: ESCWA.

Mehryar, A. 2004. "Primary Health Care and the Rural Poor in the Islamic Republic of Iran." Paper presented at Scaling-Up Poverty Reduction: A Global Learning Process and Conference, Shanghai, May 25–27, 2004.

Ministère de la Santé. 2008, 2007. Santé en Chiffres (Health Statistics). Rabat, Morocco: Royaume du Maroc, Ministère de la Santé,

Roberts, P., K. C. Shyam, and C. Rastogi. 2006. "Rural Access Index: A Key Development Indicator." World Bank Transport Paper.

Shlash, Amal. 2009. Iraq High Committee for Strategy Reduction Draft Strategy Review. Powerpoint presentation. Amman.

Uchida, H., and A. Nelson. 2008. "Agglomeration Index: Towards a New Measure of Urban Concentration." World Bank. http://sitere sources.worldbank.org/INTWDR2009/Resources/4231006-1204741572978/Hiro1.pdf.

UNESCO. 2007. Gender Parity Index for Net Primary Enrolment Rate. Institute for Statistics.

WHO-UNICEF. 2008. "Joint Monitoring Report for Water Supply and Sanitation." http://www.wssinfo.org/resources/documents.html?type=country_files.

World Bank. 1999. *Democratic and Popular Republic of Algeria; Growth, Employment and Poverty Reduction.* Washington, DC: World Bank.

———. 2002. *Algeria Low Income Housing Project. Mid-term Review Mission Report.* Washington, DC: World Bank.

———. 2004. *Jordan: Poverty Assessment.* Washington, DC: World Bank.

———. 2006a. *Tunisia: Agricultural Policy Review.* Washington, DC: World Bank.

———. 2006b. *World Development Report 2006: Equity and Development.* Washington, DC: World Bank.

———. 2007. *Making the Most of Scarcity: Accountability for Better Water Management in the Middle East and North Africa.* Washington, DC: World Bank.

———. 2009. *World Development Report 2009: Reshaping Economic Geography.* Washington DC: World Bank.

Index

Boxes, figures, notes, and tables are indicated by *b*, *f*, *n*, and *t*, respectively.

Eco-Audit

Environmental Benefits Statement

The World Bank is committed to preserving endangered forests and natural resources. The Office of the Publisher has chosen to print *Poor Places, Thriving People: How the Middle East and North Africa Can Rise Above Spatial Disparities* on recycled paper including 50% post-consumer recycled fiber in accordance with the recommended standards for paper usage set by the Green Press Initiative, a nonprofit program supporting publishers in using fiber that is not sourced from endangered forests. For more information, visit www.greenpressinitiative.org.

Saved:

- 14 trees
- 384 lbs. of solid waste
- 6,325 gallons of water
- 1,313 lbs. of CO_2 equivalent of net greenhouse gases
- 4 million BTUs of total energy

green press
INITIATIVE